ALL THE BEST IN BELIZE

EASY BELIZE

How to Live, Retire, Work and Buy Property in Belize, the English Speaking, Frost Free Paradise on the Caribbean Coast

By LAN SLUDER

EASY BELIZE How to Live, Retire, Work and Buy Property in
Belize, the English Speaking, Frost Free Paradise
on the Caribbean Coast
by Lan Sluder

Published by Equator Publications, Asheville, NC.

Revised and fully updated 2010.

EQUATOR PUBLICATIONS/ASHEVILLE
287 Beaverdam Road • Candler, NC 28715 USA
E-mail: lansluder@gmail.com • www.belizefirst.com

Notice: This work does not purport to give legal, medical, tax or
other professional advice. Seek competent professional counsel
and perform due diligence before acting on information contained
herein.

ABOUT THIS BOOK

Easy Belize How to Live, Retire, Work and Buy Property in Belize, the English Speaking, Frost Free Paradise on the Caribbean Coast by Lan Sluder is the complete guide for anyone considering relocating or retiring to Belize, and for anyone thinking of buying property or building a home in Belize.

In more than 35 chapters, it covers everything you need to know: What things cost in Belize, how to find the best deals on real estate, health care in Belize, safety and security, options for residency and how to stretch your dollars in Belize.

It provides detailed information on all the major areas of Belize, whether inland or on the coast and cayes: Corozal Town and Corozal District, the islands of Belize including Ambergris Caye (San Pedro) and Caye Caulker, San Ignacio and Belmopan in Cayo District, Hopkins and Placencia in Stann Creek District, and the Punta Gorda area in Toledo District.

Author Lan Sluder has been banging around Belize since 1991. He's visited every area of the country. Sluder is the author of more than half a dozen books on Belize, including *Fodor's Belize, San Pedro Cool, Adapter Kit Belize, Belize Islands Guide* and *Living Abroad in Belize.* He is the founder and editor of *Belize First,* now an on-line magazine at www.BelizeFirst.com.

TABLE OF CONTENTS

View of the Belize Barrier Reef and Caribbean from North Ambergris

INTRODUCTION: WHY CHOOSE BELIZE?

Over the years, I've interviewed, talked with or heard from via e-mail hundreds of people who have moved to Belize or who plan to do so, and I've asked them this question: "Why did you choose Belize?" I've gotten many answers, but these are the most common:

"I like speaking English." You don't have to learn a new language to live in Belize, because English is the official language. You don't have to struggle with grammar and syntax in an unfamiliar tongue. While Spanish and several other languages are widely spoken in Belize, and many Belizeans are bi- or trilingual, everything from street signs and newspapers to official government documents are in English. From your first day in Belize, you can shop, dine, chat and gossip without having to thumb through a dictionary or cast about for the right verb ending.

"I love the warm, sunny climate." It never frosts or snows in Belize. The climate ranges from sub-tropical to tropical, similar to that of South Florida. As long as you're comfortable with warm to hot temperatures, perhaps tempered by cooling breezes from the sea, you'll like Belize weather. As a bonus, you'll never have to pay for heating oil again.

"I feel welcome here." Belize is not a Never-Never Land where everyone loves everybody in perfect harmony, but the fact is, by and large, Belizeans are as friendly a bunch of people as you'll ever find. Belizeans take

people one at a time. Whether you're black, white, brown or green, short, fat, ugly or beautiful, rich or poor, you'll find acceptance in Belize. Your neighbors will say hello to you on the street, check on you if you're sick and share a joke with you over a Belikin at the bar. And they may try to hit you up for a loan. For the most part, Belizeans genuinely like Americans (and Canadians and Europeans). At the official level, the Belize government welcomes retirees and others, especially if they bring some resources to the country. The Qualified Retired Persons Incentive Program (see below) is administered not by a bureaucratic immigration department but by the Belize Tourist Board, and they generally provide approvals within three months.

"I enjoy the lifestyle here, doing things outdoors and on the water." Belize offers relatively little in the way of cultural activities — museums, art galleries, the arts. But it makes up for it with a wealth of options for those who love the outdoors. You can garden year-round. The saltwater fishing is some of the best in the world. Boating, diving, swimming and snorkeling can be as close as your back yard. For the more adventurous, there are caves and ancient ruins to explore, rivers to canoe and mountains to hike.

"I can live better here for less money than where I came from." Belize is not the cheapest place to live, and in some areas of Belize an American lifestyle will cost U.S. prices or higher. Overall, however, expats in Belize say they can live larger than back home, enjoying some luxuries such as a housekeeper or meals out. Investment income, pensions and Social Security checks seem to stretch a little farther in Belize. While some items such as gasoline, imported foods and electricity cost more in Belize, other things including medical care, housing, insurance and household help are significantly cheaper in Belize than in the U.S., Canada or Western Europe. Although Belize has a few half million dollar houses and condos, you can rent a little house for US$200-$400 a month, set up a made-in-Belize cabin for US$15,000, build an attractive new home for US$75,000 to $125,000 and buy a waterfront lot for US$50,000 to $100,000.

"I thought I could never afford to live on the beach ... but I can in Belize." If you've seen the prices for beachfront lots in Florida, South Carolina, Massachusetts or California – often hundreds of thousands, even millions of dollars – you know that oceanfront living in the U.S. is out of the question for most people. In Belize, beachfront lots aren't as cheap as they used to be, or as cheap as they still are in places like Nicaragua, but you can still buy a buildable lot on the Caribbean for US$50,000 to $100,000. Lots a row or two back from the sea start at US$15,000 to $20,000. And you can put a storm-resistant concrete house on the lot for US$50 to $85 a square foot. So, with a little patience and planning for around US$150,000 to US$200,000, you can own a small new home right on the water.

"I appreciate the fact that Belize has a stable, democratic government." You don't have to worry about a coup in Belize. Politics in Belize is highly personal and can be rough and tumble, even dirty, but Belizeans take their democracy seriously. The voter turnout in the last national election was almost 75%. Along with Costa Rica, Belize has the most stable political sys-

tem in the region.

"I'm glad I escaped from America's consumer society." In Belize, you won't find Starbucks, McDonald's or Wal-Mart. Global franchise businesses are almost unknown. That can be frustrating when you're trying to find a cheap home appliance or a quick meal, but on the plus side you don't need to spend your life accumulating stuff.

"I like living on Belize time." Like many sub-tropical and tropical countries, Belize offers a slower way of life than the frenetic pace of life in many more developed countries. If you don't get it done today, there's always tomorrow. Slow down. Be cool. Don't make your blood boil. "I'll be here at 7:30 Monday morning" really means, "I'll try to get there early Monday but if I decide to go fishing I'll be there sometime Tuesday." Not everyone can adjust to this way of living, but for those who do it has a lot of appeal.

"I feel healthier here." As I discuss in detail later in this book, Belize does not have the high-tech, state-of-the-art medical care available in the U.S. or even in countries like Costa Rica or Panama. But the Belizean lifestyle can be very healthful. You eat fresh fruit and unprocessed food. You walk more and ride less. You stay outside in the clean, unpolluted air rather than being cooped up in a climate-controlled box all day. You go home for lunch or take a nap at mid-day. In Belize's balmy climate, your arthritis and other aches and pains seem to fade away. Many people who move to Belize start feeling better within a few weeks. Quite a few lose weight. Blood pressure levels go down. Of course, you can also live an unhealthy life in Belize — watching cable TV all day, drinking all night and eating fried foods and lardy beans and rice.

"I like the people of Belize." If you're a people person, you can't help liking Belizeans. Belizeans come in every shape, background and color, but nearly all are open and friendly. They love to have fun, and there's always an excuse for a party or a celebration. Expats in Belize are also an interesting bunch, usually with an independent streak and sometimes downright eccentric.

"There's always something to do or see here." If you're bored in Belize, it's your own fault. Belize is a natural wonder. You could spend the rest of your life just learning about the flora and fauna of the country. Belize is home to thousands of species of trees and flowers, hundreds of kinds of birds and butterflies. The culture of Belize is wide and deep. The history of the Maya in Belize goes back thousands of years. Garifuna came to Belize in the early 1800s; Hispanics have trickled in over the past several hundred years; Mennonites came here in the 1950s. Every group in Belize has a fascinating history to explore. When you tire of intellectual pursuits, you can take trips to the enchanting corners of the country, to the high hills of the Mountain Pine Ridge, to the endless caves of the Chiquibul wilderness, to the lush rainforest of Toledo, to the many islands in the Caribbean Sea and to the 190-mile long Belize Barrier Reef.

"I like the wide open spaces of Belize." With around 330,000 people

in an area the size of the state of Massachusetts (population: 6,400,000), Belize is one of the least densely populated countries in the Western Hemisphere. Outside the cities and towns, you can often drive for miles without seeing another human being. In that regard, Belize is like a little, subtropical Alaska. Or like Florida 50 years ago.

"I don't have to worry about losing my property here." Property rights are protected in Belize through the traditions of English Common Law. In some countries, if you leave your house or land unoccupied, squatters can move in, and it's almost impossible to get them out. Legal documents may be written in a language you don't understand. Powerful local interests can take your property through tricky legal — or illegal — means. In many parts of Latin America and Europe, the legal system is Civil Law based on the Napoleonic Code, very different from the system in the United States. But Belize shares with America, Canada and the United Kingdom a legal system based on English Common Law. In Belize, private property is respected and protected. Foreigners can own property virtually anywhere in Belize, with exactly the same rights and protections as exist for Belizeans. Squatters cannot take your property. The Belize legal system isn't perfect, and lawyers in Belize are almost as costly as those in the U.S., but it's a far better system than, for example, in Honduras.

"The U.S. dollar is accepted everywhere in Belize." Belize has its own currency, the Belize dollar, so technically the American greenback is not the official monetary unit of the country. As a practical matter, though, the U.S. dollar is accepted anywhere and everywhere in Belize, and the Belize dollar has been pegged for decades at the rate of 2 Belize to 1 U.S. dollar. Anything of substantial value, such as real estate, is priced in U.S. dollars. This means that prices in Belize are more stable for American dollar holders than they would be if the Belizean currency floated against the dollar. It also means that in periods when the value of the U.S. dollar declines sharply against the euro, yen and many other hard currencies, prices in Belize remained about the same as always for Americans. (Of course, during periods of appreciation of the value of the U.S. dollar, prices in Belize do not become cheaper for U.S. dollar holders.)

What Some Do NOT Like About Belize

I've also talked with many people who came to Belize and decided not to stay, or who were unhappy with their life in Belize but couldn't afford to leave. Here are their major gripes and complaints. Keep in mind that some people who are unhappy in Belize would be just as unhappy where they came from. You can move to a new place, but you can't run away from yourself.

"We can't get anybody to do anything here." If you're expecting a Minnesota-style work ethic in Belize, everything prompt and efficient, you're in for a surprise. People have their own ways of doing things and their own time frame for doing them. In remote areas, many Belizeans have never held a regular job. Belizeans have their own methods of work, sometimes developed over hundreds of years. It may take them longer to finish, but they'll get

it done. Eventually. Also, decades of "brain drain" with more than 100,000 of the most ambitious Belizeans moving to the U.S. in search of better jobs means that you may occasionally run into folks who are a little less motivated or skilled.

"We're tired of getting ripped off." One of the most common subjects of cocktail party conversation among expats in Belize is how to protect their homes and property from petty theft. "Tiefin" (as it's said in Creole) is unfortunately common in Belize, as it is in many poor, developing countries. Leave a tool or a bicycle out overnight, and it's likely to be gone the next day. Leave your house unattended for a week or two, and you'll likely come back to a home stripped of everything of value. You have to acclimate yourself to an environment where petty theft is going to happen, and you have to protect your possessions. Hire a dependable caretaker, put up a fence around your property and get a big black dog.

"Things cost more than we thought they would." Belize is a small, inefficient marketplace. Little is manufactured locally, shops are mostly small mom 'n pop places and shipping costs to Belize are expensive. Import duties are high. All this adds up to an economy where most anything imported is likely to cost more than where it was produced: automobiles, wine, cement, cornflakes, books, shoes. If you come to Belize thinking everything across the board will be cheaper than back home, you'll be sorely disappointed. To duplicate a Scottsdale lifestyle in Belize, down to the Stoly in the liquor cabinet, the Carrier turned to frigid and an SUV in the drive, you'll spend a lot more than in Arizona. To live in Belize on the cheap, you have to live like a Belizean — eat rice and beans, take the bus, go the local clinic for health care. You can move up a bit from the Belizean lifestyle without paying a ton of money, but you have to buy wisely: Dump the dishwasher, use the ceiling fan instead of the A/C, drink rum instead of Russian vodka, order from Amazon.com, eat the healthful local foods — cheese, brown eggs and watermelons from Mennonite farms, mangoes and oranges off your backyard trees, tortillas from the corner *tacqueria.*

"We hate the telephone company." Probably no single fact of life in Belize causes more grouching and griping than telcom service. Belize Telemedia Ltd. no longer enjoys a complete legal monopoly on telecommunications in Belize, but it still controls most of the telephone and Internet service in Belize. Unlike its U.S. counterparts, it's still a money making machine. Long-distance and Internet costs in Belize are much higher than in more competitive markets. BTL's service really isn't bad, and most of BTL's infrastructure is modern, but for those, especially in business, who depend on telephone and e-mail, the high costs and sometimes-arrogant attitude of BTL is a real thorn in the side.

"Belizean politicians are corrupt." Belize isn't Mexico. Petty bribery is rare. The average Belizean official wants respect, not a few bucks. But corruption certainly exists in Belize, especially at the higher levels of government. In the first months of 2005, accusations of alleged corruption were at the heart of a series of demonstrations and strikes against the party then in

power, the People's United Party headed by Prime Minister Said Musa. These culminated in demonstrations in Belize City, during which several people were injured, about 100 were arrested and some stores in the city centre were looted. Since then, further reports of government corruption and waste have come to light. The new United Democratic Party government, which won the 2008 national elections, tried (without much success) to prosecute some members of the former PUP government. The Old Boy network is alive and well in Belize, too. It's accepted, even expected, that senior government officials will do favors for their cronies and family, everything from awarding lucrative contracts for cruise ship shore excursions to selling prime land at bargain basement prices. Not every government official takes advantage of office, but some do. Many expats in Belize get sick and tired of this aspect of Belize reality (especially since as non-voters they benefit not at all from the political corruption.)

"We can't make any money here." If you want to go into business and make a lot of money, do it in the U.S. America is still the land of opportunity for the entrepreneur, with a huge, wealthy market for any product or service you can imagine. By contrast, the entire country of Belize has the buying power of a small town of 40,000 people in the U.S. There are some opportunities in tourism and agriculture, but the scale is small – for example, Myrtle Beach, S.C., gets 60 or 70 times as many tourists as does the whole country of Belize. As the saying goes, if you want to make a small fortune in Belize, come here with a big fortune. Belize has some very successful home-grown business people, and some expats have built successful businesses in Belize, but it's not an easy country in which to get rich. Make your bucks before you come to Belize.

"We don't have the juice and connections we had back home." When you move to Belize, you lose the network of contacts – personal, business and political – you used to have. Unless you become a Belizean citizen, you can't vote in national elections and, in any case, you don't have the political connections that many Belizeans have built up over the course of their life. In short, nobody cares what you think about local matters. You're not so much at the bottom rung of the ladder as not even close to the ladder.

Fruit stand near the capital of Belmopan – pineapples US$1

CHAPTER 1:
WHAT YOU NEED TO KNOW – BELIZE A TO Z

I'm not going to bore you with a long narrative on the history of Belize, or provide a laundry list of trivia about the country. If you want to know more about Belize's past, present and future, (and much of it is fascinating) see the Recommended Reading section in the Appendix of this book.

Here are the basic facts to get you up to speed on Belize:

Acclimatization: How long does it take the typical expat to acclimatize to Belize? The answer varies from immediately to never. In terms of the weather, it usually takes new residents about six months to a year to get used to the warm, humid subtropical climate, assuming they didn't come from a similar climate. Belize is superficially similar to the U.S. in many ways – from the use of English in official documents to the same standards of measurement – miles, feet, gallons and ounces rather than kilometers, meters, liters and milliliters. You drive on the right and cable TV offers HBO, CNN and other U.S. channels. But, below the surface, the differences are more subtle and significant (see Getting Along in Belize chapter below.)

Bargaining: In general, prices in Belize stores are fixed, and there is no bargaining. At street markets, you may do some light bargaining, but haggling is not a way of life in Belize as it is some other parts of the world. Hotels and other tourist services may offer discounts – it never hurts to ask. Of course, when buying real estate, bargaining is the order of the day in Belize as most everywhere.

Business Hours: Most businesses open around 8 a.m. and close at 5 or 6 p.m. on weekdays. Some close for lunch, usually from 1 to 2 p.m. Many stores are open on Saturday, or at least on Saturday mornings. On Sundays, most stores and other businesses are closed, except in tourist areas like San Pedro. Banks typically are open until 1 p.m. Monday to Thursday and until 4 or 5 on Friday.

Capital: Belmopan, a small town (now technically a city) of around 20,000 people in the central part of the country, is Belize's capital and home to many government offices. The capital was moved from Belize City following the terrific destruction and loss of life caused by Hurricane Hattie in 1961. However, while Belmopan is growing fast, Belize City remains the cultural, social and commercial hub of the country, and many government offices remain in Belize's only sizeable city.

Cell Phones: In addition to an older analog system, Belize Telemedia Limited now offers "DigiCell," a digital service on the GSM dual band 850/1900 Mhz technology. As with cell phone service nearly everywhere, cell plans in Belize are complex and change frequently, but in general Belize cell service, especially texting, is more costly than in the U.S. or most other countries. Currently BTL offers a package (DigiCell Gold) for US$50 a month that includes 250 anytime minutes, and 30 text messages, and a US$75 a month (DigiCell Platinum) plan that includes 500 minutes and 30 text messages. Excess minutes are US12 ½ to 25 cents, and excess text messages are US12 ½ cents each. You can also purchase pre-paid cell service at a higher minute rate – US42 1/2 cents per minute for most minutes and US12 ½ cents for text messages. Visitors to Belize can buy a SIM card for their unlocked GSM 850/1900 cell phone for US$25, which includes BZ$10 of air time, or rent a DigiCell phone from BTL for US$5 a day (not including outgoing call usage). SpeedNet is another digital cell service that began operating in 2005 and may offer slightly lower rates than BTL. All charges shown are plus 10% GST. *See also Internet and Telephone entries below.*

Churches and Religion: Although Belize was a British colony, the Catholic Church, not the Anglican Church, is dominant in Belize. About one-half of Belizeans are at least nominally Catholic; Anglicans represent about 6% of the population. Other religious groups in Belize include Methodist, Church of Christ, Mennonite, Presbyterian, Jehovah's Witnesses, Assembly of God and Seventh Day Adventist. Belize has one Muslim mosque. There is no temple, but Jews meet in local homes in Belize City.

Climate: Most of Belize has a sub-tropical climate similar to that of South Florida. Frost-free Belize usually enjoys lows in the 60s to 70s, with highs in the 80s to low 90s. More rain falls as you go south, with average annual rainfall in the north being about 50 inches, similar to Atlanta, Georgia, but increasing to 160 inches or more in the far south. Generally the rainiest months are June through October, with the driest months being February through April. January sees the coolest temperatures of the year, while May has the hottest. In general, daytime temps are higher inland, due to the influence of prevailing winds from the sea on the cayes and coast. The humidity is high year round in all parts of the country.

Drugs: Despite its reputation as a source of marijuana and, more recently, as a transshipment point for cocaine and other drugs from South America, Belize has strict laws on the use of illegal drugs, with prison terms and fines for offenders. Quite a few Belizeans smoke marijuana, some fairly openly, but it is illegal. Unfortunately, crack, heroin and other hard drugs are a fact of life in Belize, as they are in many countries. Much of the crime in Belize City and in other parts of the country is related to drugs.

Economy: Belize's Gross Domestic Product in 2009 was estimated at US$1.4 billion, or around US$4,250 per capita. By comparison, U.S. GDP in 2009 was US$14.4 trillion, and per-capita GDP in the U.S. in 2009 was about US$47,500. Thus, per-capita income in Belize is less than one-tenth that in the U.S. Belize's GDP growth averaged nearly 4% annually between 1999 and 2007 but fell to an estimated 2.4% in 2008 and was slightly negative at -1.1% in 2009. Major concerns include a large public debt relative to government income and GDP, and a sizeable trade deficit. More than one-third of the population is below the poverty line. The entire Belize national economy is about the size of the economy of a small U.S. metro area of 40,000 people.

Tourism and agriculture/marine products are the two major industries, each representing about one-fifth of GDP. Due to recent growth, tourism is now slightly larger. Ambergris Caye, Cayo and Placencia are the major areas developed for tourism. Belize gets about 240,000 international visitors a year, with 61% coming from the U.S. These figures do not include almost three quarter of a million annual day visitors on cruise ships, which call on Belize City. The main agricultural crops are sugar cane, citrus, marine products and bananas. Aquaculture, mainly shrimp farming, has grown in importance in recent years.

Belize has a labor force of around 144,000. The official unemployment rate in 2009 was about 12.6%, but in many rural areas of Belize it is much higher. Even so, there is a shortage of skilled workers in some areas. Inflation in Belize has been low to moderate in recent years; it was 4.5% in 2007 but increased to over 6% in 2008, before dropping to a negative 1.1% in 2009. The government has been running a large budget deficit in recent years. The deficit has been about 15% of the total government budget of about US$400 million. External debt is over US$1 billion. That is high given the small size of the Belizean economy. In 2006, the government reached agreement with most international creditors to restructure its external debt, issuing new bonds at lower interest rates.

Key Economic Numbers:
(All figures for 2009):

GDP: US$1.4 billion
GDP Per Capita: US$4,200

Inflation Rate: -1.1%
Unemployment Rate: 12.6%

Education: Belize's educational system is generally based on the English system. Students move through forms, from first form in primary school to sixth form (a kind of junior college), although some schools, following U.S. and Caribbean Community practices, use the grade system -- grades 1-12. The Catholic Church, through an agreement with the government, operates many of Belize's public schools. Nearly two-thirds of Belize's population are teenagers or younger, so in every part of Belize you'll see school kids in their khaki or blue school uniforms. In Belize City and elsewhere, there are both Catholic and government-run high schools. A few private or parochial schools run by Protestant denominations also exist. The best schools are in Belize City and in larger towns, and many of the worst schools -- with untrained teachers and few books or equipment -- are in the far south. One study found that lack of supplies was a major problem for schools in Toledo, and that about one-half of the teachers in the district had no educational training beyond high school. Only one in two Toledo children even finish primary school. In 2004, more than 85,000 students were enrolled in Belize schools and colleges at all levels, including almost 4,000 in preschools, 63,000 in primary schools, and more than 13,000 in high schools. Close to 5,000 students were in post-secondary studies.

Primary education is free and compulsory through age 14. However, a sizable minority of Belizean children does not complete primary school. Only about 60% of teachers are professionally trained, though the number if growing. Even teachers with four-year college degrees earn only about US$1,000 a month. Secondary education, consisting of a four-year high school, is competitive, requiring passage of a comprehensive exam. The student's percentile ranking on the admissions test in part determines which school the student can attend. Charges for books and fees at secondary schools are beyond the reach of many Belizean families.

About three-fourths of primary school students do go on to secondary schools, though not all graduate. The typical tuition cost for private schools in Belize is around US$15 per month. The Belize government pays this tuition if the student is a child of a citizen or permanent resident. Some expats choose to do home schooling. Private schools are available in a few areas. The Island Academy on Ambergris Caye, as an example, which goes through grade 8, charges US$3,000 a year per student. This school has an excellent reputation. Belize Elementary School in Belize City is one of the best private elementary schools on the mainland. Saint Catherine Academy for girls and St. John's High School for boys, both in Belize City, are recognized as among the best high schools. Belize also has community colleges and junior colleges. Despite the name, community colleges such as Corozal Community College and Toledo Community College, and also some other schools with college in the name, are usually secondary schools (high schools). Junior colleges may have secondary school programs but also offer tertiary, post-high

14

school programs. Most are patterned after the "sixth form" in Britain. They usually offer associate or two-year college degrees. St. John's College in Belize City has educated many of Belize's leaders. Corozal Junior College in Corozal and Muffles College in Orange Walk Town are other examples. Corozal Junior College and St. John's Junior College also offer evening and extension programs directed primarily to adults.

Until the 1990s, Belize did not have a true four-year university system. The colleges in Belize City and elsewhere were more like American high schools or two-year community colleges. However, in 2000, provisions were made for the development of the University of Belize, which combines several existing Belize educational facilities. A small private college, Galen University, is in Cayo near San Ignacio. The University of the West Indies also offers courses in Belize. In addition, several small for-profit offshore medical schools have set up base in Belize – currently one in Belize City, one in Corozal Town and one in Belmopan.

A sampling of education costs in Belize. All figures are in US dollars:

Primary School
Public schools (often run by the Catholic Church): Free except for uniforms & books
Island Academy, San Pedro -- private school: $3,000+ a year
High School
Saint Catherine's Academy, Belize City: $500 a year (tuition & fees)
Mount Carmel High School, Benque Viejo: $300 a year (tuition)
Four-Year College
University of Belize, Belmopan and Belize City: $675 (tuition for 15 credit hours) per semester for Belizean citizens and permanent residents; $1,350 for students from developing countries; $2,025 for students from developed countries; all plus fees of $210 per semester and plus living expenses

Electricity: 110 volts AC/60 cycles, same as in the U.S., and outlets are like those in the U.S. and Canada. However, electricity is at least twice as expensive in Belize as in the U.S., at around 21 U.S. cents per kilowatt-hour.

Embassies: The U.S. Embassy in Belize moved from Belize City to Floral Park Road in Belmopan in late 2006. The new embassy is a compound constructed at a cost of US$50 million. In 2005, George W. Bush picked Rob Dieter, Bush's former roommate at Yale, as the new ambassador to Belize. Dieter was a professor at the University of Colorado law school. He went to law school at the University of Denver and before that roomed for four years with W as an undergraduate at Yale. President Barrack Obama also picked a former college roommate, at Occidental College, Vinai Thummalapally, an Indian-American businessman from Colorado Springs, Colo., as new ambassador.

The embassy's telephone number is 501-822-4011, fax 501-822-4012, and the web site is www.belize.usembassy.gov. The U.K., Mexico, Guatemala, Costa Rica, Taiwan and about a dozen other countries have ambassadors or other representatives either in Belize City or Belmopan.

Family Life: With so many different ethnic groups in Belize, you can't generalize about family life. However, as in many countries, Belize faces social problems relating to the disintegration of traditional family life. Especially in Belize City and other urbanized areas, a large percentage of babies are born out of wedlock and the traditional nuclear family is becoming less the norm.

Government: Formerly a British colony, and known as British Honduras from 1862 to 1973, Belize became independent from Britain in 1981. It is now a democratic member of the British Commonwealth, with a Westminster-style government system with a prime minister, an elected house of representatives and an appointed senate. The current prime minister is Dean Barrow, a Jamaica- and U.S.-educated lawyer. He heads the United Democratic Party (UDP), which swept national elections in 2008. The opposition party is the People's United Party (PUP). Both parties are generally centrist. The "George Washington of Belize" is George Cadle Price, an ascetic Creole who helped found the PUP and was Belize's first prime minister. Politics in Belize is a freewheeling affair and often intensely personal. Belize has strong ties with the United States and Britain, but it also has cultivated ties with Taiwan, Cuba, Venezuela, Japan, Mexico and other countries, often out of the need to seek foreign aid or development funding.

History: The human history of Belize can be divided into four broad periods: the ancient Maya period, the Spanish conquest, the British colonial period and modern Belize.

The ancient Maya, whose ancestors likely came originally from Asia, settled in what is now Mexico at least 2,000 years before the birth of Christ. The Maya civilization was influenced by and grew out of the Olmec culture farther north. The Maya migrated to what is now Belize about 3,000 years ago. During the height of the Maya empire, called the Classic Period, roughly 300 BC to 900 AD, the area that is now Belize had a civilization that included large-scale agriculture, sizeable cities of up to several hundred thousand people, formalized religion and a sophisticated knowledge of architecture, art, science and mathematics. As many as a million people lived in Belize during the late Classic period, compared to less than one-third that number today. Caracol likely was the largest city-state in Belize, with a population perhaps several times larger than that of Belize City today. Then, rather quickly, in a matter of at most a few hundred years, most of the great Maya cities were depopulated and the Maya civilization went into decline. There are many theories as to why this happened, among them that there was a change in weather patterns that disrupted agricultural, that epidemic diseases swept the region, or that social changes – perhaps revolutions – transformed the society. It could have been a combination of reasons. Whatever the reasons, by around 1000 AD most of the major cities in Belize had been at least partially abandoned, though a few settlements, such as Lamanai in northern Belize, lasted for many more centuries.

The Spanish Conquest of Mexico and Central America began in the first quarter of the 16th Century. Spanish troops and missionaries destroyed much of what was left of the Maya civilization, including burning nearly all of the Maya books they found. Soldiers killed many, and the European diseases they brought such as smallpox killed even more. Belize offered little to the Spanish in the way of gold or other riches, so Spain never paid much attention to it.

By the early 17th Century, Belize drew the attention of a motley group of British loggers and adventurers. The original Brits in Belize sought logwood, a valuable hardwood used to make dyes. These Brits also did a little buccaneering on the side. One of the most fearsome was Edward Teach, called Blackbeard for his huge black beard. According to legend, Blackbeard used Ambergris Caye for his hideout, continuing to terrorize ships of all nations, until he was finally killed off the coast of North Carolina. By around 1700, several hundred British loggers and hangers-on had settled around the mouth of the Belize River, near the bay of what is now Belize City. The Brits were known as Baymen. British logging settlements grew over the course of the next 100 years or so. The loggers imported slaves from Jamaica to help cut logwood and mahogany.

There was continuing conflict between the British and the Spanish. Finally, in early September 1798, a Spanish fleet of 32 ships with about 2,000 men came to settle the score and wipe out the British once and for all. But it didn't work out that way. A ragtag band of Baymen assisted by a Royal Navy battleship on September 10, 1798, defeated the larger Spanish force in the Battle of St. George's Caye. That event helped end Spain's claims to Belize once and for all and is now celebrated as National Day. Spain acknowledged British sovereignty in Belize in the Treaty of Amiens in 1802.

Thus began the British era in Belize, which lasted until the mid-20th Century. British Honduras, as it was then known, officially became a British colony in 1862, at the time of the U.S. Civil War. Following the Civil War, about 1,500 Confederate supporters came to British Honduras and established the town of New Richmond. Much of the British period was marked by the traditional colonial approach of exploiting the natural resources of the colony. Though slavery was abolished in Belize in 1838, two decades before it was abolished in the United States, English and Scottish companies employing hard-working Belizean blacks continued to log the native forests, exporting the timber back to Europe.

During this time, Belize began to become a melting pot of races and ethnic backgrounds. The old Baymen families, with names like Usher and Fairweather, married former slaves, creating a kind of provincial Creole aristocracy in Belize City. Some Mayas, fleeing the Caste Wars of mid-19th Century Mexico, intermarried with the Spanish, and were then called Mestizos. Hundreds of Garifuna from Honduras, with African and Caribbean Indian heritage, settled in southern Belize. As the 20th Century dawned, British Honduras was a sleepy backwater of the British Empire. But underneath the sleepiness, things were stirring. Jamaican-born Marcus Garvey helped raised black consciousness in Belize, as he did elsewhere in the Caribbean. The worldwide Great Depression and a terrible hurricane in 1931, which killed some 2,000 people in and around Belize City, both had a great impact on Belize.

The end of World War II sparked anti-colonial feelings, and the first major political movements favoring independence from Britain arose. Of these, the People's United Party (PUP) under George Price, a Creole educated at St. John's College in Belize City, was the most important. In 1954, a new constitution for the colony was introduced, for the first time giving all literate adults the right to vote (until then only about 3 in 100 Belizeans were allowed to vote.) In 1964, George Price negotiated a new constitution, which granted British Honduras full internal self-government, although it remained a British colony.

In 1973, the country's name officially was changed to Belize. On September 21, 1981, Belize became an independent nation, with George Price as prime minister. Small by international standards, unpopulated and undeveloped, modern Belize has struggled to create a viable economy and infrastructure. The country several times faced off with Guatemala, which had long maintained that Belize was simply a province of Guatemala. It was not until 1991 that Guatemala finally recognized Belize as a sovereign state, although even up until today populist flag-wavers in Guatemala occasionally threaten to invade Belice (as it is known in Spanish).

In the 20th Century, agriculture, especially citrus, bananas and sugar, replaced logging as the country's main industry. More recently, tourism has supplanted agriculture as the primary industry.

Democracy found fertile roots in Belize, and the little country has a dynamic two-party system. The United Democratic Party (UDP), under the former schoolteacher Manuel Esquivel, first defeated the PUP in the 1984 national elections, and again in 1993, but the PUP under Said Musa regained power in 1998 and held it until 2008. The current UDP prime minister is Dean Barrow, the first black to hold the office.

Important Dates in Belize History
300 BC to 900 AD Classic Maya period, when what is now Belize was the heart of the Maya empire with a population of one million

1508-1511 First Europeans — Spaniards — come to Belize; Maya resist

1798 Baymen defeat Spanish at Battle of St. George's Caye on September 10, Belize's National Day

1838 Slaves emancipated

1862 Britain declares British Honduras a colony and a member of British Commonwealth

1931 Worst hurricane in Belize history strikes on September 10, kills about 2,000

1949 Protests against devaluation of British Honduras dollar lead to formation of People's United Party headed by George Price, sowing seeds of independence

1961 Hurricane Hattie nearly levels Belize City on the night before Halloween, kills more than 250

1973 Name changed to Belize; capital moved to Belmopan from Belize City

1981 On September 21, Belize becomes fully independent member of British Commonwealth, under Prime Minister George Price

1984 UDP wins national elections; Manuel Esquivel becomes PM; for next 14 years, parties alternate election wins

1998 Said Musa becomes Prime Minister

2001 Hurricane Iris hits southern Belize, on October 9, killing 21

2005 Charging corruption and fiscal mismanagement by the PUP, labor unions and the opposition UDP stage strikes and demonstrations

2008 UDP sweeps national elections in February, and Dean Barrow becomes prime minister.

Holidays: The following are legal public holidays in Belize:
New Year's Day - January 1
Baron Bliss Day - March 9 (date of celebration varies)
Good Friday
Holy Saturday
Easter Sunday
Easter Monday
Labour Day - May 1
Commonwealth Day - May 24
St. George's Caye Day - September 10
Independence Day - September 21
Columbus Day - October 12
Garifuna Settlement Day - November 19
Christmas Day - December 25
Boxing Day - December 26

Hurricanes and Other Natural Disasters: June through November technically is hurricane season in the Western Caribbean, but the September and October period is the most likely time for tropical storms and hurricanes. The worst hurricane in modern Belize history struck in September 1931, killing as many as 2,000 people in and around Belize City. About two-thirds of all tropical storms that have visited Belize in modern times have struck during those two months.

Since 1889, some 52 tropical storms and hurricanes have made landfall in Belize, an average of about once every 2.3 years. During the last half of the 20th century, only five serious hurricanes struck Belize, with the worst being Hattie in 1961. With the new millennium has come an increase in storm activity. Hurricane Keith hit Ambergris Caye in late September 2000, killing five and doing some US$150 million in damage, mainly on the backside of the island. Hurricane Iris in early October 2001 devastated the Placencia peninsula and rural Toledo District in southern Belize, killing 21 people, all in a live aboard dive boat. Hurricane Dean, in August 2007 hit Northern Belize, destroying some crops and homes.

Hurricanes can have a serious economic impact on Belize. For example, the Caribbean Development Bank estimates that in 2000 costs associated with hurricane damage were 13% of Gross Domestic Product and in 2001 6% of GDP. Even without hurricanes and tropical storms, flooding does frequently occur in low-lying areas, especially at the beginning of the rainy season, typically in June or July. Heavy rains from June through September in southern Belize can also cause flooding at any time during this period. Happily, Belize is not much subject to that other scourge of Central America – earthquakes. While earthquakes have occurred in Belize, notably in southern Belize – there were two minor earthquakes in 2009 -- no severe *terremotos* have occurred in Belize in modern times. Likewise, there are no active volcanoes in Belize. Forest fires are a risk at the end of the dry season, typically April and May.

Internet: There are about 35,000 Internet users in Belize. Internet access in Belize has been greatly improved over the past few years. BTL now offers DSL in most of the country, for either PC or Mac. However, costs are higher than in the U.S. or most other countries. Rates range from US$50 a month for 128 kbps to US$150 for 512kbps to US$250 for 2meg bps. These are download rates, and in practice you may not get these speeds. In addition, there is an installation charge of US$100 (US$500 deposit for non-residents) and a monthly modem rental fee of US$15 (or you can buy a modem for around US$155.) DSL is currently available in the Belize City area, San Pedro, Caye Caulker, Corozal Town, Belmopan, San Ignacio, Benque Viejo, Orange Walk Town, Punta Gorda and Placencia areas, plus in a number of outlying areas. Check www.belizetelemedia.net for current DSL coverage. Note: DSL may not be available in all areas of these cities, towns and villages. Dial-up accounts are also available from BLT. Connection speed is slow, usually 28 to 52 kbps. Internet via digital cable is available in Belize City and San Pedro for around US$50 a month and may soon be available in a few other areas. Some Internet users in Belize go with a satellite service, mainly HughesNet. Setup, installation and activation fees vary but currently are in the US$1,000 range, with monthly fees for unlimited service of around US$60. There are issues with getting import permits for satellite service. Most businesses and nearly all hotels in Belize have Internet access. Internet access is also available at cybercafés in San Pedro, Caye Caulker, Placencia, San Ignacio, Punta Gorda, Belize City, Corozal Town and elsewhere. BTL also has installed Internet kiosks for public Internet access in several locations around the country. There are a number of wireless hotspots in Belize.

Language: The official language of Belize is English, and English speakers have little or no trouble communicating anywhere in the country. However, Creole, a combination of mostly English vocabulary with West African grammar, syntax and word endings, is used daily by many Belizeans of all backgrounds. Spanish is widely spoken as well, and tends to be the dominant language in areas bordering Mexico and Guatemala. The Belize government has called on all Belizeans to learn both Spanish and English. Garifuna and Maya languages also are spoken, and some Mennonites speak a German dialect. As many as two-thirds of Belizeans are bi- or tri-lingual.

Largest Cities and Towns: Populated areas in Belize are officially designated as a city, town or village. Belize City is the largest city, with an official population of 66,700, according to the 2009 update of the Belize Census. Including its outskirts, the city is home to about 80,000 people. Belmopan, the capital, also has been designated a city; it has a population of 20,000. San Ignacio and Orange Walk are among the country's largest towns, with San Ignacio having 19,900 residents, and Orange Wal Town 16,700, according to 2009 figures. However, the fast-growing San Pedro area of Ambergris Caye may soon surpass these towns in population. Official estimates put the island's population at 12,900 in mid-2009, but others put it close to 20,000, if you include temporary workers and expat snowbirds. The country's urban areas, in order of population from largest to smallest, as of mid-2009, are:

Urbanized Areas Population, 2009:

Belize City	66,700 (urban area 79,600)
Belmopan	20,000
San Ignacio/Santa Elena	19,900
Orange Walk	16,700
San Pedro	12,900
Dangriga	12,500
Corozal Town	9,400
Benque Viejo	9,300
Punta Gorda	5,500

According to the Belize Statistical Institute's 2009 estimate about 52% of Belize's population lives in urban areas and 48% in rural areas.

Belize is divided into six political districts, which function a little like U.S. counties. The six districts, from north to south, are Corozal, Orange Walk, Belize, Cayo, Stann Creek and Toledo.

Location, Size and Population: Belize is on the Caribbean Coast of Central America, bordered by Mexico to the north and Guatemala to the west and south. To the east is the Caribbean Sea. In Belize waters are as many as 400 islands, most unpopulated specks of sand or mangrove. Belize is about the size of the U.S. state of Massachusetts or Wales in the U.K. — 8,866 square miles — with a population estimated at around 330,000 in 2009, about as many people as live in metro Savannah, Georgia. From north to south Belize is less than 200 miles in length, and at its widest point it is less than 70 miles across.

Mail Service: Mail service to and from Belize is reasonably reliable and not too slow. Mail between the U.S. and Belize City usually takes less than a week. To outlying areas, however, it can take much longer – often several weeks. There are post offices in Belize City and in all towns and some villages. Many areas do not have home delivery. Unlike some of its Latin neighbors, Belize's postal service does not usually suffer from theft and lost mail. However, never send cash by mail. To mail an airmail letter from Belize to the U.S. costs 30 cents U.S., and 15 cents for a postcard. For fast, dependable but expensive international express delivery, DHL Worldwide Express is one choice. Federal Express is another.

Maps: The best maps of Belize are these:

Belize Traveller's Map, ITMB. Scale 1:250,000. The best general map to Belize, last updated as 6th edition in 2005. US$10.95. Available from www.itmb.com, www.amazon.com or at larger bookstores. Other general maps of Belize are *Insight Fleximap Belize* (2003); *Laminated Belize Map* by Borch (2008) and *National Geographic Belize Adventure Map* at 1:400,000 scale (2009).

Driver's Guide to Beautiful Belize, by Emory King. This mile-by-mile guide to most roads in Belize is really handy if you are traveling around the mainland. It's a 40-some-page booklet in 8 1/2" x 11" format. It was updated annually until Emory King's death in late 2007. It also has maps of Belize City and major towns. If you can find a copy, the price is around US$10 in Belize.

Belize Topographical Map, British Ordnance Survey, 1:250,000-scale. Beautiful map, in two flat sheets, with Belize City and town maps on reverse sides. Also, there are 44 individual topo maps to most of Belize, at 1:50,000 scale. These are excellent maps but in most cases haven't been updated since the early 1980s. Most are now out of print.

Google Earth has satellite images of Belize. Some areas are in fairly high resolution; others, not.

Media: Belize has six television stations, several radio stations and a number of weekly and monthly newspapers. There is no daily newspaper in the country. Cable television companies operate in most populated areas. Most of the weekly newspapers in Belize are based in Belize City, but a few other towns have weekly or monthly newspapers. The two best national newspapers in Belize are *Amandala* and *The Reporter.* These two weekly tabloids are independent and outspoken, though coverage runs to strident political and crime news, and since they are based in Belize City both have a Creole, port city orientation that does not fully reflect the views of all of Belize's diverse society. Both have Web editions: www.belizereporter.bz and www.amandala.bz. *The Guardian* and the *Belize Times* are operated by the two leading political parties in Belize. The weekly *Belize Times* is the United Peoples Party paper, and *The Guardian* is the United Democratic Party's organ.

Ambergris Caye has two weekly newspapers. The *San Pedro Sun* (tel. 501-226-2070, www.sanpedrosun.net) is operated by expats from the U.S. *Ambergris Today* (tel. 501-226-3462, www.ambergristoday.com) is run by Dorian Nuñez. There also are small newspapers in several outlying towns and villages: *Placencia Breeze* in Placencia, *The Star* in San Ignacio, *Howler* in Toledo and others. None of these newspapers has extensive classified listings for real estate or other items of interest to prospective expats, although the *San Pedro Sun* usually has a page or so of classified items for sale, and *Amandala* usually has some Belize City home rental and homes for sale listings.

Two Belize City TV stations, Channel 5 and Channel 7, may also be picked up in a good part of the country, though these stations are not carried on all cable systems. Channel 5 has an informative text version of its nightly news broadcast on-line at www.channel5belize.com. Channel 7, which has more of a UDP political slant, also has an on-line news summary at www.7newsbelize.com. Streaming video versions of the evening newscasts are now also available, though the quality can be spotty. Channel 3 in Orange Walk Town, affiliated with Centaur Cable (www.ctv3belizenews.com) offers some news of Northern Belize and the nation. LOVE-FM radio also has a TV arm. While some of the equipment is primitive, it has some good locally produced programming. Plus TV and Open TV, both in Belmopan, cover capital news.

KREM-FM 96.5 and LOVE-FM 95.1 (frequencies vary around the country) are the two most popular radio stations in Belize. KREM-FM has a morning talk and call-in show from 6 to 8:30 a.m., with host Evan Hyde Jr. During the day it broadcasts an eclectic mix of local music, rap, soul and other music, along with Belize news. LOVE-FM offers "easy listening" music during the day, with a morning call-in and talk show hosted by station owner Rene Villanueva from 6 to 8 a.m. This station has three full newscasts at 6:45 a.m., 12:30 p.m. and 6 p.m., Monday to Saturday, and news updates frequently. Both stations offer Internet broadcasts (you have to install Real One media player.) Web site for KREM is www.krem.bz, for LOVE www.lovefm.com. Another station, this one with a UDP slant, is WAVE-FM. *Belize First Magazine,* an on-line magazine about Belize founded by Lan Sluder, has hundreds of pages of articles and archives at www.belizefirst.com. Among its offerings are eBooks on Belize and a news archive going back more than eight years. Most of these media can be accessed through links from www.belizenews.com. *San Pedro Daily* is an on-line "newspaper" that mainly runs unedited articles picked up from other media. *Ambergris Daily* is another daily online newsletter/blog on San Pedro. Cable TV, typically with some 50 channels from the U.S. and Mexico, is available in many areas of Belize, offered by local companies. You pay around US$20 to $30 monthly for cable service. Some Belize residents have satellite TV.

Medical Care: Belize City is the center for medical care in Belize. A number of dentists and private medical clinics are available there. Many serious problems can be treated at Karl Heusner Memorial Hospital in Belize City (Princess Margaret Dr., tel. 501-223-1548), a modern public hospital albeit one plagued by equipment problems and supply shortages, and it has also had some management problems. It's hard to beat the rates, though – under US$50 per day for a hospital room. There are seven other public hospitals in

Belize, including two regional hospitals: the Southern Regional Hospital in Dangriga, and the Northern Regional Hospital in Orange Walk Town. Altogether, there are about 600 public hospital beds in Belize. The public hospitals provide the four basic medical specialties: internal medicine, surgery, pediatrics and OB-GYN. Karl Heusner Memorial also provides neuro, ENT, physiotherapy, orthopedic surgery and several other services.

The quality of these hospitals varies considerably. Karl Heusner Memorial -- named after a prominent Belize City physician -- opened in 1997 and has much modern equipment, such as a CAT-scan, though some Belizeans and expats complain that even this hospital is chronically short of supplies, including at times toilet paper. In 2004-2005, it added new facilities including ones for neurosurgery and trauma care. The Southern Regional Hospital in Dangriga, which opened in 2000, is another modern facility, with much of the same medical technologies and equipment as you'd find in a community hospital in an American town. However, other hospitals leave a lot to be desired. The Northern Regional Hospital in Orange Walk, for example, though it is being upgraded, still looks more like a refugee camp than a hospital, with low concrete block buildings and limited equipment. Several small medical clinics, one essentially a small hospital, operate in San Pedro.

Besides these hospitals, Belize has a network of around 60 public health clinics and rural health posts in many towns and villages around the country, providing primary medical and dental care. Most of these suffer from inadequate staffing, too many patients for their available resources and lack of equipment and medicine. Doctors may diagnose health problems accurately, but they may not be able to provide the proper medications to cure them. In addition to these public hospitals and clinics, Belize has two private hospitals -- La Loma Luz, a not-for-profit Seventh Day Adventist hospital in Santa Elena near San Ignacio, and Belize Medical Associates, a for-profit facility in Belize City. Universal Health Services, a third private hospital, is being merged into Karl Heusner Memorial. Altogether these private hospitals have fewer than 50 hospital beds. There also are a number of physicians and dentists in private practice, mostly in Belize City.

Starting in the late 1990s, health care in Belize got a boost, thanks to the arrival of a group of several dozen medical volunteers from Cuba. Currently almost 100 Cuban nurses and physicians are in Belize.

Most physicians and dentists in Belize are trained in the U.S., Guatemala, Mexico or Great Britain. There are three so-called offshore medical schools in Belize, but their graduates are unlikely to practice in Belize. A nursing school, affiliated with the University of Belize, trains nurses for work in Belize. While many expats do go to Guatemala, or to Chetumal or Mérida, Mexico, for specialized treatment, others who can afford it go to Houston, Miami, New Orleans or elsewhere in the U.S. *(Also see the chapter on Health in Belize below.)*

Money: The Belize currency is the Belize dollar, which for many years has been tied to the U.S. dollar at a fixed 2 Belize to 1 U.S. dollar rate. Moneychangers at the borders often give a slightly higher rate than 2 Belize for 1 U.S. dollar, sometimes as much as 2.1 or 2.2 to 1, depending on the current demand for American greenbacks. U.S. dollars (bills, not coins) are accepted everywhere in Belize, although you often will receive change in Belizean money, or in a mix of Belizean and U.S. money. There has been talk for years of dollarizing the Belize economy, but so far that move hasn't gotten traction. The Belize dollar is difficult if not impossible to exchange anywhere outside of Belize (except at border areas of Guatemala and Mexico). Paper-money Belize denominations are the 100-, 50-, 20-, 10-, 5- and 2-dollar bills. Belize coins come in 1-dollar, 50, 25, 10, 5 and 1 Belizean cent units. The 25-cent piece is called a shilling.

Mennonite school children near Little Belize in Corozal District

People of Belize: Belize is truly a multicultural society. Mestizos make up about 49% of the population. These are persons of mixed European and Maya heritage, typically speaking Spanish as a first language and having social values more closely associated with Latin America than with the Caribbean. Mestizos are concentrated in northern and western Belize. There is often a distinction made between Mestizos who came to Belize from the Yucatán during the Caste Wars of the mid-19th century and more recent immigrants from Central America. Mestizos are the fastest growing segment of the population.

Creoles, once the dominant ethnic group in the country, now make up only about 25% of the population. These are people usually but not always of

25

African heritage, typically speaking Creole and English and often having a set of social values derived from England and the Caribbean. Creoles are concentrated in Belize City and Belize District, although there are predominantly Creole villages elsewhere, including the village of Placencia.

Maya constitute about 11% of the population. There are concentrations of Yucatec Maya in Corozal and Orange Walk districts, Mopan Maya in Toledo and Cayo districts, and Kekchí Maya in about 30 villages in Toledo. Garifuna (also known as Garinagu or Black Caribs) make up about 6% of the Belizean population. They are of mixed African and Carib Indian heritage. Most came to then British Honduras from Honduras in 1830s. Dangriga and Punta Gorda are towns with large Garifuna populations, as are the villages of Seine Bight, Hopkins and Barranco.

The "Other" group, making up about 8% of the population, includes several thousand Mennonites who came to Belize from Canada and Mexico in the 1950s. Divided into conservative and progressive groups, they farm large acreages in Belize. Conservatives live mostly in Shipyard, Barton Creek and Little Belize, avoid the use of modern farm equipment and speak German among themselves. Progressives live mostly in Blue Creek, Progresso and Spanish Lookout. Belize also has sizable communities of East Indians, who live mainly around Belize City and in Toledo, Chinese, mostly from Taiwan, living in Belize City and elsewhere, Lebanese and "Gringos," mostly expats from the U.S. and Canada concentrated in San Pedro, Placencia, Cayo and around Corozal Town.

Belize predominantly is a country of the young. More than two out of five Belizeans are under 15 years of age, and the median average age is around 19 years.

Pharmacies: There are drug stores in Belize City and in all towns. Many prescription drugs cost less in Belize than in the U.S., though pharmacies may not stock a wide selection of drugs. In general, in Belize prescriptions usually are not needed for antibiotics and some other drugs that require prescriptions in the U.S., although pharmacies owned by physicians or operated by hospitals (common in Belize) may require or suggest a consultation with the doctor.

Satellite Radio: Yes, satellite radio is available in Belize. Although Sirius and XM Radio have merged, and most of their programming is now shared, the two services use different satellites. Currently, Sirius can be picked up better than XM in most of Belize.

Taxes: The main taxes you'll face in Belize are:
• National Goods and Services Tax (GST) of 10% on nearly all products and services. The GST replaced a 9% sales tax in mid-2006. A few items are exempt: basic foodstuffs such as rice, flour, tortillas, eggs and beans; some medicines; school textbooks; transportation on buses and airplanes, items being exported and hotel stays taxed under the hotel tax system. Like a value-added tax, the GST is supposed to be included in the final purchase price, rather than added on like a sales tax, but many businesses quote prices without the GST and just add it on at the cash register. Very small businesses,

such as street vendors, don't have to register for the GST and don't charge the tax. There are additional taxes on alcohol, cigarettes and a few other items. More than one-half the cost of gasoline is due to government tax.

• Import duties of up to 80% on imported items, with some items such as computers and books having no duty (though you pay sales tax) and most having 25% or less duty. The average duty on imported items is around 20%.

• Personal income tax ranges from 25% to up to 45%, with those making about US$10,000 or less per year effectively paying no tax. The 45% rate kicks in on an income of about US$47,500. Personal income tax is only on income derived in Belize; there is no Belize income tax on income generated outside Belize.

• Corporate or business tax on gross revenues (without any deductions) rather than earnings, with the percentage tax depending on the category of business. The rate for what is actually a turnover tax ranges from 0.75% to 25%. For most businesses it is 1.5% of gross revenue; for most professions it is 3% of gross revenue. Revenue taxes for several types of businesses were increased in early 2005 and again in 2008.

• Property taxes vary but are about 1% to 1 1/2% of the value of the undeveloped land, payable annually on April 1. Property taxes on homes and other developed land are very low. For example, the property tax on a nice four-bedroom North American-style home would likely be in the range of US$100 to $200. Many people with simple homes pay only US$10 or $20 property tax annually. There is a 5% speculation tax on land of 300 acres or more, payable annually on April 1 based on the value of the land. Since 1999, there has been a move to make property taxes based on the market value of the property, but implementation has been spotty at best.

• Property transfer tax (often called "stamp duty") of 5% of property value payable at time of closing. This 5% tax applies to existing homes, most lots and land, whether purchased by a Belizean or a foreigner. If you are buying a newly built, or substantially renovated (typically about 80% renovated) home or condo, in addition to the 5% transfer tax you will also owe the 10% GST, for a total of 15% due on closing. This GST also applies, in some cases, to the first sale of lots in a subdivision, but not to their resale.

• No inheritance tax.

• No capital gains tax.

• Hotel tax of 9% on hotel stays.

Belize has signed double taxation agreements with many countries, including: United Kingdom, Bahamas, Barbados, St. Vincent and the Grenadines, Dominica, Grenada, St. Kitts and Nevis, Suriname, Guyana, Jamaica, Trinidad and Tobago and St. Lucia.

Note: This very brief overview of Belize taxation should not be relied on for your actual situation, for which professional tax advice is recommended.

Telecommunications: Belize has one of the best telephone systems in the region, with a combination of fiber optic cable and microwave, plus

27

cell service in most of the country. There are some 100,000 cell phone subscribers and 33,000 landlines. You can dial to or from even remote areas of Belize and usually get a clear, clean line. That's the good news. The bad news is that telephone service in Belize is expensive, both for users and for Belizean taxpayers who are the footing part of the bill.

Belize Telemedia, Ltd. (BTL) is a company with a checkered history dating back to 1956, when a British firm, Cable & Wireless, set up the first telecommunications system in what was then British Honduras. After several changes, it became Belize Telecommunications, Ltd. in 1987. In 2001, majority ownership in BTL was purchased from the Belize government by Carlisle Holdings, Ltd., a U.K. company under the control of Michael Ashcroft, a British lord and Conservative politician. BTL retained a legal monopoly on all types of telecommunications services in Belize until the end of 2002, when its license to operate all forms of telecommunications in Belize expired. It is no longer the monopoly it once was, since BTL now has some limited competition, but it's still the 800-pound gorilla of Belize telcom -- and if you live in Belize, you can't escape its clutches. Lord Ashcroft's Carlisle Holdings sold its interest in BTL back to the Belize government in 2004. Later that same year, the Belize government sold BTL to Innovative Communications Corporation (ICC), an American company based in the U.S. Virgin Islands. ICC added 5,000 new landlines and claims to have brought on thousands of new cell users. Then, BTL/ICC and the Belize government got into a row, culminating in a lawsuit in Miami.

In 2006, Lord Ashcroft, a friend of some top Belizean officials, moved to repurchase some of BTL. However, in 2009 the Belize government under Prime Minister Dean Barrow renationalized Belize Telemedia Ltd. The government has taken over the operations of BTL, supposedly pending the sale of company stock to Belizean and other private investors. The amount the government will have to pay Lord Ashcroft and other owners is in dispute. Stay tuned.

In spring 2005, a new Belizean-owned wireless company, Speednet, began offering digital cell service in Belize, with an interconnect to BTL. Speednet, or Smart as its consumer brand is called, now offers wireless voice and Internet service in most of Belize. In 2009, it was disclosed that Michael Ashcroft also had an interest in Speednet.

It costs about US$50 for BTL to install a telephone in your home, plus a US$100 refundable deposit. If you are not a citizen or official resident, the deposit jumps to US$500. There is a US$10 a month residential service fee. Local calls in Belize are charged by the minute (each local minute costs US5 cents, after some free units.) Costs for calls to other parts of Belize vary from US 10 to 20 cents a minute during the day, and half that at night. A 10-minute daytime call to Belize City from San Pedro is US$1. Costs of direct-dialed long-distance calls to the U.S. currently are US40 to 63 cents a minute, less at night, and also less if you use BTL's 10-10-199 service.

With Belize and international long-distance and cell phone rates so high, some Belizeans with personal computers are turning to Voice over Internet Protocol (VoIP) services, such as Skype. However, BTL attempts to block Skype and other VoIP. In 2007, BTL began offering its own VoIP service, naturally at much higher cost than most other services.

A seven-digit dialing system was introduced in 2002. Formerly, telephone numbers in Belize had five digits, plus a two-digit local exchange number in Belize. Now to reach any number in Belize you must dial all seven digits. All numbers begin with a district area code: 2 for Belize District, which includes Ambergris Caye and Caye Caulker, 3 for Orange Walk District, 4 for Corozal District, 5 for Stann Creek District, 6 for mobile phones, 7 for Toledo District and 8 for Cayo District. The second digit of the phone number is a service provider code: 0 for prepaid services, 1 for mobile services and 2 for regular telephone service. So a number like 22x-xxxx indicates that it is in Belize District and is a regular telephone, not a cell phone and not a prepaid service. When dialing from outside Belize, you must also dial the country code and international calling prefix. The country code for Belize is 501. When dialing from the U.S., add 011. Pay phones in Belize now operate only with a prepaid BTL calling card. These cards are sold in many shops in denominations from US$5 to $25. BTL provides a single telephone directory for Belize, published annually in the spring. Most numbers can be looked up on the online directory on BTL's Web site, www.btl.net. *(See also Internet above.)*

Time: Local time is GMT-6 year-round, the same as U.S. Central Standard Time. Belize does not observe daylight savings time.

Big new service station and convenience store near Belmopan

CHAPTER 2:
WHAT THINGS COST IN BELIZE

Belize doesn't have a cost of living. It has several costs of living. The traditional view is that Belize is the most expensive country in Central America, yet one of the least expensive in the Caribbean. While there's truth to that, it really doesn't take into account that the actual cost of living in Belize can vary from almost nothing to very high. You can live in a luxury four-bedroom house on Ambergris Caye, with air conditioning, telephones and faxes, a dishwasher, microwave and cable TV, U.S. food in your pantry and imported vodka in your glass, and you can spend thousands a month. Or you can live in a small house in Cayo, or around Corozal Town, with no phone or internet, eat beans and rice and rice and beans, and drink local rum for US$600 a month or less. Most expats in Belize choose somewhere in between. Some condos in Belize go for more than US$750,000, but I know one expat who built and equipped his small house, using his own labor, with thatch from nature and timbers from a lagoon, for US$4,000, and that includes furniture and kitchen equipment.

After all, per capita income in Belize is a fraction of that in the U.S. A weekly wage of US$125 to $150 for six days of work is considered pretty good. Tens of thousands of Belizeans live, and in many cases live comfortably, on a few thousand dollars a year. You can, too. Or you can compromise, forsaking those high-cost icons of civilization such as 80,000 BTU air conditioners, while keeping the family car, boat or other toys that you enjoy. Live partly on the Belizean style, partly in the U.S. style, and enjoy the benefits of both, and you'll get more, for less. One American expat, who returned to Colorado after living in Belize for five years, said he was surprised at how the cost of living in the U.S. had increased since he left. "Compared to Colorado Springs, ANYTHING in Belize is cheap. And I can't wait to get back — I just don't have enough money to live here in anything but poverty!"

Price Sampler: What Things Costs in Belize

Here's a sampler of costs for common items in Belize, as of 2009. *All prices are shown here in U.S. dollars.* As in other countries, prices for many items vary depending on where and when you buy them.

Transportation

Gallon of regular unleaded gas: $4.65 (the pump price varies slightly by area, and fluctuates frequently reflecting the international price of oil – in 2008 and 2009 the price ranged from around US$2.50 to over $5)

Gallon of diesel fuel: $4.25

Bus fare from Belize City to San Ignacio: $2.50 regular, $3 express

Water taxi from Belize City to San Pedro, Ambergris Caye: $10

One-way adult airfare from Belize City municipal airport to Placencia: $84

One-way adult airfare from Belize City municipal airport to San Pedro: $35

Taxi fare within Belize City: $3-4

Utilities/Telecommunications

1-kilowatt hour of current (electricity): $0.21

"Current" (electrical service) for 1000 KW monthly: $210

Installation of residential telephone: $50 plus $100 deposit ($500 if you are not a Belizean citizen or permanent resident)

Monthly charge for residential telephone: $10

10-minute call from Corozal to Belize City: $1

10-minute daytime call to U.S.: $6

DSL Internet access: $50 to $200 a month

Digital cellular service: $50 for 250 anytime minutes (incoming calls are free) plus 30 text messages

Water and sewer service: $10-$30+ (varies by area)

Butane, 100-pound tank, delivered: $50 (varies by area)

Bottled water, delivered: $2.50/gallon

"Dirt" (trash) pick-up: Free to $10 a month (varies by area)

Staples in Grocery Stores (Prices Vary by Store)

Red beans: $0.90 per pound

Coffee (Belizean, Gallon Jug): $8 per pound

Milk: $2.25 1/2 gallon

Ground steak (lean ground beef): $1.50 per pound
Pork chops: $2 per pound
Chicken: $1.25 per pound
Loaf of white bread: $1 (whole wheat $2.50-$3)
Corn tortillas, freshly made: $0.02-$0.04 each
Bananas: 10 to 20 for $1
Avocados (pears): 6 for $1 (varies seasonally)
Flour, bulk, 1 lb.: $1
Onions: $0.60 per pound (varies seasonally)
Soft drink, Coca-Cola, 12 oz.: $0.50 - 0.75 each
Local rum, liter: $7 - $12
Sugar: $0.27 per pound
Crackers (Premium Saltines): $3.32
Cigarettes, Independence local brand: $3 a pack
Canned soup (Campbell's Chicken Noodle): $1.80
Cereal (Raisin Bran): $5
Cooking oil (1-2-3 brand from Mexico), 1/2 liter: $1.75

Household Items
Mennonite-made wood dining table: $175
Music CD (pirated): $5
Whirlpool 12,000 BTU air-conditioner: $700
Mabe (Mexican) frost-free 16 cubic foot refrigerator: $675
Small home appliances at Mirab, Courts, Brodies, Hofius or other stores: about 25% to 50% more than prices in the U.S.

Entertainment
Fish and beans and rice at local restaurant, Hopkins: $4
Fish, French fries and cole slaw dinner, San Pedro: $12
Lobster dinner at nice restaurant, Belize City: $30
Movie theater ticket, Princess, Belize City: $8.50
Rum drink at bar, Placencia: $3
Belikin beer at bar in Cayo: $2.50

Shelter Costs
Rent for simple two-bedroom house in Corozal Town: $200 to $400
Rent for modern two-bedroom apartment in San Pedro: $800 to $1,800
Cost to build a reinforced concrete home: $40 to $100 per sq. ft., finished out moderately
Small concrete house and lot in Belmopan or Cayo: $30,000 to $100,000
Modern three-bedroom house and beachview lot in Consejo: $145,000--$250,000
Two-bedroom condo on Ambergris Caye: $200,000 to $750,000

Medical Care
Office visit, private physician: $25
Teeth cleaning, private dentist: $40
Root canal and crown, private dentist: $250 - $500

Building Supplies
50# bag of cement: $6 to $7
"Prefab" Mennonite House, 800 sq. ft, set up on your lot, $16,000+

Family Budgets in Belize
As noted, the cost of living varies greatly in Belize, depending on your lifestyle, preferences and place of residence. Here are several different budgets.

Monthly Budget (in U.S. Dollars) for Affluent Couple in San Pedro
This budget reflects the cost of living for a 45-year-old affluent expat couple that rent a two-bedroom condo on Ambergris Caye. Assumption: The couple owns a golf cart for transportation, owns a small boat and spends freely for entertainment and personal expenses.

Rent	$1,250
Electricity (1000 KW)	210
Telephone (including long distance)	150
Water	100
Bottled water	80
Butane	50
Groceries	400
DSL or Cable Internet	50
Entertainment and dining out	400
Cable TV	25
Golf cart maintenance	100
Boat expenses	350
Health insurance	378
Out-of-pocket medical/dental care	150
Flights to Belize City (monthly)	140
Other travel expenses	300
Clothing	100
Household help	350
Other personal expenses	250
Total	**$4,833**

Monthly Budget (in U.S. Dollars) for Middle-Class Couple
This budget reflects the cost of living for a 55-year-old expat couple that owns their own home in Placencia. It assumes that the couple has paid for their US$150,000 house and therefore do not have a house payment. Also assumed: their 2002 Ford Explorer is paid for and that they choose to pur-

chase health insurance, which includes medevac coverage, from an international insurer.

Electricity (750KW a month)	$158
Telephone (including long distance)	110
Butane	45
Groceries	320
Cable TV	25
Internet	50
Entertainment and dining out	200
Property tax	24
Auto insurance	20
Health insurance	300
Out-of-pocket medical expenses	150
Home insurance (at 2% of value)	300
Gasoline (40 gallons a month @ $4.50)	180
Auto maintenance	100
Clothing	75
Other personal expenses	150
Household help/care taker (part-time)	200
Other	125
Total	**$2,532**

Barebones Budget

This budget is for a single 60-year-old permanent resident in a Belizean-style rented house near San Ignacio. Assumptions: The individual uses public transportation and takes advantage of local public health care system.

Rent	$250
Transportation (bus and taxi)	40
Telephone	40
Groceries	150
Entertainment	75
Butane	20
Water, dirt (trash) pick-up	25
Electricity (400 KW)	84
Local health care and medicines	95
Cable TV	20
Clothing	20
Other personal expenses	50
Total	**$859**

CHAPTER 3:
CRIME AND SAFETY IN BELIZE

I don't won't to scare you, because things aren't as bad as they sound when you read about them from afar, but you need to know: the dark underbelly of life in Belize (and indeed in most developing countries) is crime, especially property crime. As a cautionary tale, I'm presenting some of the most negative reports, so you'll be prepared for the worst. Most expats in Belize say that while they have to be mindful of the possibility of thefts and burglarlies that they don't spend much time worrying about it.

An American who owns a second home on Ambergris Caye posted this plaintive note on one of the message boards on www.ambergriscaye.com.

"I'd like to know why the [San Pedro] town council or town board can't do anything about getting the thieves and thugs off the island. I just received a call today saying our house had been broken into again. This time they broke into a locked closet, then broke into a large metal lock box with heavy duty locks on it. Took everything of value again. The same thing had happened in July. That time they didn't get into the lock box. Sometimes they break in just to put graffiti on the walls. They also broke into our little guesthouse, with nothing of value in it, (just painted and fixed up) punctured the waterbed and destroyed the inside. We've tried the caretaker thing and have gone thru six caretakers in five years. We pay them good money to live there free, but the only thing they did was steal from us, too. My neighbor was also robbed every time we were. All of his stuff was also locked up, but they have all the time in the world to go thru your things and break into everything. These thieves live in the dump, have no job and live to rob people. After a couple of months with no proof of a job can't they deport them? These are the same ones who have robbed tourists (even at gun point) on the beach. There have been three within the last few months. I'm about ready to sell my place and start talking … about this terrible (true) situation. When the tourists or people planning to vacation in San Pedro, or buy houses or property, find out the reality of what's really happening, maybe they'll decide to go elsewhere."

This kind of comment, unfortunately, is common among those who own vacation or second homes in Belize. And it's not unheard of among expats who live full-time in Belize, either. Gaz Cooper, who lived on Ambergris Caye for many years, formerly operating a small hotel and dive shop on North Ambergris, says: "My house has been broken into four times and if I were to reveal the whole story it … would make your hair curl. One guy got caught in the house and still got away with it, God knows how."

Another resort owner on the south end of Ambergris Caye said her house was broken into while she was sleeping, and her wallet was stolen. These accounts are from Ambergris Caye, but the situation is similar in most parts of Belize. When I meet homeowners in Placencia, Cayo or Corozal Town often the talk turns to the latest break-in at a neighbor's home. Residents and tourism operators in Placencia village, Caye Caulker and Corozal are reporting increased problems with burglaries and thefts, a trend that mirrors a similar situation taking place in San Pedro.

One tourism operator in Placencia said that of the last five guest parties the operator had booked in Placencia village, all five had been hit with thefts, usually in the daytime. On Caye Caulker, two hotel owners reported that break-ins at hotels, businesses and homes were occurring almost nightly. "In Corozal, I conducted an informal survey of expat residents and found ... 84% of those living in Corozal Town had experienced at least major burglaries or worse, some victimized more than once [over the past four years]," noted Margaret Briggs, who formerly operated a web site for expats in Corozal, but who in summer 2005 sold her home in Corozal and moved to New Mexico.

The San Pedro Chamber of Commerce, following a series of high-profile robberies and burglaries that culminated in the murder of a security guard at Fido's, developed a list of 20 steps -- including screening new arrivals to the island coming from the mainland, registering street vendors and strengthening community watch programs -- it recommends to help stop the crime wave.

Burglaries and petty theft in Belize are disturbingly common. Of course, this isn't unique to Belize. There are about 2.2 million burglaries reported in the United States annually. When you add together burglaries, auto thefts and larcenies/thefts, the total for the U.S. is around 10.5 million. That's one theft-related crime for every 10 households. So, in the U.S., in a decade the chance of your household being a victim of theft is statistically 100%.

But the situation is perhaps more acute in Belize, in part because often the police do little about the problem. This can be because they are incompetent, or lack the necessary training or, in some cases, they know the culprits and refuse to arrest them. Most often I think it is due to lack of resources. In many cases constables don't even have the basic tools to do their jobs. There have been a number of reports about police cars that simply sat at the police station because there wasn't money to buy gas for them.

In many cases, the local authorities do have a good idea who is responsible, but in a society such as Belize where most people in a village are at least distantly related, police have to go along to get along, and this may mean turning their eye if they think a cousin is doing the "teifing" or drug dealing. One American expat in Placencia had to briefly leave the peninsula because drug dealers thought this person had found and kept a shipment of cocaine. Local constables probably knew who the drug dealers were but were reluctant to take any action. They felt powerless to offer protection, so they recommended this American go away on vacation until things cooled down.

What can you do to avoid being a burglary victim in Belize? Several things can help:

Put burglar bars on your windows and doors. These are available from local hardware stores and cost around US$50 to $75 per window. If your house is in a remote area, the bad guys may just attach a chain to the burglar bars and pull them off with a truck, but in most areas they offer a good first line of defense.

Get a dog. A dog is THE most effective deterrent to break-ins in Belize. It doesn't have to be a vicious dog, but it should sound vicious. A big, black dog is considered the best deterrent.

Put a fence or wall around your property. This won't deter serious thieves, but it may slow them down.

Hire a caretaker you can trust. Though there are irresponsible or crooked caretakers, there also are many who are dependable and will look out for your property when you are away. Ask around, especially among fellow expats and at local churches, for an honest individual or family. Remember, the mango doesn't fall far from the tree. You will usually have to provide free living quarters and a monthly stipend, typically about US$100 to $300 a month, depending on what you require of the caretaker. There can also be issues related to your role as an employer, including the requirement to provide social security payments, severance pay, vacation time and other employment issues.

Install an alarm system with motion detectors. Belize has several security companies that install and monitor residential security systems. Among the security companies in Belize are:

AAA Security Services Corp., Belize City; tel. 501-223-4900, www.aaasecurity.net.

Elite Security Services, Belize City with an office in Dangriga; tel. 501-223-0202, email essbelize_staff@yahoo.com.

KBH Security Systems, Belize City, with offices in Belmopan, Corozal, Punta Gorda, Dangriga, Orange Walk Town, San Ignacio, San Pedro, Placencia and Independence; tel. 501-227-2263, www.kbh-security.com.bz.

Check the Belize telephone directory for other security companies.

Personal Safety

The homicide and violent crime rate in Belize is higher than in most large urban areas of the United States. Typically, there are 90 to 100 murders a year in Belize. That's a murder rate about five to six times higher than the average in the U.S., which has an annual rate in the range of 6 murders per 100,000 population, which itself is very high compared to Canada (about 2 homicides per 100,000) or Western Europe. However, most of the murders are concentrated in Belize City, and much of the other violent crime involves a farm worker getting drunk on Saturday night and knifing or machete chopping somebody in a cool spot (bar.)

To put the Belize crime rate in perspective, Guatemala City sees about 100 murders a WEEK. Also, although there are gangs in Belize City, Belize does not have the severe youth gang problems that plague Mexico, Guatemala, Honduras and El Salvador. In Central America alone, it is estimated there are 250,000 members of *maras,* Spanish for species of swarming, aggressive ants. While there are gangs in Belize City, the situation nothing like that in Honduras, where the number of gang members is higher than the total population of Belize City.

A recent report by non-governmental organizations in Central America puts the murder rate for Guatemala, Honduras and El Salvador as follows: El Salvador 55.5 homicides per 100,000 inhabitants; Honduras, 40.6; and Guatemala, 37.5. In 2009, Belize's rate was around 33 per 100,000.

While most expats are concerned about burglaries and thefts, most retirees and foreign residents in Belize express little concern about their personal safety. Certainly, it's wise to use common sense: Don't walk on in unlit areas at night; don't pick up strangers in your car; put up exterior lighting around your home driveway and entrance.

Colonial-era buildings in the Fort George area of Belize City

CHAPTER 4:
GETTING ALONG IN BELIZE

If you're looking for a place to live or to retire that's just like back home, only better, for a United States or a Canada on the cheap, for Florida with ruins, reefs and rum, you may get a rude awakening when you move to Belize. Because Belize isn't just like the U.S. or Canada. It does have cheap rum, awe-inspiring ruins, beautiful Caribbean seas and much more. But the rules are different. The people who make and enforce the rules are different. Sometimes there are no rules. Sometimes there is a set of rules for you, and a different one for everyone else. Just about every expat resident of Belize has some story to tell about problems he or she faced in adjusting to life in Belize -- or, in not adjusting. Let's look at some of the differences, and what they mean to you as a potential resident or retiree.

Population of a Small City

First, Belize is a country with a population hardly bigger than a small city in the U.S. Even including recent illegal and uncounted immigrants from El Salvador, Guatemala and Honduras, the population of the entire country is only about 330,000. Imagine the difficulties your hometown would have if it suddenly became a country. Belize has to maintain embassies, establish social, educational and medical systems, raise a little army, and conduct affairs of state and international diplomacy, all with the resources of a small city.

You can see the difficulties Belize faces in just getting by in a world of mega states. It lacks the people resources, not to mention the tax base and financial resources, to get things done in the way North Americans expect. If you're a snap-to-it, get-it-done-right kind of person, you're going to wrestle with a lot of crocodiles in Belize.

No More Power

Most expats seeking retirement or residency in Belize are white middle-class North Americans, from a society still run by white middle-class North Americans. Belize, on the other hand, is a truly multi-cultural society, with Creoles, Mestizos, Maya, Garifuna, Asians, and what in the rest of Latin America would be called Gringos, living together in complex and changing relationships, living together in probably more harmony than anyone has a right to expect. In several areas, Creoles dominate; increasingly, in other areas Spanish-speaking Belizeans and immigrants dominate. One thing is for certain, though: In this mix, North Americans, Europeans and Asians have very limited power. Money talks in Belize, of course, as it does everywhere. Most of Belize's tourism industry is owned by foreign interests. Much of its industry and agriculture is controlled by multinational companies or by a few wealthy, well-connected Belizean families.

Politically, however, the typical North American resident of Belize is powerless. He or she has no vote and is truly outside the political process. That's the fate of expats everywhere, but some who come to Belize, seeing a country that is superficially much like back home, are shocked that they no longer have a power base and are, in a political sense at least, truly powerless. The North American or European is not so much at the bottom rung of Belizean society, as off the ladder completely. If you like to pick up the phone and give your congressional representative a piece of your mind, you're going to miss this opportunity in Belize.

Culture Shock

Culture shock is what happens when everything looks about 20 degrees off kilter, when all the ways you learned were the right ways to deal with people turn out to be wrong. It is a state, someone said, of temporary madness. Usually it happens after about six months to a year in a new situation. At first, you're excited and thrilled by the new things you're seeing. Then, one day, you just can't stand one more dish of stew chicken and rice and beans.

In Belize, culture shock is sometimes masked by the surface familiarity. Most Belizeans speak English, albeit a different English. They watch -- such a shame -- American television. They drive big, old Buicks and Chevrolets or Japanese cars. They even accept U.S. currency. But, underneath the surface sameness, Belize is different, a collection of differences. Cases in point: The ancient Mayan view of time, cyclical and recurring, and even the Mayan view today, are grossly different from the linear way urban North Americans view time. The emerging Hispanic majority in Belize has social, religious and political views that are quite different from the views of the average North American, or, even of the typical Belizean Creole. A Belize Creole saying is "If crab no walk 'e get fat, if 'e walk too much 'e lose claw." Is that a cultural concept your community shares? In many cases, family connections and relationships are more important in Belize than they are in the U.S. or Canada. Time is less important. Not wanting to disappoint, Belizeans may say "maybe" when "no" would be more accurate. Otherwise honest men may take money under the table for getting things moving. Values North Americans take for granted, such as "work hard and get ahead," may not apply in Belize in the same way. Physical labor, especially agricultural work and service work, because of the heritage of slavery and colonialism, is sometimes viewed as demeaning among some Belize groups. A Belizean may work long hours for himself - fishing or logging can be backbreaking labor - but be reluctant to do so for an employer.

Respect, Not Money

Respect is important in Belize. If you make a pass at a friend's girl, you may end up on the wrong end of a knife or machete. If you diss one of your employees or neighbors, you may find yourself in a bad situation on a dark night. Just when you least expect it, you may get jumped on a back street and beat nearly to death. If you say something bad about a politician or a business owner, it may come back and bite you years later. Belizeans have long memories, and they don't take well to criticism, especially not from outsiders. On the other hand, Belizeans can be surprisingly rough and tumble in their personal relationships. They'll say the nastiest things to each other, just run the other guy down for being stupid and a total fool, and then the next day both parties forget about it and act like they've been friends or cousins all their lives, which they have been. The best advice is to make as many friends in Belize as you can. Sooner or later, you'll need them.

No Wal-Marts in Belize

Belize has no Wal-Marts. No K-Marts. No Home Depots. No Circuit Cities. No McDonalds fast food restaurants. While this lack of homogenization is in Belize's favor, it also means that you can't go down to your neighborhood hyperstore and select from 40 kinds of dish soap, or 18 brands of underwear. Rum may be US$7 or $8 a bottle, but Cheetos may be US$5 a bag. Every CD player, nearly every piece of plumbing and electrical equipment, every car and truck, every pair of scissors, every bottle of aspirin, is imported, and often transshipped thousands of miles from one port to another before it gets to the final destination in Belize. Then it's carried on a bus or under a Cessna seat somewhere else.

Some items simply aren't available in Belize, or supplies may be spotty. Bags of cement, for example, sometimes are in short supply, and the cost, around US$7 for a 50-pound bag, is higher than you'd pay back home. To get ordinary items such as building nails or a certain kind of auto part, you may have to call several different suppliers. Belize's small population is spread out over a relatively large area, served by a network of bad roads (though they are getting better), old planes and leaky boats. Although the government is shifting its focus from excise and import taxes more to income and consumption taxes, much of government revenue still comes from import taxes, so the prices you pay may reflect a tax of 20% to 80% or more. In short, Belize is an inefficient market of low-paid consumers, a country of middlemen and mom 'n pop stores, few of which could last more than a month or two in a highly competitive marketplace like the U.S. This is what gives Belize its unique flavor in an age of franchised sameness. But, you better Belize it, it also provides a lot of frustration and higher prices.

Human remains at Actun Tunichil Muknal Maya site

CHAPTER 5:
YOUR HEALTH IN BELIZE

A major issue for expats, especially retirees, is health care. Health care in Belize is a mixed picture. On the positive side, health and hygiene standards in Belize are considerably higher than in most other countries in Central America or in Mexico. However, as a developing country Belize's medical resources are in no way comparable to those offered in the United States, Canada and Western Europe. If you are older and especially if you face chronic health problems, you will have to look closely at the health care tradeoffs — a healthier way of living, lower medical costs and more person- alized care in Belize versus the high-tech, low touch, high cost of health care and health insurance back home.

Hospitals and Other Health Care Facilities in Belize

Belize has a mixed public and private health care system. The vast majority of Belizeans get medical care through a system of government-run hospitals and clinics.

Public Hospitals in Belize

There are eight public hospitals in Belize. Karl Heusner Memorial Hospital in Belize City functions as the main public hospital in the country and as a national referral center. Also, there are two regional hospitals: the Southern Regional Hospital in Dangriga, and the Northern Regional Hospital in Orange Walk Town. In addition, there are district public hospitals in Belmopan, San Ignacio, Punta Gorda and Corozal Town. Rockview Hospital in Belize City is a psychiatric center. Altogether, there are about 600 public hospital beds in Belize. The public hospitals provide the basic medical specialties: internal medicine, surgery, pediatrics and OB-GYN. Karl Heusner Memorial also provides neuro, ENT, physiotherapy, orthopedic surgery and several other services. The quality of these hospitals varies considerably.

Karl Heusner Memorial -- named after a prominent Belize City physician -- opened in 1997 and has much modern equipment, such as a CAT-scan, though some Belizeans and expats complain that even this hospital is sometimes short of supplies, including at times toilet paper. In 2004-2005, it added new facilities including ones for neurosurgery and trauma care.

The Southern Regional Hospital in Dangriga, which opened in 2000, is another modern facility, with much of the same medical technologies and equipment as you'd find in a community hospital in an American town. For example, the hospital's printed materials and Web site boast that its surgical operating rooms have "Narkomed anesthesia and Bovie electrosurgical units with laryngoscope sets, ECG monitoring spacelabs, Vilatert monitoring systems, resuscitators and 'Shampaine' surgical tables." However, other hospitals leave a lot to be desired. Some other hospitals, however, still look more like refugee camps than hospitals, with basic buildings and limited equipment. A medical "polyclinic" has opened in San Pedro, but the island still lacks a hospital.

Besides these hospitals, Belize has a network of around 60 public health clinics and rural health posts in many towns and villages around the country, providing primary medical and dental care. Most of these suffer from inadequate staffing, too many patients for their available resources and lack of equipment and medicine. Doctors may diagnose health problems accurately, but they may not be able to provide the proper medications to cure them.

Medical Personnel

Government figures show Belize has fewer than one physicians per 1,000 population, less than one-half the rate in the U.S. Belize has about 500 nurses, or one nurse per 700 population. Altogether there are perhaps 800 trained medical personnel in Belize. They are not distributed evenly around the country, however. More than one-half are in Belize City, which has only about one-fourth of the population. About three-fourths of trained medical people work in the public sector, and the rest in the private sector. Starting in the late 1990s, health care in Belize got a boost, thanks to the arrival of a group of several dozen medical volunteers from Cuba. Currently almost 100 Cuban nurses and physicians are in Belize. These doctors and nurses were assigned to clinics in areas of Belize, which, until then, did not have full-time medical personnel available to the local people. These hardworking Cubans, who exist on stipends of only a few dollars a month, have won many new friends for Fidel in Belize, regardless of what Belizeans may think of his politics. Medical and dental volunteer teams from the U.S. and Canada also regularly visit Belize to provide short-term care. Also, Nigeria and Venezuela have been helping provide medical care for Belize.

Medical care professionals in Belize earn very modest incomes compared with those in the U.S. Physicians employed by the government start at under US$15,000 a year, though they may supplement their income in private practice. Nurses start at around US$8,000.

Most physicians and dentists in Belize are trained in the U.S., Guatemala, Mexico or Great Britain. There are several so-called offshore medical schools in Belize (see the chapter on Language and Education) but their graduates are unlikely to practice in Belize. A nursing school, affiliated with the University of Belize, trains nurses for work in Belize. Belize medical professionals, like Belizean society, come in every shape and flavor. "My dentist is Garifuna, my ear doc is Mayan, my eye doc Mestizo and my OB-GYN is Spanish," says Katie Valk, a former New Yorker who now lives in Belize City.

The following regulatory bodies are established under the laws of Belize: The Medical Board responsible for the registration of medical practitioners, dentists, opticians and nursing homes. The Nurses and Midwives Council, responsible for the registration and regulation of nurses and midwives; and The Board of Examiners of Chemist and Druggists, responsible for the examining and registration of Chemist and Druggists and for carrying out other matters provided for in this Ordinance. The Nursing School participates in an accreditation program within the CARICOM countries.

What you won't find in Belize is topnotch emergency care. Karl Heusner Memorial Hospital in Belize City has added a trauma care center. While there are ambulances, a helicopter transfer surface using Astrum Helicopters near Belize City and an emergency air transport service operated by Wings of Hope, a U.S.-based charitable organization with an operations center in Belize City, Belize's spread-out population means it could take hours to get you to a hospital. In specialist care, such as for heart disease or cancer, Belize is behind the U.S. and Canada and even its larger Latin neighbors such as Mexico, Guatemala and Honduras. "The big minus in Belize is that there is not adequate medical care for chronically ill people who need regular visits to specialists," said Judy duPlooy, who owns a lodge near San Ignacio. She said that for people in Western Belize, Guatemala has "excellent care and is the quickest place to get to in an emergency." While many expats do go to Guatemala, or to Chetumal or Mérida, Mexico, for specialized treatment, others who can afford it go to Houston, Miami, New Orleans or elsewhere in the U.S. For example, when Barry Bowen, the wealthy Coca-Cola distributor and Belikin beer brewer in Belize, had an automobile accident on the way to his shrimp farm in Placencia, he was first treated and stabilized at Karl Heusner Hospital in Belize City. Then, he and his family opted to have him flown to Miami where he underwent treatment for his back injury.

Private Hospitals and Private Care

In addition to the public hospitals, Belize has two private hospitals -- La Loma Luz, a not-for-profit hospital in Santa Elena near San Ignacio, and

Belize Medical Associates, a for-profit facility in Belize City. Altogether these hospitals have fewer than 50 hospital beds.

La Loma Luz Medical Center, Santa Elena, Cayo; tel. 501/824-2087; fax 501/824-2674. La Loma Luz is a not-for-profit hospital operated by the Seventh Day Adventists. It has 17 hospital beds, a primary care clinic and 24-hour emergency services.

Belize Medical Associates, 5791 St. Thomas St., Kings Park (P.O. Box 1008), Belize City; tel. 501/223-0302; fax 501/223-3827; www.belizemedical.com. Established in 1989, Belize Medical Associates has a 25-bed hospital, along with two surgical suites, X-ray and ultrasound machines, a clinical lab, emergency services, and pharmacy. It is affiliated with Baptist Health Systems of Miami.

Owned by a group of Belizean physicians and businesspeople, a third private hospital, Universal Health Services ran into financial difficulties and is being merged into Karl Heusner Memorial Hospital.

Pharmacies and Prescriptions

There are drug stores in Belize City, in all towns, and in some villages. Many prescription drugs cost less in Belize than in the U.S., though pharmacies may not stock a wide selection of drugs and some drugs cost more in Belize than in the U.S. or Canada. In general, in Belize prescriptions usually are not needed for antibiotics and some other drugs that require prescriptions in the U.S., even some painkillers containing codeine. However, pharmacies owned by physicians or operated by hospitals, a common situation in Belize, may require or suggest a consultation with the doctor. Among the larger drug stores in Belize are Community Drug Stores, which has three locations in Belize City; Val-U-Med, Family Health Pharmacy and First Choice Pharmacy, all in Belize City; and The Pharmacy in San Ignacio. Also, Brodies supermarkets in Belize City and Belmopan have pharmacies. In addition, especially if you are in Northern Belize, crossing the border to Chetumal is an option. Chetumal has large *farmacias* that have most medications at prices significantly lower than in the U.S., and often lower than in Belize. If you are taking prescription medications, when you come to Belize you should be sure you have the generic name of the drug, as local pharmacies may not have the same brand names as back home.

Medical Records

If you have preexisting health conditions, you should bring a copy of your medical records with you when you move to Belize or come for an extended stay. It is also a good idea to have a letter from your physician outlining your conditions and past treatments.

Cost of Medical Care

Even if medical care isn't always up to snuff in Belize, at least it is cheap. The majority of health care is provided at little or no charge. Belizeans who can't afford to pay are treated in about the same way as those with more means. Only a tiny percentage of Belizeans have medical insurance. Private medical insurance coverage in Belize begins at US$150 to $200 a month, above what the average Belizean can pay. Rarely in the public health system in Belize will anyone be turned away for lack of cash or insurance, as thousands routinely are in the U.S. every day. Public hospitals and clinics may bill nominal amounts for tests and procedures -- for example, a woman's clinic in northern Belize charges US$10 to $20 for a Pap smear, cervical exam and breast exam, and under US$15 for an ultrasound -- or they may ask for a donation. In some waiting rooms you will see a box where you can leave a donation. But even visitors are routinely treated for free. A British friend was injured in a boating accident off Dangriga. In great pain, he was taken to the hospital in Dangriga where he was he was diagnosed as having broken ribs. He was then transported by air to Belize City where he was hospitalized for several days. His total bill, including X-rays, hospital stay, transport and medications: Zero.

If you can accept long waits and less than state-of-the-art medical technology, you won't have to spend all of your pension income to afford care. "Medical, dental and eye care is a fraction of the cost of the U.S. I have my teeth checked and cleaned for US$40, pay U.S. $10 to $20 for an office visit to my physician, and medications are cheap," says one Californian who now lives in Belize full-time. Even if you opt for private care, office visits to a physician generally are just US$20 to $40. A root canal with crown might cost US$250 to $500, although some Belize dentists charge more. Hospitalization runs under US$100 per day. Prescription drug costs vary but generally are less expensive than in the U.S. A few years ago, I paid just US$5 for a course of antibiotics. Pharmacies are in Belize City and in all towns. By the way, prescription drugs in Belize are usually dispensed in plastic baggies or envelopes rather than in bottles. While it is difficult to compare costs between Belize and the U.S., since the quality of care is different and the amount of medical tests done in Belize pales beside those routinely ordered in America, it's probably fair to say that even in the private sector overall costs for health care in Belize are one-fourth to one-third that in the U.S., and may be even less.

National Health Insurance

The medical care system in Belize is in a transitional period. A National Health Insurance scheme, proposed in the 1990s, is gradually being put in place. Under the scheme, through the Belize Social Security system, all Belizeans and permanent residents would get medical care through a system somewhat similar to that in Britain. Eventually, the scheme calls for individuals and businesses to pay into Social Security system for health care. The benefit, with the individual's Social Security card the identity card, would be comprehensive universal medical care. The system would pay for care, or at least part of it, at either public or private hospitals and clinics. Initially, a pilot project in Belize City, which started in 2002, was funded by the government and was free to all residents of the Belize City South Side. Later, residents of the North Side were added. It provided for care at a group of clinics, free drugs from participating pharmacies, and free lab tests at participating clinics. Unfortunately, the Social Security system in Belize has been troubled for several years, with charges flying back and forth about management and financial accountability of the system. The Belize government also is running a high budget deficit. Together, these factors are hampering and delaying expansion of the NHI.

The Social Security Board is the only public health insurance provider for labor force in the country. According to the Pan American Health Organization, Social Security has 55,000 contributors, representing 68% of the estimated labor force. Private health insurance is limited in Belize but has increased rapidly during the past two decades. Many of the insurance companies are affiliates of large international firms. The benefit packages are fashioned to cover expenses for medical care acquired in and outside of Belize, depending on the premium.

Health Insurance

For routine primary care, most foreign residents in Belize make do with the low-cost public system, or they go to a private physician, dentist or clinic. Mostly they pay cash. Many "self-insure," taking a calculated risk that what they save in medical insurance premiums will more than pay for their actual medical costs in Belize. Health insurance policies for care in Belize are available through a few insurance companies in Belize:

RF&G Insurance, 81 N. Front St., Belize City; tel. 501/227-3744; fax 501/227-2202; www.fandginsurance.com.   RF&G, the largest firm in Belize, the result of a 2005 merger of Regent Insurance and F&G Insurance, is based in Belize City and has other offices around Belize, including branches in Corozal Town, Belmopan, Punta Gorda, Dangriga, Placencia and Orange Walk Town.

Belize Insurance Center. 212 North Front St., Belize City; tel. 501-227-7310; www.belizeinsurance.com. This group offers a variety of insurance products including health.

Several international insurance companies and insurance brokers write health care policies for expatriates, with the premiums sometimes covering medical transportation back to the home country along with actual health care. One that specializes in coverage for foreigners living in Latin America and the Caribbean, including Belize, and which has gotten good reviews from those in Belize who have used it, is:

Bupa (which absorbed **Amedex**). 7001 Southwest 97th Avenue, Miami, FL 33173; tel. 305-398-7400; www.bupalatinamerica.com. This company says it has more than 10 million policyholders around the world. It usually works through medical insurance brokers such as **Pacific Prime,** based in Hong Kong (www.pacificprime.com). Bupa took over Amedex, which formerly had more than 1 million policyholders in Latin America. Most policies cover direct payment to hospitals, reimbursement for outpatient care and medical evacuation. Premium costs vary based on age, but an individual $1 million (annual limit) major medical policy with a US$500 to $1,000 deductible for a person in his or her mid-50s could be around US$2,000-$6,000 annually, depending on the details of the policy, and assuming that you live most of the year in Belize or elsewhere outside the U.S. Most but not all policies exclude coverage in the U.S. Coverage in the U.S. typically doubles the premium cost.

Here are estimates from several underwriting companies, provided by a medical insurance broker in early 2010, of the cost of coverage annually for persons aged 54 and 49. Note that these are just representative examples only, and your particular situation could be different, with very different premiums and coverage. They are also subject to change each renewal period.

Aetna (Foundation plan). US$1.6 million annual limit; US$100 deductible *per condition* per year; worldwide coverage except U.S.; hospitalization; out-patient care; emergency evacuation; chiropractor visits; chronic conditions covered in acute phase only.

Age 54: $4,305 per year
Age 49: $3,381 per year

IHI Danmark (ISM Plan). US$1 million annual limit: US$1,350 deductible per year; worldwide coverage *including U.S.;* hospitalization with 10% co-insurance; out-patient care; no emergency evacuation; chiropractor visits; chronic conditions covered.

Age 54: $6,949 per year
Age 49: $6,764 per year

Healthcare International (Plus Plan). US$1 million annual limit; US$1,000 deductible *per condition* per year; worldwide coverage except U.S.; hospitalization; out-patient care; emergency evacuation; chiropractor visits; chronic conditions covered only up to US$20,000 lifetime.

Age 54: $1,885
·Age 49: $1,683

Allianz (Classic Bronze Plan). US$1.6 million annual limit; US$280 deductible per year; worldwide coverage except U.S.; hospitalization; out-patient care; emergency evacuation; chiropractor visits; chronic conditions covered.

Age 54: $3,964
Age 49: $3,104

Interglobal (Comprehensive Plan). US$1.7 million annual limit; US$85 deductible *per condition* per year; worldwide coverage except U.S.; hospitalization; out-patient care; limited dental; emergency evacuation; chiropractor visits; chronic conditions covered with some limits.

Age 54: $3,733
Age 49: $2,931

Vanbreda (Globe Plan). US$1.25 million annual limit; US$125 deductible per year; worldwide coverage *except North America*; hospitalization; out-patient care with 20% co-insurance; emergency evacuation; chiropractor visits; chronic conditions covered.

Age 54: $2,914
Age 49: $2,174

Medicare

Medicare and Medicaid do not pay for medical care outside the U.S., except for some limited situations in Canada and Mexico. The U.S. Department of Veterans Affairs will pay for coverage outside the U.S. only if you are a veteran with a service-related disability. For Americans, this is a major drawback of expat life in Belize, or indeed anywhere else outside the U.S. and its territories. For visitors and short-term residents, some private insurance policies including some Blue Cross policies do cover you regardless of where you become ill or have an accident. Also, some credit cards pay for medical evacuations back to the cardholder's home country.

Health Issues in Belize

Bad water and poor sanitation are major causes of illness in much of the Third World. In Belize, happily these are less of a problem than in Belize's larger neighbors, Mexico and Guatemala. All residents of Belize City and nearly all towns have access to safe and adequate water supplies — "pipe water" as it's called in Belize — and close to 70% of rural residents do, according to the Pan American Health Care Organization. Thanks to the plentiful rain in Belize — from 50 to 200 inches or more per year — drinking water literally falls from the sky, so even if you decide to live in an area without a community water system you can collect drinking water in a cistern. Concrete or plastic cisterns, with accompanying pipes and drains to gather rain from your roof, are sold in building supply stores or can be constructed by local workers, if your home does not already have one. To be safe, rainwater should be treated by filtering or with a disinfectant such as chlorine bleach. Overall, about 85% of Belizeans have access to potable water. In short, in most areas of Belize, including nearly all areas of interest to expats, you can drink the water and not worry about getting sick. Increasingly, municipal water supplies in Belize are being privatized. In San Pedro, for example, the water system is run by a company based in the Cayman Islands.

In many areas, sewage disposal is less adequate. The Belize Water and Sewerage Authority (WASA), which was privatized in 2001, with majority ownership by a European consortium called CASCAL, operates sewerage systems in Belize City, Belmopan and a few other areas. There is still a lack of facilities in rural areas, and even in urban areas more than one-third of houses do not have adequate sanitation, according to Belize government figures. In rural parts of Belize, refuse disposal is not organized at the community level; households are responsible for the disposal of their own solid wastes. While many homes have reasonably effective septic systems, or at least well-maintained pit latrines, in poorer areas Belizeans dump their household wastes into rivers or the Caribbean Sea. Life expectancy at birth in Belize is about 70 years, only a little lower than that in the U.S. Heart disease is the leading cause of death from illness for both males and females, but Belizeans, as are Americans, are paying more attention to the causes of heart disease, such as smoking, lack of exercise and a diet high in fats, and the incidence of death from heart illnesses is declining.

There are no reliable statistics on how many Belizeans smoke. Certainly, the antismoking crusade hasn't progressed as far as it has in the U.S. Few businesses, public buildings or restaurants are smoke free, and many Belizeans feel it is their right to light up anytime and anywhere. My own very unscientific survey of foreigners resident in Belize suggests that a large number, maybe as many as one-half, smoke. Perhaps some of these came to Belize just to be able to smoke without being harassed by the lifestyle police? However, with local brands of cigarettes costing US$15+ a carton and imported brands US$20 to $25 or more, the vast majority of Belizeans can't afford the habit.

The leading cause of death in Belize is not illness but traffic accidents. About one-fourth of all deaths in Belize are now due to traffic accidents, even though the vast majority of Belizeans don't own cars. Often the cause of accidents is alcohol-related. Such speed limits as there are in Belize — and most roads have no posted speed limit — don't mean much because Belize has very few traffic enforcement officers. The use of seat belts is now required in Belize, but this rule too is rarely enforced. Finally, many Belizeans simply aren't good drivers. Driver's education programs are virtually unknown. Normally you must pass a short written test to get a driver's license and have a medical exam. However, some residents say they have gotten one simply by showing up at your local Transport Department office with the necessary forms, including a certificate from a doctor that you are in good health and two passport-size photos, and paying US$10.

AIDS has become a serious epidemic in Belize, according to health officials. Although government figures are lower, AIDS workers estimate that as many as 7,000 people in Belize are HIV positive. Given Belize's small population of a little over 330,000, this estimate means that one in about 43 Belizeans is HIV positive, thought to be the highest infection rate in Central America. Worldwide, about one in 120 persons is believed to be HIV positive. In Belize, nearly three-fourths of HIV infection is spread by heterosexual contact. The highest number of reported AIDS cases is in Belize and Stann Creek districts. All blood for transfusion in Belize is screened for HIV, with the cost absorbed by the government.

At one time, Belize had on a per capita basis one of the highest incidences of malaria in the world, and the highest in Central America. Thanks to a widespread program of spraying for mosquitoes, the incidence of malaria in Belize has been declining from its peak of more than 10,000 reported cases in 1994. In recent years, the number of reported cases has fallen to under 1,000 annually, mostly in remote bush areas and typically among recent immigrants from Guatemala or elsewhere in Central America. Another good thing is that more than 95% of the malaria cases in Belize are the *Plasmodium vivax* strain, which is less dangerous than *Plasmodium falciparum* and which can be prevented with the use of chloroquine, a time-tested and fairly inexpensive drug. Dengue fever is transmitted by another type of mosquito. It causes flu-like symptoms that are unpleasant but which in most cases are not life threatening. Dengue has become epidemic at the end of the rainy season in many countries of Central America, including Costa Rica and Honduras. Dengue exists in Belize, especially during the rainy season, but happily it is not very common. However, in 2009 there was an outbreak of dengue in western Belize. There is at present no preventative medication for dengue, but its symptoms can be treated effectively with Tylenol or its generic equivalent. Avoid taking aspirin if you think you have dengue, as aspirin can exacerbate internal bleeding sometimes associated with dengue.

Both cholera and typhoid fever are occasionally present in Belize, but only a handful of cases have been reported in recent years.

The Healthy Belize Lifestyle

Belize could be good for your health. A positive side to the typical Belize lifestyle, especially outside urban areas, is that compared to the usual way of living in developed countries you tend to walk and exercise more, get more fresh air and eat simpler, healthier meals of complex carbohydrates and fresh fruits. One Canadian says that after a year in Belize he went for a health check-up. He found his blood pressure was down 15 points and his weight down 15 pounds. "But what do you expect?" he asks, smiling. "I live on the beach, walk 25 feet to work and eat almost nothing but fresh fish and fruit."

The use of herbal remedies also is common in Belize. Bush doctors or snake doctors often have an extensive knowledge of plants with healing properties. Don Elijio Panti was one of the best known of the herbal healers. He was a Guatemalan by birth but a long-time resident of Cayo in western Belize who died in 1996 at over 100 years of age. His work was popularized by Rosita Arvigo (with Nadine Epstein and Marilyn Yaquinto) in the 1993 book, *Sastun, My Apprenticeship with a Maya Healer*. Dr. Arvigo today operates a herbal healing facility near San Ignacio. Many other herbal or snake doctors operate in Belize.

CHAPTER 6:
OPTIONS FOR RESIDENCY IN BELIZE

There are three options for those wishing to live or retire in Belize or to spend extended periods of time in the country. Each has advantages and disadvantages.

TOURIST CARD

This is the easiest, cheapest way to live in the country for a while, and it requires no long-term commitment. The procedure is simple: You get a 30-day entry free (via a passport stamp) when you arrive in the country by air, land or sea. After 30 days, you can go to an immigration office (or police station in remote areas) and renew the tourist card monthly for US$25 a month for up to six months, and then US$50 a month after that. After six months, you also must register as an alien. Citizens of the U.S., European Community, the U.K., Canada, Australia, New Zealand, Mexico, Costa Rica, Guatemala, Suriname, Fiji, Hungary, Iceland, Kenya, Latvia, Lithunania, Seychelles, South Africa, Singapore, Slovakia, Solomon Islands, Malawi, Malaysia, Maldives, Mauritius, Czech Republic, Namibia, Papua New Guinea, Chile, Norway, Sierra Leone, Sweden, Tanzania, Turkey, Uganda, Uruguay, Zambia, Western Samoa, Zimbabwe, Tuvalu, Venezuela, Hong Kong, CARICOM member states and some other countries get a tourist card without having to apply in advance for a tourist visa. Nationals of more than 75 other countries must apply in advance for a tourist visa, and there is a fee. See the Belize Tourism Board web site, www.travelbelize.org for details.

As a tourist cardholder, you can enjoy Belize without a long-term commitment. You can buy or rent property, but you cannot work for pay. In theory, when you renew your tourist card, you are supposed to be able to prove that you have sufficient resources, set at US$60 a day, to stay in Belize, but this requirement is not usually enforced. Of course, there is no guarantee that you will be able to renew your card indefinitely, as rules and conditions can change, as you have no official residency status. If you fail to renew your permit in a timely way, or if you overstay your allotted time, technically you are in violation of Belize law and can be deported. As a practical matter, if you can offer a good reason why you failed to follow the law, and are very friendly to Immigration officers, you'll probably be let off with a short lecture from the official, and perhaps a fine. However, some people who overstay their tourist cards *are* sent packing.

QUALIFIED RETIRED PERSON STATUS

The Qualified Retired Persons Incentive Act passed by the Belize legislature in 1999 is managed by the Belize Tourism Board. The program is designed to attract more retirees to Belize. In the first years of operation, the program attracted considerable interest and a number of applications. But the Belize Tourism Board now declines to disclose publicly how many applications it has received and how many have been approved. However, we understand that there are only a few hundred participants in the program. Interest in the program appears to be fairly high, but because of the income requirement, inability to work for pay in Belize, lack of official residency status and other factors, the actual number of retirees under the program in Belize is as yet relatively small and far fewer than are in programs in Costa Rica, Panama, Mexico and elsewhere. In 2010, the BTB was said to be reviewing the program to see how it can be improved.

For those who can show the required monthly income from investments or pensions, this program offers benefits of official residency and tax-free entry of the retiree's household goods and a car, boat and even an airplane. This program also eliminates some of the bureaucratic delays built into other programs. The BTB guarantees action on an application in no more than three months, but we have heard of qualified retirees getting approval for this program in only a few weeks.

Who qualifies? Anyone at least 45 years old from anywhere in the world can qualify for the program. A person who qualifies can also include his or her dependents in the program. Dependents include spouses and children under the age of 18. However, it can include children under the age of 23 if enrolled in a university.

Main benefits: Besides prompt approval of residency for qualifying applicants, import duties and fees for household goods and a vehicle, airplane and boat are waived.

Duty-free import of personal household effects: Qualified Retired Persons under the program can qualify for duty and tax exemptions on new and used personal and household effects admitted as such by the Belize Tourism Board. A list of all items with corresponding values that will be imported must be submitted with the application. A one-year period is granted for the importation of personal and household effects.

Duty-free import of a vehicle, aircraft and boat:

a. Motor Vehicle: Applicants are encouraged to import new motor vehicles under the program, but the vehicle must be no more than three years old. (An exception may be made in the case of an older vehicle with low mileage, but this would be decided on a case-by-case basis.) A Qualified Retired Person may also buy a vehicle duty-free in country.

b. Light Aircraft: A Qualified Retired Person is entitled to import a light aircraft less than 17,000 kg. A Qualified Retired Person is required to have a valid Private Pilot license to fly in Belize. This license can be obtained by passing the requirements set by the Civil Aviation. However, if the participant has a valid pilot's license, that license only has to be validated by Civil Aviation Department in Belize.

c. Boat: Any vessel that is used for personal purposes and for pleasure will be accepted under this program. If for whatever reason a Qualified Retired Person decides to sell, give away, lease, or otherwise dispose of the approved means of transportation or personal effects to any person or entity within Belize, all duties and taxes must be paid to the proper authorities. The Belize Tourism Board states: "Qualified Retired Persons must note that only after three years and upon proof that the transportation that was previously imported to Belize was adequately disposed off, will another concession be granted to import another mode of transportation."

Income requirement: To be designated a Qualified Retired Person under the program, the applicant must have a monthly income of at least US$2,000. A couple does not need to show US$4,000 a month – just US$2,000, as the applicant is normally an individual and the applicant's spouse is a dependent under the program. The income rules for Qualified Retired Persons are, like many things in Belize, a little confusing. On first reading, it looks like the income must derive from a pension or annuity that has been generated outside of Belize. The rules do not specifically say so, but according to Belize Tourism Board officials U.S. Social Security income can be included as part of this pension requirement. This pension and annuity information then has to be substantiated by a Certified Public Accountant, along with two bank references from the company providing the pension or annuity. These substantiations may not be required if your pension and/or annuity is from a Fortune 500 company. Several retirees have told me that they were able to include other forms of income, including investment income, in the US$2,000 figure, if supported by a CPA's statement that the income would continue indefinitely. In this latter case, the US$2,000 a month income (US$24,000 a year) can be substantiated by showing records from a bank or other financial institution in Belize that the retiree has deposited the necessary money.

Background check: All applications are subject to a background check by the Ministry of National Security.

Application: Applications for the program must be made to the Belize Tourism Board in Belize City and include the following:

• Birth certificate: A certified copy of a certificate for the applicant and each dependant.

• Marriage certificate if applicant is married and spouse is a dependant.

• Police record: A police record from the applicant's last place of residency issued within one month prior to the application

• Passport: Color copies of complete passport (including all blank pages) of applicant and all dependents that have been certified by a Notary Public. The copies must have the passport number, name of principal, number of pages and the seal or stamp of the Notary Public.

• Proof of income: An official statement from a bank or financial institution certifying that the applicant is the recipient of a pension or annuity of a minimum of US$2,000 per month.

• Medical examination: Applicants should undergo a complete medical examination including an AIDS test. A copy of the medical certificate must be attached to the application.

• Photos: Four front and four-side passport size photographs that have been taken recently of applicant and dependents.

The application form for the Qualified Retired Persons Program is available for download on the Belize Tourism Board Website at www.belizeretirement.org. Application fees and costs for the QRP program total US$1,350 for an individual or US$2,100 for a couple.

For information on the program, contact: Belize Tourism Board, P.O. Box 325, Belize City, Belize, Central America; tel: 501-223-1913 or 1-800-624-0686; fax: 501-223-1943. If you have questions or problems, try contacting the Program Officer. The current Program Officer is Romy Haylock (email romy@travelbelize.org). She is said to be very helpful.

OFFICIAL PERMANENT RESIDENT

Application requirements and most benefits are similar to those of the Retired Persons Incentive Act, but there are some important differences. The application process itself and the supporting documents needed are similar to those for the QRP, although the applications are processed by different organizations.

Here are the main differences: As a regular permanent resident, you have two major advantages over a participant in the QRP program. First, you do not have to deposit any particular sum in a bank in Belize. However, you do have to show financial resources sufficient to obtain residency status. Second, as a permanent resident, you can work for pay in Belize. You also enjoy some advantages as a resident rather than a "long-term visitor" as you are considered as a QRPer, such as not having to pay the land or sea exit tax when departing Belize. As a permanent resident, you can vote in local (not national) Belize elections.

You must live in Belize for one full year before you can apply for regular permanent residency. During this period, you cannot leave the country for more than 14 days. Even a short, two-hour visit to Chetumal counts as one day's absence. Note, however, that the Immigration and Nationality Department sometimes interprets this requirement only as meaning that you cannot leave the country for 14 or more CONSECUTIVE days.

Here are the documents you must have to apply for permanent residency (photocopies of original documents must be submitted along with the original documents):

- Application form.
- Passport.
- Evidence, such as passport pages with immigration stamps, that you have been in the country for one year.
- Recent police record for yourself and all members of your family over the age of 16.
- Evidence you have acquired property in Belize if you are claiming that you have – but owning property in Belize is NOT required to obtain permanent residency.
- Alien registration for yourself and all members of your family if you have resided in Belize for six months or longer.
- Certificate of health including HIV and venereal disease tests for you and all members of your family – these tests must be conducted in Belize.
- Three passport-size photos of yourself and all members of your family.
- Birth certificates of all applicants.
- Marriage certificate (if applicable).
- Recent local bank statement if means of financial support is not otherwise demonstrated.
- Temporary work permit if you are planning to work for pay.
- Income tax statement.

After approval, you have up to one year to bring in household effects duty-free, on a one-time basis. However, the duty-free exemption does not apply to a vehicle, boat and airplane, as it does for the Qualified Retired Persons program.

It is somewhat expensive to apply for regular permanent residency. Application fees for Permanent Residency vary by nationality, ranging from US$250 to $5,000. For Americans, the fee is US$1,000 per person. There is also, upon approval, a fee of US$150. In addition, if you use an "expediter" in Belize to help you with the paperwork, you'll likely pay a fee of around US$1,500, plus several hundred dollars in travel and photocopying fees and taxes. Note that these fees are per-person, not per-application, as is the case for the Qualified Retired Persons program. For example, an American married couple applying for permanent residency would pay US$2,000 with the application and US$300 for residency cards after approval. Some applicants also have been required to post a bond, supposedly to guarantee the cost of repatriation to their home country, should that ever be required. The bond amount varies, ranging from several hundred dollars to as much as US$2,000. Other applicants say they have not been required to post the bond. Residency cards are no longer provided -- instead, your passport is stamped.

You apply to the Belize Immigration and Nationality Department rather than through the Belize Tourism Board. For information and application form, contact: Immigration and Nationality Department Ministry of National Security and Immigration, Belmopan City, Belize, Central America; tel.: 501-222-4620; fax: 501-222-4056.

Time for approval of a permanent residency application varies. Some find that the process goes fairly quickly, taking only a few months. Others say it took up to a year, or longer, for approval.

Pros and Cons

Each option has pluses and minuses. The main advantages and disadvantages are as follows:

Tourist Card

Pros: No commitment, no financial requirement, flexibility, little red tape.

Cons: No tax advantages, no official status, inconvenience of having to renew periodically, monthly fee of US$25 to $50 per person to extend, possibility rules may change, can't work for pay in Belize.

Qualified Retired Persons Incentive Program

Pros: Quick approval, application through Belize Tourism Board rather than Immigration Department, some residency rights (except voting), tax-free entry of household effects, car, boat and airplane, only have to live in country for one month a year.

Cons: Must deposit US$24,000 a year in a Belize bank, somewhat costly application process, can't work for pay in Belize, must be 45 or over, still have to pay tourist exit taxes when leaving the country.

Official Permanent Residency

Pros: Full residency rights (except voting in national elections -- you can vote in local elections), can work, open to anyone regardless of age, tax-free entry of household effects.

Cons: Year-long residency before applying, more red tape, costly application process, and some people are turned down for minor details; you can bring in household goods but NOT a car, boat or airplane free of duty.

The controversial Economic Citizenship program, under which foreigners were able to buy a Belize passport and residency rights for a fee of US$25,000 to $50,000, was discontinued in 2002.

In addition to these programs, regular citizenship in Belize is a possibility for those living in Belize over a long period. To acquire citizenship, applicants must have been a resident or have permanent residency status for a minimum of five years. Applicants for citizenship need to provide essentially the same supporting documentation as those applying for permanent residency. Applicants also must demonstrate a knowledge of Belizean history. Note that for citizenship residency purposes, stays in the Belize under the Qualified Retired Persons program do NOT qualify. To become a citizen, you would have to give up QRP status (perhaps having to pay back the duties you escaped under QRP), apply for permanent residency, and begin the five-year residency from scratch.

Caution: Rules and regulations and the interpretation of them change frequently in Belize. Do NOT assume that this information is the last word on any matter pertaining to entering or staying in Belize.

Quiet street in the village of Sarteneja

CHAPTER 7:
HOMES AND LAND IN BELIZE

The good news is that real estate costs less in Belize than it does in the U.S., Canada or Western Europe. To be sure, in a few prime areas you can spend hundreds of thousands of dollars on North American-style luxury home, but you can also buy raw land at prices not seen in the U.S. since the 1970s and in some areas find a simple but pleasant rental house near the sea for under US$400 a month. More good news: There are few restrictions on the purchase or use of real estate by foreigners, legal documents are in English and follow English common law traditions.

Shopping for Housing

Except for occasional ads in the *San Pedro Sun* on Ambergris Caye and in Belize City newspapers, and listings on the Internet, few properties are advertised for sale. Real estate agencies do maintain listing brochures, and you can contact them to request a copy. Most real estate brokers use the Internet as the primary way of presenting listings and of getting prospective buyers. See the real estate agent listings below for addresses of real estate Web sites in Belize.

Even with the Internet, however, you'll miss one-half or more of available properties. To find out what's really for sale, you'll have to spend time on the ground in Belize. Many properties are for sale by owner, rather than being listed with a broker. In many cases, you will see no sign or other indication that a property is for sale. Just start asking around, and before long you'll have more deals being offered you than you can even begin to consider. This goes double for rentals. It is rare to see a house advertised for rent in a newspaper, except in San Pedro or Belize City, and brokers handle only the most expensive rentals.

About the only way to find a house or apartment to rent is to spend some time in the area where you wish to rent. Drive around and look for vacant homes, or ask foreign residents or Belizeans for tips on what's available.

Note: Several web sites not affiliated with a real estate company have Belize real estate listings. Belize First maintains a section of free listings of Belize real estate for sale, wanted and trades. Visit www.belizefirst.com/indexrealestate.html. Also on the site are some rental listings. Another interesting site for free listings of Belize real estate is www.realestateinbelize.org.

Real Estate Brokers

In Belize, anyone can be a real estate broker. No license needed. No schooling, no bonding, no continuing education. All you need is enough money to print business cards, and, presto, you're a broker. Selling real estate is a popular first job for expats in Belize, and some do it on the side without a work permit. Quite a few hoteliers, dive shop operators and taxi drivers peddle real estate to tourists on the side. One of the best-known real estate guys in Placencia, until he left to sail his boat around the Caribbean, was also the proprietor and barkeep of one of the most popular bars on the peninsula.

Efforts have been made to require some basic licensing of real estate brokers, but as of this writing this is still a work in progress. The Belize National Association of REALTORS® has been established – the group's web site is www.belizenar.org. Agent members, of which there are more than 100 in Belize, subscribe to a code of ethics and are supposed to follow other professional guidelines. Another group, the Association of Real Estate Brokers in Belize (www.arebb.com), was established in 2006 and has more than 80 agent members.

Not surprisingly, the quality of agents varies. Some are professional and honest. A few are out for a fast buck. Some are just not very knowledgeable. The ones we've listed here are among the best we know about, but even so your mileage may vary. Real estate commissions in Belize are similar to those in the U.S. Agents typically charge the seller 7% commission on residential property, and around 10% on raw land. Of course, rates are negotiable. Because many properties are in remote areas, brokers often charge prospective buyers expenses for travel and transportation incurred in connection with showing properties.

Selected Agents

These are some of the best real estate agents and companies in Belize:

Bayshore Limited, 100 Embarcadero road, Maya Beach, Placencia

Peninsula, Stann Creek District, tel. 501-523-8019; e-mail jwildman@lincsat.com, www.bayshorebelize.com. Jenny Wildman and her agents specialize in property on the Placencia peninsula.

Belize Land Consultants, P.O. Box 35, Corozal, tel. 501-423-1005, fax 423-1006, email consejoshores@gmail.com, www.consejoshores.com. Bill Wildman, a land surveyor, developed Consejo Shores near Corozal Town and also has more than 30 years of real estate experience in Belize.

Diane Campbell, San Pedro, Ambergris Caye, tel. 501-226-5203 or 501-610-5118; email dcampbellbz@gmail.com. Diane is a former Californian who with her husband has built a number of homes on Ambergris Caye, including the Los Encantos development. She is very well informed about real estate on Ambergris Caye.

Charlotte's Casa Belize, 78 5th Ave., Corozal; tel. 501-422-0135, cell 501-607-0456; email charbelize@yahoo.com, www.charlottescasabelize.com. Charlotte Zahniser has been in Belize since around 1999. She can probably help with rentals in the Corozal area, too.

Ceiba Realty (Jonathan Lohr), 119A Western Highway, Santa Elena Town, Cayo; tel. 501-824-4050 or cell 501-610-4458; email ceibarealty@gmail.com, www.ceibarealtybelize.com.

Emerald Futures Real Estate, Mile 3 ½, Northern Hwy., Belize City, tel. 501-670-6818, fax 501-223-2609; email emeraldbelize2006@yahoo.com, www.emeraldfutures.com. Emerald Futures has properties in most areas of the mainland. Owners Madeleine and John Estephan were born and raised in Belize.

Pelican Properties, San Pedro, Ambergris Caye, tel. 501-226-3234, fax 226-3434, www.pelicanbelize.com.

Rainforest Realty, P.O. Box 195, San Ignacio, Cayo; tel. Macarena Rose at 501-670-4045, USA direct: 727-490-7710; www.rainforestrealty.com, email macarenarose@gmail.com. Macarena Rose is the founding president of the Belize National Association of REALTORS®.

Regent Realty, Ltd., 81 N. Front St., Belize City; tel. 501-227-0090, fax 227-2022, email regent@btl.net, www.regentrealtybelize.com. Regent Realty was formerly associated with Regent Insurance Co., one of largest Belize-based insurance companies, before it merged with F&G Insurance to become RF&G Insurance.

Southwind Properties, P.O. Box 1, San Pedro, tel. 501-226-2005, fax 501-226-2331, email southwind@starband.net, www.southwindproperties.net. Specializes in property on Ambergris Caye. Southwind is also a real estate developer, having done Belizean Shores, Coral Bay and Coco Beach condos.

Sunrise Realty, #1 Barrier Reef Dr. (P.O. Box 236), San Pedro; tel. 501-226-3737, fax 501-226-3379, email info@sunrisebelize.com, www.sunrisebelize.com. Brokers Chris Berlin and Amanda Syme are San Pedro residents. They focus on properties on Ambergris Caye.

Tropic Real Estate, P.O. Box 453, Belmopan, Cayo, tel. 501-824-3475, fax 501-824-3649, email tropic@realestatebelize.com, www.realestatebelize.com. This is one of the oldest real estate agencies in Cayo. The owner is originally from Texas.

Katie Valk, P.O. Box 1108, Belize City; tel. 501-223-0376, 501-610-1923 or 561-210-7015 in the U.S., email info@belize-trips.com, www.belize-trips.com. Katie Valk has a home in the Cocoplum development (a first-rate place) in Placencia and offers lots and homes for sale there.

Other Real Estate Agents

Here are other real estate agents in Belize. In many cases, we have no personal knowledge of these agents. They may be excellent; we just aren't knowledgeable about them. They are listed for your convenience. Also check the Belize National Association of REALTORS® web site at www.belizenar.org for other real estate agents.

Ambergris Seaside Real Estate, P.O. Box 163, San Pedro, Ambergris Caye, tel. 501-226-4545, fax 501-226-3545, www.ambergrisrealestate.com.

Alpha & Omega International Realty & Consultants, Corozal Town, tel. 501-207-8887; www.AlphaOmegaBelizeRealEstate.com.

Arabella Chambers Limited, Real Estate Agents & Home Builders (Luigi Lungarini and Alexia Malo), San Ignacio, Cayo; tel. 501-824-2161 or 501-624-0951; www.arabellachambers.org.

Belize Land Properties Ltd. (Hector Romero), 9 Third Street, King's Park, Belize City, tel./fax 501-223-4807; www.belizelandproperties.com.

Belize North Real Estate, P.O. Box 226, Corozal Town, tel. 501-422-0284 www.belizenorthrealestate.bz.

Belize Property Agents Ltd. (Managing Partner David Gobeil), Box 273 Dangriga, Physical Address: Mile 6 Hummingbird Highway, tel. 501-522-0512, cell: 501-665-2412, www.belizepropertyagent.com.

Belize Realty Services, 29 Burns Avenue, San Ignacio, Cayo, tel: 501-801-0195 or 501-610-2265, www.belize-real-estate-services.com.

Belize Shores Realty (Paul and Karol Kammeyer) San Pedro, Ambergris Caye, tel. 501-226-2825, www.Belizeshoresrealty.com.

Blue Diamond Realty (Janelle Castillo), # 1 Barrier Reef Dr., San Pedro, Ambergris Caye, tel. 501-226-3933 or 501-620-4149; www.bluediamondbelize.com.

Buy Belize Real Estate, (Estevan Perera), 2.5 Miles Western Highway (P.O. Box 2276), Belize City, www.buy-belize.com.

Alex Canalez, Buyers' Agent/Real Estate Advertiser, 3781 Marina Drive, San Pedro, Ambergris Caye, tel. 501-608-5535, www.affordablebelizerealestate.com, www.realestateinbelize.org.

Caribbean Properties Consultants, P.O. Box 149 Dangriga, Stann Creek District, tel. 501-523-7299 or 669-9000, www.belizeproperty.com.

Casa Cayo Real Estate (Richard McMinimy), San Pedro, Ambergris Caye; tel. 501-226-2791, www.casacayorealestate.net.

Cayo Connection (Jose Mendoza), #1 Bullet Tree Rd., San Ignacio, Cayo; tel. 501-670-3296 or 824-4691, www.ownlandinbelize.com.

Century 21 Isla Bonita, San Pedro, Ambergris Caye; tel. 866-589-4618; www.century21belize.com.

Caye Caulker for Sale, Caye Caulker, 501-622-3254, www.CayeCaulkerforSale.com.

Coldwell Banker Belize, (Jonathon Mullen) San Pedro, Ambergris Caye; tel. 501- 226-3400; www.ColdwellBankerBelize.com.

Coral Beach Realty, Barrier Reef Drive, San Pedro, tel. 501-226-2681, fax 226-2875; www.coralbeachrealty.com.

Eden Isle & South Point Developments, Caye Caulker, 501-622-3254, www.CayeCaulker.net.

Hopkins Bay Real Estate, 1613 Pelican Lakes Point, Windsor, CO 80550 USA, tel. (877) 467-2297, fax (970)-674-5090; www.hopkinsbayrealestate.com.

IVORR Real Estate Agency, 7145 Slaughterhouse Road, Belize City, tel. 501-223-5560, cell 501-620-3711, www.ivorr.com.

Premier Real Estate, Mile 2 Western Highway, Belize City, tel. 501-224-4075 or 225-9052, cell 501-610-4343, fax 501-222-4150, www.premier-realestatebelize.com.

Realty Management of Belize Ltd., 24 Daly Street, Belize City, tel. 501-223-3523, fax 223-3375, www.realtymanagementofbelize.com.

RE/MAX Isla Bonita (Daryl Carlson), 10 Coconut Drive, San Pedro Town, Ambergris Caye tel. 501-226-4400, fax 501-226-440, www.owninbelize.com.

RE/MAX Property Center (Looey Tremblay), San Ignacio, tel. 501-824-0550, cell 519-241-1230 (Canada), fax 501-824-0447, www.belizepropertycenter.com.

Sirena del Mar Ltd. Real Estate & Development Services, Front Street, Caye Caulker, tel. 501-226-0404, www.realestateofbelize.com.

South Belize Realty, www.southbelizerealty.com. Tel. 512-382-6779 in the U.S. Ron Forrester at rrf2001@yahoo.com.

Southern Belize Real Estate, www.southernbelizerealestate.com.

Triton Properties, Barrier Reef Dr., San Pedro, Ambergris Caye; tel. 501-226-3783, fax 501-226-3549; e-mail triton@btl.net.

Vista Real Estate, 122 Eve St. (P.O. Box 2383), Belize City, tel. 501-223-2427, fax 223-2228, www.vistabelize.com or www.belizerealestate.bz.

Yearwood Properties, General Delivery, Placencia, tel./fax 501-523-3462, e-mail brian@belizebeachfront.com.

Few Restrictions on Ownership

Belize imposes few restrictions on ownership of land by non-nationals. Unlike Mexico, which prohibits the direct ownership of land by foreigners on or near the coast, in Belize foreigners can buy and hold beach-front real estate in exactly the same way as Belizeans. Formerly an alien landholder's license was needed for purchases of 10 acres or more (or more than 1/2 acre within a town or city.) However, such a license is no longer needed.

The only limitations on ownership by foreign nationals are these: Government approval is required from the Ministry of Natural Resources before the purchase of any island, regardless of size. In a few coastal and caye areas such as Caye Caulker there are rules limiting purchases by non-locals, and approval by the local village council or board must be obtained in advance.

Real Estate Prices

Property prices vary greatly in Belize from one area to another. They generally are highest in Belize City, on Ambergris Caye and in Placencia, and lowest in remote rural areas.

In large tracts, raw land is available in Belize for under US$300 an acre, but for this price access may be poor and surveying costs may exceed the cost of the land itself. Agricultural land might range from US$500 to $3,000 an acre, depending on quality and access.

Home prices range from under US$25,000 for a simple Belizean-style home in a small village to US$750,000 or more for a luxury home on the beach in San Pedro. Finished, newer homes typically sell for from US$75 to $150 per square foot, though of course the location of the lot or land also is a major factor.

The condominium type of ownership is new to Belize, and most condos are on Ambergris Caye. There are a few condos in Placencia and Belize City and on Caye Caulker, and a handful in Corozal Town. Prices start at around US$125,000 for a one-bedroom unit and go up to well over half a million dollars. On a square foot basis, you can expect to pay US$200 to $300 per square foot for a two-bedroom condo with sea views.

Belize has a few timeshares and "fractional ownership" properties, mostly on Ambergris Caye. These are generally not a good investment, in our opinion.

Property in Belize has appreciated over the past two decades, but by exactly how much is more difficult to say. Real estate agents say that some beachfront property in Placencia, San Pedro and elsewhere that was selling for a few hundred dollars a front foot in1980 is now going for US$3,000 to $5,000 or more a front foot. Real estate agents naturally talk up the appreciation potential, but keep in mind that the Belize economy is closely tied to the economy in the U.S.

Since the U.S. and world economies went into a tailspin in 2008, real estate sales in Belize have slowed, especially in beach areas. Condo sales in particular have stalled. A few condo developments in Placencia and on Ambergris have shut down, at least temporarily. Other have stopped or postponed construction. Lot sales also have slowed significantly. "Very little is selling in Placencia," one agent said. However, there still seems to be interest in small tracts of land in inland areas such as Cayo.

Despite the slowdown, price levels seem to have held up in most areas. The only big cuts in asking prices are on properties that were overpriced to begin with, real estate agents say.

As of this writing (early 2010), very little new condo or new home construction is going on in formerly "hot" areas of Ambergris Caye and Placencia.

Even with appreciation, real estate prices in Belize are still inexpensive by the standards of the U.S. or most of Western Europe. That's especially true of beachfront prices. Waterfront lot prices on the Eastern seaboard of the U.S. or in Florida rarely are less than US$200,000 to $500,000, and in places like Hilton Head, S.C., or Ft. Lauderdale, Fla., can easily reach US$1 million or more, whereas beachfront building lots on Belize's Caribbean are still available for US$100,000 to $200,000.

Precautions and Pitfalls

Most of the same rules of thumb that apply when looking for a home, land or apartment in the United States or Canada also apply in Belize. But Belize also has its own special situations:

Be prepared to get out and hunt. You're not going to get a deal if you only go to a real estate agent. Most properties in Belize aren't listed with brokers. You'll need to go out and look for available properties. Just start asking around, and you'll soon have plenty of choices. In Belize, money talks, and if you have the cash some people who have never considered selling may decide it's time to cash in.

Understand that the Belize real estate market is small and inefficient.

Someone asked me why a piece of property near Placencia was still on the market three years after he had first seen it advertised. "Was there something wrong with the property?" he asked. No, I told him, nothing wrong with the property. It's just Belize. The real estate marketplace in Belize is even more inefficient than it is elsewhere. The pool of financially capable real estate buyers in Belize is small, leaving many sellers dependent on foreign buyers. There is little real estate classified advertising, and most properties are sold or rented by word of mouth. Multiple listing services are just in their infancy in Belize. There is no computerized database of real estate sales with prices. Thus, it's not easy to find out exactly what is on the market or what the prices are. There are relatively few well-trained real estate agents, appraisers and surveyors. Mortgage financing is not easily available for foreign buyers, further reducing the size of the buying pool and requiring cash sales or owner financing.

All this means that prices for similar properties can be all over the board. Also, the time to sell a property may be measured in years rather months. Which is something to think about as you buy real estate, which you may someday want to sell.

Negotiate. If you're a good horse trader, you'll likely get a better deal in Belize than the guy who isn't. Keep in mind that in most parts of Belize there is far more available real estate than buyers with cold cash; so don't jump at the first deal that comes your way. Remember, too, that in real estate you almost always make your money when you buy, not when you sell. The more you know, the better price you'll get. A common saying among expats in Belize is that the second house you buy or rent is twice as large as the first and costs one-half as much. The real estate market in Belize is so thin that many sellers just pull an asking price out of the air -- similar properties can vary widely in asking price. Unscrupulous real estate agents also sometimes change the asking price in mid-negotiation, in many cases without telling the owner. Spend as much time in Belize as you can before you put any money in real estate.

Caveat emptor. Buyer beware applies as much in Belize as anywhere else. Real estate agents in Belize still aren't licensed, although licensing efforts are under way. That beachfront lot that looks wonderful in the dry season may be under two feet of water in the rainy season, and there are no laws in Belize that provide for you to get your money back if the real estate agent didn't provide full disclosure. In addition, as soon as the word gets out that you're in the market for a place to live, everybody and his brother will tell you about this little piece of property owned by a cousin of theirs. It may be a great deal, but look before you leap.

In Belize, especially outside resort areas, there are sometimes two prices: one price for locals and another price for foreigners. The difference may only be a few dollars, but sometimes the Belizean price may be one-half or less of the "rich foreigner" price. From the expat's point of view, this is unfair. From the Belizean point of view, this is perfectly kosher and reflects the reality that Americans (or Canadians or Europeans) make far more money for the same work as Belizeans and can well afford to pay more. One way around this problem is to get a trusted Belizean friend to find out the "local price" for you. Another is spend enough time in the country to get a feel for the difference between the Belizean price and the non-Belizean price, so that at least you can bargain with your eyes open.

What You Get for Your Real Estate Dollar in Belize

Here's a sampler of what you can expect to get for your money in Belize in 2009:

Under US$20,000
5 to10 acres of land in Orange Walk District or other rural area
One-half acre building lot in Corozal, Belize, Toledo or Cayo districts

Under US$30,000
Seaview lot on far North Ambergris Caye (no utilities, boat access)
15-acre farm with small very basic dwelling in rural area

Under US$50,000
Small beachfront lot on far North Ambergris Caye
Beachfront lot in some areas of Hopkins or Corozal
Small concrete home in Belmopan, Corozal or Cayo
Mennonite "prefab" small house on lagoon or riverfront lot on southern coast (including lot)

Under US$125,000
50-acre farm with small dwelling and outbuildings in northern Belize,

Cayo or Toledo

Modern 1,000 square-foot home, possibly with waterview in Corozal or Hopkins area

One-bedroom condo on Ambergris Caye or Caye Caulker

Under US$250,000

Two-bedroom condo with seaview on Ambergris Caye

Deluxe 2,000 square-foot home on nice lot in San Ignacio or Corozal

150-acre farm with nice home, outbuildings and equipment in rural area

Under US$500,000

Luxury 5,000 square-foot home on small estate in Cayo

Luxury 3,000 square-foot home on with sea view on Ambergris Caye

1,000-acre farm with home, outbuildings and equipment in rural area

Small private island

Fees and Costs of Purchase

Besides the cost of the property, you are likely to incur charges associated with the purchase that total 6% to 17% of the purchase price. These include the following:

Stamp Duty: This real estate transfer tax formerly was 15% for most foreign nationals. In 2006, however, it was reduced to 5% across the board, regardless of the nationality or residency status of the buyer. This tax is due at closing and is calculated on the gross sales price of the property, or, in the case of property being transferred at less than market value, of the actual value of the property. There is no stamp duty due on the first US$10,000 of the sale – so if a property is sold for US$50,000 there would be a transfer tax of 5% on US$40,000.

GST: The GST of 10% applies to the FIRST-TIME sale of new or substantially renovated property. This applies, for example, to newly constructed condos and houses. Substantially renovated means that 60% or more of the property was renovated. It also applies in some cases to residential lots selling for the first time in a subdivision. It does NOT apply to the sale of other land or previously occupied homes. In some cases, the GST is rolled into the sales price.

Attorney's fee: For around 1% to 2% (usually 2%) of the purchase price, the attorney will draw up sales agreements, transfer documents and ascertain that the title is sound.

Thus, if you are buying a new condominium for US$200,000 at the time of closing you will pay the 5% stamp duty, 10% GST and 2% attorney's fee, for a total of 17% of the sales price, or US$34,000. On the purchase of an existing home or tract of land, the total would be around 7% of the sales price.

In addition, there usually are nominal other fees and charges associated with transferring a title, such as for photocopying or filing.

Property taxes: Property taxes vary but are about 1.5% of the assigned value (NOT market value) of the undeveloped land, payable annually on April 1. In Belize, property taxes outside cities are based on land value rather than the developed value of the property, to encourage development. Property taxes on homes and other developed land even in cities are low, although the government has been increasing them in some areas. For example, the property tax on a nice four-bedroom North American-style home would likely be in the range of US$200 to $400, but in some areas the tax might be under US$100. Some property owners pay as little as US$20 or $30 property tax.

Speculation tax: There is a 5% speculation tax on land of 300 acres or more, payable annually based on the value of the land.

Capital gains tax: There is no capital gains tax in Belize.

Registration and Title

There are three different real property title systems in Belize:

Registered Land Act system, in which application for transfer is made, and a new Land Certificate is issued to the purchaser. Belize is moving to this system throughout the country, but at present it is not yet available everywhere. Under this system, an application is made for title transfer and a new Certificate of Title is issued to the grantee. Any existing "charges" will be shown on the Land Register for that parcel of land. The owner holds a Certificate of Title, and this, together with the relevant Land Register entries is the proof of ownership.

Conveyance system, which involves the transfer of land by conveyance and registration. This is the system used in much of the United States. In order to assure that the seller actually owns the land, a title search must be made in the Lands Unit in Belmopan to unearth the chain of title and to uncover any encumbrances such as uncanceled mortgages. This search usually is done by an attorney or a paralegal. Unfortunately, it is sometimes difficult or impossible to trace old conveyances with any degree of certainty of results, due to the condition of the index books.

Torrens system, which involves a First Certificate of Title followed by Transfer Certificates of Title. Unlike the Torrens system in use in parts of the U.S. and elsewhere, the Belize systems is not backed up by a fund, which guarantees title. Under this system, the uncanceled charges or encumbrances and the transfers from the title are shown on the relevant Certificate, so no further search is normally needed before the new Transfer Certificate of Title is issued, following the application for transfer.

Which system you use depends on where your property is located. You won't have a choice. If for example your property is located in an area of Belize where the Registered Land Act system is in place, such as around Belmopan or in a planned subdivision, your property will be registered under that system. Land in Belize is being put into this system area by area until eventually the entire country will be included in it. Each year, more of Belize is converted to this system.

Some property purchasers in Belize complain that it can take many months or even years for the Lands Department to provide them with their Certificate of Title.

Title insurance is available in Belize, though most buying property don't use it. RF&G Insurance and other insurance companies offer title insurance. Typically, title insurance costs 1% of the purchase price. Stewart Title, a U.S.-based title insurance firm, does not have an office in Belize but provides title insurance for some properties through Belizean firms.

Need for a Lawyer

In Belize, attorneys remain trusted advisors. They're usually well-connected, well-paid pillars of the community who wield real power. Fees are not all that different from what you would pay in a small or mid-size city in the U.S.

A roster of attorneys in Belize *(see Appendix)* reveals the surnames of prominent families with histories in Belize going well back into colonial times along with those of today's political leaders including Barrow, Young, Shoman, Musa, Courtenay and Godfrey.

In any real estate transaction, you should have your own Belize attorney.

Caution about Buying Leased Land

Many Belizeans own property under a leasehold from the government. The Belize government provides building lots and other small pieces of land to Belizean citizens on a lease basis. After the Belizean clears the property and improves it with a building, he or she can apply for a conversion to a fee simple title. However, some Belizean owners never get around to doing this or cannot afford the cost. Be sure that you are buying a fee simple, freehold property, not a leasehold property. Again, this is an area where a Belizean attorney can help you.

Financing

It is difficult for a non-resident to get a mortgage loan from a bank in Belize for buying or building, so you should be prepared to pay cash, arrange owner financing or get financing through a loan from a non-Belize financial institution on your assets back home. Acreage and building lots in Belize are often purchased on terms under an Agreement for Sale or Contract for Deed whereby the seller keeps title to the property until it has been paid for in full. Terms vary but can range from 10% down with 10 years to pay at 10% simple interest per annum — about the best deal you can hope for — to 50% down and three years to pay at 12 to 14%, with perhaps a balloon at the end. Residential property may also have owner financing, although commonly the lowest price will be for all-cash deals. A few owners of condos and homes in San Pedro and elsewhere offer financing, typically with around 20% down.

For citizens and official permanent residents of Belize only, the Development Finance Corporation (DFC), a financial institution owned by the government of Belize, formerly made loans of US$2,500-$50,000 or more for building or buying housing. Terms were for up to 25 years at interest rates of 8.5 to 13%. The DFC also developed housing subdivisions near Belmopan on Ambergris Caye, on the Northern Highway in Belize District, and in Corozal Town. These subdivisions offered new homes, such as a small, three-bedroom, concrete house near Belmopan for US$35,000 and a three-bedroom, two-bath home of 925 square feet at Ladyville for about US$47,000. Financing was at 12% for up to 25 years.

Belizeans did not seem to care much for most of these subdivisions, and many homes were never sold. Some of the houses were poorly constructed and located in undesirable areas. In 2004, the DFC ran out of financial string. As of this writing in 2010, plans are under way to reorganize and restart the DFC.

Real Estate Foreclosure Auctions

From time to time there are foreclosure auctions in Belize. They sell property put up as security for bank or other financial institution loans. Usually these are advertised in the weekly newspapers in Belize City. Foreigners can participate in these auctions. There may be no particular problems in buying at a foreclosure auction, other than those ordinarily associated with auctions, such as the fact that among the savvy bidders may be local people who know more than you do about the property and its value. However, in Belize sometimes the owners of the property will still be in possession at the time of the auction. If so, you may face a real problem getting the owners out. Before putting up your money, you may want to consult with an attorney conversant with real estate property law (see Appendix for a list of attorneys in Belize.)

Rentals

Rental levels in Belize also vary widely, being highest on Ambergris Caye and in Belize City. In upscale areas of Belize City, you can expect to pay around US$.80 to $1.50 per square foot per month, or about US$800 to $1,500 a month for a 1,000 sq. ft. two-bedroom apartment. On Ambergris Caye, a one-bedroom apartment goes for US$500 to $900 and a two-bedroom US$700 to $1,500.

Elsewhere, rentals are much lower. In rural areas and low-cost towns such as Corozal, you can find a small house in a safe area for under US$400 a month and sometimes for as little as one-half that amount. Modern three-bedroom homes near the water go for US$500 to $1,000 a month. We know of expats in Corozal who rent for under US$300 a month, and while their homes are not fancy they are comfortable, typically of concrete block construction with a couple of small bedrooms, bath, a living room and a kitchen with stove and refrigerator. In all areas, North American-style housing with air conditioning, modern appliances, and security systems will be several times more expensive than a traditional Belize rental, simple concrete or wood house, with only basic amenities and probably no appliances except for a butane stove and a small fridge.

Short-Term Rentals

If you're coming to Belize on a scouting expedition of a few weeks to a few months, consider a short-term rental. Staying in a house or apartment rather than in a hotel can help you decide if Belize is really for you. Unfortunately, there are not a lot of short-term vacation rentals in Belize. Most of them are concentrated on Ambergris Caye, but there are a few in other areas including Placencia and Corozal. In most areas, however, you can find a hotel with housekeeping facilities.

Free Land?

You may have heard about a program of homesteading or otherwise getting free land in Belize. Yes, there is such a program in place, but there are big catches: First, you must be a Belizean citizen or have lived in the country as an official resident for at least three years. Second, land is only available in certain areas. Mainly it is small tracts or building lots. This is not the homesteading hundreds of acres of prime farm land that you read about in the your American history book. Third, you have to lease the land from the government, clear it and actually construct a home. At that point, for a nominal amount you can buy the property from the government, and you will get title.

Given all the time and red tape involved, and the low cost of land in Belize, it's hardly worth it to get a small piece of land worth a few thousand dollars. Frankly, if the only reason you moved to Belize is to take advantage of such a scheme, it's unlikely you'll have the financial resources to make it in Belize long enough to qualify for the program.

Kitchen cabinets custom-made of Belizean mahogany

CHAPTER 8:
BUILDING YOUR OWN HOME IN BELIZE

Building is usually cheaper than buying, especially if you act as your own general contractor. As a rule, you will get more for your housing dollar in Belize by building rather than buying a completed home. You'll often get a lot more home. However, you'll also get a lot more headaches. If you can put up with construction hassles – which are many — you can build a house with details such as built-in furniture, exotic tropical hardwood floors and ceilings and custom-made mahogany cabinets that in the U.S. would be found only in the most upscale homes.

What Does It Cost?

Construction costs vary depending on such factors the cost of transportation of materials to the building site, the terrain and quality of work. In Belize, construction costs are higher on the coast and cayes, because of the need to use hurricane resistant construction. In the case of the cayes, it costs extra to transport building materials out to the islands by boat. Building costs also are higher in southern than in northern Belize. Inexpensive building materials are more readily available in northern Belize since some can be imported from Chetumal, Mexico.

Labor in Belize is much less expensive than in the U.S., with carpenters and masons typically getting around US$25 to $40 a day or less. Unskilled construction workers may only get US$15 to $20 a day.

While labor may be cheap, jobs usually take longer in Belize. Workers may be skilled at construction techniques common in Belize but may lack knowledge about building in the American style. Outside of urban areas, it is difficult to find qualified craftspeople such as electricians and plumbers. Building materials vary but are mostly no cheaper than in the U.S., except for locally produced items such as tropical hardwoods which run about US$1,000 for 1,000 board feet. Also, locally produced plywood is roughly one-half the cost in the U.S. (though plywood prices vary over time due to fluctuating demand.) Cement is more expensive than in the U.S., — a 50 lb. bag typically costs around US$6 to $8 — as are most bathroom and kitchen fixtures that have to be imported. Flooring materials such as salt tiles from Guatemala and Mexico are moderately priced and of high quality. Overall, building costs in Belize range from around US$30 to $150 a square foot, not including the cost of land. At the bottom end, that would be a simple Belizean-style cinderblock house or frame construction, and at the top it would be high-quality concrete construction with hardwood floors and trim and with many custom details such as hand-made doors and windows. Most commonly, you'd expect to pay about US$50 to $90 a square foot, so a 1,500 square foot home would cost US$75,000 to $135,000 to build, not including land. That's about one-half or less of typical costs for construction in the U.S.

Costs can vary tremendously from builder to builder. One resident of San Pedro said he got quotes for the construction of a five-bedroom reinforced concrete home that varied from US$60 to $130 a square foot.

Regardless of where or how you build, you need to be on-site to manage and oversee the construction, or pay someone you trust very well to do that for you. Expect that the process will take roughly twice as long as you expect – eight to ten months, or longer, to build a house is not uncommon.

Especially in rural areas or on the coast, a lot of the cost of building is underground – foundations, pilings, cisterns, septic tanks. You may need two or more septic tanks for a large house. Cisterns for your drinking water cost roughly US$50 cents to $1 a gallon to construct.

Of course, if you have a nose for saving money you can build for much less than that. We know one fellow who built a small house on a lagoon north of Corozal for about US$4,000. He collected building materials such as old planks and boards that were floating in the lagoon, scrounged others from old houses and did most of the actual construction work himself. The charity organization Habitat for Humanity has constructed a number of affordable homes in Belize. Habitat says the cost of a two-bedroom, one-bath 528 sq. ft. concrete block house with a septic tank is about US$11,000, and US$15,000 for a 720 sq. ft. three-bedroom house. That's a little less than US$21 a square foot.

In areas at risk of hurricanes and tropical storms, you'll have to put in deep pilings and raise the first floor above ground level to avoid water damage. Depending on the area and the depth and type of pilings, these can cost as much as US$3,000 to $5,000 each.

Reinforced concrete is the preferred construction. Hurricane straps and rafter ties are inexpensive protection against having the roof blown away. Most insurance companies in Belize no longer will cover traditional thatch construction, and some also will not cover wood frame construction if the house is on the coast or cayes.

Insurance if available at all will vary with the construction: Wood frame construction in coastal or island areas will incur annual premiums of up to 2 to 4% of value, whereas steel construction will see premiums of around 1.25% of value and reinforced concrete about 1.5% or less.

In the past, the only building codes in Belize have been those imposed by local municipalities. Many rural areas had no codes at all, and builders often ignored any existing codes. However, Belize has developed a national building code calling for nation-wide standards of construction. The Central Building Authority (CBA) is starting to take a tougher stance to ensure that builders follow the building code. Now before construction for a house can be approved, drawings must be presented (including an electrical plan approved by the Public Utilities Commission) to the CBA, an application for construction made and the appropriate fees paid.

The CBA has authority nationally, although it works with local building authorities. Varying local codes apply. For example, in Belmopan City only concrete new construction is permitted, not wood. More developed areas such as San Pedro and Belize City have stricter building permit and code systems. In most areas now, a licensed electrician must sign off on the electrical work before the building can be hooked up to Belize Electricity Ltd.

In general, though, Belize's building codes and permitting and inspection processes are still less intrusive and financially onerous than those in the U.S.

Trailers and Manufactured Homes in Belize

Trailer trash? Not in Belize. You won't find many mobile homes, trailers or "manufactured homes" (except from the Mennonites – see below). There are several reasons for this: For one, trailers aren't known for durability or safety in hurricanes. For another, the cost of shipping prefab units to Belize is high. Also, mobile homes and trailers don't stand up well to the hot, humid semitropical climate – rusting, abandoned RVs you see in the bush are proof of that. Perhaps most importantly, import duties make bringing in trailers an unattractive option compared with building locally. However, some expats do decide to import prefab buildings. The original owner of the Nautical Inn beach resort in Seine Bight on the Placencia peninsula brought in prefab hexagonal buildings from North Carolina and had them set up on the beach by local laborers.

Mennonite Prefab: Cheap Alternative to Regular Construction

An inexpensive alternative to building from scratch in Belize is to have a prefabricated Mennonite house set up on your lot. Mennonite builders in Spanish Lookout and elsewhere build and sell small frame buildings, which they will deliver and install on pilings on your site. This is an inexpensive and quick way to get a home up in Belize, and even some resorts such as the Green Parrot on the Placencia peninsula use these buildings. These buildings typically are made of local hardwoods and come with mahogany or glass louvered windows. You can get them as unfinished shells or complete down to electrical wiring, ceiling fans and plumbing. Usually there is a choice of roofing materials – zinc, tin or asphalt shingles. The cabins are set up on 6x6 posts 8 feet apart and about 3 feet off the ground. You may want to upgrade the specs to your own standards -- for example using 2x4 framing rather than smaller boards. You can buy them from standardized plans or custom order.

Prices vary, but here are typical prices, including set up on your mainland lot:

20 ft. x 24 ft. (480 sq. ft.) US$10,000-$12,000
20 ft. x 30 ft. (600 sq. ft.) US$12,000-$14,000
20 ft. x 40 ft. (800 sq. ft.) US$14,000-$18,000

Delivery and set up to the cayes and to remote areas could increase the price substantially.

Sources of prefab Mennonite houses include:

Linda Vista Lumber & Houses, Spanish Lookout, Cayo; tel. 501-823-8052; email lvly@btl.net

Midwest Lumber Mill, Spanish Lookout, Cayo; tel. 501-823-8000; email mim@btl.net

Plett's Homebuilders, Spanish Lookout, Cayo: tel. 501-823-0447; http://plettshomebuilders.com/default.aspx

Franz Weib, Weib-Camara Construction; tel. 501-671-5885

Tobar's Home Construction, Spanish Lookout, Cayo; tel. 501-824-2660; www.belize-construction.com

Household Expenses

You'll get some good--and some bad--surprises when you open your household bills in Belize. On the positive side, you won't be getting a bill for fuel oil or gas to heat your home. Very few houses in Belize even have a furnace or heater, since winter temperatures rarely fall even into the 50s. If a cold front comes through, just put a blanket on the bed or pull on a cotton sweater.

However, electricity (it's usually called "current" in Belize) is much pricier than in the U.S. or Canada. Figure about US$.21 per kilowatt-hour, which is about twice the average in the U.S. High electric rates are why most Belizeans don't have air conditioning, or if they do have A/C, it's only in the bedrooms. Belize Electricity, Ltd., is the sole provider in Belize. About 40% of the electricity used in Belize is purchased from Mexico.

The newly constructed Chalillo Dam in Cayo, along with three others, is supposed to help Belize become energy-independent, but at the cost of wildlife habitat. So far, the dam has not lowered electrical costs in Belize, nor as it made the grid significantly more reliable. Outages and surges still occur fairly frequently. If you're off the grid, as many still are in remote rural areas, either you do without power or run a diesel generator. Wind, hydro, and solar energy are making some headway in Belize, though initial set-up costs are high. A small community of some 20 homes on Caye Caulker generates all its power from alternate sources, mainly wind turbines. Due to the cost of batteries and other materials, they say that their long-term costs are about US$1 a kilowatt.

Water and sewerage bills vary around the country, but a typical monthly cost per household is about US$10-$20. "Pipe water," as it's known in Belize, is costlier on Ambergris Caye. If you live in a rural area, you'll probably have your own water system, either a well or a cistern to collect rainwater, and a septic tank for wastes. Thus, your only expenses will be the initial cost of the systems, plus any electricity you use. Most households in Belize run stoves and hot water showers on butane. (Butane is sold in Belize instead of propane.) Rates vary according to energy prices, but on average, a small household may use US$30-$60 worth of butane a month. Trucks deliver butane tanks to your home, or at least to the road in front of your home. Aside from your telephone, electric and butane bills, the only other utility expense you may face is garbage pickup. Belizeans refer to it as "dirt." Your dirt bill will probably not run more than US$10, and pickup is free in some areas. Also, cable television bills generally are a little lower in Belize than you're used to back home. Typical monthly rates are US$20-25.

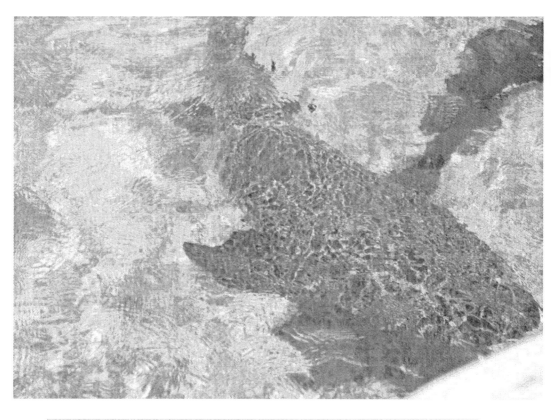

Nurse shark at Hol Chan – also beware the land sharks

CHAPTER 9:
OVERVIEW OF BEST PLACES TO LIVE, RETIRE OR BUY PROPERTY

Here, in thumbnail sketches, are your main choices for living, retiring and investing in Belize. In the chapters that follow, we'll explore in more detail the options in each of these areas, including a closer look at what each area offers, the cost of living, price and availability of real estate, examples of property for sale and rent and other practical matters.

NORTHERN CAYES

The two largest of the Northern Cayes are Ambergris (pronounced Am-BUR-griss Key) and Caye Caulker, sometimes known as Caye Corker.

Ambergris Caye

Ambergris Caye is the most popular place for retirees and other expats to live in Belize. It offers the beauty of the Caribbean in a fairly compact, accessible package. You can dive, snorkel, swim and fish to your heart's content. San Pedro, Ambergris Caye's only town, has Belize's biggest selection of restaurants and nightlife.

Island life, however, presents its own special set of pleasures and problems. On Ambergris Caye, residents say island fever strikes from time to time. Most residents go into Belize City regularly to conduct business, shop for items not available on the island or to get dental care. Many expats take vacations in the U.S., or long weekends in Cayo district or elsewhere in Belize.

While beachfront house and lot prices are no longer the bargain they once were, they are not too expensive by U.S. coastal standards. You can buy a buildable beach lot on North Ambergris for US$75,000 and up, or build a small but pleasant seaside home for US$200,000. Costs on the back or lagoon side are lower.

Prices for quality beachfront land, especially near San Pedro, rose rapidly (at least until the big recession hit the U.S. in 2008-2009) and now are in the US$3,000 to $5,000 a front foot range. As of 2008, more than 700 new condo units were under development on the island, mostly on North Ambergris Caye. Some of these projects were completed, but others were delayed.

Most of the island's economy is focused on tourism. If you aren't busy selling real estate or running a hotel, the island offers some volunteer opportunities. Some expats help out at the local library, or do church work (the island has one Catholic church and several Protestant denominations). The San Pedro chapter of the Lions Club is the island's most active civic organization. Its weekly barbecue is delicious, cheap and a fund-raiser for the group's good works.

Caye Caulker

Ambergris Caye's sister island is smaller and, if anything, even friendlier. Residents here have managed to maintain close ownership of land on the island, though some lots and houses are available on the open market. A few condos are going up. We see Caulker as a real growth area for real estate over the next few years, barring a major hurricane. A few apartments are for rent, starting at around US$300 to $500 a month.

COROZAL IN NORTHERN BELIZE

Most visitors to Belize either never get to Corozal or pass through quickly en route somewhere else. But Corozal Town and nearby Consejo village offer a lot for those staying awhile: low prices, friendly people, a generally low-crime environment, the beautiful blue water of Corozal Bay and the extra plus of having Mexico next door for shopping. There's even a new Sam's Club in Chetumal, just across the border. Corozal is one of the undiscovered jewels of Belize. There's not a lot to do, but it's a great place to do it.

The Sugar Coast – sugarcane is a main agricultural crop here as it is in the adjoining Orange Walk district – is a place to slow down, relax and enjoy life. The climate is appealing, with less rain than almost anywhere else in Belize, and fishing is excellent. The sunny disposition of residents – Mestizos, Creoles, Maya, Chinese, East Indians and even North Americans – is infectious. Real estate costs in Corozal are among the lowest in Belize. Modern North American-style homes with three or four bedrooms in Corozal Town or Consejo Shores go for US$100,000 to around US$250,000, but Belizean-style homes start at less than US$35,000. Waterfront lots are available for US$75,000 or less, and big lots near the water are US$15,000-$30,000.

Rentals are relatively inexpensive – US$1200-$350 for a nice Belizean-style house or US$400-$800 for a modern American-style house.

ORANGE WALK DISTRICT IN NORTHERN BELIZE

Orange Walk Town — the name came from the orange groves in the area — could be any number of towns in Mexico. There's a formal plaza, and the town hall is called the Palacio Municipal. The businesses and houses along the main drag — Queen Victoria Avenue or the Belize-Corozal Road — have barred windows, and some of the hotels and bars are in fact brothels. In this setting, conservative Mennonites from Shipyard and Blue Creek who come to town to sell produce look strangely out of place. However, Orange Walk Town is a gateway to a magical area of Belize — the wide sky, fertile land and unpeopled forests of Belize's northwest shoulder, pressed against the Guatemala border.

CAYO DISTRICT IN WESTERN BELIZE

Cayo has a lot going for it: wide open spaces, cheap land, few bugs and friendly people. This might be the place to buy a few acres and grow oranges. The major towns are San Ignacio/Santa Elena, with a population of nearly 20,000, about 10 miles from the Guatemala border, and Belmopan City, the miniature capital of Belize, with a population of around 20,000. Agriculture, ranching and, increasingly, tourism are the major industries here. About 30 years ago, the first small jungle lodges began operation around San Ignacio. Now there is a flourishing mix of hotels, cottages and jungle lodges near San Ignacio and in the Mountain Pine Ridge, along with a lot of natural attractions and outdoor activities – canoeing, caving, hiking, horseback riding, to name a few. The country's most accessible Maya ruins are here, as well as Caracol, in its heyday a larger city-state than Tikal. Between Belize City and San Ignacio, Belmopan is the downsized capital of Belize, but the attractions are in the surrounding countryside. The Belize Zoo is nearby, as are several excellent jungle lodges. Along the scenic Hummingbird Highway are barely explored caves, wild rivers and national park areas. Small farms are available for US$25,000-$75,000.

PLACENCIA ON THE SOUTHERN COAST

Placencia has the best beaches on the mainland, and it's an appealing seaside alternative to the bustle of Ambergris Caye. This peninsula in southern Belize has some 16 miles of beachfront along the Caribbean, a backside lagoon where manatees are frequently seen, two small villages, a few dozen hotels and restaurants and an increasing number of expatriates and foreign-owned homes. In recent years, the Placencia peninsula has been undergoing a boom, a boom that was slowed only temporarily by Hurricane Iris in 2001. Building lots by the score have been sold to foreigners who think they'd someday like to live by the sea. Beginning around 2004-2005, condo development on the peninsula took off, and now some 1,500 condos are either under construction or planned, though construction slowed down dramatically as the housing crunch and recession seized up markets in the U.S. and elsewhere, and one large condo project shut down, at least temporarily.

Seafront real estate costs are higher in Placencia than anywhere else in Belize, except Ambergris Caye. Beachfront lots cost US$2,500 to $3,500 per front foot, making a seaside lot around US$100,000 or more. Lots on the lagoon or canal are less expensive. There is little North American-style housing available for sale or rent, and many expatriates are building their own homes, with building costs ranging upwards of US$100 per square foot, depending on type of construction. A contract to pave the peninsula road, a monster that everyone loved to hate, was signed in 2007, and as of this writing the road is paved from Placencia village to Maya Beach. It is expected to be completed by 2011. A new airport is under construction just north of the peninsula. It is supposed to open in late 2010, with limited international service. It's too early to say whether the international service will actually materialize.

HOPKINS ON THE SOUTHERN COAST

On the southern coast of Belize in Stann Creek District between Dangriga and Placencia, Hopkins today is what Placencia was like just a decade or so ago. Expatriates are moving to Hopkins, a friendly Garifuna village that got telephones only in the mid-1990s, and to real estate developments nearby. New small seaside hotels and condo developments are going up in Hopkins and Sittee Point. Although at times the sand flies can eat you alive here, you can get in some excellent fishing and beach time, with day trips to the nearby Cockscomb jaguar reserve and boat trips to the reef. You'll love Hopkins if Placencia is too developed for you.

PUNTA GORDA AREA IN SOUTHERN BELIZE

Rainy, beautiful and remote, Punta Gorda in far southern Belize is the jumping-off point for unspoiled Maya villages and for onward travel to Guatemala and Honduras. Over the next few years as paving of the final 5-mile portion o the Southern Highway to Punta Gorda is completed and the road is extended into Guatemala, this area is expected to take off, both in terms of tourism and as a place for expatriate living. "PG," as it's known, is Toledo District's only population center, with about 5,500 people, mostly Garifuna, Maya and immigrants from Guatemala. Maya villages, hardly changed for centuries, are located around PG. Cayes and the south end of the barrier reef offer good snorkeling and fishing. Lumbering and fishing are about the only industries. Undeveloped land is inexpensive, with acreage beginning at a few hundred dollars an acre. Few North American-style homes are for sale. Quality rentals are fairly expensive due to demand from missionaries and lack of supply.

PRIVATE ISLANDS

The days of buying your own private island for a song are long gone, but if you have money to burn and the willingness to rebuild after the next hurricane, one of Belize's remote islands could be yours, beginning at about US$100,000 and going up to several million. In 2005, Leo DiCaprio, the star of "Titanic," bought Blackadore Caye, a 104-acre island near San Pedro, for a reported US$2.4 million, or about US$23,000 an acre.

Developers have been selling lots on a few small cayes. Keep in mind that transporting materials to the island, building there and maintaining the property likely will be much, much higher than on the mainland.

■■

Beachfront Land Costs in Belize

Many dream of living on a Caribbean beach. Here's the reality of what you'll pay for beachfront lots in Belize today. These are typical selling prices per front foot on the beach. If the lot has 75 feet of beach frontage, multiply that by the per-front foot cost in U.S. dollars. While the overall size and depth of the lot affects the total price, a 200-foot deep lot may be only a little more expensive than a 100- or 150-foot deep lot. It's the frontage on the water that matters most. The top end of the price range is for better-quality, buildable lots on higher ground. Large tracts with extensive beachfront typically would be less that prices shown here.

Corozal Town Area: US$800-$2,000
Cerros/Sarteneja Peninsula: US$750-$1,800
Ambergris Caye: US$2,500-$5,000
Placencia Peninsula: US$2,500-$3,500
Hopkins/Sittee Point Area: US$2,000-$2,500
Toledo District: US$500-$1,500

CHAPTER 10:
THE NORTHERN CAYES IN DETAIL

The first area we'll look at is the best-known destination in Belize for both visitors and prospective expats -- Ambergris Caye.

GRADING THE AREA FOR RETIREMENT, RELOCATION AND INVESTMENT Ratings are on an A to F scale, just like your old high school report card. A is the top grade; F is failing. Grades are on a curve, relative compared to other areas in Belize.

Popularity with Expats	A
Safety	B
Overall Cost of Living	C-
Real Estate Costs	D
Investment Potential	B+
Leisure Activities	B+
Restaurants	A
Cultural Activities	D
Infrastructure	C+
Business Potential	B+
Medical Care	C+
Shopping	C+

ADVANTAGES OF AMBERGRIS CAYE: • Largest expat community in Belize • Busy resort island atmosphere with the country's best restaurants • Offers some of Belize's best beaches • Provides excellent water sports opportunities – diving, boating, fishing • No need for a car • Reasonably safe though burglaries are common

Ambergris Caye is the most popular destination in Belize, for expats and travelers. There are good reasons for that: Ambergris Caye has a pleasant, laid-back attitude. Folks are friendly. There's a wide selection of hotels and restaurants and quite a few little shops. And of course, there's the Caribbean – big and blue and beautiful. This isn't a large island. It's only 25 miles long and 4 miles wide at its widest point, about one-half the size of Barbados. Much of the island is low mangrove swamp, and there are a dozen lagoons.

A Tour of the Island

The experienced Caribbean traveler will recognize San Pedro Town immediately: In some ways, it's the Caribbean of 30 years ago, before the boom in international travel, a throwback to the days before cruise ships turned too many Caribbean islands into concrete mini-malls hustling duty-free booze and discount jewelry. There are just three north-south streets. Wood houses and shops, painted in bright tropical colors fading quickly in the sun, stand close together. Newer buildings are reinforced concrete, optimistically girded for the next big hurricane. Many people still get around by foot and bicycle, though the packed sand and concrete cobblestone streets are busy with golf carts – keep a close eye, as the electric ones sneak up behind you silently – and, unfortunately, an ever increasing number of pickups and cars. In fact, there are so many taxis and private cars that there are occasional traffic jams downtown.

The name of Front Street (dozens of Caribbean islands have main streets named Front, Middle and Back) was changed a few years ago to the more romantic-sounding Barrier Reef Drive. It is one-way, with carts and vehicles allowed to go north only for most of its distance, to Caribena Street. On weekends, the street is closed to all but pedestrians. Middle Street, or Pescador Drive, is one-way south from the intersection with Caribena Street.

Many hotels, restaurants and larger businesses are on Front Street. Just beyond the primary school and the bite-sized San Pedro Library (here, you don't need a library card, and even visitors can check out books, free, or a buy a used paperback for a dollar or two), you'll see Rubie's, also spelled Ruby's, Celi's Deli, Holiday Hotel, Spindrift, home of the chicken drop, and then, near "Central Park." Big Daddy's and Jaguar's clubs are across the street from each other, and the Catholic church, cool and welcoming stands guard. Farther up on the right there's Fido's, a popular bar and restaurant, and the Mayan Princess. On the left is the big, modern Belize Bank building. As Barrier Reef Drive peters out, dead ahead is the new Phoenix condos and comfy Paradise Villas.

To the east, beyond the line of buildings, only a few feet away, accessible through many alleys, is the Caribbean. There's a narrow strip of beach and seawall between the buildings and the sea, used as a pedestrian walkway. A number of piers or docks jut out into the sea. The patch of white you see a few hundred yards out is surf breaking over the barrier reef. Even if you're a strong swimmer, don't try swimming out to the reef from the shore, especially not in or near town. There is a lot of boat traffic inside the reef, and over the years several swimmers have been killed or injured by boats.

Middle Street, or Pescador Drive, the other main north-south venue, is also busy. It's home to several restaurants, including Elvi's Kitchen, Cocina Caramba, The Reef and other worthies. As you go farther north on Middle Street, San Pedro becomes more residential, and more local. You'll see the San Pedro Supermarket (which usually has better prices than the larger Island Supermarket south of town), electric and telephone facilities, a small high school, playground, and then the Boca del Rio or "the river" or "the channel."

Cross the New Bridge to North Ambergris

In early 2006, a new bridge opened over the river. Until then, you crossed the channel on a hand-pulled ferry. The bridge is for golf carts, bikes and pedestrians only. Golf carts are charged BZ$5 each way, pedestrians BZ$1. For longer-term stays you can buy a monthly pass. A small golf cart and walking path wends its way north, mostly on the back side of the island, past several new and under-construction condo developments, expat homes, restaurants and resorts. The cart path, badly washed when it rains, is often bumpy and muddy. Plans are afoot to improve it. One of the first things you see after crossing the bridge is what is possibility the ugliest developments in all of Belize, Reef Village.

You can usually drive your cart past Captain Morgan's, made briefly famous by the "Temptation Island" reality TV program and still abuilding with new timeshares and condos, as far as Belizean Shores, Seascape, Las Terrazas, Journey's End Resort, Rendezvous restaurant, Rojo Lounge and Azul Resort, Mata Chica and Portofino. In good weather you can actually go all the way to Robles Point beyond Blue Reef Island Resort. But it is a long, long drive, some of its inland and some on the beach, which unfortunately is littered with trash in many places. Be sure to take plenty of bug spray, and wear light-colored clothes, because on North Ambergris away from the water, mosquitoes can be terrible, especially in the late summer and fall, after seasonal rains.

There are now two ferry services, Island Ferry and Coastal Xpress, that provide boat transportation up and down the island. The boats carry pedestrians only, between Pelican Reef at the south to Blue Island at the north, generally from 6 a.m. to 2 a.m. Rates vary according to distance travelled, from US$5 to $20 per person one-way.

Beyond most of the resorts is a large area that is beginning to develop for private homes, but some of it is undeveloped. Over the years, many schemes have been floated for this part of the island, once part of a private holding called the Pinkerton Estate. A large chunk of this area has been saved from Cancunization thanks to establishment of the Bacalar Chico national park and marine reserve. The park, which opened in 1996, comprises 12,000 acres of land and 15,000 acres of water. At present the park is accessible by boat from San Pedro, from the Belize mainland at Sarteneja and elsewhere and from the Mexican port village of Xcalak. The park is home to a surprisingly large population of birds and wildlife, and there are a number of Maya sites. This northern tip of the island is separated from the Mexican Yucatán only by the narrow Bacalar Chico channel. Indeed, Ambergris Caye once was physically part of the Yucatán peninsula, the channel having been dug by the Maya. In recent years, several remote beachfront resorts have opened some 8 to 12 miles north of town, including Blue Reef and Tranquility.

Heading South

Head south from town rather than north, and you're on Coconut Drive. A cluster of hotels and other businesses are near the airstrip, including SunBreeze, The Palms and Ramon's Village, with its annex, the cleverly named Steve & Becky's Cute Little Hotel, painted in bright Caribbean colors, on the right side of the street. Tropic Air's new terminal, which opened in 2009, even has an aquarium in the waiting area. In 2008, Coconut Drive as far south as Victoria House was paved with concrete cobblestones.

You'll pass the Belize Yacht Club, Changes in Latitudes B&B, Exotic Caye with its thatch condos, Corona Del Mar, Coconuts Hotel and Caribbean Villas. You'll also see the Island Supermarket, San Pedro's largest, spiffiest grocery, and soft-drink and beer magnate Barry Bowen's turf and his warehouse facility. At the warehouse you can buy Belikin, soft drinks and bottled water by the case for less than you'd pay in groceries. Some of the buildings, you'll note, are painted Belikin green. Nearby is a modern new service station, selling gas for all the cars owned by Sanpedranos. The road veers sharply right, then back left. The area west of the main drag here, or to your right going south, is the San Pablo residential area, and on the lagoon a cluster of cheap prefab homes put up by the government in a flood plain, after Hurricane Keith.

Considerable development is taking place along the sea. Villas at Banyan Bay (taken over by its lender, Belize Bank, in late 2008), the newer Grand Colony condos (they start at over half a million US), Banana Beach, Mata Rocks, Royal Palm, the beautifully upgraded Victoria House, Royal Caribbean, Caribe Island Resort, Sunset Beach, Miramar, Athens Gate and Pelican Reef are also in this area. By this point, you're some 3 miles south of the center of San Pedro Town. If you continue farther south, by foot or cart, you're back in a residential area, with a number of upmarket houses including one owned by musician Jerry Jeff Walker, along with shacks, mansions and other assorted digs. A little farther on is the planned site of South Beach Belize, a controversial development by the guy who built Reef Village. If it ever comes to pass, it eventually is supposed to have houses, condos and other accommodations for up to 7,000 people. Where all these people are supposed to come from, no one is sure.

No Longer a Fishing Village

Once a fishing village, San Pedro and the entire island are now mostly focused on tourism and real estate development. The island has more than 60 hotels and dozens of restaurants. Most of the hotels are owned by Americans, Canadians and Europeans; a study showed that only about 15% are owned by Belizeans. Expats still of working age who aren't involved in the hospitality industry often gravitate to selling real estate. For those who can't find enough to occupy themselves, substance abuse is always a risk, more so in San Pedro's freewheeling resort atmosphere than in most other areas of Belize. "Booze is ubiquitous here, and bar-hanging quite the social custom. And, in San Pedro as much as in most U.S. cities, you can now add other chemicals. If you're vulnerable, unimaginative, not a self-starter, passive-dependent, maybe Peoria would be a better bet," said John Lankford, a former New Orleans lawyer who lived on the island for several years, but who recently passed away in Alabama.

In the past, expats used to say that their hospitals were TACA, American and Continental airlines. For top-flight medical care, Americans on the island may still fly to Miami or Houston, or at least pop over to Belize City, but there are now full-time physicians on the island, along with a medical clinic that is not quite a full-fledged hospital.

Most residents and visitors say they feel safe on the island. Burglary and petty thefts are relatively common (see chapter on crime, above), but violent crime isn't. Probably the worst crime in modern island history occurred in 1994, when, late at night, American expat Ann Reilly, a gardening writer with some 30 books to her credit, and her British husband, Alan Dines, were attacked and brutally beaten to death in a dark area of beachfront south of San Pedro. The attacker, a Belizean from Punta Gorda, was eventually caught, tried, convicted and sentenced to hang.

Ambergris Caye Practicalities

Banks: Retail banks on the island include Belize Bank, Alliance Bank, First Caribbean International and Atlantic Bank, all on Barrier Reef Drive. Scotia Bank is across from Tropic Air on Coconut Drive. Caye Bank, on Coconut Drive south of town, is an international (offshore) bank and cannot do retail banking in Belize.

Groceries: There are a number of small groceries on the island. The largest are San Pedro Supermarket at the north end of town, Richie's (across the street from San Pedro Supermarket) and Island Supermarket south of town. Island Supermarket is the largest and fanciest of the three but usually the most expensive. Other small groceries are located around the island, including Marina's south of town. Super Buy on Back Street is where many locals shop. These and other shops each have approximately the inventory of a large convenience store in the U.S., plus items such as frozen meats. In addition, there are small stores that specialize in meats, including excellent sausages at the Sausage Factory. A good local bakery is Casa Pan Dulce (formerly La Popular). Fruits and vegetables can be purchased from street vendors or at small specialty shops. Costs for most food items, especially imported items, are considerably higher than in the U.S., often twice as high. Belikin beer can be ordered by the case from the Belikin distributor just south of town, near the Island Supermarket. However, even by the case beer in Belize isn't cheap – you'll pay about a U.S. dollar a bottle, but that's still a savings over supermarket prices. Liquor is sold in grocery stores – imported brands cost about twice U.S. prices, but local rum is under US$10 a fifth.

There are two wine shops on the island, Wine DeVine, on Tarpon Street near the airstrip, and Premium Wines & Spirits (a branch of a Belize City store) on Barrier Reef Drive. You'll generally pay twice U.S. prices for most wines.

Other Stores: Ambergris Caye has hardware stores and other shops that provide the basics, but for some items you'll want to visit Belize City.

Medical: There is now a clinic on the island and several physicians, nurses and other medical professionals. The San Pedro Polyclinic II (501-226-2536) was established in great part due to the long-time efforts of the San Pedro Lions Club. In 2005, the year the new clinic opened, the San Pedro club was named the Lions Club of the Year, selected from more than 46,000 clubs in 193 countries.

Some of the other medical services on the island:
Ambergris Hopes Clinic – 501-226-2660
Rene Hegar, DDS – 501-226-4595
Hyperbaric Chamber – 501-226-2851
Los Pinos Clinic — 501-226-2686
Lerida Rodriguez, MD — 501-226-2197
Otto Rodriguez, MD – 501-226-2854

Island Ferry Emergency--501-226-3232, Ch. 11 marine radio

Two small offshore medical schools on the island didn't make it, and closed their doors.

•••

Real Estate on Ambergris Caye

Property prices on Ambergris Caye are among the highest in Belize. As elsewhere, prices vary tremendously depending on location and on the specific property. Houses and lots in predominantly Belizean areas, mostly on the back or lagoon side of the island, tend to be much less expensive than seafront property preferred by foreign investors and residents. Demand in recent years generally has been strong for beachfront lots and beachfront homes. Appreciation has run 10 to 20% per year for many years, according to local real estate brokers, although this appreciation rate slowed in the 2001-2003 period, due to the economic slowdown in the United States, and stalled completely in 2008-2009, with the worldwide deep recession.

Agents point to beachfront property on North Ambergris, which went for US$450 a front foot in the late1980s that is offered for US$3,000 or more a front foot now.

Prices in Belize are to a great extent dependent on economic conditions in the United States and, to some extent, in Canada. When the U.S. sneezes, Belize catches cold.

Upfront taxes, especially on new condos and homes, can discourage middle-income buyers. With the 15% surcharge up front (5% stamp duty and 10% GST), buying a US$300,000 condo would entail an additional US$45,000 cash outlay upfront, although in some cases the GST and stamp duty is rolled into the offering price.

Condo development continues on the island. Some 700 new condo units have been constructed recently or are currently under construction, most on North Ambergris Caye. A number of hotels have converted some or all of their units to "condotel" status. The idea is to sell now for immediate cash, then make 40 to 60% of revenues in management fees for running the hotel for absentee owners. Sales, however, have not always met expectations, as some investors are wary of condominium laws in Belize – condos are fairly new to Belize – and some have been burned by disputes with developers. At least one condotel project on North Ambergris has shut down, and a couple stopped construction before completion of all phases. A few developers offer limited financing, typically 20% down, with the balance payable over 10 years at around 12% interest. Usually, there's a balloon payment at the end of the term.

Timeshares have not fared well on Ambergris Caye or anywhere in Belize, though a number of condo hotels offer timeshares in a low-key way. Buyers have been few, and many who did buy quickly became dissatisfied with their purchase. The town council has passed regulations restricting activities of timeshare touts.

Building lots: Caribbean seafront building lots range from around US$3,000 to $6,000 per beachfront linear foot, and some are even higher.

Less-expensive lots generally are on upper reaches of North Ambergris, which is accessible only by private boat or water taxi and has no electricity or other utilities. There you can find small beachfront lots from around US$50,000 and sometimes less; lots one row back from the beach from around US$20,000; and back lots from around US$10,000 to $15,000. Water-front lots on the lagoon or backside of the island start at around US$500 per waterfront foot, with most under US$1,500 a foot. In general, lots a row back from the sea are just 30% of those directly on the water. Buyers should be aware that some beachfront lots have mangroves, not sand, on the waterside, and a permit is required to cut mangroves (though many mangroves have been illegally removed). Higher ground not subject to flooding obviously is more desirable, and more expensive, than low-lying property.

Homes: Two- or three-bedroom modern houses on the beach on North Ambergris Caye (access via water taxi or ferry) range from around US$200,000 (generally for a simple, wooden Belizean-style house) to well over US$1 million. Those south of San Pedro Town on the sea start at around US$250,000. Homes not on the water but with sea views are available from around US$100,000, but many run several hundred thousand dollars. At the top end, deluxe, recently built beachfront three and four bedroom homes may go for US$750,000 to $1,500,000 or more. Homes with "sunset views" – that is, on the west side or lagoon side of the island – start at around US$75,000 for a simple house.

Condos: Small one-bedroom condos without sea view start at around US$100,000, though most are US$125,000 or more. One-bedroom condos with sea views run about US$135,000 to $200,000. High-quality two- or three-bedroom condos with sea views range from around US$250,000 to $500,000 or higher. With the 10% GST on new condos, plus 5% transfer tax, and a surplus of inventory, the condo market in San Pedro and elsewhere has been hit hard, and some developers and owners are cutting prices.

Home construction: Building costs on Ambergris are relatively high, due to the need to dig deep foundations and install pilings for stability in the sandy soil, and to build with hurricane protection in mind. Bringing building supplies in by barge also adds to the cost. Expect to pay US$75-$150 or more a square foot for quality reinforced concrete construction. As elsewhere in Belize, labor costs are lower than in the U.S., but most building materials are more expensive. An exception is native hardwood lumber, which is beautiful and cheap.

Builders: Several builders have become very well off building vacation and second homes for Americans and other expats. Among the builders and construction management companies on the island are the following. Ask other owners their experiences with these builders:

Armando Graniel, Graniel Construction, San Pedro; tel. 501-226-2632, e-mail sunset@btl.net. Graniel has built many of the homes and resorts on island.

Bob Campbell, San Pedro; tel. 501-226-5203. The Campbells built El Pescador Villas, Seascape and other upper-end projects on the island.

Jim Hanna, San Pedro; tel. 501-226-3117.

Tom Harding, Harding General Contracting, San Pedro; tel. 501-226-2184; e-mail harding@btl.net. Harding supervised the construction of Barry Bowen's famed Chan Chich Lodge and with his wife, Josie, ran this lodge for many years before moving to San Pedro.

Daniel Camal, San Pedro; tel. 501-226-2563, fax 226-2040; e-mail dcamal@btl.net.

Wayne Alfaro, San Pedro; tel. 501-226-2097.

Blazing Hammers, Dennis and Judie Fisher; tel. 501-226-2922; judie@blazinghammers.com.

Belize Tropical Homes, Ivo Tzankov; tel. 501-610-0222; www.tropicalhomesbelize.com.

Properties for Sale

Here are some sample listings offered by individuals and real estate companies in 2009. Prices shown are asking prices. Due to issues of timeliness, we have not included the offering individual or real estate agent. Consider these as representative of property on the market at this time. For similar offerings go to the real estate websites listed in this book. Also, check out the new Ambergris Caye MLS, a local multiple listing service – www.mlsambergriscaye.com.

Beachfront lot with 200 ft. of sea frontage, Robles Point 14 miles north of San Pedro. US$330,000

Lagoon front lot in San Pablo area 1½ miles south of San Pedro, 50 x 102 ft., with road access, electricity, telephone, municipal water and cable TV. Sunset views of San Pedro Lagoon. US$80,000

Beachfront lot with 75 ft. of sea frontage, 125 ft. deep, 7 miles north of San Pedro, annual taxes US$435, electricity to lot. US$279,000

Fourth row 100 x 100 ft. lot in Palm Bay, 22 miles north of San Pedro, US$18,000

Large commercial seafront parcel suitable for condo or resort development, 400 ft. beachfront x 600 ft. (approx. 5½ acres), 8½ miles north of San Pedro. US$1,800,000

Three-bedroom, three-bath 2,385 sq. ft. condo at Grand Caribe, 1½ miles north of San Pedro, second floor unit with seaviews, use of three pools, marina. US$635,800

Two-bedroom, two-bath 1,275 sq. ft. furnished beachfront condo at Pelican Reef, 2½ miles south of San Pedro, air-conditioning, all utilities including cable TV available, use of all hotel amenities including pool, pier. Annual property tax US$193. US$349,000

Two-bedroom, one-bath furnished 600 sq. ft. seafront condo at Banana Beach Resort 1½ miles south of San Pedro, air-conditioning, all utilities including cable TV available, use of all hotel amenities including two pools, guaranteed rental income. US$145,000

One-bedroom, one-bath furnished 580 sq. ft. seafront condo at Mayan Princess, in San Pedro, ground floor, air-conditioning, all utilities including cable TV available. US$108,000

Beachfront three-bedroom, three and a half bath, 2,300 sq. ft. concrete house on ¼ acre 9 miles north of San Pedro at Palmero Point. Reef and sea views from wrap around second-story veranda. Fully furnished. Separate one-bedroom caretaker's house. Total annual property tax US$128. US$798,000

Lagoon side two-bedroom, two-bath 1,250 sq. ft. home with water views, on 75 x 75 ft. lot in Tres Cocos area, 1 mile north of San Pedro. All utilities available. US$295,000

Small three-bedroom, one-bath government-built concrete house with lagoon view, on 50 x 75 ft. lot 1½ miles south of San Pedro. Needs some repairs. US$57,000

Real Estate Developments

Here are selected new condo and real estate developments in Ambergris Caye. Most market primarily to foreign buyers.

Grand Baymen, www.grandbaymen.com. This condo development on 4 acres about ½ mile south of San Pedro focuses on moderately priced condos, not on the water. One-bedroom (720 sq. ft.) and two-bedroom (1,070 sq. ft) condos are priced from US$159,000 to $244,000. Financing is available for 10 to 15 years, at 11.5% for the first three years, and then U.S. prime rate plus 5.5%, with 50% down.

Grand Belizean Estates, residential lots, tel. 501-226-2260; www.grandbelizeanestates.net. Grand Belizean Estates goes for the low end of the market, with lots starting at under US$8,000. It is located about 5 miles north of San Pedro. The development has 1,193 lots. Lots 60 x 75 ft. start at US$7,925 and the most expensive lots are US$13,000 US each. The developer claims 350 of the lots sold in the first 70 days. At this price, you don't get water views, paved roads or a clubhouse. In fact, currently there is no road at all to the development. The developer says electricity will be available "soon." Homes will have to have a septic tank system, and water likely will be sky juice. Property taxes are expected to be around US$25 a year.

Grand Caribe, 1½ miles north of San Pedro, tel. 501-226-4726; www.grandcaribe.com. This high-quality upscale condominium development has 74 one-, two- and three-bedroom units in eight three- and four-story buildings in a horseshoe arrangement. It is on 5 acres with 500 ft. of beachfront. All units have sea views. There are three fresh-water swimming pools and a striking curved dock and pier. Rare in Belize, one of the buildings has elevator access to upper level condo units. Prices range from around US$395,000 to $715,000.

South Beach Belize, www.southbeachbelize.com. Developers of this controversial mega-project claim it will have condos, villas, hotels, a marina, casino, a theater, restaurants and retail space at the south end of the island, about 4 miles south of San Pedro. Everything will be done in an Art Deco style imitative of Miami's South Beach. Eventually, if it comes to fruition, the developer says it will be home to as many as 7,000 people. At present, nothing has been built.

San Pedro Real Estate Agents

Ambergris Seaside Real Estate, P.O. Box 163, San Pedro,

Ambergris Caye, tel. 501-226-4545; www.ambergrisrealestate.com.

Belize Shores Realty (Paul and Karol Kammeyer) San Pedro, Ambergris Caye, tel. 501-226-2825, www.Belizeshoresrealty.com.

Blue Diamond Realty (Janelle Castillo), # 1 Barrier Reef Dr., San Pedro, Ambergris Caye, tel. 501-226-3933 or 501-620-4149; www.bluediamondbelize.com.

Alex Canalez, Buyers' Agent/Real Estate Advertiser, 3781 Marina Drive, San Pedro, Ambergris Caye, tel. 501-608-5535, www.affordablebelizerealestate.com, www.realestateinbelize.org.

Casa Cayo Real Estate, Corner of Buccaneer and Pescador, San Pedro, tel. 501- 226-2791; www.casacayorealestate.net.

Century 21 Isla Bonita, San Pedro, Ambergris Caye; tel. 866-589-4618; www.century21belize.com.

Coldwell Banker Belize, (Jonathon Mullen) San Pedro, Ambergris Caye; tel. 501- 226-3400; www.ColdwellBankerBelize.com.

Coral Beach Realty, Barrier Reef Drive, San Pedro, tel. 501-226-2681, fax 226-2875; www.coralbeachrealty.com.

Diane Campbell, San Pedro, tel. 501-226-5203 or 610-5118; e-mail diane@dianecampbell.net.

Pelican Properties, San Pedro, tel. 501-226-3234; www.pelicanpropertiesbelize.com.

RE/MAX Isla Bonita (Daryl Carlson), 10 Coconut Drive, San Pedro Town, Ambergris Caye tel. 501-226-4400, fax 501-226-440, www.owninbelize.com.

Southwind Properties, P.O. Box 1, San Pedro, Ambergris Caye, tel. 501-226-2005; www.belize-real-estate.net.

Sundancer Properties, Pescador Dr., San Pedro, tel. 501-226-4473; www.sundancerproperties.com.

Sunrise Realty, P.O. Box 236, #1 Barrier Reef Dr., San Pedro, Ambergris Caye; tel. 501-226-3737; www.SunriseBelize.com.

Triton Properties, Barrier Reef Dr., San Pedro; tel. 501-226-3783; www.triton-properties.com.

Short-Term Rentals on Ambergris Caye

The best way to find a rental house or apartment on Ambergris Caye is to come to the island and look around in person. The *San Pedro Sun* and *Ambergris Today* newspapers have a few rental classifieds, and Ambergris-Caye.com (www.ambergriscaye.com) has occasional rentals posted. Here are some sources of short-term house rentals:

Caye Management (Barrier Reef Drive, San Pedro, tel. 501-226-3077, www.cayemanagement.com) has many rental houses and condos on the island.

B-Lease (P.O. Box 184, San Pedro, tel. 501-226-2186, www.ambergriscaye.com/blease/) is a property management company that specializes in longer-term rentals of at least six months. Six-month rentals start at around US$400 per month and go up to over US$2,000 a month.

Also consider short-term condo rentals. One good option is **Banana Beach** (P.O. Box 94, San Pedro, tel. 501-226-3890, fax 226-3891; www.bananabeach.com). Banana Beach has one-bedroom efficiencies from around US$900 a month plus utilities, or US$1,300 with utilities including air-conditioning. Other condo developments including **Paradise Villas** and **Royal Palm** may offer monthly rentals, especially in the off-season between Easter and early December.

Frenchie's Dive Shop, Caye Caulker

Caye Caulker

GRADING THE AREA FOR RETIREMENT, RELOCATION AND INVESTMENT Ratings are on an A to F scale, just like your old high school report card. A is the top grade; F is failing. Grades are relative compared to other areas in Belize.

Popularity with Expats	C+
Safety	B-
Overall Cost of Living	B
Real Estate Bargains	B
Investment Potential	B+
Leisure Activities	C
Restaurants	B
Cultural Activities	D

Infrastructure	C
Business Potential	C+
Medical Care	D+
Shopping	D

ADVANTAGES OF CAYE CAULKER: • Small, laid-back island atmosphere • Provides excellent opportunities for water activities – boating, fishing, diving • Less expensive than San Pedro • No need for a car

Caye Caulker is Ambergris Caye's "little sister" island – smaller, less developed and a cheaper date. Caulker, whose name derives from the Spanish word for coco plum, hicaco, has the kind of laidback, sandy-street, tropical-color, low-key Caribbean charm that travelers pay thousands to experience, but here they can have it for peanuts. Less than 10 miles, and about 30 minutes by boat, from San Pedro, Caye Caulker is definitely worth a visit, and perhaps you'll like it well enough to stay.

Here are some of the key comparisons between Caye Caulker and Ambergris Caye:

• Caye Caulker is physically much smaller, under 5 miles long and half a mile wide at its widest point, roughly one-tenth the size of Ambergris Caye. Hurricane Hattie in 1961 divided the island in two parts. North of "the Split" it is mostly uninhabited mangrove, and this area is protected as a nature reserve. As on many islands, there are basically just three streets running down the island, Front, Middle and Back streets being the main ones, though there are few street signs and locals usually give directions just by saying "go down to yellow house and turn right." Most of the 300 or so listings in the Caye Caulker section of the Belize telephone directory don't even include a street name or address, just the person's name and phone number. Nearly all of 1,500 people on the island live in the village on the south end.

• Unlike Ambergris Caye, where a few of the main streets are now paved with concrete cobblestones, Caye Caulker has streets of hard-packed sand and far fewer cars than San Pedro. Almost everybody gets around on foot or bike.

• As on Ambergris, a majority of local residents are Mestizos who originally came to the island from Mexico, and who until recently made their living by fishing, but the island also has Creoles, some of whom consider themselves Rastafarians, gringos and others.

• While it is gradually going upmarket, Caye Caulker remains very much a budget island. In the 1960s and 1970s, the island was on the "backpacker trail," a cheap place for longhaired visitors to relax and smoke a little weed or sip a beer. Today, the most expensive hotel on Caulker goes for around US$160 a night, and most of the hotels charge under US$75 double, with some as low as US$10. Many of the older buildings on the island are wooden clapboard, often painted in tropical colors, but more recently constructed houses and hotels are of reinforced concrete. Only a few hotels on the island have a swimming pool.

94

• Caye Caulker has much the same mix of tourist-oriented businesses as San Pedro, but in most cases there are fewer of everything. The island has perhaps 20 simple restaurants, if you include those that operate out of somebody's back window, a few casual bars, a handful of dive shops and tour guides, several pint-sized groceries, a few gift shops, two banks, several cybercafés.

• Beaches? Caulker has much less beachfront, and what beaches it has don't compare with some of the better stretches of beach on Ambergris Caye. A beach reclamation project in 2000 did widen and improve the beach along the east side of the village (storms since have taken away and then given back sand). Swimming in the shallow water close to shore is mainly from piers and at "the Split."

• The pipe water on Caulker is not as good as on Ambergris Caye. On Caulker, it often has a sulfur smell and comes from shallow wells, which may be close to septic systems, which can be overloaded. A reverse osmosis water plant is under construction and should open by late 2010. Caye Caulker also has sandflies. Especially on calm days, they can be a real nuisance.

Real Estate on Caye Caulker

Most of the development on Caulker is concentrated in the one small village. Many families have long ties with the island and aren't interested in selling. Thus, the number of available properties is small. When properties do come on the market, the owners sometimes have an inflated idea of their value. One small budget hotel has been offered for US$3,500,000 for not much less than the total annual gross tourism revenue of the entire island!

Properties on Caye Caulker

Most of the real estate companies in San Pedro also have occasional listings on Caye Caulker. Here are some of the properties for sale on Caye Caulker in 2009, offered both by individuals and by real estate companies:

Residential lot south with sea views through park, fourth lot back, 68 x 80 ft., about 250 ft. from sea. US$40,000

Residential lot north, 1¾ miles north of the Split, 75 x 70 ft., access by boat, no utilities, US$20,000

Beachfront lot north, within walking distance of Split, 65 x 150 ft., no utilities. US$110,000

Two-bedroom, one-bath house on Middle Street in Caye Caulker village. Wood construction, with Ply-Sem (cement) exterior and galvanized roof. Lot 50 x 90 ft. US$225,000

Two-bedroom, two-bath wood house south, in Bahia Puesta del Sol area. Views of lagoon. Property needs some repairs and fill. US$69,000

CHAPTER 11:
OTHER ISLANDS IN DETAIL

GRADING THE AREA FOR RETIREMENT, RELOCATION AND INVESTMENT Ratings are on an A to F scale, just like your old high school report card. A is the top grade; F is failing. Grades are relative compared to other areas in Belize.

Popularity with Expats	B
Safety	B
Overall Cost of Living	D
Real Estate Bargains	D
Investment Potential	B
Leisure Activities	B-
Cultural Activities	F
Infrastructure	F
Business Potential	D
Medical Care	F
Shopping	F

ISLAND ADVANTAGES: • Beautiful island living • Easy access to recreational activities on the water

Belize has at least 400 islands in the Caribbean. The vast majority are small spits of sand and mangroves. Most are either privately owned (by old Belize families or by wealthy foreigners) or are government property.

Islands Properties Offered

Drowned Caye in the Drowned Caye Range, 75 acres, 10 minutes by boat from Belize City. US$2,500,000

Dangriga Island, 5 miles off Dangriga Town, 3 acres. US$650,000

Serene Caye, at northwestern tip of Turneffe Atoll, 45 acres, perfect location for fishing lodge. US$2,500,000

Bakers Rendezvous Caye, about 12 miles off Placencia, about 2 acres. US$395,000

Water Caye, 12 miles off Belize City near deep water channel used by cruise ships, 511 acres, day resort for up to 800 already built, asking US$17,000,000

Real Estate Agents

Real estate agents all over Belize occasionally offer islands for sale. In addition, companies specializing in islands for sale also offer Belize cayes. These companies include **Private Islands Online** (www.privateislandsonline.com), **Caribbean Island Brokers** (www.caribbeanislandbrokers.com) and **Private Islands Bz.** (www.privateislands.bz).

CHAPTER 12:
COROZAL IN MORE DETAIL

GRADING THE AREA FOR RETIREMENT, RELOCATION AND INVESTMENT Ratings are on an A to F scale, just like your old high school report card. A is the top grade; F is failing. Grades are relative compared to other areas in Belize. Note: Scores for Corozal reflect its proximity to Chetumal.

Popularity with Expats	B
Safety	B
Overall Cost of Living	B
Real Estate Bargains	A
Investment Potential	C
Leisure Activities	C+
Restaurants	C
Cultural Activities	C+
Infrastructure	B
Business Potential	C
Medical Care	B+ (Chetumal)
Shopping	B+ (Chetumal)

ADVANTAGES OF COROZAL TOWN AREA: Low housing costs whether you're renting or buying • Proximity to Chetumal, Mexico, for medical care and shopping • Sizeable (several hundred) and growing expat community • Pleasant location on the Bay of Chetumal (sometimes called Corozal Bay) • Few sandflies in most areas and fewer noxious bugs • Pleasant sub-tropical climate with lower rainfall than southern Belize • Generally safe, friendly area • Easy access by car, bus, water taxi and air to Ambergris Caye and other areas of Belize and to the Yucatán

Few Belize casual visitors to Belize, except medical missionaries and tourists passing through from Mexico, pay much attention to Corozal District and its main population center, Corozal Town. Yet this part of Northern Belize is one of the friendliest, safest, least expensive and most interesting areas of the entire country. For visitors, it's a place to slow down, relax and enjoy at least a few days of easy living by the beautiful turquoise waters of Corozal Bay and the Bay of Chetumal. True, there's not a whole lot to see here, not many tourist sites, no real beaches though nice swimming is yours in the bay and lagoons, and few memorable hotels or restaurants. But the climate is appealing, with less rain than almost anywhere else in Belize, and the sunny dispositions of residents are infectious. Corozal Town and environs is one of our top picks for expatriate living. It offers inexpensive rentals and affordable real estate. You'll want to be sure to visit here, if you are interesting in living or retiring in Belize.

Corozal District is 718 square miles in area, with a district population of 37,300, according to the Belize Statistical Institute. The largest town by far is Corozal, with 9,400 residents. Spanish is spoken more widely than English here, although you can get by in English at least in Corozal Town. The town is laid out on a small grid, with the most appealing part along the bayfront, with its colorful houses and parks. Nearby on and near the Northern Highway are "suburbs" — the small villages of Ranchito, Xaibe, Calcutta, San Antonio and others. The Corozal Free Zone, just south of the Santa Elena border crossing from Mexico, is starting to make a name for itself as a place for businesses to set up free from many of the restrictions and high import duties of the rest of Belize. Mexicans come here for cheap gas. The Free Zone now employs more than 1,000 Belizeans. There are three casinos open at the border, including a branch of the Princess and a large casino, Las Vegas. These casinos, like the Free Zone, mostly depend on business from Mexico.

The district can be divided into two main sections. The west part is still sugar cane country, once anchored by Libertad, the now-closed sugar cane processing plant and farther north by Corozal Town on Corozal Bay. The main road artery of this hemisphere is the Northern Highway, a good two-lane paved road. From the southern edge of Corozal District near San Pablo village, it is about 28 miles to the Mexican border at Santa Elena. The border is about 9 miles from Corozal Town. The Consejo area about 7 miles north of Corozal Town on an all-weather unpaved road, on Corozal Bay, has attracted a small number of expats at Consejo Shores, Mayan Sands and other residential developments.

The east hemisphere consists of the Cerros/Copper Bank area and Sarteneja peninsula. This peninsula has far more trees than people. It is an area mostly of swamp and savannah, with the bulk of the peninsula's small population living in villages along the beautiful Progresso Lagoon and Chetumal Bay. Little Belize, a Mennonite area, is the largest population center, with around 2,000 residents. For visitors, a main reason to come here is the Shipstern Nature Preserve, a 22,000-acre park managed by the Belize Audubon Society. The little fishing village of Sarteneja (pop. 1,700) is charming as well. An all-weather mostly unpaved road runs from Orange Walk Town to Sarteneja village, a distance of about 40 miles. You can also get to the peninsula from Corozal Town via a free, hand-pulled vehicular ferry across the New River and another hand-pulled ferry over the mouth of Laguna Seca. Several residential developments, including Cerros Sands and Orchid Bay, are on the bay, and Progresso Heights is on the Progresso Lagoon. While a number of lots have been sold at these developments, so far there are only a handful of homes built.

Corozal is one of the safer places in Belize. Even so, burglary and property theft are fairly common. One survey of expats in Corozal Town found that about 80% had been victims of theft, burglary and even home invasions in the past four years. The town of Corozal and surrounding villages are on the power grid and generally have municipal water supplies with potable water. Sarteneja and other remote areas have less modern infrastructures.

One of Belize's two main land border crossing points is north of

Corozal Town at Santa Elena (the other is at Benque Viejo del Carmen in Cayo.) The Rio Honda marks the boundary between Belize and Mexico. Once across the border, some knowledge of Spanish is helpful. Chetumal has large supermarkets (San Francisco is one) and a modern mall with department stores, a multiplex cinema and food court. There are McDonalds and a Burger King fast-food restaurants in Chetumal, along with a Sam's Club and other big box stores.

Corozal Practicalities: Banks: Scotia Bank, Belize Bank and Atlantic Bank have branches in Corozal Town.

Groceries: Corozal Town has more than a dozen small groceries and tiendas and a market with fruits and vegetables. Large supermarkets are in Chetumal.

Restaurants: Among the best of the small bunch of restaurants in Corozal Town are Patti's Bistro, Cactus Plaza and the bayside restaurant at Tony's Inn.

Other Stores: Corozal has a selection of small home furnishings, construction supplies and hardware stores, many run by Chinese immigrants. Chetumal across the border has larger stores of all kinds.

Medical: Corozal Town has a district hospital and several doctors and clinics. Nearby Chetumal offers low-cost and often high-quality dental and medical care.

Real Estate

Corozal Town and environs has some of the best property bargains in Belize – whether you are renting or buying. Rentals in Corozal Town start at under US$300 a month, and for US$300 to $500 you can get a comfortable house in town. In **Consejo Shores**, a nice development on the Bay of Chetumal about 7 miles from Corozal Town, U.S.-style three- and four-bedroom homes rent for US$500 to $900 a month. Bayfront building lots are available for $75,000 or less, though prices for these are rising, and those back a row or two from the bay are US$15,000 to $25,000. Modern three- and four-bedroom homes sell for as little as US$75,000, and US$300,000 gets you close to the top end of the market.

Corozal District, like the rest of Belize, has its share of blue-sky real estate peddlers, often operating via the Internet. Watch out for sellers of lots in remote areas. Some are claiming that their lots on a part of a golf or hotel development. Such developments may be years or decades in the future, if they are ever built at all.

Properties in Corozal

Here are some of the property listings offered by individuals and brokers in 2009-2010:

Building lot with views of Progresso Lagoon, in Progresso village, 75 x 150 ft. US$50,000

50 x 100 ft. building lot in small subdivision off road to Mexican border. Electricity and other utilities available. US$12,000

Bayfront building lot in Cerros/Copper Bank area. Approx. 1/3-acre with 65 ft. on bay, 200 ft. deep. US$48,000

Bayfront lot on Bay Front Drive (aka Gringo Trail), 75 x 200, filled and ready to build. US$120,000

36-acre farm 4 miles from Copper Bank, with 18 acres in mangos, oranges, avocados, limes, bananas and other fruit, and 5 acres in sugar cane. Mostly fenced, with well. US$70,000

5-acre farmette off Consejo Road near Corozal Town, zone for residential and agricultural use. US$12,500

496-acre tract in Progresso area, partially cleared. Owner financing available with 50% down. US$248,000 (US$500 an acre)

Two-bedroom, two-bath 2,300 sq. ft. concrete house in Consejo Shores, on small 9-hole golf course, tiled and mahogany floors, furnished and ready to move in, garage. US$245,000

Small wood (treated pine) house on ¼-acre fenced lot in Mayan Seaside development near Consejo. Community water system, cisterns, electricity, satellite TV and Internet. Includes appliances. US$99,000

Three-bedroom, two-bath, 2,200 sq. ft. adobe-style hurricane-resistant concrete block house in Consejo shores, open concept kitchen/living/dining area, mahogany cabinets, concrete roof, 16,000-gallon cistern. US$189,900

Real Estate Agents

Belize Land Consultants, P.O. Box 35, Corozal, tel. 501-423-1005. Bill Wildman developed Consejo Shores near Corozal Town, www.consejoshores.com. Wildman, a land surveyor, has more than 40 years of real estate experience in Belize.

Charlotte's Casa Belize, 78 5th Ave., Corozal; tel. 501-422- 0135, cell 607-0456; www.charlottescasabelize.com. Charlotte Zahniser has been in Belize since around 1999. She can probably help with rentals in the Corozal area, too.

Belize North Real Estate Ltd. (Gregg Turrentine), P.O. Box 226, Corozal Town, tel. 501-422-0284; www.belizenorthrealestate.bz.

Mayan Seaside (Art Higgins), Consejo, tel. 501-602-2686; www.mayanseaside.com.

Real Estate Developments

Here are selected real estate developments in Corozal District. Most market primarily to foreign buyers. Keep in mind that Cerros Sands, Orchid Bay and Progresso Heights are all a 30 to 45-minute or more drive on unpaved roads from Corozal Town. Consejo Shores and Mayan Seaside are about a 10-minute drive on an unpaved road from Corozal Town.

Cerros Sands, near Cerros, tel. 501-670-8724; www.cerrossands.com. Cerros Sands is a 92-acre development near the Cerros Maya ruins, across the bay from Corozal Town. Lots start at around US$19,000, with some bayfront lots starting around US$49,000. There are at present no public utilities at the development. While some lots have been sold, there have been no homes built in the development yet. A 22-unit condo development has been announced, with prices from US$138,000.

Consejo Shores, Consejo, tel. 501-423-1005; www.consejoshores.com. Consejo Shores, with 350 acres and 7,000 ft. of bayfront, is the premier residential development in Northern Belize. About 75 homes have been built in the community. Most homes for resale in Consejo Shores are in the US$150,000 to $300,000 range. Bayfront lots now are available only as resales, but ½-acre lots with bay views or near the water are still being sold by the developer, starting at around US$35,000.

Mayan Seaside, Consejo, tel. 501-602-2686; www.mayanseaside.com. This development near Consejo village has about 105 lots, most of which have been sold. A couple of dozen small homes have been built, or are under construction or are about to begin construction. Lot owners in the development pay a US$250 per year maintenance fee.

Orchid Bay, between Copper Bank and Sarteneja, tel. 313-454-3113; www.orchidbaybelize.com. Some 200 lots are offered for sale in the planned community. Lot prices range from around US$39,000 to over $200,000. Home prices range from around US$90,000 to over $500,000. So far, only a few casitas have been constructed.

Progresso Heights, on Progresso Lagoon near Progresso Village, tel. 888-235-4934 or 561-859-1433; www.progressoheights.com. Hundreds of lots, mostly around ¼-acre in size, are included in the master plan, and more than 300 lots have been sold. Lot prices start at around US$16,000 for cash, or US$20,000 with financing (at up to 15 years at 6.99%). Lot owners in the development pay a US$250 per year maintenance fee. A club house with swimming pool, a community pier and marl roads have been constructed. About 10 homes have been built or are under construction in the development.

Rentals

Charlotte Zahniser, owner of Charlotte's Casa Belize real estate company (www.charlottescasabelize.com) can be helpful in finding you a rental, for a relatively modest fee. In addition, Belize North Real Estate (www.belizenorthrealestate.bz) handles some rentals. Paradise Bay Villas, across from Corozal Bay Resort, offers two-bedroom apartments on a weekly basis. E-mail shaunybelize@hotmail.com or call 501-422-0209.

CHAPTER 13:
ORANGE WALK IN MORE DETAIL

GRADING THE AREA FOR RETIREMENT, RELOCATION AND INVESTMENT Ratings are on an A to F scale, just like your old high school report card. A is the top grade; F is failing. Grades are relative compared to other areas in Belize.

Popularity with Expats	D
Safety	B-
Overall Cost of Living	B+
Real Estate Bargains	B+
Investment Potential	C-
Leisure Activities	C
Restaurants	C-
Cultural Activities	D
Infrastructure	C+
Business Potential	C
Medical Care	C+
Shopping	C

ADVANTAGES OF ORANGE WALK: • Very low land prices in rural areas • Offers some of the most natural areas of Belize, with excellent birding and wildlife spotting • Proximity to Mennonite areas of Shipyard and Blue Creek • Good agricultural area

In what is now Orange Walk District, the early greatness of the Maya empire was on display at Lamanai and elsewhere. During the centuries before the time of Christ, the Maya built temples that were higher than any modern building in Belize, and one at Lamanai still stands about 100 feet above the jungle floor. Many Maya sites in Orange Walk were occupied up to colonial times. For a while the Maya were even able to resist the Spanish conquistadores, in the 17th century driving the Spanish out of the area around Lamanai and burning Catholic churches. Mestizos fleeing the Maya rebellions in the Yucatán settled modern Orange Walk around 1849, and Corozal about the same time.

Mahogany logging in the late 18th and early 19th centuries was the first major modern industry of the region, with some 5,000 giant mahogany trees harvested every year. A big British-based company, Belize Estate and Produce Company, once owned one-fifth of the land in Belize and was a major force in British Honduras' economy and politics until the mid-20th century. When the mahogany industry died down due to over logging, sugar cane and citrus became staple crops. But boom and bust continued, and with the global of supply of sugar, small Orange Walk farmers turned to marijuana cultivation. The U.S. government, with its take-no-prisoners approach to drug control, forced Belizean authorities to shut down airstrips, spray chemicals on fields and destroy this cash crop. Today, subsistence agriculture and the remnants of sugar cane and citrus farming occupy the time of rural residents. Rum is distilled near Orange Walk Town, logging still is going on and Mennonites farm productively in the Shipyard (home to conservative Mennonites) and Blue Creek (progressive) areas.

The road west from Orange Walk Town, past Cuello distillery, Yo Creek, and then back south to August Pine Ridge village and San Felipe village leads through agricultural areas to the 240,000-acre Programme for Belize Rio Bravo Conservation area and the 250,000-acre private estate of Barry Bowen. Or, if you go southeast from San Felipe, you end up at Lamanai near Indian Church village. Two world-class jungle lodges, Chan Chich at Gallon Jug, and Lamanai Outpost Lodge on the New River Lagoon, await you in this part of Orange Walk District. Another route is via Shipyard, on an unpaved road just south of Orange Walk Town.

Orange Walk Practicalities

Banks: Scotia Bank, Atlantic Bank and Belize Bank have branches in Orange Walk Town.

Groceries: M & A Supermarket and P & P Supermarket, both fairly small, are among your choices.

Medical: Orange Walk Town has a regional hospital, though it is not one of the more modern hospitals in Belize. Chetumal, Mexico, about an hour away, offers low-cost and often high-quality dental and medical care.

Real Estate

The real estate market in Orange Walk District is not very active. Undeveloped land in large tracts starts at under US$200 an acre and goes up to around US$2,000 an acre for well-sited medium-sized tracts with good road and utility access.

Property Listings

Here are properties available in 2009-2010 in Orange Walk District:

145 acres near Honey Camp Lagoon. Property has 871 ft of lagoon frontage, road access and is high ground. US$145,000

2 acres fronting on Northern Highway, near Tower Hill Bridge. US$25,000

Two-bedroom, two-bath concrete house on 150 x 200 ft. lot in Carmelita village, 45 minutes from international airport. US$90,000

Real Estate Agents

Real estate companies in Belize City and elsewhere in Belize occasionally handle property in Orange Walk.

Sign at Belize Zoo

CHAPTER 14:
CAYO AND WESTERN BELIZE IN MORE DETAIL

GRADING THE AREA FOR RETIREMENT, RELOCATION AND INVESTMENT Ratings are on an A to F scale, just like your old high school report card. A is the top grade; F is failing. Grades are relative compared to other areas in Belize.

Popularity with Expats	B
Safety	B-
Overall Cost of Living	B
Real Estate Bargains	B+
Investment Potential	C+
Leisure Activities	B
Restaurants	B
Cultural Activities	C
Infrastructure	B
Business Potential	B
Medical Care	C+
Shopping	C+

ADVANTAGES OF CAYO: • Relatively low cost for rural land and for houses in San Ignacio and Belmopan • Offers some of Belize's most beautiful inland scenery • Access to outdoor activities on beautiful rivers and mountains • Friendly mix of Mestizo and Maya residents • Good agricultural area for citrus and other crops • Good place to escape from hurricanes

Cayo is the "Wild West" of Belize. For would-be expats, it's an area where you can buy a small spread (or a large one) to raise citrus or Brahma cattle. For tourists, it is the turf in the traditional "surf 'n turf" visit to Belize — a few days on the cayes, typically Ambergris Caye or Caye Caulker, combined with some time on the mainland exploring ruins, rivers and rainforests.

Cayo District has an area of more than 2,000 square miles, beginning near Belmopan and extending west and southwest to the Pine Ridge and into the Chiquibul wilderness and Maya Mountains. Belmopan City, Belize's capital, about 48 miles west of Belize City, has a reputation as a Nowheresville. Truth to say, the capital is not exactly a jumping place, but nearby is the Hummingbird Highway, the most scenic road in Belize. Also in the area are several top-notch jungle lodges. Belmopan is also in a growth spurt, with the population reaching around 14,000 and a lot of new development going on. San Ignacio, with its sister town Santa Elena, total population near 20,000, have an unassuming small town atmosphere. Nothing here will knock your boots off. There are no big cultural sights or museums, and the shopping and other urban activities are limited. But San Ignacio, often just called Cayo or El Cayo, is a pleasant little burg. Locals are friendly, easy-going folk, mostly Mestizos with the usual Belizean mix of other, from Maya to Creoles to Chinese and Americans. Here you can buy groceries, check your e-mail and get a good cheap meal.

Mennonites have a sizable farming and commercial presence in the Spanish Lookout area northeast of San Ignacio. Some of the largest stores in Belize are in Spanish Lookout, with some of the lowest prices. Around San Ignacio, mostly to the southwest, are the green rolling hills of cottage country. Some of Belize's best lodges are here. With a few exceptions, to call them jungle lodges is a misnomer. Most are set in partially cleared pastures or fields.

Much of the land here is in cattle farms and citrus orchards. As you go west, you begin to see the influences of Guatemala. Maya women wash clothes in the river, and Benque Viejo del Carmen strikes many as a more Spanish and less Caribbean than most Belizean towns. But cross the border to Melchor de Mencos, and you're really in another world, one of much more intensive poverty and where English is rarely spoken.

This part of Cayo offers some of the best caving in Central America (Actun Tunichil Muknal is a must-see), along with great hiking, biking, canoeing and horseback riding. There are important Maya sites, including Caracol and Xunantunich.

In mid-2005, an oil drilling company, Belize Natural Energy, then run by two Irishwomen and three geologists, found oil near Spanish Lookout. The well currently is pumping light sweet crude at the rate of several thousand barrels a day. BNE is exploring for oil in other areas of Belize.

About a half an hour from San Ignacio is the Mountain Pine Ridge reserve. Visitors here are surprised by what they find. Instead of low-lying, bug-infested tropical vistas, they find hills and low mountains with few mosquitoes and temperatures that can dip into the 40s and 50s F. in winter. Instead of lush Tarzan-style jungle, in some parts of the region they find pinewoods, sparse grass and red clay mindful of the Southern Appalachians. Many of the Mountain Pines trees in this area have been killed by the Southern Pine Beetle, but the pines are quickly coming back. Once into the Chiquibul wilderness, the vegetation turns to broadleaf rainforest, more like the jungle you've seen in the movies. It is beautiful country, with isolated waterfalls where you can slip in for a skinny dip, incredible cave systems, unpolluted streams and blue skies.

Except for a small settlement at Augustine/Douglas de Silva, groups of workers living at the area's four lodges and some remote squatter settlements occupied by illegal immigrants from Guatemala, few people live in the Mountain Pine Ridge. Some of the land is government property, and some is owned, mostly in large tracts, by foreign interests or wealthy Belizeans. The roads in the region are former logging roads, most hardly better than dirt tracks. Controlled logging continues, and the area is also the site of occasional Belize Defence Force or U.S. Army training exercises. In the dry season, usually March to late May or early June, the area sees higher temperatures (though still cooler than in most of the rest of inland Belize), and forest fires are a threat.

Cayo District Practicalities

Banks: All five Belize banks, Caribbean International Bank, Alliance Bank, Scotia Bank, Belize Bank and Atlantic Bank, have branches in San Ignacio; Alliance Bank, Atlantic Bank, Caribbean International Bank and Belize Bank have offices in Belmopan. Currently, there are no banks in Benque Viejo.

Groceries: In San Ignacio, Celina's Superstore has a pretty good selection of groceries plus some dry goods and other items.

Restaurants: San Ignacio has many good small dining spots, including Ko-Ox Han-Nah (formerly Hannah's), Sanny's, Erva's, Mom's Place, Mr. Greedy's Pizzeria, Hode's, Serindib and others. Benny's Kitchen in San José Succotz is a local favorite. Belmopan has several good places to eat, including Ristorante Puccini's and Bull Frog Inn.

Medical: A private hospital, La Loma Luz Hospital, is in Santa Elena. Among public facilities, there are district hospitals in San Ignacio and Belmopan, and Mopan Clinic is in Benque Viejo.

Real Estate

Cayo covers a fairly large area, with a lot of agricultural land along with wild bush. It includes the capital, Belmopan, and the largish town of San Ignacio, plus Spanish Lookout and Benque Viejo. Thus property values vary widely. Land in tracts of under 50 to 100 acres along the beautiful Hummingbird Highway is selling in the range of US$1,000 to $2,000 an acre. These tracts have some road frontage and electricity. Larger accessible tracts are going for US$500 to $1,000 an acre. Homes start at under US$25,000 and go up to half a million or more for a mansion on an estate tract.

Property Listings

Here are a few of the properties available, offered by individuals and real estate firms:

188 acres in Clarissa Falls village, on year-round creek. Property has hilltop building sites and two small wood houses. US$188,000 (US$1,000 an acre)

187 acres on Yalbac Creek, formerly a cattle ranch. US$205,700 (US$1,100 an acre)

323 acres near Los Tambos, wooded with year-round spring and rolling hills with legal access from public road. Parcel is only a few miles from Spanish Lookout. US$179,000 (US$554 per acre) cash or possible contract for deed with substantial down payment.

100 x 100 ft. residential lots in Bullet Tree village. US$6,500

Building lot (100 x 100 ft.) in Santa Familia village, US$3,750

Approx. 8 acres in Mountain Pine Ridge, two small creeks on property. US$65,000

Small 945 sq. ft. all concrete house in Santa Familia village. Nice lot planted with mango, nani, craboo, lime and other fruit trees. Electricity and water available. US$39,000

One-bedroom, one-bath studio cottage at duPlooy's Lodge, on ¼-acre lot. Financing available with 30% down. US$99,000

Four-bedroom concrete home in Kon Tiki section of San Ignacio, sunken living room, mahogany cabinets and ceiling in kitchen, fenced. US$93,500

Real Estate Agents

Real estate firms in Belize City also offer extensive listings in Cayo.

Belize Realty Services, 29 Burns Avenue, San Ignacio, tel: 501-801-0195 or 501-610-2265, www.belize-real-estate-services.com

Ceiba Realty (Jonathan Lohr), 119A Western Highway, Santa Elena, tel. 501-824-4050 (normal working hours) or cell 501-610-4458; www.ceibarealtybelize.com

Rainforest Realty, P.O. Box 195, San Ignacio, Cayo; tel. Macarena Rose at 501-670-4045, USA direct: 727-490-7710; www.rainforestrealty.com, email macarenarose@gmail.com

Tropic Real Estate, P.O. Box 453, Belmopan, tel. 501-824-3475, fax 824-3649; www.realestatebelize.com

CHAPTER 15:
DANGRIGA AND HOPKINS AREA IN MORE DETAIL

GRADING THE AREA FOR RETIREMENT, RELOCATION AND INVESTMENT Ratings are on an A to F scale, just like your old high school report card. A is the top grade; F is failing. Grades are relative compared to other areas in Belize.

Popularity with Expats	C+
Safety	B
Overall Cost of Living	B
Real Estate Bargains	C+
Investment Potential	B
Leisure Activities	B
Restaurants	C+
Cultural Activities	C
Infrastructure	C+
Business Potential	C+
Medical Care	C+
Shopping	C+

ADVANTAGES OF HOPKINS/DANGRIGA AREA: • Lower prices for beachfront property than on Ambergris Caye or Placencia • Friendly, interesting Garifuna culture • Provides excellent opportunities for water sports – boating, fishing, diving • Proximity to Cockscomb Jaguar Preserve and other natural areas

This part of Stann Creek District is Belize at its most exotic, with Garifuna settlements that may remind you more of a coastal village in Senegal than Central America and Maya villages that look much as they might have hundreds of years ago. A few miles inland are a wild jaguar preserve and highest mountains in Belize. The Cockscomb Basin Preserve west of Hopkins is real rainforest jungle, and the highest peaks in Belize, Doyle's Delight at 3,688 feet and Victoria Peak at 3,675 feet, are in the Maya Mountains.

Unlike most of the rest of Belize's mainland coast, the Hopkins area has real beaches. The beaches here are similar to those in Placencia (see below) — narrow ribbons of khaki-colored sand, with a good deal of seagrass in the water off the beach. Swimming is possible, especially in areas where the seagrass has been removed, as at the end of a dock. The snorkeling off the shore usually is not very good, although you can see some fish and possibly even a manatee.

The barrier reef is about 12 to 15 miles offshore from Hopkins and Dangriga, so it takes a while to get out to the reef for diving.

The Garifuna (pronounced Gah-RIF-oo-na) people who settled in this area have a fascinating history. Before the time of Columbus, Indians from the South American mainland came by boat to the island of St. Vincent in the southeast Caribbean. They conquered, and then intermarried with, Arawak Indians, adopting much of the Indian language. They went by the name Kwaib, from which the names Carib and Garifuna, meaning cassava-eaters, probably evolved. Then, in the 17th century, slaves from Nigeria were ship-wrecked off St. Vincent. They too mixed with the Caribs or Garifuna. For years, Britain tried to subdue these free people of color, but the Garifuna, with the support of the French, fought back until the late 1700s, when the French and Garifuna finally surrendered to the British. In 1797, several thousand surviving Garifuna were taken by ship to Roatán in Honduras. Over the 150 years or so, many Garifuna moved from Roatán up the coast of Central America to Belize, where they worked in logging. The largest migration to Belize took place in 1823, and today that year is commemorated on November 19 as Garifuna Settlement Day. Many settled in what is now Dangriga. Punta Gorda, Hopkins, Seine Bight and Barranco also have sizable Garifuna populations. Initially, Dangriga was called Black Carib Town and then Stann Creek. The Garifuna in Belize are working hard to continue their language and culture. They have a complex system of religious beliefs, combining African and South American elements as well as Catholicism. Dugu or "Feasting of the Dead" is one of the ancestral rites practiced by Garifuna.

Dangriga is not a popular area for expats, but the Hopkins/Sittee Point area south of Dangriga is attracting a lot of attention, especially among those wanting a beachfront or riverfront home. An American developer based in Texas, British-American Cattle Company, subdivided a large tract near Hopkins and over the years sold a sizeable number of lots. Not too many homes have yet been built in this area, but more building is likely to take place over the next few years. Several upscale developments, including Belizean Dreams and Hopkins Bay, have opened, with units sold to investors who let a management company rent out the units on a nightly or weekly basis.

Hopkins is a delightfully friendly and still mostly unspoiled village, though it is changing fast. In Hopkins and nearby are several excellent beach resorts, such as Hamanasi, and you'll find some good spots for dining as well. The Sittee River and the Caribbean waters offer some of Belize's best fishing. The barrier reef isn't close to shore here, but once you get to the reef there's good diving. There's also good diving in the South Water Marine Reserve. Inland you're only a few miles from the world's first jaguar preserve, Cockscomb. Also within a short drive are Maya ruins at Mayflower.

In Dangriga you'll find some shopping and a regional hospital for medical care. The access roads to Sittee Village and Hopkins Village from the Southern Highway are partly paved. If there's a rub to this paradise, it's the sand fleas, which can be fierce in this area.

Dangriga/Hopkins Practicalities

Dangriga is the hub of this area, and for medical care, shopping and other services this is where you will need to go. Hopkins has only a few small shops.

Banks: Belize Bank, First Caribbean International and Scotia Bank have branches in Dangriga. There are no banks in Hopkins.

Groceries: Try Southern Pride (Court House St., Dangriga).

Restaurants: Hopkins has several small restaurants owned and operated by local ladies, such as Iris's and Ruthie's, that serve good local food and low prices. The restaurant at Beaches and Dreams is excellent, as is Hamanai's restaurant.

Medical: The Southern Regional Hospital (tel. 501-522-2078) at Mile 1 1/2 of the Stann Creek Valley Road opened in 1999. Dangriga is a regional medical center for southern Belize, including Placencia.

Real Estate

Prices have gone up considerably in recent years in the Hopkins/Sittee area, due to resort development in and around Hopkins. Beachfront lots generally go for US$100,000+ though occasionally one is available for less. Larger lots of more than half an acre with both Caribbean and canal or lagoon access are around US$150,000. Seaview lots are around US$35,000 and lots on the Sittee River are around US$40,000. These lots have utilities (electricity, telephones, public water and cable TV) and road access. Small recently built homes in this area, near but not on the water, are going for US$125,000 to $300,000, occasionally with some owner financing available. Several new beachside condos are going up in the area, with prices over US$300,000.

Properties in Dangriga/Hopkins

These are offerings by individuals and real estate agencies in 2009-2010:

1.6 acres on Sittee River, deep-water access, with water & electricity on the lot. US$89,000. Owner would consider dividing the lot in half, the riverfront for US$50,000 and the back portion for US$39,000.

Small working farm off Hummingbird Highway at Mile 25 in the Stann Creek District. Property is 19 acres with around 1,575 fruit trees including 1,200 orange trees and 375 grapefruit trees and with about 3 acres still as jungle. US$45,000

Two-story concrete house in Dangriga with seaview. US$139,000

Real Estate Developments

Here are selected real estate developments in the Dangriga-Hopkins area. Most market primarily to foreign buyers.

Dreamscapes of Belize, North Palm Beach, FL, tel. 888-359-8629; www.dreamscapesofbelize.com. This 400-acre development on the Mullins River near Dangriga, has a lot of plans, including a proposed golf course, but so far little but some land clearing has been done. Lots are priced from around US$30,000 to $50,000.

Hopkins Bay, Hopkins village, tel. 877-467-2297; www.hopkinsbayresort.com. Developers of the successful Belizean Dreams condos near Jaguar Reef Resort put together the Hopkins Bay project at the north end of Hopkins village. To date, however, it hasn't proved as successful, and a number of condo units, which range in price from US$229,000 to $729,000, remain unsold. A master plan calls for a casino, marina and golf course, but those are years in the future if they materialize at all. To move unsold units, developers say they offer a "guaranteed 5% return" to buyers with a triple net lease payment of 5% per annum, but only for three years.

Sanctuary Bay, P.O. Box 260, Dangriga, tel. 501-520-7565, or 855 N. Wilton Place, Los Angeles, CA 90038, tel. 949-533-0010; www.sanctuarybay.com. Sanctuary Bay, on a 14,000-acre tract of land located between the Placencia peninsula and Hopkins, bordering the Sapodilla Lagoon and the Sittee River, has a checkered history. In May 2007, two Americans involved in Sanctuary Bay were jailed in the U.S. Andris Pukke, founder of a U.S. credit counseling company accused of cheating 300,000 debtors out of millions of dollars and allegedly the original owner/developer of Sanctuary Bay, and Peter Baker, a long-time Pukke friend and associate who was also a principal in Sanctuary Bay, were jailed by U.S. District Court Judge Peter Messitte in Maryland. Pukke was held in contempt of court for failing to turn over assets to a fund set up, in a U.S. Federal Trade Commission agreement, to repay the debtors. Robb Evans Associates was appointed by the court to attempt to collect monies from Pukke and his associates. Peter Baker, the son of Joan Medhurst, whose firm in the 1990s had the international public relations contract for the Belize Tourism Board, was jailed because the judge concluded Baker and Pukke colluded to shield assets both in Belize and in California. For a while after the U.S. legal action, sales and development at Sanctuary Bay were essentially put on hold. Today, with new management, headed by John Usher, a Belizean, in place and a fancy new website, Sanctuary Bay is trying to regain traction. Sanctuary Bay Estates has approximately 220 building lots of 1 acre or more in its initial phases, surrounded by a 11,000-acre wildlife sanctuary. A number of lots have been sold, and some of the development infrastructure, such as graded roads, is in place. Originally offered for under US$80,000 to US$229,000, some resale riverfront lots are on the market for around US$150,000-$190,000. A marina, yacht club, 9-hole golf course and equestrian center are among the amenities planned.

Real Estate Agents

Belize Development Company (formerly British-American Cattle Co.), 4600 Spicewood Springs Rd., Suite 102, Austin, Texas 78759; tel. 512-346-7381; www.bacc.com

Belize Property Agent, Mile 6, Hummingbird Hwy., Dangriga, tel. 501-522-0511; www.belizepropertyagent.com.

Caribbean Property Consultants, P.O. Box 149, Dangriga, tel. 501-523-7299; www.belizeproperty.com

Pier at Robert's Grove in Placencia

CHAPTER 16:
PLACENCIA IN MORE DETAIL

GRADING THE AREA FOR RETIREMENT, RELOCATION AND INVESTMENT Ratings are on an A to F scale, just like your old high school report card. A is the top grade; F is failing. Grades are relative compared to other areas in Belize.

Popularity with Expats	B
Safety	B
Overall Cost of Living	C+
Real Estate Bargains	C
Investment Potential	B
Leisure Activities	B
Restaurants	B
Cultural Activities	D
Infrastructure	C
Business Potential	C+
Medical Care	C
Shopping	D

ADVANTAGES OF PLACENCIA: • 16 miles of beaches on the peninsula • Growing number of expats buying property and building here • Excellent fishing and water sports • Popular resort area

Placencia's boosters boast that it has the best beaches on mainland Belize. The 16 miles or so of beaches on the peninsula are a beautiful resource, a narrow, long loaf of toast-colored sand. Like most beaches in Belize, these are only fair for swimming, as there's a good deal of seagrass, except where hotels have removed it around piers. You can snorkel here and there, but for world-class snorkeling you'll have to take a boat out to the reef or to one of the small offshore cayes, a 10- to 20-mile boat trip. (There is closer snorkeling at False Caye off Maya Beach and in a couple of other areas.)

Several marine national parks and reserves are within an hour or two by boat, including Laughing Bird Caye, South Water and Port Honduras. The Caribbean is incredibly beautiful, above and below the surface. Above, the crystal clear water sparkles in the sun. Poke your head below, and you find a whole new universe of color and activity, from tiny tropical fish to dolphins, manatees and whale sharks.

The peninsula is beginning to take off in development, but contradictions abound. Unpainted wood shacks stand next door to luxury resorts, where a week's stay costs more than a local worker might earn in a year. Local families who a few years ago fished for a living have opened restaurants, bars and hotels, and they don't always have all the management skills down pat. There's a modern water system, and most of the peninsula is on the power grid, yet local schools barely have any books and, until a Cuban volunteer medical team came to the peninsula, locals had to go to Independence or Dangriga to see a doctor.

The big change is that after years of promises the road from the Southern Highway to Riversdale and then down the peninsula is at last being paved. As of early 2010, the road was paved between Maya Beach and Placencia village, an excellent road except for way too many giant *topes* or speed bumps. Completion of the paving is expected in late 2011. Another development is that a new international airport, funded by private interests on the peninsula and elsewhere in Belize, is under construction just northwest of Riversdale. Whether this airport actually will handle international flights is still, well, up in the air.

In October 2001, Hurricane Iris did extensive damage to the southern part of the peninsula. Except for a few open spaces where trees have not been replanted or houses rebuilt, the peninsula is back to normal now. The area is attracting a mix of expats: A few with cash and a dream have opened resorts. Some are middle-class baby boomers that are buying lots and hope to build a vacation or retirement home. Others are marginalized escapees from the North American rat race, who live hand-to-mouth and seem to spend most of their time boozing.

Hundreds of condo units are under construction or planned, though some of the projects have been stalled by the 2008-2009 recession. Several major projects were announced and then cancelled. At least one large project, Bella Maya, closed at least temporarily in January 2010; developers say it will reopen later in 2010.

Tourism is still a hit-and-miss seasonal thing on the Placencia peninsula. Except for a few well-marketed properties, annual occupancy at peninsula hotels is well averages under 35% (it was 32% in 2008, the last year for which statistics are available.) During the winter, especially around holidays, hotels fill up and it can be tough to find a decent room. But, off-season, the peninsula slows down, some hotels and restaurants close and most of the peninsula reverts to its sleepy self. Many peninsula resorts are, actively or passively, up for sale. Many have been on the market for years; nearly all continue with business-as-usual, regardless of sale status.

Land on the peninsula is low-lying and flat. The Maya Mountains are visible to the west. Placencia, a Creole village, with a population of about 600, is at the southern tip of the peninsula. A long concrete sidewalk runs up the center of the village. A stroll up and down the sidewalk will give you a good introduction to life in the village. A Garifuna village, Seine Bight (population over 1,000), is a little farther north. Maya Beach, not a village but a collection of houses and small resorts, is known for its good beaches.

Placencia Practicalities

Shops and services, such as they are, mostly are clustered in Placencia village, though a few are located in Seine Bight and in Maya Beach.

Banks: Atlantic Bank, Belize Bank and ScotiaBank have branches and ATMs in Placencia.

Groceries: There are several groceries on the peninsula, none of them much larger than your living room. Wallen's Market (on the main road in Placencia village, across from the soccer field), which now has air-conditioning, is the largest. For a bigger selection of groceries and better prices, you'll have to go to Dangriga or Belize City. A truck from Dangriga makes regular deliveries selling fresh fruit and vegetables.

Restaurants: The dining scene on the peninsula has greatly improved in recent years. The Bistro at Maya Beach Hotel is one of the best restaurants in Belize. The French Connection in Placencia village (at a new location next to the police station) makes a good stab at contemporary Euro cuisine, and Rumfish y Vino is a nice spot for drinks and little plates. Several of the larger hotels, including Inn at Roberts Grove and Turtle Inn, do an excellent job with food and beverage. Among the more modest spots, Wendy's, De Tatch, Omar's and Yoli's offer good food and good value. Tutti Fruitti has authentic Italian gelati, by far the best we've tasted anywhere in Central America.

Other Services: There is a Shell gas station in Placencia village, a Texaco a little north of the village, a fairly well equipped building supplies store, Professional Builders Supply, and several Internet cafés.

Medical: A small medical clinic is located near the school in Placencia village, and another clinic is in Seine Bight. Cuban doctors, on loan from Fidel, may still be in residence when you are there. Otherwise, for medical attention you may need to go to Dangriga or across the lagoon to Independence.

Real Estate: Real estate has been booming on the Placencia peninsula, though with the 2009-2009 global recession the boom has diminished to a whimper. With limited land on the narrow peninsula, and considerable demand from Americans seeking a place on the Caribbean, prices zoomed upward in recent years. Desirable beachfront lots are now going for US$2,500 to $3,500 a front foot, or around US$185,000 to $260,000+ for a deep lot with 75 ft. of beachfront, while lots a row or two back are US$50,000 to $100,000. Lagoon and canal lots are US$35,000 to $75,000, and some more. Most condos are also expensive – US$150,000 to $225,000 for a one-bedroom and US$200,000 to $400,000+ for a two-bedroom. Small wood homes in Placencia or Seine Bight villages might be had under US$100,000, but modern reinforced concrete homes farther north on or near the beach are US$200,000 to $400,000 and up, often way up. Rentals are few and far between on the peninsula. You may be able to find a rental in Placencia village for around US$300 to $500 a month. A nicer home north of village may go for US$700 and up.

Real Estate Developments

Among the real estate developments on the peninsula are these:

Coco Plum (www.cocoplumbelize.net): This is *the* quality residential development on the peninsula. Established by Stewart Krohn, who for years operated Channel 5 TV and Great Belize Productions, and his partners, the 224-acre master-planned community is a low-density development with most lots over one-half acre. All roads are paved, and utilities are underground. Eventually it will have a resort hotel and other amenities. Lots range from around US$100,000 to over $400,000. Several homes already have been built. Villas at Coco Plum, a condo development, was carved out of Coco Plum land but is separate from the Coco Plum residential development.

The Placencia, The Placencia Residences and Copal Beach (www.theplacencia.com, www.theplacenciaresidences.com and www.copalbeach.com). The Placencia is an ambitious hotel, condominium and residential development north on the peninsula. Condos on the seaside are offered from US$350,000 to $950,000. Some of the these condos are part of The Placencia hotel, which must have one of the lowest occupancy rates on the peninsula; we've never seen more than a handful of guests here. Residential lots on the filled lagoon side are US$113,000 to $540,000. Home construction packages (in addition to lot cost) range from US$395,000 to $825,000. The Placencia developer is also associated with the planned international airport northwest of the peninsula and the high-rise Copal Beach luxury development, under construction just north of The Placencia condos. Copal Beach, expected to open in 2012, will have 106 condo units ranging in price from US$1.3 to $4.3 million. Who buys these things, anyway?

Sunset Pointe (www.sunsetpointebelize.com). This is a 12-unit condotel project on the lagoon side of Placencia village, with construction by Albert Lowen, who has built a number of upscale hotels and houses in Belize.

Inn at Robert's Grove (www.robertsgrove.com/html/condos.html). Phase 2 of the condos at Robert's Grove features two- and three-bedroom units for US$385,000 to $485,000. Condo owners have access to all the resort amenities at Robert's Grove.

Properties on the Placencia Peninsula

Here is a selection of properties offered by individuals and real estate companies in 2009-2010:

Two-bedroom condo at Villas at Coco Plum, 1,392 sq. ft., one of 12 finished units out of planned 35 on the beach. US$315,000

4.25 acres, sea to lagoon, north of Seine Bight village, 255 ft. beachfront, US$565,000

54 ft. x 70 ft. lot in Placencia village, US$98,000

Beachfront residential lot at Coco Plum, 120 ft on the beach by 235 ft. deep, US$360,000

Short-Term Rentals

Barnacle Bill's, Maya Beach (tel. 501-523-8010, www.barnaclebills-belize.com) has two nice one-bedroom cottages on the beach at Maya Beach, for around US$665 a week May to November and around US$770 the rest of the year. These rates include utilities but not 9% tax.

Real Estate Agents

Bayshore Limited, 100 Embarcadero road, Maya Beach, tel. 501-523-8019; www.bayshorebelize.com

Katie Valk, International Sales Associate/Travel Info, Coco Plum, US tel. 561-210-7015, Belize tel. 501-610-1923, e-mail info@belize-trips.com, www.cocoplumbelize.net

Yearwood Properties, Placencia; tel. 501-523-3174; www.belizebeachfront.com

Brits Kate and Ian Morton Run Hickatee Cottages in PG

CHAPTER 17:
PUNTA GORDA AND SOUTHERN BELIZE IN MORE DETAIL

GRADING THE AREA FOR RETIREMENT, RELOCATION AND INVESTMENT Ratings are on an A to F scale, just like your old high school report card. A is the top grade; F is failing. Grades are relative compared to other areas in Belize.

Popularity with Expats	D+
Safety	B+
Overall Cost of Living	B
Real Estate Values	B
Investment Potential	C
Leisure Activities	C
Restaurants	D+
Cultural Activities	C-
Infrastructure	C+
Business Potential	C
Medical Care	C
Shopping	C-

117

ADVANTAGES TO PUNTA GORDA AREA: • Lush, beautiful tropical scenery • Excellent fishing • Diverse mix of Maya, Garifuna and other cultures • Moderate land prices • Proximity to Rio Dulce area of Guatemala • Increasing interest in area for tourism due to completion of Southern Highway

You've probably heard stories about Punta Gorda being the end of the earth and all that. You may be surprised, then, at how inviting a town it is. With about 5,500 people, it has a mix of Mopan and Kekchí Maya, Garifuna and a dollop of Creoles, Lebanese and Chinese, plus a few American expats, missionaries, and dreamers.

PG, as it's known in Belize is (all things being relative) colorful and friendly. There's usually a breeze blowing from the Bay of Honduras. On Wednesdays and Saturdays, the downtown market draws Maya from surrounding villages. PG's waterside setting is, like that of Corozal Town, truly pleasant, even beautiful.

Business activity in the town is not exactly hot and hopping. Hotels in and around PG stay empty most of the year, though several new ones have opened -- hope springs eternal. The official occupancy rate is around 28%. As yet, only a few tourists make it all the way down the Southern Highway from Belize City or Placencia. Some backpackers do pass through on their way to cheaper towns in Guatemala and Honduras. With the paving of the Southern Highway (only about 5 miles near Big Falls remain unsurfaced), conventional wisdom is that PG will explode with new hotels, real estate developments and other businesses. We're not so sure that will happen to any great extent, but certainly things will get busier.

Outside of PG, the land in Toledo District is lush, wild and wet, fed by 160 inches or more of rain each year — the only dry months are February through May. Emerald green valleys lay between low peaks of the Maya Mountains. Rice grows in flooded fields, and giant bromeliads line the roads. There are no beaches to speak of around PG, but the rocky shorelines are cooled by near constant breezes from the Bay of Honduras. Offshore are isolated cayes and the straggling end of the barrier reef.

The Maya have lived in this part of Belize for millennia. Among the Maya ruins here are Lubaantun ("Place of the Fallen Stones") Lubaantun was occupied only from around 700 to 900 AD. The famous, or infamous, "crystal skull" was supposedly discovered here in 1926 by F.A. Mitchell-Hedges, on assignment from the British Museum, though most experts believe the skull is a hoax. Nim Li Punit ("Big Hat") was occupied about the same time as Lubaantun, in the Late Classic period. At its height, several thousand people may have lived there. Among other notable Maya sites in the area is Uxbenka (pronounced Ush-ben-ka and meaning "Ancient Place").

The Maya were joined in the early 19th century by Garifuna from the Bay Islands of Honduras and, after the American Civil War, by a group of former Confederate soldiers and their families who attempted to settle here, with relatively little success. In modern times, Punta Gorda has held an attraction for missionary groups, mostly fundamentalists from the U.S. Who knows? You may find PG is precisely your kind of place, too.

Punta Gorda Practicalities

Banks: Belize Bank and ScotiaBank have branches and ATMs in PG.

Groceries: Wallace Supaul Store on Main Street and Southern Grocer on King Street may have what you need.

Restaurants: Mangrove Inn, Earth Runnin', Marian's Bayview, Emery's, Gomier's, Grace's and the restaurants at Hickatee Cottages and Machaca Hill Lodge are among the best.

Medical: Punta Gorda Hospital (south end of Main Street) can provide basic emergency care; you may want to upgrade to the Southern Regional Hospital in Dangriga or to hospitals in Belize City.

Real Estate

Toledo does not have a very active real estate market, and it is difficult to establish market value. Accessible land in smaller tracts (under 50 acres) often goes for US$1,000 to $2,000 an acre. Larger parcels with access and river frontage are usually US$500 to $1,000 an acre. Building lots in or near Punta Gorda not on the bay are inexpensive – usually no more than a few thousand dollars, but waterfront lots are more expensive. Smaller concrete houses on the bay in PG have sold for under US$75,000.

Properties Offered in Toledo

Here are a few properties offered by individuals and real estate companies in 2009-2010:

200 acres on the Moho River, with all-weather road access, located on the road to Barranco. US$210,000, some owner financing.

Seafront building lot in Punta Negra, about 30 miles north of PG by boat (no road access). US$50,000

10 acres with seaview, just north of PG in Cattle Landing area. US$60,000

Small two-bedroom cinderblock house with unfinished kitchen in Indianville area near PG. Electricity, cable and telephone to house. US$14,500

Real Estate Agents

Real estate companies in Belize City and elsewhere have some listings for Toledo. PG tourism operators and entrepreneurs sometimes hustle real estate on the side.

Traffic in Belize City

CHAPTER 18:
BELIZE CITY IN MORE DETAIL

GRADING THE AREA FOR RETIREMENT, RELOCATION AND INVESTMENT Ratings are on an A to F scale, just like your old high school report card. A is the top grade; F is failing. Grades are relative compared to other areas in Belize.

Popularity with Expats	D
Safety	D
Overall Cost of Living	C-
Real Estate Bargains	C-
Investment Potential	B-
Leisure Activities	C+
Restaurants	B+
Cultural Activities	A-
Infrastructure	B+
Business Potential	B
Medical Care	A-
Shopping	A-

ADVANTAGES TO BELIZE CITY: • Access to good restaurants and social and cultural activities • Business and transportation hub of the country • Access to more stores and shopping, with lower prices • Good medical care

Belize City has a bad rep among visitors and even among Belizeans from other areas, who sometimes dread visiting the "big city" with its rude layabouts and drug touts. In truth, the city is hardly more than an oversized town, with ramshackle buildings set close to the street in the central areas but also with its share of stately old colonial houses in the Fort George section and early 19th century landmarks such as St. John's Anglican Cathedral and the House of Culture. And while crime is a considerable problem – hardly a weekend goes by without a murder or three – crime in Belize City is nothing like that you'd experience in the much bigger and meaner cities of the region such as Guatemala City and Tegucigalpa.

The city has an energy of its own. By day, Front, Queen and Albert streets swarm with shop clerks and shoppers. Restaurants are packed at lunchtime. On Regent Street you'll find lawyers and judges dressed in British-style robes. Day trippers from the cruise ships that now call on Belize City – about 650,000 passengers make port here annually, much to the dismay of many resort and ecolodge owners who fear the impact of hordes of cruise tourists on environmentally sensitive ruins, caves and cayes – get on vans and boats for their shore excursions.

Everywhere you'll hear the sound of Creole being spoken, as local residents greet friends and lovers amid a happy Caribbean-style gumbo of sounds and smells. At night, despite the street crime, Belize City lights up with parties, gallery openings and political and professional meetings, as Belize City remains in all but name the true political, as well as cultural and social, capital of the country.

Belize City Practicalities

As the largest urban area and commercial hub of the country, Belize City offers most of the amenities of a town of similar size in the U.S. or Canada.

Airlines: Belize City is the transportation hub of the country and offers more than 50 domestic flights a day by Maya Island Air and Tropic Air from two airports to major destinations in Belize. Internationally, it is served by American, Continental, Delta, TACA and USAir.

Buses: National Transport and more than a dozen other bus companies leave from the terminal in the Collet Canal area west of the city center. This terminal is still called Novelo's, though the Novelo's bus line is out of business.

Taxis: Most taxi trips within the city cost US$4 or less. The rate to and from the city and the international airport is fixed at US$25 (for the cab, not per person).

Banks: Alliance Bank, Atlantic Bank, Belize Bank, First Caribbean International and ScotiaBank all have offices in Belize City. The larger banks have multiple offices. Branches in the "suburbs" even have drive-up windows.

Embassies: Some diplomatic missions to Belize maintain their offices in Belize City rather than Belmopan. However, the U.S. Embassy moved to its new US$50 million compound in Belmopan in late 2006.

Groceries: The two largest supermarkets in the Belize City area — indeed in all of Belize — are Save-U (San Cas Plaza by Belcan Bridge, tel. 501-223-1291) and Brodies (Mile 2 1/2 Northern Hwy. tel. 501-223-5587). Both are modern supermarkets with air-conditioning and free parking. Brodies was greatly expanded and redone in 2006. They both have pharmacies and sell liquor, beer and wine, and Brodies has a fairly extensive dry goods section. There is another, older Brodies downtown. Premium Wine & Spirits (166 Newtown Barracks, tel. 501-223-4984) has a good selection of imported wines.

Restaurants: Belize City has many good restaurants in all price ranges. Among our favorites are the Riverside Tavern, Sumathi, Smoky Mermaid, Harbourview and Chon Saan Palace.

Other Stores: While there at present is no Wal-Mart or K-Mart, Belize City does have a number of larger stores where you can buy appliances, hardware, home furnishings and construction supplies. Among them: Mirab Department Store (tel. 501-223-2933, for appliances, home furnishings and other items); Courts (tel. 501-223-0775 for electronics and other goods); Benny's Home Center (tel. 501-227-3347, for construction supplies); Dave's Furniture World (tel. 501-227-5312, furniture); Hofius (tel. 501-227-7231), a hardware store with a good reputation for appliances and kitchen equipment.

Car Dealers: Among the new car dealers in Belize City are those selling Ford, Toyota, Mitsubishi, Land Rover, Suzuki, Hyundai, Kia, Isuzu, Nissan, Dodge and Jeep.

Medical: Belize City is the medical center of Belize, with the largest hospital (Karl Heusner Memorial Hospital, Princess Margaret Dr., tel. 501-223-1548) and by far the largest number of physicians, dentists and other healthcare professionals. Belize Medical Associates (5791 St. Thomas St., Kings Park, tel. 501- 223-0302) is a 25-bed private hospital. (*See the Health chapter for other listings.*)

Among the several dozen physician practices in the city are Family Medical Center (3 Newtown Barracks, tel. 501-223-2647, e-mail b.e.bulwer@btl.net) and Caribbean Shores Medical Center (5756 Princess Margaret Dr., tel. 501-224-4821, e-mail fdsmith@btl.net). Among recommended dentists are Dr. Osbert O. Usher Dental Clinic (16 Magazine Rd., tel. 501-227-3415) and Heusner's Professional Dentistry (42 Albert St., tel. 501-272-2583).

Real Estate

Few expats will choose Belize City as a place to live, unless they need to be there for business reasons. Those that do likely will live in the suburbs north and west of the city, such as Bella Vista and Belama, or in the more up-scale areas of town along Princess Margaret Street, King's Park and West Landivar. Homes in these areas are priced similarly to homes in nice areas of mid-sized U.S. cities, with prices of several hundred U.S. dollars for homes not being unusual.

Secure apartment rentals also are not cheap: You can expect to pay around US$.80 to $1.50 per square foot per month, or about US$800 to $1,500 a month for a 1,000 sq. ft. two-bedroom apartment, and more for luxury condos such as those in Renaissance Towers and Marina Towers.

Residential areas around Belize City range from upscale suburbs to poor villages. Ladyville near the international airport has subdivisions and a variety of businesses. Farther north in Belize District, Crooked Tree is a pleasant Creole village with a lagoon setting. To the west, Hattieville is a sprawling residential area that sprang up after Hurricane Hattie in 1961. To the south off the Coastal Highway, Gales Point, another Creole village, enjoys a beautiful setting between the sea and lagoons.

Properties Offered in and around Belize City

Here are some offerings, from individuals and real estate firms in early 2010:

Renovated two-story house in Buttonwood Bay, with 5 bedrooms and 3 bathrooms. US$137,500

Modern concrete two-story home in Bella Vista, around Mile 3 of the Northern Highway, across from the Biltmore Plaza. Four bedrooms, 2 ½ baths in 2,750 sq. ft. of floor space. Fenced. Possible conversion to commercial. US$337,500

49 acres on Western Highway at Mile 11. Potential for tourism site. US$300,000

10,500 sq. ft. luxury home on seafront in Buttonwood Bay. Eight bedrooms, 6 bathrooms, private pier. US$2,000,0000

Real Estate Agents

Belize Land Properties Ltd. (Hector Romero), 9 Third Street, King's Park, Belize City, tel./fax 501-223-4807; www.belizelandproperties.com.

Buy-Belize Real Estate, (Estevan Perera), 2.5 Miles Western Highway (P.O. Box 2276), tel. 501-222-4190, Belize City, www.buy-belize.com.

Emerald Futures Real Estate, Mile 3 ½, Northern Hwy., Belize City, tel. 501-670-6818, fax 501-223-2609; www.emeraldfutures.com.

IVORR Real Estate Agency, 7145 Slaughterhouse Road, Belize City, tel. 501-223-5560, cell 501-620-3711, www.ivorr.com.

Premier Real Estate, Mile 2 Western Highway, Belize City, tel. 501-224-4075 or 225-9052, cell 501-610-4343, fax 501-222-4150, www.premier-realestatebelize.com.

Realty Management of Belize Ltd., 24 Daly Street, Belize City, tel. 501-223-3523, fax 223-3375, www.realtymanagementofbelize.com.

Regent Realty, Ltd., 81 N. Front St., Belize City; tel. 501-227-0090, fax 227-2022, www.regentrealtybelize.com.

Vista Real Estate, 122 Eve St. (P.O. Box 2383), Belize City, tel. 501-223-2427, fax 223-2228, www.vistabelize.com or www.belizerealestate.bz.

CHAPTER 19:
HOTELS AND RESORTS FOR SALE

Many people have a dream of owning and operating a small beach hotel or jungle lodge. Many people have also lost their shirts in this kind of operation. A surprising number of hotels are actively for sale in Belize.

By our count, more than 60 hotels, lodges, inns and B&Bs are currently for sale in Belize. Aside from these properties that are actively on the market via media advertising or listings with real estate companies, a number of other hotels are for sale but currently are not being promoted. The largest concentration of hotel properties for sale is in Cayo District, followed by Caye Caulker and Placencia. Despite its ranking as the number one tourism destination in Belize, with the largest number of hotels in the country, Ambergris Caye has relatively few hotels for sale.

Below are hotels and related businesses offered or advertised for sale in late 2009 and early 2010. Several restaurants are also included, although this is not a complete list. All asking prices are in U.S. dollars. Prices are those set by the owner and in some cases may bear little relationship to actual market value. Most properties, if they sell at all, do not sell at full asking price.

We attempt to provide current and accurate information, but such information is subject to change, and owners *do* change their minds. To correct any listing or to add a listing, email lansluder@gmail.com. Note that these were on market in late 2009 and may have since been sold or removed from market.

CAYO DISTRICT

Pook's Hill Lodge, Belmopan, 11 cabañas on 100 acres, asking US$2,300,000

Gumbo Limbo Village Resort, Mountain Pine Ridge Road, San Ignacio, 4 cottages, restaurant, pool on 40 acres, US$660,000

Falconview Backpackers Adventure Hostel, Santa Elena, asking US$328,000

Roaring River Golf Course, 9-hole golf course on 20 acres with restaurant and five tourist rental cottages, asking US$1,800,000

Aguada Hotel, Santa Elena, 22 rooms, owner's apartment, restaurant and bar, pool, asking US$850,000

Royal Mayan Resort and Spa, Benque Viejo, 25 rooms on 8 acres with pool and spa, asking US$1,750,000

Belmopan Hotel and Convention Center, Belmopan, on 2 acres, asking US$1,200,000

Macaw Bank, Cristo Rey, 5 cabañas/cottages with owner's house on 50 acres on Macal River, asking US$550,000

Five Sisters Lodge, Mountain Pine Ridge, 18 units with restaurant on about 15 acres, asking US$2,500,000

Windy Hill Resort, San Ignacio, 16 cottages and 9 rooms on 97 acres, pool, tour operation, asking US$1,800,000

Belize Jungle Dome, Belmopan, 7 rooms, pool, on 2.88 acres on Belize River, asking US$850,000 (owner's villa not included but is available at an additional US$275,000)

Belmopan Bed and Breakfast, Belmopan, 3 units plus owner's residence, pool, asking US$330,000

Mopan River Resort, Benque Viejo, asking US$2,850,000

Eva's, San Ignacio, restaurant, leased, asking US$150,000

Amore Mio Italian restaurant, San Ignacio, leased, asking US$35,000

Iguana Junction, Bullet Tree, 4 rooms and main house on 1 acre, asking US$315,000

B&B, Succotz, residence and three guest houses, café (leased) in San Ignacio also included, asking US$190,000

Cedar Cabins Resort, Frank's Eddy Village near Belmopan, camping, restaurant, gift shop, botanical garden and butterfly farm, asking US$1,600,000

Cha Chalaga Inn, Bullet Tree

Tract near Maya Mountain Lodge, San Ignacio, approx. 46 acres, asking US$915,620

duPlooy's Lodge, near San Ignacio, 7 cottages/units for sale individually from US$99,000 to $250,000, not entire lodge

CAYE CAULKER

Seaside Cabanas, 16 rooms on seafront, asking US$2,299,000

Belize Odyssey Hotel, 22 rooms, asking US$4,000,000

Tropical Paradise Resort, 25 rooms, restaurant and bar, asking US$2,500,000

Popeyes Beach Resort, 20 rooms, restaurant and bar, seafront, asking US$1,800,000

Iguana Reef Inn, 13 rooms plus owner's suite, pool, asking US$3,000,000

Tropics Hotel, 17 rooms, asking US$1,400,000

Jaguar Morning Star Guest House, 3 units plus owner's apartment, asking US$499,000

Barefoot Caribe, 14 rooms plus seafront restaurant/bar, asking US$1,900,000

Sunset View Hotel, 25 budget rooms plus bar, lagoon side, asking US$560,000

Tom's Hotel, seafront, asking US$3,200,000

Casa Rosado B&B, 3 rooms, asking US$250,000

Don Corleone Caribbean Trattoria, leased, asking US$125,000

Alamina Beach House, 3 apartments with sports bar, ice cream parlour, café and gift shop, asking US$750,000

AMBERGRIS CAYE

The Pink Motel & Hideaway Bar, 13 cabañas, pool, asking US$400,000

Seven Seas Resort, 1-bedroom units on seafront, pool, RCI timeshare affiliation, asking US$1,950,000

Lagniappe Provisioning, asking US$50,000

Casa Picasso Restaurant, (leasehold) asking US$150,000

Winnie Estelle charter boat, asking US$185,500

Conch Shell, 10 rooms, seafront, asking US$850,000

Jungle Jack's restaurant and bar, leasehold, asking US$35,000

Mr. Joe's Grocery and Grill, includes owner's living quarters, asking US$500,000

Palapa Bar, leased, with owner's house, asking US$700,000

Mayan Secrets Day Spa, asking US$175,000

Stadium Bar & Grill, asking US$145,000

Hidden Treasure Restaurant, plus home, asking US$825,000

REMOTE CAYES & ATOLLS

Slick Rock Adventure Lodge, Long Caye, Glovers Atoll, seafront, asking US$995,000 for leased dive resort only or US$2,195,000 for 5.2 acre island with resort facilities

Blackbird Caye Resort, Turneffe Atoll, 18 cabañas on 44 acres, seafront, asking US$4,000,000

Manta Reef Resort, Glovers Reef Atoll, 15 cabañas plus house and restaurant on 12 acres, seafront, asking US$5,500,000

Unopened fishing/dive resort on Long Caye, Lighthouse Atoll, 27 units, asking US$1,950,000

Gaviota's Resort, Tobacco Caye, 7 rooms, seafront, asking US$495,000

Royal Belize, Hermit Caye, private resort island with four cottages, asking US$2,775,000

Water Caye, largest private island in Belize, 511 acres, 12 miles from Belize City near deep water channel, with day resort for cruise ship passengers, asking US$12,000,000

HOPKINS

Kanantik, all-inclusive seafront resort with 25 cabañas on 300 acres, asking US$8,400,000

River House Lodge, Sittee, 6 units on 2 acres, asking US$890,000

Sir Thomas' at Toucan Sittee, Sittee, 6 cottages plus owner's house, restaurant on 1 acre, asking US$950,000

Caribbean Shores Bed & Breakfast, Hopkins, 6 rooms, asking US$400,000

Parrot Cove Lodge, 6 rooms, 2 houses, pool, restaurant and bar, asking US$1,750,000

DANGRIGA

Mama Noots Jungle Resort, Mayflower, 48 acres, asking price US$1,600,000

PLACENCIA
Pickled Parrot, 2 cabañas, restaurant, owner's apartment, asking US$395,000

Manatee Inn, asking US$375,000

Ranguana Lodge, 5 cabañas, seafront, asking US$1,250,000

Seaspray Hotel, 21 rooms, seafront, asking US$1,500,000

La Chapelle Suites, 6 units plus 3-bedroom unit, asking US$1,200,000

South Waters Resort, 4 cabañas, restaurant and bar on 2 acres, asking US$3,000,000

Green Parrot Beach Houses & Resort, 8 units, seafront, asking US$1,495,000

COROZAL TOWN
TJ's Guesthouse, 10 rooms with manager's apartment, restaurant and pool, asking US$275,000

Las Palmas, 29 rooms, space for restaurant, asking US$2,900,000

Hok'ol K'in Guesthouse, asking US$598,000

Oasis Bed & Breakfast, 21 rooms, asking US$275,000

Bay Breeze Hotel (Seabreeze Hotel), 7 rooms, asking US$330,000

PUNTA GORDA
Sea Front Inn, Punta Gorda, 14 rooms and 6 apartments, restaurant, asking US$1,100,000

BELIZE CITY AND BELIZE DISTRICT
Belize River Lodge, 8 rooms on 47 acres, with fishing gear, boats and a live-aboard motor yacht, asking US$2,000,000

El Chiclero Inn, asking US$1,000,000

Maruba Lodge & Spa, Old Northern Highway, 18 units, two villas, 2 pools, spa, 700 acres, asking US$8,000,000

Bakadeer Inn, Belize City, asking US$375,000

Bacab Eco Park, Belize City, asking US$2,600,000

Tiger Point, Southern Lagoon, eco-lodge on 359 acres, asking $1,700,000

Cheers, near Belize Zoo, 3 cabañas and restaurant and owner's house, asking US$1,083,000

Altun-Ha Ecotourism Resort and Maskall Golf Course, (formerly Pretty See) Old Northern Highway, lodge building with apartment, 14 cabañas, 9-hole golf course on 1,320 acres, asking US$5,500,000

Seaside Guest House, Belize City, 8 budget rooms, asking US$375,000 with US$75,000 down, balance owner-financed

Riverbend B&B, asking US$750,000

CHAPTER 20:
YOUR MONEY AND HOW TO HOLD ON TO IT IN BELIZE

Belize's official currency is the Belize dollar, which for many years has been pegged to the U.S. dollar at a rate of 2 Belize dollars to 1 U.S. dollar. However, moneychangers often give a slightly higher rate than 2 Belize for 1 U.S. dollar, sometimes as much as 2.1 or 2.2 to 1, or even higher, depending on the local demand for American greenbacks. Generally, though, the premium is only 2 or 3 percent.

That brings us to a key fact about Belize and your money: Hard currencies, like the U.S. dollar, euro and yen, are good. Soft currencies, and the Belize dollar is one of them, are not so good. The Belize dollar is difficult to exchange anywhere outside of Belize (except at border areas of Guatemala and Mexico).

For years there has been talk of dollarizing the Belize economy, making the U.S. dollar the official currency of Belize, similar to what El Salvador and Ecuador and, to a degree, Guatemala have done, but so far that talk hasn't translated into action. There are several possible reasons. For one, the Belize government is reluctant to do away with its Central Bank and surrender so much of its financial control to Uncle Sam. That's understandable. For another, Belize politicians may think that in a tough economic pinch it's a lot easier to just print money than to actually earn it. That's also understandable.

Technically, according to Belize law, only the Central Bank of Belize is permitted to deal in foreign currencies including the U.S. dollar. But this rule is widely, almost universally, flaunted in Belize, and businesses routinely take U.S. dollars in payment for goods and services and have been doing so for decades. In any event, U.S. dollars (bills, not coins) are accepted everywhere in Belize, although you often will receive change in Belizean money, or in a mix of Belizean and U.S. money.

Paper-money Belize denominations are the 100-, 50-, 20-, 10-, 5- and 2-dollar bills. Belize coins come in 1-dollar, 50, 25, 10, 5 and 1 Belizean cent units. The 25-cent piece is called a shilling.

Currency Exchange Regulations

The U.S. Embassy in Belize provides this summary of currency regulations in Belize:

Under the Exchange Control Regulations (Chapter 43 of the Laws of Belize - 1980), only the Central Bank of Belize and authorized dealers/depositories (i.e., commercial banks and Casas de Cambio, if permitted) may deal in foreign currencies. In order to pay for goods and services procured outside of Belize in a foreign currency, a foreign exchange permit must be obtained from an authorized dealer or directly from the Central Bank of Belize. The permission of the Central Bank of Belize is also required to secure a loan from outside Belize that involves a foreign currency, and also to service repayment of foreign debt. According to the Belize Investment Guide, "the necessary approvals can be easily secured in the case of genuine, approved enterprises." Foreign investors are required to register any investments made in Belize with the Central Bank in order to facilitate the repatriation of profits, dividends, etc. Officially, no person, other than authorized dealers and authorized depositories, may retain any foreign currency in their possession without the consent of the Central Bank of Belize. In practice, however, many local businesses accept payment in U.S. currency.

Foreign exchange controls can be summarized by the following rules and guidelines: Residents and non-residents need permission to buy foreign currency for whatever purpose; Authorized dealers (i.e., commercial banks) are allowed to sell foreign currency up to US$2,500 for private travel and up to US$10,000 for business travel per calendar year; requests in excess of these amounts must be approved by the Central Bank of Belize; Exporters are required to register their exports with the Central Bank, guaranteeing delivery of their foreign exchange earnings; Authorized dealers may authorize payments for imports, where goods are paid for through letters of credit or bank collection. They may also authorize payments for imports against copies of invoices and customs entries, where the documents show that the goods were obtained on credit; Belizean residents, who wish to borrow abroad and where debt service will be in hard currencies, must apply to the Central Bank of Belize for permission to do so.

Banks and Banking in Belize

Belize has five commercial banks, not including offshore banks. Three are based in Belize – Alliance Bank, Belize Bank and Atlantic Bank — and two, First Caribbean Bank (formerly Barclays) and ScotiaBank, are large multinational banks with branches in Belize. The local banks are small, about the size of a small-town local bank or savings and loan in the U.S. Belize also has several credit unions and small mortgage lending institutions.

Here are the basic facts, including contact information for the main offices, about each bank in Belize:

Alliance Bank of Belize is the newest of the commercial banks in Belize. It has eight offices -- in Belize City, Belmopan, Caye Caulker, San Pedro, Orange Walk, San Ignacio, Independence and Pomona (near Dangriga). It formerly was associated with Glenn D. Godfrey, a well-connected Belizean businessman and attorney. In 2009, Alliance Bank reportedly was sold to a group of mostly foreign investors from Mexico and the Caribbean. The bank then ran a contest to rename the bank. At press time, the new name has not been announced. The bank has assets of around US$100 million. Main Office: 106 Princess Margaret Drive, Belize City; tel.: 501-223-6783, fax 223-6785. www.alliancebank.bz.

Atlantic Bank was founded in 1971. It is majority owned by Sociedad Nacional de Inversiones, S.A., a Honduran company, along with some individual stockholders in Belize and Honduras. Atlantic Bank has 13 offices in Belize — in Corozal, the Corozal Free Zone, Belize City (three offices), International Airport, Belmopan, Ladyville, Caye Caulker, Orange Walk, San Pedro, Placencia and San Ignacio. Main office: Atlantic Building, Freetown Road; tel. 501-223-4123, fax 223-3907; www.atlabank.com. Atlantic Bank's international banking operation is Atlantic International Bank.

Belize Bank traces its history back to 1902 when it was founded as the Bank of British Honduras. It is owned by BB Holdings, shares of which trade on the Alternative Investment Market of the London Stock Exchange in the United Kingdom under the symbol BBHL. Lord Michael Ashcroft, a British billionaire and Conservative party officer who holds dual citizenship in the UK and Belize, is chairman and a large stockholder in BB Holdings. Belize Bank bills itself as the largest commercial bank in Belize, with assets if around US$440 million, and around 40% share of loans and deposits in Belize. It has 12 offices around the country — in Corozal, the Corozal Free Zone, Orange Walk, International Airport, Belize City (two offices), Belmopan, San Ignacio, San Pedro, Dangriga and Punta Gorda. Main office: 60 Market Square, Belize City; tel. 501-227-7132, fax 227-2712; www.belizebank.com. Belize Bank also has an international banking division, Belize Caribbean International Bank.

First Caribbean International Bank (formerly Barclays) was formed in 2003 by the merger of the Caribbean operations of Barclays, the giant U.K.-based financial service firm, and those of another large bank, Canadian Imperial Bank of Commerce (CIBC). Operations in 17 Caribbean countries including Belize were rebranded as First Caribbean International Bank. First Caribbean has assets of around US$11 billion. In Belize, First Caribbean has five offices, in Belmopan, Belize City (two), San Pedro and Dangriga. Main office in Belize: Albert Street, Belize City; tel. 501-227-7211, fax 227-8572; www.firstcaribbean.com.

ScotiaBank, formerly Bank of Nova Scotia, is a large Canadian bank with operations in 50 countries and with worldwide assets of more than US$500 billion. In Belize, it has 13 offices -- in Corozal Town, San Pedro, Orange Walk, Belize City (two offices), Belmopan, Spanish Lookout, Placencia, Punta Gorda and Dangriga. Main Belize office: Albert Street, Belize

City, tel. 501-227-7027, fax 227-7416; www.scotiabank.com.

Offshore Banks

In addition to commercial banks in Belize serving local customers, Belize has developed a small but growing community of offshore banks (or international banks as they like to be called.) These offshore banks were authorized by the Banks and Financial Institutions Act, 1995, and the introduction of the Offshore Banking Act, 1996, and the Money Laundering (Prevention) Act, 1996.

These banks are regulated by the Belize Central Bank, have physical offices in Belize and offer various services including international bankcards and demand, savings and time deposit accounts. Accounts maintained with these banks are not subject to local taxes or exchange control restrictions and may be denominated in any major currency, including U.S. dollars, euros and others. International banks tout their privacy for their customers, although if the Belize courts find that funds in the banks are proceeds of crime the banks are required to release the identity of the account owner. Funds are transferred into and out of Belize in foreign currencies with no conversion to Belize dollars taking place.

These banks are prohibited from doing business with Belize citizens or legal residents. The offshore banks also comply with UN sanctions and don't accept deposits from citizens of Iran, North Korea, Somalia, Sudan, Ivory Coast and several other countries. Most customers of international banks first establish an International Business Company (IBC). Here's information on some of the larger offshore banks in Belize:

Atlantic International Bank: Owned by Atlantic Bank, this bank offers demand deposit accounts, personal savings accounts (minimum US$1,000) paying around 2.25% at the time of this writing; savings accounts with US$25,000 or more earn 3% interest; time deposits with a minimum of US$20,000 paying between 2.25% and 6%, depending on amount and term; corporate accounts; credit cards and investment/brokerage accounts. Other services include offshore trust services and establishing International Business Companies (IBCs). Main office: Cleghorn St. & Freetown Rd., Belize City; tel. 501 223-0681, fax 223-3528; www.atlanticibl.com.

Belize Caribbean International Bank: A division of Belize Bank Holdings, Belize Caribbean International Bank Ltd. was licensed in 2006. The offshore bank, shares of which are traded on the Trinidad and Tobago Stock Exchange, offers personal demand deposit accounts with a US$1,000 minimum, and CDs with a US$25,000 minimum. It also offers credit cards, corporate accounts and loans. Accounts may be in U.S. dollars, Canadian dollars, euros or U.K. pounds. Main office: 60 Market Square, Belize City; tel. 501-227-0673, fax 227-0983; www.bcbankinternational.com.

Caye International Bank: Opened in 2003, Caye Bank is located in San Pedro. Currently, the bank offers a mix of deposit and loan services to non-residents of Belize, including demand (checking) deposits (minimum US$5,000) currently paying 0.5% to 1.25%, savings deposits (minimum US$5,000) paying .75% to 3%, and CDs (minimum deposit US$25,000, rates subject to negotiation. Main office: Coconut Drive, San Pedro; tel. 501-226-2388, fax 226-2892, www.cayebank.bz.

Provident Bank and Trust: This bank, with an office in Belize City, has been associated with Glenn D. Godfrey, a prominent but controversial attorney and businessman in Belize, and his companies. Demand deposits may be opened with a minimum of U$3,000, savings accounts with US$500, premium savings accounts with US$5,000 and time deposits with a minimum of US$25,000. The bank also offers on-line banking, credit cards and other services. Main office: 35 Barrack Road, Belize City; tel. 501-223-5698, fax 223-0368; www.providentbelize.com.

Belize Banking Differences

Most expats find that banking is a little different in Belize. In most cases, you can't just sashay in to your local bank office and open an account. You usually will be asked for references, including a letter from your former bank. There is no standard format for this reference letter, but it should state something along these lines: "Mr. Jones is currently a customer of our bank and has maintained a satisfactory banking relationship here since 1985. His savings, time and demand deposit accounts with us current total about US$xxx,xxx." The letter should be on the institution's letterhead and signed by an officer.

Commercial banks in some cases may also require that you have some reason before you can open a banking account in Belize, such as owning property, building a house, living in Belize part- or full-time, etc. The off-shore banks in Belize are just the opposite – you can't be a citizen or resident and bank of Belize.

All of which brings us to another key fact about your money and Belize: Keep the bulk of your liquid assets out of Belize. You will probably want to open a checking account in Belize to have easy access to spending money and for handling routine local transactions, such as paying your Belize telephone or electric bill. And if you are in Belize under the Qualified Retired Persons Incentive Program, you are required to deposit US$24,000 a year in a Belize bank. But the savvy expat will maintain a banking relationship in the U.S. or similar country, with the bulk of your demand and deposit cash accounts there. You can then transfer funds by wire or other means to your account in Belize, as needed.

CAUTION: Deposits in Belize banks are not protected by deposit insurance, as they are in the U.S. under the FDIC, and in many other countries. All of your deposits are at risk should the bank fail.

Belize Bank has 12 ATMs around Belize that accept foreign-issued ATM cards on the Visa, MasterCard, Plus, Cirrus and Visa Electron systems. Atlantic Bank has 16 ATMs that accept foreign-issued ATM cards on the Visa, MasterCard, Plus and Cirrus systems. ScotiaBank has 14 ATMs around the country accepting foreign-issued ATM Cards. First Caribbean Bank's six ATMs also accept foreign ATM cards.

You can use these ATMs to tap your bank accounts back home, although you will get cash in Belize in Belize dollars. Alliance Bank (the name is expected to change soon) has ATMs but at present do not accept ATM cards issued outside Belize.

Banking hours are shorter in Belize, typically only until 2 p.m. most days, and in other cases banks close for lunch. Most bank offices have modern conveniences such as ATM machines. While bank personnel in Belize are usually very friendly – this is Belize, after all – you can't always say the same about bank policies, especially for loans. Loan interest rates are high. Even as the U.S. prime rate was down to 4%, Belize banks were getting 12% to 16% or more on business loans and even higher on some personal loans. And the hidden fees and charges can add several percentage points to the loan interest. Modern consumer protection laws haven't all made it to Belize yet.

Savings earn higher interest in Belize than in the U.S. or Canada. In late 2009, for example, money in regular savings accounts in commercial bank in Belize (not offshore banks) earned 5 to 6%. CD rates were higher.

On the road in Cayo District

CHAPTER 21:
MECHANICS OF MOVING TO BELIZE

If you decide to move to Belize, you have several options, including driving down with your household goods and other possessions or shipping them by sea or land. This chapter covers the mechanics of moving, including bringing pets.

Driving to Belize

The drive from Brownsville, Texas, the nearest entry point in the U.S. to Belize, is about 1,250 miles and usually takes three to four days. Total non-stop driving time is around 28 hours.

The fastest route from Brownsville/Matamoros is via Tampico, Tuxpan, Veracruz, Villahermosa and Chetumal. From the border, take Mexico national route 101 to highway 180. Just north of Veracruz, take 150D (a toll road) to Villahermosa. (Alternatively you can stay on highway 180). At Villahermosa, take route 186 for 360 miles to the Belize border (the last 5 miles may be signed as route 307). The toll roads are expensive, around US$10 to $12 for each 100 miles, but you can make 70 mph on them, much faster than on the regular roads.

Driving in Mexico can be confusing, as road through towns and elsewhere are often poorly signed. In general, avoid going through the town centers *(Centro)*, as you can easily get lost and the hotels are more expensive. To enter Mexico (and later, Belize) by car, you need the original plus two copies of your passport, valid driver's license, vehicle registration card, original vehicle title, or if your vehicle is not paid for, a notarized letter of permission from the lien holder. Besides paying the Mexico tourist entry fee of about US$20, which allows entry for up to six months, you have to provide a credit card in lieu of posting a cash bond to guarantee that you will bring the car back out of Mexico. Your credit card (Master Card, Visa, American Express, Diners, which must be in the name of the driver) will be charged US$22.

Upon arrival at the Belize-Mexico border, if you are not returning to the U.S., you must have the Mexican temporary entry permit canceled at Mexican customs. If entering Mexico by car as a tourist, as a resident of the U.S. or Canada you can bring in such personal items as luggage, binoculars, laptop computer, TV, camping equipment, up to three liters of alcohol and fishing equipment. Do NOT even think about bringing in a gun, as you will find yourself in serious trouble. If you are transporting goods of a value of US$1,000 or more and/or are going through Mexico to Belize to stay permanently, you are supposed to use the services of a customs broker at the U.S.-Mexico border and get trans-migratory status, which costs money in fees and, some say, in bribes to Mexican federal officers along the way. A broker at the U.S.-Mexico border will cost you about US$150 to $200. Unless you plan to stay in Belize, it is best just to enter Mexico as a tourist and not go the trans-mig route.

Except on toll roads, driving after dark in Mexico is not advised. You may be stopped frequently for inspections. You should exchange enough U.S. dollars to get you through Mexico, as U.S. dollars are not widely accepted, or are accepted at a low rate of exchange. The exchange rate for U.S. dollars in early 2010 was around 13 pesos to the dollar. Gasoline stations in Mexico usually do not accept credit cards.

Mexican auto insurance is required; liability costs from around US$50 for five days. Collision insurance coverage can add to the cost, depending on the value of your vehicle. Insurance for a month or two, or even six months, is not much more than for a few days.

Here's a typical quote for 7 days:
Liability only: US$85.31
Full coverage for vehicle valued at US$15,000: US$114.25

Six months: US$225.97 for liability; US$391.43 for full coverage
One-year: US$273.84 for liability; US$514.15 for full coverage

Full coverage includes US$150,000 in liability, with a deductible of 2% and minimum of US$500 for cars and US$1,000 for trucks and SUVs; collision and fire and theft up to value of vehicle, with 5% deductible, minimum of US$500 for cars and US$1,000 for trucks and SUVs; some medical; bail bond; towing

You MUST have Mexican auto insurance. Your U.S. or Canadian insurance is NOT valid in Mexico (or Belize.)

Sanborn's (tel. 800-222-0158; www.sanbornsinsurance.com) is a well-known source of information on travel in Mexico and for Mexican auto insurance, although their insurance tends to be more expensive than insurance from most other companies.

Do a Google search for other companies selling Mexican auto insurance, some of which can be purchased on-line in advance. One such is www.mexicanInsurance.com.

Sanborn maps, and in fact most maps to Mexico, may not be completely accurate. The Guia Roji (Red Guide) maps to Mexico are probably the best available, although ITMB maps also are good. A website with all types of helpful information on Mexico is www.mexconnect.com.

On arrival at the Mexico-Belize border, you again need your original title (no photocopies) for your vehicle, or, if you do not own it free and clear, a notarized statement from the lien holder that you have permission to take the car out of the U.S. You also have to buy Belize auto insurance, which is required by law in Belize. There are brokers at the border. Three months of insurance should cost about US$60 to $100, or one month or less about US$35. The cost may be higher depending on the coverage you get. Crossing the border you probably will have to have your car sprayed to kill hitchhiking bugs — the fee is around US$5. If you plan to stay in Belize and keep your vehicle there, you have to pay import duty. The rate varies by number of cylinders and type of vehicle, but it runs about 20% to nearly 80% of book value. *(For more information, see below.)* If you are just visiting, you should not have to pay the import tax, but the car is entered on your passport so you cannot sell it in Belize. Some say that if you want a lower appraisal of value of the vehicle, have it appraised in Belize City. You can have a customs officer drive with you to Belize City for around US$20. However, others claim that appraisals are lower at the border.

If you bring your vehicle in as a tourist and do not pay import duty, and then later decide you want to keep the vehicle in Belize, you may be hit with a fine of US$250 in addition to import duty. So, if you are pretty sure you want to keep the vehicle in Belize, it's usually best to go ahead and pay the import duty when you first enter Belize.

Your Vehicle in Belize

Because Belize is lightly populated and fairly spread out, it's very useful to have a car or truck in Belize. A four-wheel drive is ideal, due to the many unpaved secondary and tertiary roads, which can get very bad during the rainy season. Many people consider a small four-wheel drive truck, such as Toyota Hi-Lux, as the perfect vehicle for Belize. Import duties are only 10% on trucks or vans (not SUVs, which are taxed at the higher auto rates), plus GST of 10%. It is relatively inexpensive to buy new -- US$22,000 to $28,000 including duty. It gets good mileage, which is important when fuel is near US$5 a gallon. The Toyota is a rugged vehicle that holds up well to tough conditions in Belize. Even better is to get a diesel-engine version, as diesel fuel costs about one-third less in Belize than gasoline. Other small cars and trucks are popular in Belize, including Suzuki, Mitsubishi and the smaller

American models such as Ford Ranger and the Jeep Cherokee. With Belize's British heritage, the Range Rover is also popular, especially older models. However, many Belizeans drive older, larger U.S. cars that were brought into Belize before the price of gas went up to its present high levels. Most of the new car dealers in Belize are located in Belize City, with a couple in Belmopan and Spanish Lookout. Among the brands available new are Ford, Toyota, Suzuki, Kia, Land Rover, Jeep, Hyundai, Dodge, Nissan and Mitsubishi. Some Chinese brands are available in Belmopan or Spanish Lookout. Other car brands are in Chetumal, Mexico.

If you live on an island, you probably will not need a car. Smaller islands do not have any roads or vehicles. Caye Caulker has only a few emergency vehicles. Ambergris Caye has too many vehicles for its small size and limited road system and is currently limiting the import of more vehicles to the island. On Ambergris, Caulker and other islands a golf cart is a useful way to get around. You can expect to pay around US$2,000-$4,000 for a used cart in Belize. Maintenance tends to be costly due to the salt air. Replacing the six batteries alone costs US$300 or more.

Liability insurance is mandatory in Belize. If you don't have it and are stopped at a road check, which are common in Belize, you are likely going to be arrested and will spend at least a little time in jail. Happily, auto insurance in Belize is fairly inexpensive. You likely won't pay more than US$200 to $300 a year. Your U.S. or other driver's license is good for up to three months in Belize. After that, you are supposed to get a Belize license. You must be 18 to get a driver's license in Belize. You can obtain a driver's license in Belize City or in larger towns for a fee of US$10. You will have to provide a doctor's statement that you are in good health.

Getting Your Household Goods to Belize
What to Bring
Foreign residents in Belize are split on how much to bring to Belize. Some see a savings in bringing everything you may need to Belize, especially if you have a duty exemption on household goods as an approved permanent resident or as a participant in the Qualified Retired Persons program. On the other hand, many who have moved to Belize say it's best to bring as little as possible with you. After all, you won't need a lot of clothes. You can buy furniture cheaply in Belize, and you can find appliances and other household goods either in Belize City or in Chetumal, Mexico. Amazon.com and other companies will ship books, CDs, and other items to Belize, though international shipping charges may be high. You may want to store most of your household goods in a storage facility back home. Then, after you've been in Belize for a while, on a trip back home you can get items you decide you really need.

Items you probably will want to bring to Belize if you are setting up housekeeping, as these are hard to find or expensive in Belize, or will be expensive to ship later:
  • good-quality sheets and towels
  • high-quality mattresses

- good dishes
- high-quality pots and pans, silverware and other kitchenware
- hobby equipment
- specialized hand and power tools
- fishing and diving gear
- top-end electronics
- books

Shipping Options

You can ship bulky items by sea or overland. Small items can be shipped via the postal system or an air freight service. You can drive your vehicle down through Mexico or ship it by sea.

Ocean Freight

Sending goods in a 20-foot container from Miami is likely to cost you about US$2,000--$2,500, not including import duties. A 40-foot container may cost you US$4,000-$5,000 by the time you get it to your home in Belize, again not including any import duties.

Hyde Shipping is probably the most used and recommended shipping company serving Belize. It offers freight sailings from Port Everglades near Miami to Belize once and sometimes twice a week. Both 20-ft. and 40-ft. containers are available. Contact Hyde in Florida at: 10025 NW 116th Way, Suite 2, Medley, FL 33178; tel: 30-/913-4933, fax 305-913-4900; www.hydeshipping.com. **Tropical Shipping** also offers weekly freight service from Miami Belize. Contact Tropical Shipping, 9505 N.W. 108th Avenue, Miami, FL 33178; tel. 305/805-7400 or 888/578-5851; www.tropical.com.

Other Options for Smaller Shipments

Another good choice is **Sterling Freight** (Mile 63, Western Hwy., Cayo Air Center, Central Farm Airstrip, Cayo; tel. 501-824-2496; www.sterlingfreight.com), which ships to Belize from Houston. Sterling ships via cargo ship and air freight. FCL (Full Container Load) shipments usually are weekly, LCL (Less than Container Load) shipments are approximately monthly, and air freight shipments are twice weekly. If you are not in the Houston area, you can ship to Sterling there. See the website for details. Rates for LCL are charged by the cubic foot. A one-quarter container (667 cubic ft.) from Houston to Belize is around US$4.95 per cubic ft. or a total of US$3,300. One-half and full container rates per cubic foot are lower. Rates include a Belize warehouse storage period up to two free weeks. Any storage after two weeks will incur a charge of US$12.5 cents per cubic foot per week with a minimum charge of US$25. Goods can arrive in Houston anytime before sailing without charges.

There are freight consolidators in Miami who will assemble your goods, crate them where necessary and put them in a full or partial container, for a price. Small items can be shipped to Belize by air or surface mail, which is fairly dependable, or by a fast but expensive airfreight service such as FedEx or DHL. **Speed Cargo** in Miami (9950 NW 17 St., Miami, FL 33172; tel. 305-463-4800) can ship small boxes via freighter - a 20 cubic foot box might cost under US$100.

Overland Freight

You can also move goods to Belize overland, usually from Houston, Texas. An often-recommended mover is **Elbert Flowers,** Cayo Adventure Tours, Santa Elena, Cayo, tel. 501-824-3426, e-mail cattours@btl.net.

Preparing Items for Shipment

When shipping individual packages to Belize, new items require an invoice and used items require a packing list. A packing list is simply a list of the items enclosed in the package with their reasonable resale values. You need to insert one copy of the invoice or packing list into an envelope and tape it to the outside of the package, and mail or fax one copy of it to the freight company in advance of your shipment.

Customs Brokers

Customs brokers in Belize can be very helpful in smoothing the way and in getting materials quickly released from customs. They will meet your goods when they arrive in Belize, fill out the paper work and have the goods forwarded to their final destination in Belize. It will make your life a lot easier if you have a local customs broker working for you. Be sure to check references. Here are some brokers and freight-forwarding agents who have received recommendations from folks moving to Belize:

Billy Valdes, 160 N. Front St. (P.O. Box 4), Belize City, tel. 501-227-7436

George Bradley, 117 Albert St., Belize City, tel. 501-227-0702, fax 501-227-0727

Calbert Reynolds, Belize City, tel. 501-227-0381

Lulett Ramara, Belize City, tel. 501-223-4807, email svet@btl.net

Steve Kuylen, Corozal Town, tel. 501-422-3624 or 501-610-4213

Storage in Belize

What do you do with your goods after you get them to Belize, if your home isn't ready for occupancy? Freight companies usually will store your shipped items in their warehouse, for a fee of around US$12.5 cents per cubic ft. per week. This can add up; storage of a half-container would cost nearly US$700 a month.

Storage facilities in Belize, other than those owned by the government or freight companies, are few and far between. **Edgar's Mini** Storage (1235 Rockfish Dr., Ladyville, tel. 501-602-4513, www.edgarsministorage.com) in the Vista Del Mar area of Ladyville, near Belize City, was the first mini-storage facility in the country. Dave Edgar established it in 2002. The steel storage building has 32 10 x 20 ft. spaces, each with around 1,800 cubic ft. of space. Current rates for a space are US$100 a month on a 12-month lease, US$125 a month on a six-month lease and US$150 on a three-month lease. Rates are plus 10% tax.

Another storage facility is on Ambergris Caye. **Grumpy & Happy Storage** offers an 8-feet wide, 12-feet deep, and 10-feet high container for US$150 a month, plus tax. Larger spaces are also available. Contact Caye

Mini Storage at 501-226-3420, www.belizestorage.com.

Moving with Pets

Dogs and cats can be brought into Belize without quarantine.

Bringing a pet into the country falls under live animal importation and is regulated by the Belize Agricultural Health Authority (BAHA). Dogs and cats are allowed to enter the country provided that owners have a valid import permit, international veterinary certificate, valid rabies vaccination certificate and inspection by quarantine officer at the port of entry. Owners must get a certificate from a veterinarian at the owner's home country. The vet examination must take place within 14 days before arrival in Belize, and the certificate must state that the animal is in good health, is free from infectious diseases and has been vaccinated for rabies not less than one month and no more than one year prior to departure for Belize.

Kittens and puppies under three months of age that can't be vaccinated for rabies can be brought in but must be confined at the owner's home in Belize until they are three months old, at which time they must be vaccinated and then confined at home an additional 30 days.

For other pets, such as ferrets or birds, check with BAHA for the current regulations.

To apply for an import permit, request application form from:

Permit Unit Belize Agricultural Health Authority (BAHA)
Agricultural Showgrounds
Belmopan City, Belize
Tel. 501-822-0197, fax 501-822-0271
www.baha.bz
Email baha@btl.net or animalhealthbz@gmail.com

Return the completed form to Permit Unit of BAHA. The date of arrival must be specified. There is a US$37.50 entry and inspection fee plus US$17.50 fax fee. Approved permits will be faxed to applicant at a cost of US$17.50 to be paid at the point of entry on the day of arrival. If you don't follow this application process, you will be subject to a US$100 violation fine in addition to the US$37.50 entry and inspection fee. In addition, any pet arriving without a valid permit or without a valid rabies vaccination may be confined at the owner's expense until the vaccination is valid.

More information about pets in Belize may be available from vets in Belize, including the following:

Animal Medical Centre (Michael Deshield and Jane Crawford), 1 Lancaster St., Belize City, tel. 501-223-3781

Corozal Veterinary Clinic, 16 San Andres Rd., Corozal Town, tel. 501-422-2519

Transporting Pets to Belize

Small dogs and cats can usually be carried in the cabin of scheduled commercial airlines. Reservations in advance are required, to assure that no more than seven animals are on the flight.

For larger animals, American and Continental are two of the airlines flying into Belize that ship pets. Pets are transported in the pressurized cargo hold. The kennel must be large enough for the animal to turn around in. Pets may not be accepted by the airline if the forecast temperature is above 85 or below 45 degrees F. at any point on the air itinerary; in some cases, the airline may accept a letter from a vet stating that the animal can stand temperatures above or below these points. Charges vary depending on the weight of the animal. Continental, for example, charges about US$250 to fly a 40-pound dog from the U.S. to Belize. Contact the airline in advance to be sure you are following all its rules for pet travel; otherwise, you may be denied boarding.

Yes, There Can Be Import Duty on Pets!

You will not be charged Belize import duty on pets that accompany you on your flight. However, if you ship your pets separately, you will be charged an import duty based on a combination of the freight charges and the value of the animal, plus sales tax. The duty plus sales tax rate is about 50%. Check with Belize Customs to determine the amount of duty.

In-Country Transport

In Belize, both Maya Island and Tropic Air will carry your pet in its kennel. Tropic Air currently charges you for three seats for the pet, plus your own ticket. Maya Island Air currently charges you only for one seat for your pet, plus your town ticket. You must notify the airlines in advance that you are transporting a pet. To San Pedro and Caye Caulker, the Caye Caulker Water Taxi Association boats allow pets to be carried like luggage, at no charge. The San Pedro-Belize Express boats charge US$10. Note that these charges are subject to change.

You can drive through Mexico with your pets. Some cargo services also transport animals.

Will Your Pet Adapt to Belize?

Not all pets adapt well to Belize's subtropical climate. Mange and venereal disease are endemic. Snakebites and scorpion or bee stings can be dangerous or fatal to your pet. Rabies occasionally shows up in rural areas, vectored by vampire bats and other wild things.

Belizean Attitudes Toward Pets

Belizeans generally do not have the same view of pets as do Americans. They rarely allow dogs in the house, for example. Dogs are used more as watchdogs than as companions. You don't see that many cats kept as pets in Belize. In some areas, feral cats are a problem, hunting birds and other wildlife. In rural areas, often you will see a number of wild animals including howler and spider monkeys and the smaller wild cats kept as pets (even though it is may be against the law).

Moving with Children

Belize is a country of young people -- the average age of the population is only 19 -- so your kids will probably have a lot of friends. Belizeans love kids, and kids are welcome almost everywhere. It's rare to find a restaurant or any business that doesn't accept kids. In many respects, most of Belize is the way the U.S. was in the 1950s or earlier: Kids play outside all the time, walk or ride bikes to the store or school, and hang out with friends. There are very few "soccer moms" in Belize spending their days driving their offspring here and there.

Whether your kids adapt well to Belize, or not, depends on what expectations they -- and you -- have. If their lives have revolved around going to the mall, seeing movies every weekend, and eating fast food, they're probably facing a serious adaptation problem, as there are no malls or fast-food places in Belize, and only three movie theaters in the country, one in Belize City at the Princess Hotel with two screens, a new one on Ambergris at Reef Village with two screens and one tiny one with 20 seats in San Ignacio. On the other hand, if they like to be outdoors, and especially if they enjoy activities on the water (no place in Belize is more than a few miles from the sea, a lagoon or bay, or a river) they'll be in heaven.

Young kids do have to be watched, as they may not know the dangers from scorpions, snakes, Africanized bees, and other wild creatures. In Belize City, in some neighborhoods, kids are in danger from gangs and crack heads. Finding toys, children's books, and children's clothes may be a challenge in Belize, especially in rural areas. Libraries are few and far between, and none is large.

Schooling obviously is an issue for expats with children. Schools vary widely in quality of teachers, equipment, and facilities. In rural Toledo, your local school may have few textbooks, no library, and perhaps not even electricity or running water. In Belize City, the best schools are quite good indeed, and motivated students will be well prepared for a rigorous college. Most Belizean schools do teach religion as part of their daily curriculum, and that may be an issue for some families. Some expats home school their kids.

CHAPTER 22:
WORKING OR OPERATING A BUSINESS IN BELIZE

Imagine you're living beside the blue Caribbean Sea. You spend your days snorkeling, diving and fishing. Now imagine you get paid to do this. You pay your way through paradise by working as a dive master, or guiding tourists, or tending bar in a little thatch hut. Or you run a little hotel by the sea, welcoming guests and raking in the dough.

I'm afraid reality check is required. About one in ten Belizeans is out of work, and those with jobs often don't make enough to live above the poverty level. The few good jobs that are available in Belize are mostly reserved for Belizeans. Many occupations, including tour guiding and waiting tables and bartending, are reserved for Belize citizens only. Residents under the Qualified Retired Persons Incentive Act can't work for pay at all. Even if you were able to legally get a job, salaries in Belize are far below those in the U.S., Canada or Western Europe, and even physicians, college teachers and other professionals may earn under US$15,000 a year. While some hotel and resort owners and other expat business owners in Belize do pretty well, others barely eek out a living. Costs are higher than they planned for, and the frustrations of doing business in Belize are far more numerous than they expected.

I do know expatriates who have carved out a comfortable niche for themselves in Belize, either working for an established Belizean company or running their own business. It is possible to do so, but it's not easy. After all, it's the United States that is the land of opportunity for job seekers and entrepreneurs. Millions of people around the world vie to get a green card to let them live and work in the States. More than 100,000 Belizeans have left Belize to work and find their fortunes, legally or illegally, in the U.S. You're going to leave the U.S. with all its opportunity, resources and huge base of consumers and set up shop or find a job in poor little Belize, with its tiny population and economic resources of a small American town? If you can't make it in the U.S., how do you expect to make it in Belize?

There are good reasons why someone might decide to move to Belize and work or invest there, mostly having to do with quality of life, but economic rewards and an easy road to fortune are not among them.

The Reality of Investing in Belize

John Lankford, a New Orleans lawyer who lived for several years in San Pedro before selling his property and moving back to the U.S., put the situation bluntly: "As to investing, first realize that when Belize's government or general population speaks or thinks of foreigners 'investing in Belize' they mean bringing money and handing it over. They also contemplate a long-term, possibly permanent, commitment. They are not so solicitous of your expectations to realize a RETURN on your investment, and in some cases tend to think it craven of a 'rich' first-world person to try to make money off poor Belize. The approved motivation for investing in Belize is for the benefit of Belize. The investor's benefit is gratification at helping Belize advance, and any other motivation may be seen as exploiting rather than investing. As a general rule, don't even dream of investing in Belize unless you plan to be present with your eyes on your investment every day."

Starting and Running Your Own Business

With good-paying jobs few and far between, most foreigners who want to generate an income in Belize will be looking at operating a business. The Belize government says it welcomes investors who can contribute to the Belize economy and provide work for Belizeans, particularly in tourism, agriculture and manufacturing. But it's rarely simple or easy to do business in Belize. A timeworn saying in Belize, worth repeating again, is that if you want to make a small fortune in the country, better start with a big one. Belize's small domestic market, inefficient distribution and marketing systems, heavy-handed government red tape and other factors make it difficult for entrepreneurs to achieve great success in Belize.

What Type of Business?

Several types of businesses require special permits or licenses, and these may not be granted to non-Belizeans. The idea is to avoid permitting non-Belizeans to take jobs from Belizeans. The following businesses are, in varying degrees, are not usually open to foreigners: Commercial fishing, sugar cane cultivation, restaurants and bars (not associated with a resort), legal and accounting services, small retail shops, beekeeping, beauty shops, sightseeing tours and operation of bus, water taxi or domestic airlines.

Businesses that are most likely to succeed in Belize include export-oriented operations whose main markets are outside Belize. The Belize market itself is small and spread out, and average Belizeans don't have the income to buy much beyond the basic necessities of life. Niche export products such as specialty or organic agricultural products may have a future. Also workable are well-marketed resorts or lodges that target international visitors and, in addition, the companies that cater to them — for example, companies that provide specialty herbs, fruits and gourmet vegetables to larger resorts.

However, the difficulty of making a go in tourism in Belize is shown by the number of hotels that are actively on the market at any one time. In the San Ignacio area, for example, at any one time about one-fourth of the hotel properties are actively for sale, and other owners likely would quickly sell for the right offer. With hotel occupancies in Belize averaging only about 40% occupancy nationally, it is difficult to earn an adequate return. Only in San Pedro, which gets a regular flow of tourists year-round, do hotels appear to be more consistently profitable. The typical small hotel in Belize can't afford to do the international advertising and marketing necessary to compete with larger, better-capitalized resorts in other parts of the Caribbean.

Quite a few expats gravitate to selling or developing real estate. Some have been successful; many have not.

Unemployment in Belize is stubbornly high, yet many of the best-trained and ambitious Belizean workers have moved to the U.S. This brain drain means that it's difficult to find skilled, motivated employees. In rural areas, many Belizeans have never held a regular job. Training must start with the basics like showing up on time and coming to work every day. Another problem is that the cost of labor in Belize, while low compared with the U.S., is relatively high compared with some other developing countries. The minimum wage in Belize is around US$1.50 an hour for most workers, but that's several times the minimum wage of workers in Honduras or Nicaragua. The minimum wage in Mexico is around US$4 a day, less than one-half that of Belize. Most workers in Belize do earn more than the minimum wage.

Belizean workers also have comparatively strong workplace protections, including mandatory two weeks' paid vacation and participation in Belize's Social Security system, mostly funded by employer contributions of about 5% to 6.5% of wages (the percentage varies depending on the wage of the worker), 13 paid holidays, 16 days of sick leave annually and a required two weeks' notice or pay in lieu of that notice should the employee be terminated after having been on the job at least a year. The workweek cannot exceed six days or 45 hours. Businesses in highly competitive export industries may be at a disadvantage if they are located in Belize.

Capital for Business

In Belize as in most countries it is difficult to borrow money to start a business. For successful, on-going businesses loans from Belize banks may be available but typically at higher interest rates than prevailing in the U.S. In recent years, 12 to 16% has been the usual rate for business loans. Business people in Belize complain that in some cases hidden fees and charges for business loans add to the overall cost. The Belize Development Finance Corporation, a government-owned entity whose mission is to help develop the Belize economy, did make loans for developing new tourism and agricultural projects, but the DFC is now in reorganization following scandals about management and its lending practices under the last PUP government.

Incentive Programs

Belize has several incentive schemes designed to encourage investment in the country, including the Fiscal Incentives Act, the International Business and Public Companies Act, Export Processing Zone Act and Commercial Free Zone Act. However, a U.S. Commerce Department advisory notes, "many foreign investors have complained that these investment promotion tools are rarely as open and effective as they are portrayed." The programs of most interest to those thinking of starting a business in Belize are the Export Processing Zone Act, the Commercial Free Zone Act and the Fiscal Incentives Act. For more information on these programs, you should contact Belize Trade & Development Service (BELTRAIDE), 14 Orchid Garden St., Belmopan; tel. 501-822-3737; fax 822-0595; e-mail beltraide@belizeinvest.org.bz, www.belizeinvest.org.bz.

The International Business Companies Act (IBC) makes it possible for foreign companies to get tax exemptions on all income of the IBC, all dividends paid by an IBC, all interest rents, royalties to non-Belizean residents and capital gains realized. There are several thousand companies registered as IBC's in Belize. However, IBCs are not available to citizens or official residents of Belize.

Working in Belize

In theory, unless you are a Belize citizen or a permanent resident under the regular permanent residency program (as a resident under the Qualified Retired Persons Incentive Act program you can't work for pay, though you can own a business or rental property in Belize) you cannot work in Belize without a work permit from the government. You also need a Belize Social Security card. In practice, we have heard about a few foreigners without work permits who have part-time jobs and take in-kind or cash payments. If you're caught working without a permit, however, both you and your employer could be in trouble. You could be deported, or even jailed, and fines are imposed on employers found with illegal workers. The new UDP government has cracked down on foreigners working in Belize, and on at least a couple of occasions senior management at resorts alleged to be working without a work permit were arrested and jailed.

There are two types of work permits. One is a work permit that is obtained by an employer in Belize for an employee. The employer has to prove that the company can't fill the job with a Belizean and has exhausted all avenues for finding a qualified Belizean applicant, including advertising the position for at least three weeks. Examples of jobs that may require a foreign applicant are hotel restaurant chef or a specialized computer software engineer. Application must be made by the employer to the Immigration Department with proof that the foreign employee is qualified, three passport photos, a valid passport and a small application fee.

Another type of work permit is the temporary self-employment certificate. This category applies to foreign investors and others seeking self-employment or who are starting a business in Belize, where it is assumed that the venture will lead to the creation of jobs for Belizeans. The applicant has to show proof of adequate funds for the proposed venture — for example, a bank statement. Also, the applicant has to have a reference from the relevant government Ministry or other organization showing that the venture is reasonable. If opening a tourist operation a reference from the Ministry of Tourism or the local village or town council where the operation is to be located may be required. For the temporary self-employment certificate the residency period is waived.

Work permit fees as of 2005:

Professional workers	US$1,500
Technical workers	US$1,000
Self-employed workers	US$1,000
Religious/voluntary workers	US$100
Entertainers, in groups	US$500 to $750
General workers in banana, citrus and sugar industries	US$100

Permits must be renewed annually and the above fees paid each year. With rare exceptions, work permits are not granted for waiters, domestic workers, farm hands and anyone involved in retail or other types of sales. For information and application forms, contact the Immigration and Nationality Department in Belmopan. If that sounds like a lot of red tape, it is. The Belize government is trying to discourage foreigners from working in jobs in Belize that Belizeans can perform. Belize is also trying to discourage illegal immigration from Guatemala and other Central American countries.

Tammy Martinez, who moved to Ambergris Caye from Florida, says, "It was very hard for me to find work. My husband found work as a bartender the first week we were here, but he is Belizean, so he didn't have the problem of a work permit to deal with. I found that businesses are reluctant to hire you if you don't already have a permit in hand. The problem is, the price of work permits has gone up for professionals. None of the employers want to spend that amount of money when they don't know if you will stay or go."

Another American, Katie Valk, who was an executive in the music business in New York City before moving to Belize about 20 years ago, recalls the frustrations of trying to get a work permit: "It was not at all difficult adjusting. Belize was a perfect fit for me. Finding work wasn't a problem for me, either. Getting a work permit was, however, and it took a tremendous amount of stick-to-it-ness, patience and energy. But I finally got that, then my residency and now I'm seconds away from being a citizen."

Typical Salaries in Belize

Salaries and wages in Belize vary widely, even for the same position, just as they do in the U.S. or Canada. Overall, wage levels in Belize are about one-fourth of those in the U.S., or lower, although a few business people and entrepreneurs in Belize make as much or more than their American counterparts. In general, wages are highest in Belize City and San Pedro and lowest in remote rural areas. All figures are in U.S. dollars:

Maid/Domestic Worker	$10-$20 per day
Day Laborer	$15-$25 per day
Skilled Carpenter or Mason	$25-$40 per day
Nurse	$8,000 per year
Doctor in Public Health Care	$10,000-$20,000 per year
Primary School Teacher	$8,000 a year
High School Teacher	$10,000 a year
Sixth Form or College Professor	$12,000-$18,000 a year
Shop Clerk	$90-$125 a week
Office/Clerical Worker	$100-$125 a week
Secretary	$125-$150 a week
Lodge/Resort Workers	$15-$25 a day
Minimum Hourly Wage	$1.50 a hour

CHAPTER 23:
DAILY LIFE IN BELIZE

What's daily life like in Belize? Of course, it varies from person to person in Belize as it does anywhere in the world. But here's a composite picture of a typical week in the life of an expat living in the Corozal area.

Monday You get up around 6 a.m. and watch the sun rise over Corozal Bay, while enjoying your regular breakfast of fresh fruit. This morning it's bananas and watermelon. The bananas cost about 5 U.S. cents each at the market, and the watermelon was about US$3. Here, only about 17 degrees north of the equator, the sun rises about this time every day and goes down again about 12 hours later. There's only a limited variation in the length of the day. You sit on your screened porch with a view of the bay. The weather is warm, as usual in the high 60s or low 70s F. this time of day. A refreshing breeze from the water eliminates the need for air-conditioning. The only time you turn on your small unit in your bedroom is in the summer, when there are still periods when the prevailing offshore breezes die down, sometimes for a couple of weeks at a time. After breakfast, you putter around in your yard, tending the fruit trees. You have lime, mango, star fruit and banana. Then you decide to go into town to buy some groceries and do your banking. You stop and get some gas at the Shell station. It costs nearly BZ$120, US$60, for a little over 12 gallons to fill up your Jeep. Then you go to the grocery. It's about the size of a large convenience store in the U.S. You buy two pounds of red beans (US$1.60) and a fifth of One Barrel rum (US$9). Before the ScotiaBank office closes, you stop in and cash a check on your local account. You decide to have lunch at the new location of Patty's. Stew chicken with beans and rice and a Belikin come to US$5. After lunch, you come home and take a siesta. You watch a little cable TV, and then you and your partner decide to go out to dinner. For a splurge, you decide to go to Tony's. You sit in the seaside palapa, with a breeze off the bay, and enjoy chicken fajitas and rum and tonics for under US$30 for two.

Tuesday After breakfast, you get ready to drive down to Belize City to take care of some business with your attorney. It's the maid's day to come in. You pay her US$20 a day. It's about a two-hour drive to Belize City, unless you're slowed down by the big sugar cane trucks that jam the highways at harvest time. Traffic is light all the way on the paved two-lane road. The only town of any size between Corozal and Belize City is Orange Walk Town, which looks much like a small town in Mexico. Just south of Orange Walk at the New River is Belize's only road toll -- BZ75 cents. As you approach the outskirts of Belize City, traffic tightens up. Cars pass right and left, apparently heedless of pedestrians along the road or any speed limit signs. At one of the new roundabouts coming into Belize City, traffic is backed up. Until the last few years, the entire country of Belize only had a couple of red lights. Now there are quite a few in Belize City and a handful elsewhere. As usual, you get turned around in Belize City. It's not a big city, hardly more than an overgrown town, but the narrow streets lined with ramshackle buildings confusingly end up at canals and suddenly turn one-way. The city has a colorful street life, with people of all races and backgrounds jostling for space and sharing a word. Finally you get to Albert Street, where your attorney has her office. Luckily you find a parking place on a side street, though you worry that leaving your vehicle parked here is asking for trouble. As you walk to the office, you're approached by a thin Creole who tries to sell you weed. You tell him you don't need any marijuana today, and he goes on his way. Since moving to Belize, you've picked up a little Creole -- most everybody in Belize knows how to *wap wa li Kriol,* or speak some Creole. You've also learned some Spanish, helpful in Corozal. After you finish your legal business, you return to your car and find it undisturbed. Nearby you see a tour bus full of pale-skinned, plump Americans, gawking at the street life of the city. A cruise ship must be in town. The Belize government, seeking the revenue from port charges, has encouraged the cruise companies to stop in Belize City. On some days, there are three or four ships in port at once, with thousands of day trippers tendered into the Tourist Village, built expressly for cruise industry. The harbor is too shallow to allow the big ships to dock. On your way back to Corozal, you stop for a late lunch at Victor's restaurant, at Petville near Orange Walk Town. It's a little joint serving Creole and Maya dishes. You decide just to have the roast pork with rice and beans. It's hot, close to 90 degrees, and a cold Belikin tastes good. Lunch comes to a little over US$8. After you get back home, you do some research on the Internet. With your new satellite dish, you get fast access, especially for downloads, though you notice the latency problem sometimes. You pay around US$60 a month, plus installation was about a grand. Technically, Starband isn't sold in Belize, but since you have a U.S. address for billing and a U.S. credit card, you had no problem getting it set up. A lot of businesses and hotels, along with some individuals, use satellite for Internet access, although DSL is becoming available and access via digital cable is offered in Belize City and a couple of other areas. Unfortunately, the power goes out. Power in Northern Belize comes from Mexico, and occasionally -- sometimes more than occasionally -- there are blackouts. This time, the power is off for about three hours. There's no explanation of why it went out.

Wednesday You decide to get in a little fishing today. So, early in the morning, you head out with a friend who has a small powerboat. After about an hour on the bay, you make a stop in the fishing village of Sarteneja to check out a skiff a fellow there has for sale. Sarteneja boat builders are known all over Belize. Then you grab a cold Fanta at Fernando's restaurant. You spend a few hours trolling for snapper, and you also catch and release a couple of tarpon. Your friend free dives and eventually comes up with three conchs. Heading home, you make plans next week to go diving on the reef north of San Pedro, as there's no good diving or snorkeling in the bay. After a home-cooked dinner of conch civeche and grilled snapper, you watch TV and retire early.

Thursday Today, you decide to poke around the house, doing some repairs and piddling in your garden. Not everything grows well in the thin limestone-rich soils of Northern Belize, but you've had good luck with tomatoes, peppers, several kinds of squash including cho-cho, which your neighbors say looks like the face of an old granny without teeth, and all kinds of herbs including lemongrass and basil.

Friday A lower molar is giving you a little problem, so you call a dentist you know in Chetumal, and his office says you can come in at 11 this morning. You drive to the border and then to your dentist's office in Chetumal. The office is modern and clean and seems to have all the latest equipment. Your dentist says a filling has come out, and he replaces it. The cost? US$50. It might have cost you US$200 in the States. Then you visit San Francisco, a large supermarket in Chetumal, where you pick up some antibiotics and other medicines for your partner. You don't need a prescription, and the total cost is less than one-half what you'd pay in the U.S. You have lunch at Los Cocos, where an expansive meal with good Mexican beers came to less than US$9. You take in a first-run movie (in English with Spanish subtitles) at the multiplex at the mall. At Sam's Club you buy a new blender for your kitchen. Since you're a permanent resident, the US$18.75 exit fee from Belize to cross the land border into Mexico or Guatemala doesn't apply, though coming back you pay US$5 in duty and GST on the blender.

Saturday After running errands, you stop by Xaibe village to pick up some hand-pressed coconut oil. Some locals claim the amber-colored liquid is a super food and good for all kinds of medical ailments. In the afternoon, you invite friends over for a cookout. The grind meat (Belizean for ground beef) for hamburgers isn't as good as you'd like, but it's a successful party nonetheless. After the meal, you sit out on the deck and look at the lights from Chetumal across the bay.

Sunday You go to church in Corozal Town, and then after a light lunch at home, you drive a few miles up to the Four-Mile Lagoon for a dip in the lagoon and a cold drink at the Cool Spot. After reading for a while, you snack on fresh fruit for Sunday supper, then go to bed early. You have to be rested and ready for another hard week in paradise.

Belize visitor enjoys a cold Belikin and coconut shrimp at Blue Water Grill in San Pedro

CHAPTER 24:
SEEING THE COUNTRY ON A CHECK-IT-OUT VISIT

Before you get very far along in thinking about Belize as a place to live or retire or for a vacation home, you MUST visit Belize and see it for yourself. Don't sit at your computer dreaming about this little English-speaking paradise – come see for yourself if it's for you.

Entry and Exit Requirements: You must have a valid passport to enter Belize, with at least six months before expiration, but visas are not required for citizens of the U.S., Canada, the U.K. and most Caribbean and European Union countries. You should also have an onward or return ticket. Immigration in Belize won't ask for it, but the airline you fly in on most likely will. Entry is granted for up to 30 days, with renewals of up to a total of six months permitted (renewals cost US$25 per month for the first six months, then US$50 a month.) When leaving Belize by air, there is a US$39.25 exit fee for those who are not citizens or official residents of Belize, who pay a lower rate. The fees also apply to QRP participants. Many airlines include the fee in the ticket price. When leaving by land, at either the Benque Viejo border with Guatemala or Corozal border with Mexico, or by sea, there is a US$15 border fee, plus a $3.75 conservation fee, for a total of US$18.75. Students with valid student ID pay US$7.50. Children under 12 accompanied by parents are exempt.

What to Pack and Bring: Belize is a very casual country. You don't need evening clothes or even a coat and tie or other U.S.-style business dress. You'll live in tee shirts, shorts, loose-fitting slacks and shirts. A really dressy occasion for men might require a guayaberra or collared shirt and long pants; for women a simple skirt or dress. Leave all your fancy jewelry and Rolex watches at home. They will impress only thieves. Also leave your rain gear at home. It probably will rain, but raincoats just make you sweat.

Here are ideas for your packing list:

Lightweight cotton clothes or quick-drying cotton/synthetic blends.

Comfortable walking shoes. Consider light boots or walking shoes for hiking and sandals for the beach.

Extra swimsuits.

Maps, guidebooks and reading material. If available at all in Belize, these will cost more than back home and may be out of date.

Cap or hat — be sure it's one that won't blow off in windy conditions on the water.

Sunglasses — the darker the better.

Small flashlight with extra batteries, baggies in various sizes, a roll of duct tape, a large garbage bag, pen and writing pad, and Swiss Army-style knife — with these you can go anywhere and do almost anything.

Extra film, camera battery or the digital equivalent — you'll shoot many more photos in Belize than you think you will. Film is readily available in Belize, but it's expensive.

Health kit consisting of your prescription medicines and a copy of your eyeglass prescription, plus aspirin, insect spray with 30% DEET, sunscreen (more than you think you'll need), baby oil or Avon Skin-So-Soft for sandflies, Pepto-Bismol or other tummy medicine, bandages, sun-burn lotion, toilet tissue, moist wipes, seasick pills and other over-the-counter medicines.

Optional:

Battery-operated radio if coming during peak tropical storm/hurricane season (July-November).

Snorkel mask — you can rent snorkel and dive gear in Belize, but rental masks often don't fit well.

Fishing gear.

Cotton sweater or light jacket may be needed in the winter, especially on the water or in the higher elevations of the Mountain Pine Ridge.

Frisbees and baseball-style caps with U.S. sports logos make good small gifts for kids.

School supplies also make good gifts for kids.

Money and Credit Cards: U.S. dollars (bills, not coins) are accepted everywhere in Belize, at a fixed rate of 2 Belize dollars to 1 U.S. dollar, although you often will receive change in Belizean money, or in a mix of Belizean and U.S. money. While there's no need to exchange U.S. dollars, sometimes you will get a better rate than 2 to 1 by exchanging at the border with moneychangers. Particularly in the early fall, when there is often a shortage of U.S. dollars in Belize, you may be able to get up to 2.10 to 2.20 Belize for each U.S. dollar.

Canadian dollars, Euros and other currencies are not widely accepted. These should be exchanged at banks or moneychangers. The Belize Bank branch at Goldson International Airport offers currency exchange seven days a week. Traveler's checks in U.S. dollars are still accepted by most hotels and at some stores, restaurants and other businesses, but the use of traveler's checks is becoming less common due to the prevalence of ATM machines. You usually need to show your passport when paying with a traveler's check. Banks and some businesses only give about 1.96 Belize to 1 U.S. for traveler's checks.

Visa and Master Card are widely accepted, except at small shops. American Express is accepted by some hotels and larger businesses. Discover, Diners and other cards are rarely accepted. Sometimes there is a surcharge for credit card use, usually 3 to 5% but occasionally as much as 10%. Surcharges are becoming less common, due to complaints by consumers and moves by credit card issuers. Ask about surcharges before using your card. In addition to a possible local surcharge, increasingly credit card companies are levying international currency conversion fees, from 1 to 3% or even higher. Most products and services in Belize will be charged in Belize dollars, so the currency conversion charges apply. Even if the charges are listed in U.S. dollars, some credit card companies charge an international exchange fee anytime a charge is made outside your home country.

As explained elsewhere, most bank offices in Belize have modern ATM machines, and now ATMs at Belize Bank, Atlantic Bank, First Caribbean International Bank and ScotiaBank accept ATM cards issued outside Belize. If you can't tap your funds with your ATM card, most banks in Belize will issue an advance on your Visa or MasterCard. The fee for this is usually less than US$10, depending on the bank, plus whatever fees and interest your bankcard charges. Getting a cash advance may take a little time and paperwork.

Your bank back home may levy a foreign ATM fee of up to US$5 per ATM use, plus a foreign transaction fee of 1 to 3% of the money withdrawn, and the local bank in Belize may also hit you with a fee, so try to minimize the number of ATM withdrawals you make.

Savvy travelers bring a combination of cash in small U.S. currency denominations, an ATM card and credit cards, along with a few traveler's checks, just in case.

Dress: Belize is a casual place. You don't need evening clothes or a coat and tie or other U.S.-style business dress. Heavy winter clothes are unneeded, though a light cotton sweater will come in handy at times. Most of the year, you'll live in tee shirts and shorts or other casual clothes.

Best Times to Visit Belize: Anytime is a good time to visit, but here are the "best times" for different activities and budgets:

Best time to avoid tourists: September-October
Best time to avoid rain: February through April
Best time for underwater visibility: March-June
Best time for lowest hotel prices: After Easter to U.S. Thanksgiving
Best time to visit Toledo District and the far south: February-May
Best time to visit Cayo: October-February (when it's not so hot)
Best time to visit Placencia: January-May
Best time to visit cayes: December-July
Best time to avoid hurricanes and tropical storms: December-June

Air Travel to Belize: At present, five international airlines fly to Belize: American, Continental, Delta, USAir and TACA. The gateways from the U.S. are Houston, Dallas, Miami, Charlotte, Atlanta and Newark. TACA has service from San Salvador. Maya Island Air has daily service between Belize City and Cancun, Guatemala City and San Pedro Sula, Honduras. Tropic Air has daily service between Belize City and Flores/Santa Elena, Guatemala.

The airlines use mostly 737 or other smaller equipment to Belize, with the usual tight seating in coach and grossly overpriced seating in first or business class, if there is any seating at all beyond coach.

Flights from Atlanta, Miami, Dallas, Charlotte and Houston take two to three hours. At present there is no scheduled non-stop or direct service from Canada or Europe. In-season, there is one weekly charter, in winter only, from Toronto, via Roatán. There is currently no service from Europe.

One of the chief complaints from Belize travelers is the high cost of airfare. Tickets from the U.S. to Cancun or Cozumel often are one-half the cost of tickets to Belize City. From the chief gateways you can expect to pay US$500 to $800 round-trip. Airlines flying to Belize occasionally have Internet specials with prices as low as US$300, but you have to act fast as the windows for purchase and travel are narrow.

Our advice: Sign up for Internet fare notices on the airlines that fly to Belize. Keep checking the on-line reservation sites such as Expedia.com or Travelocity.com. Also check meta-reservation sites – they compare fares from a variety of other sites – such as Kayak.com. A travel agent specializing in Belize, such as Barb's Belize (tel. 915-760-6399 or toll-free 888-321-2272, fax 915-760-6497, www.barbsbelize.com) may be able to find lower fares for you. The owner, Barbara Kasak, is very knowledgeable about Belize.

Another source of air fare deals and hotel and tour bookings in Belize is Katie Valk, an American who has lived in Belize for many years; e-mail her at info@belize-trips.com or visit www.belize-trips.com.

Another idea is to fly into Cancun or Cozumel on a cheap scheduled or charter flight and bus it from there. See below for tips on how to do this. An option that became available in 2009 is to fly from Cancun to Belize City on Maya Island Air (www.mayaregional.com).

Arriving by Air -- What to Expect: The Belize International Airport (also known as the Phillip S. W. Goldson International Airport, named after a long-time People's United Party politician) is about 9 miles north of the center of Belize City, off the Northern Highway at Ladyville. The airport is small but fairly modern, having opened in 1990. A new domestic terminal area opened in late 1998. After your airplane taxis to the terminal building, you disembark the old-fashioned way, down a set of stairs. You cross the tarmac and enter the immigration and customs area. Most days, you feel the humidity right away. The immigration officer will look at your passport and usually ask the purpose of your visit and how long you are staying. You can be granted a visitor's entry permit of up to 30 days, but that's not automatic. If you say you are staying 10 days, the officer may grant only that period or two weeks at most. If you think there's any chance you may want to stay a little longer than your current reservations, be generous about estimating the time you'll stay. The officer will then stamp your passport and enter the arrival and departure date.

From here, you move to a small baggage claim area, where there is a small duty-free shop selling duty-free liquor and a few other items. (When entering Belize, you are permitted to bring in only one liter of alcohol, but you can buy an additional four and a half liters of booze at the airport arrival duty-free shop, where you need to pay in U.S. dollars.) You then go through customs. Belize now has a Green/Red customs system. If you have nothing to declare, you can go through the Green line, though an officer may still ask to see inside your bags. On a typical flight, probably one-third of passengers have at least one bag inspected briefly. Customs and immigrations officers generally are courteous and efficient, though like government officials in most countries they are not known for being overly friendly. Treat them with respect, and you'll be treated similarly. Do not even think of offering a bribe. That is not how things work in Belize, at least not at this level. The entire immigration and customs process usually takes from 15 minutes to half an hour.

After your bags pass customs, you can go into the main airport lobby or out to the taxi or rental car area. Porters are available to assist with bags, if necessary. A tip of US$1 per bag is standard. If you are continuing on a domestic flight, move quickly to the Maya Island Air or Tropic check-in area, as the domestic carriers use small airplanes, and they fill up quickly. The rectangular passenger lobby, which is usually bustling with people, has a Belize Bank office (you do NOT need to change U.S. dollars to Belize dollars —see above), a few tourist shops and airline ticket counters. Upstairs to your left are bathrooms (clean) and a restaurant. There is another restaurant in the new terminal section.

Taxis are available right outside the passenger lobby door. The cabs at the airport – they have green license plates — are regulated and you shouldn't be ripped off. The fare is fixed at US$25 or BZ$50 to anywhere in Belize City — that's for the cab, not per person, although a small additional amount may be charged for extra luggage. In Belize, you do not need to tip taxi drivers unless they perform extra service such as carrying luggage. There are no airport shuttles into Belize City, and no buses. If you have the energy to carry your bags, you can walk almost 2 miles to the Northern Highway, or pay a taxi around US$4 to take you there, and flag down a bus to take you into Belize City (about US$1).

Rental car kiosks, including local offices of international franchised auto rental companies including Avis, Budget, Hertz and Thrifty, along with locals Crystal, Jabiru and others, are across the street on the other side of the airport parking area, a short distance. A modest hotel, the Embassy, is on the airport grounds, within walking distance just beyond the parking lot. There also is a small motel, Global Village Hotel, on the Northern Highway just south of the airport entrance road, and this hotel usually will provide a free shuttle from and to the airport.

Buses: Travel by bus in Belize is inexpensive. You can travel the whole length of the country from the Mexican border in the north to Punta Gorda in the far south for about US$20 or go from Belize City to San Ignacio in the west for US$4. It's also a good way to meet local people and to get a real feel for the country.

Bus travel in Belize falls somewhere between the chicken bus experience in rural Guatemala and the deluxe coaches with comfortable reserved seats and videos in Mexico. Buses are usually recycled American school buses or old Greyhound diesel pushers. On the Northern and Western Highway routes, a few buses are modern coaches offering "premier" express service at slightly higher rates. There is no bus service from point to point within Belize City; you either have to take taxis or walk or being going on a regular bus route out of the city.

The country has a franchised bus system, with the government granting rights for certain companies to operate on specific routes. Belize City is the hub for bus service throughout Belize. National Transport, a successor to Novelo's, is the largest of several dozen small bus companies. Bus companies authorized to operate in Northern Belize are National Transport, Belize Bus Owners Cooperative (BBOC), Russell, Tillett's, T-Line, Chell, Gilharry and Venus. Companies authorized to operate in Western Belize include National Transport, BBOC, Middleton's, D&E, Guerra's and Shaw. On the Southern Belize routes bus companies include James Line, Usher and G-Line.

In some cases you can make advance reservations with the larger bus operations by calling the bus companies, although most people don't make reservations. If boarding at a terminal, you pay for your ticket at the window and get a reserved seat. If boarding elsewhere, you pay the driver's assistant.

Air: Belize has two domestic carriers, Tropic Air tel. (501-226-2012, www.tropicair.com) and Maya Island Air (501- 223-1140, www.mayaregional.com).

Which is better? It's a toss-up. For years, Tropic was larger, but with new owners, Maya Island is expanding, adding new aircraft and building new terminals (at Belize municipal, Placencia and elsewhere). Maya Island also has added regional service to Cancun, Guatemala City and San Pedro Sula, Honduras. Both have pretty good safety records and very similar prices. For most people, the decision comes down to which airline has the more convenient flight. Tropic and Maya both fly to Ambergris and Caye Caulker as well as Dangriga, Placencia, Punta Gorda, Corozal Town, along with a few other stops. Tropic Air also goes to Flores, Guatemala.

Domestic flights from the municipal airport, about a mile from the center of Belize City, are up to one-half cheaper than from the international airport. For example, a flight to San Pedro on Ambergris Caye costs approximately US$120 round-trip from international, and US$67 round-trip from municipal. There is only a small saving on roundtrip over two one-way fares, and except for occasional off-season specials, fares are about the same year-round, with no advance-purchase or other discounts. Sometimes you can get a 10% to 25% discount by paying cash rather than paying by credit card. It pays to ask.

The airlines fly only during daylight hours, except at peak times when the airlines have permission to continue flying into San Pedro until all waiting passengers are taken care of. Currently both airlines have five or six flights a day going south, running every couple of hours from both Belize City airports, usually stopping at Dangriga, Placencia and Punta Gorda. Both airlines also have about a dozen flights a day between Belize City and San Pedro; many, but not all, flights to and from international make stops at municipal. At present flights to and from Corozal Town are through San Pedro, and flights to Guatemala City and Flores, Guatemala, Cancun and San Pedro Sula, Honduras, use the international airport only.

Are advance air reservations necessary? Except at peak high-season travel periods, you can probably get on a convenient flight without advance reservations. Even with reservations on busy days it's often first-come, first-served. Still, having a reservation gives you a little extra edge, and we recommend you book ahead. It's essential you do so at holiday periods such as Easter and Christmas.

Shuttles: If you are going to Cayo, you may want to use a shuttle service, as there is no air service to San Ignacio. Most hotels and lodges will arrange van transfers for guests to and from the international airport in Belize City for US$125-$200 for up to four passengers. The Aguada Hotel (tel. 501-804–3609), PACZ Tours (tel. 501-824-0536, www.pacztours.net) and William's Shuttle (email belizeshuttle@yahoo.com) are among several Cayo operators that offer van service to and from Belize City, at around US$45-$75 per person. A Guatemalan company, Linea Dorado, offers daily shuttle service between Chetumal and Flores, with pick-ups in Belize City at the Marine Terminal (US$35 from Chetumal to Flores). Another Guatemalan company, San Juan, also offers buses to Flores. Price is around US$25 from Belize City to Flores.

Water Taxis: If you are going to San Pedro or Caye Caulker, you have the option of taking a water taxi. Two water taxi companies, with fast boats that hold up to 100 passengers, connect Belize City with Ambergris Caye (US$12.50 one-way) and Caye Caulker (US$7.50 one-way), each with eight to ten departures a day. **Caye Caulker Water Taxi** boats depart from the Marine Terminal near the Swing Bridge; **San Pedro-Belize Express**

boats leave from a dock near the Tourism Village. Despite their names, both water taxi companies have service to both Caye Caulker and San Pedro. It's a 45-minute ride to Caulker and 75 minutes to San Pedro. Boats stop on demand at Caye Chapel. A San Pedro- Belize Express water taxi also runs twice daily between Corozal Town and San Pedro (US$22.50 one way, 2 hours), with a stop at Sarteneja on demand. Two local ferry companies, **Island Ferry** and **Coastal Xpress**, provide scheduled boat transportation up and down Ambergris Caye. To get to the water taxi terminals in Belize City from the international airport is a US$25 cab ride. There also are three water taxis daily between Punta Gorda and Puerto Barrios, Guatemala (US$20-$22 one-way). There is a weekly boat between Placencia and Puerto Cortes, Honduras, (US$55) and also a weekly boat between Dangriga and Puerto Cortes (US$50). Elsewhere, such as from Dangriga to Tobacco Caye, you can arrange a boat (US$17.50) but service is not scheduled.

Health: The standards of health and hygiene in Belize are fairly high, similar to that in Costa Rica. Not many visitors become ill from traveler's diseases or from drinking the water. While malaria, dengue fever and other tropical diseases are present in Belize, they do not frequently affect visitors in the more popular destinations of Belize. Most travelers to Ambergris Caye or Placencia and other popular areas don't get any special shots or take other precautions before they come. No shots are required for entry into Belize, except for yellow fever if you are coming from an infected area such as parts of Africa. However, it's always a good idea to keep tetanus-diphtheria, Hep A and B and other vaccinations up to date.

Malaria prophylaxis may be advised for mainland travel, especially to remote areas in southern Belize or into Guatemala. Chloroquine, taken once a week, starting two weeks before arrival, is usually all you need in most of the region. Better be safe than sorry. Check with your doctor or the U.S. Centers for Disease Control, tel. 404-332-4559 or visit www.cdc.gov for the latest information.

The biggest trip-spoiler in Belize is probably sunburn. You're only 18 degrees of latitude north of the Equator, and the sub-tropical sun is much stronger than back home.

Accommodations -- What to Expect: Belize has some 600 hotels, with about 5,000 total rooms. Most of these hotels are small, owner-operated places; about 70% have 10 or fewer rooms. Only two hotels have more than 100 rooms: the 180-room Princess Hotel & Casino and the 102-room Radisson Fort George. Both are in Belize City.

Travelers to Belize today can expect to find a variety of accommodations to fit almost any budget or preference. Among the uniquely Belizean accommodations are the so-called jungle lodges. These are mostly in remote areas, but despite the remote locations you don't have to forego life's little luxuries, such as cold beer, hot showers and comfortable mattresses. The best of these places, including Chaa Creek in Cayo, Pook's Hill near Belmopan, Hidden Valley Inn and Blancaneaux in the Mountain Pine Ridge, Machaca

Hill in Toledo, and Chan Chich in rural Orange Walk, are as good as any bush lodge in the world.

Usually, the birding and wildlife spotting around the lodges are excellent, and they offer all the amenities you enjoy after the day's adventures are done. Most, though not all, have bay thatch cabañas built with a nod to Maya-style construction, but done up in much more luxury and style than traditional Maya cottages. While the top places are first-class in every way, with rates to match — often US$200 to $300 or more a night in season — you don't have to pay much to get an authentic jungle lodge experience. Places like Clarissa Falls, Crystal Paradise, Mida's and Parrot's Nest, all in Cayo, are bargains for US$60 or less double.

Another delightful type of lodging in Belize is the casual and small seaside resort. The best of these are sandy barefoot spots, with a friendly Belizean feel you won't find in other parts of the Caribbean. A couple can spend a night at the beach for US$50 to $150 dollars.

All around Belize you can find small places with clean, safe rooms at budget prices. The Trek Stop, Aguada Hotel and Martha's Guesthouse in Cayo or Tipple Tree Beya Inn in Hopkins, are examples. At these places you can get a nice little room for US$40 or less. At the other end of the scale, for those who demand luxury, a whole wave of upmarket hotels hit Belize starting in the 1990s. No longer is it necessary to stay in a hotel with linoleum floors and mismatched furniture. On Ambergris Caye and other cayes, places like Victoria House, Cayo Espanto and Azul Resort have rooms that could earn a spot in *Architectural Digest,* with rates from US$200 to $1,500+ a night. On the mainland, Blancaneaux's villas are luxurious, as are the sea-front villas (with furnishings imported from Bali) of its sister resort, Turtle Inn in Placencia. The Inn at Robert's Grove offers all the amenities from tennis courts to rooftop Jacuzzis. In a few areas, mainly San Pedro, you can enjoy the extra space of a condo-style unit at a regular hotel-style price. Villas at Banyan Bay, Grand Colony, The Palms, Xanadu, Grand Caribe, Coco Beach, Pelican Reef and The Phoenix are great examples of small condotels. In between are all shapes and sizes of personality inns, mostly run by their owners.

Many owners are struggling to earn a decent income, and they can't always afford to have the softest sheets or new TVs in the room. But, whether the owners are Belizean, American or Canadian, they're almost always friendly and helpful, willing to sit down with you and help you plan your day.

Do You Need to Book Ahead?

Can you wing it in Belize? Or do you need to book hotels in advance? The answer, except around busy holidays such as Christmas and Easter, used to be that you could just wing it. Average annual occupancy at Belize hotels was under 40%, and rooms in all price levels were plentiful most of the time. However, beginning in the late 1990s, tourism grew to record levels. Quite a few hotels, especially those offering the best value or top service and location, were heavily booked in-season. True, with the global recession of 2008-

2009, travel to Belize fell off, and hotel rooms went begging. Still, as the recession fades, when visiting Belize in-season, roughly Christmas and March through Easter, it's a good idea to book ahead for at least the first night or two. This doesn't mean that if you arrive without reservations you'll have to sleep on the beach with the sand flies — you'll be able to find a room somewhere — but your first choices may well be booked and you may have to spend valuable vacation time hunting for a room. Tours and dive trips can easily be booked after you arrive.

Using the Internet to Find and Book Rooms: Belize is wired. Most hotels in Belize have Web sites and e-mail. You can use their Web sites (listings in this book include Internet addresses) to help you choose your accommodations, but remember that these Web sites are advertising and naturally put the best face on things. Nearly all hotels in Belize are small, and though most won't admit it for fear of alienating travel agents and travel wholesalers, they would prefer you book direct, preferably via the Internet. That saves them 10 to 25% in agent commissions, plus the cost and trouble of faxing, mailing brochures and telephoning back and forth. In many cases, booking direct also will save you money. Some, but not all, hotels offer discounts for direct bookings via the Internet. Many don't advertise this, but it won't hurt to ask.

The cheapest way to communicate with hotels in Belize is via e-mail. Unfortunately, not all hotels in Belize check their e-mail regularly and respond to messages in a timely way. Also, BTL's e-mail may be down, sometimes for several days at a time. You may have to follow up with a telephone call or fax.

Eating Well in Belize: We don't know who started the rumor that you can't get a good meal in Belize. The fact is, you can eat gloriously well, at modest prices. Rice and beans is the quintessential Belizean dish, but this are not the rice and beans your momma used to fix — unless she's from Belize or perhaps New Orleans. Rice and beans (or beans and rice, which is slightly different) in Belize means spicy and smoky, with plenty of recado (also known as achiote) and other seasonings, perhaps flavored with salt pork and some onions and peppers and cooked in coconut milk. Usually these are served with a chunk of stew chicken, fish or pork. The whole thing might cost just US$5 in a pleasant restaurant. If you're not happy in Belize, you're probably not getting enough rice and beans.

Along the coast and on the cayes, seafood is as fresh as the salt air. In-season (mid-June to mid-February) spiny lobster — grilled, broiled, steamed, even fried — is fairly inexpensive and good. But a big filet of snapper or grouper, prepared over a grill with lime juice, is just as tasty and even cheaper. Conch, in season October to June, is delicious grilled or stewed in lime juice as ceviche, but we like it best in fritters, chopped and fried in a light batter.

Every ethnic group in multicultural Belize has its own taste treats. Among them: Sere and hoodut, one of the best-known Garifuna dishes, which is fish cooked in coconut milk with plantains. Boil up is a Creole favorite, fish boiled with plantains, yams and potatoes, and served with a tomato sauce and boiled bread. The Maya dish most popular with tourists is pibil, pork and other meats seasoned, wrapped in banana leaf and cooked slowly in an underground oven. Of course, with Mexico next door, Belize has a wide variety of Mexican dishes, including tamales, burritos, garnaches (corn tortillas fried and topped with beans, salsa and cheese) and panades (deep-fried tortillas filled with fish). A few restaurants such as Macy's in Belize City serve local game, including iguana, venison and gibnut, a rabbit-like rodent dubbed "the Royal Rat" because it was once served to Queen Elizabeth II.

We find most of the beef in Belize to be poor, although you can get an excellent steak in Belize at El Divino in San Pedro and elsewhere. But the pork — it's heavenly. The pork chops are tender and flavorful, the bacon a little different from most we've had, but delicious with fresh farm eggs. Only brown eggs are legal in Belize, by the way, to protect Belize's chicken farmers — if you see a white egg it's an illegal alien. For breakfast, fruit is the thing — fresh pineapple, mango, papaya, watermelon, orange. With fry jacks (a sort of fried biscuit, the Belizean version of beignets) and a cup of Guatemalan or Gallon Jug Estates Belizean coffee, we're set for the day.

For the most part, Belize dining isn't fancy, but even Belize is branching out in some of the newer worlds of cuisine. Placencia has French (French Connection), Cayo has Sri Lankan (Serendib) and on Ambergris Caye you'll find excellent French-Thai fusion (Rendezvous) and even sushi (available at several restaurants including Blue Water Grill). Italian is tasty at Francis Ford Copolla's places in the Pine Ridge (at Blancaneaux), in San Pedro at Pinocchio's and in Placencia (Turtle Inn and La Dolce Vita), as well as at other restaurants in Placencia, Caye Caulker and elsewhere. True Italian gelato is delicious at Tutti-Fruitti in Placencia.

To drink, there's nothing more refreshing than a fresh lime juice or watermelon juice. Belikin beer may not be up to the high standards of some of the beers of Mexico and Costa Rica, but it's good enough for us, and the Belikin stout will make you strong as an ox. Local rums such as One Barrel are cheap and flavorful.

Nightlife: Many visitors to Belize, after full days of hiking, caving, diving or snorkeling, are just too pooped to stay up late and party. At remote jungle lodges and dive resorts, often the lights go out by 10 p.m. Belize City and Ambergris Caye have the most clubs and bars. Visitors thinking about a tropical romance or a visit to one of the several brothels in Belize City, Orange Walk Town, Cayo or elsewhere should be aware that AIDS is a serious and growing problem in Belize. There are an estimated 8,000 people in Belize with HIV, a large number considering the country's small population of around 330,000.

Gambling: A law passed in 1999 permitted gambling, and several casinos have opened in Belize; others are planned. Belize City has the Princess Hotel and Casino, with about 500 electronic machines plus live tables for poker, blackjack and other games. The Princess also has a branch in San Ignacio and in the Free Zone in Corozal. Two other casinos are in the Free

Zone in northern Belize, including the large Las Vegas Casino, where a near 400-room hotel is planned. San Pedro has a small casino at the Belize Yacht Club. Casinos have been proposed for Placencia in southern Belize.

In each area of Belize, I've selected my favorite hotels in all price ranges. I guarantee you'll like them.

CHAPTER 25:
CHECKING OUT BELIZE CITY AND ENVIRONS

Coming into Belize you most likely will land in Belize City. Many Belize travelers will tell you the best way to see Belize City is through your rear view window. However, with an open mind to its peculiarities, and with a little caution (the city has crack, gang and crime problems, though this rarely affects visitors, and the areas usually frequented by visitors are watched by tourist police), you may decide Belize City has a raffish, atmospheric charm. You might even see the ghost of Aldous Huxley or Graham Greene at a hotel bar.

Rates shown are plus 9% hotel tax and in some cases a service charge, usually 10%.

City Centre Area

Great House, 13 Cork St.; tel. 501-223-3400, fax 223-3444; www.greathousebelize.com. This small jewel offers spacious and well-equipped air-conditioned rooms in a modernized and expanded private house, originally built in 1927. All 12 rooms, half on the second and half on the third floor, have a balcony, private bathroom, mini-fridge, safe, TV, phone and dedicated fax line. There is also a good, if somewhat pricey, restaurant in the courtyard, the Smoky Mermaid. Owner Steve Maestre, one of Belize's most experienced hotel proprietors, takes great pride in the personal service here. Doubles around US$150.

Radisson Fort George, 2 Marine Parade; tel. 501-223-3333, fax 227-3829; www.radissonbelize.com. This is the flagship of the city's hotels, and the most expensive, though you can often get substantial reductions from the rack rates. All rooms have cable TV, fridge and minibar, and those in the Club Wing, reached by the only glass elevator in Belize, have unbeatable sea views. Most of the rooms, including those in the villa wing across the street, have been remodeled recently. There's a good restaurant, and the grounds are an oasis of calm on the edge of the sea. The hotel has two pools and a private dock. The marina can take large boats of up to 250 feet in length with a 10-foot draft. The staff is usually friendly and helpful. Rates US$169-189 double, Dec. 20-Apr. 30, about US$10 less the rest of year. But rates are often heavily discounted – ask.

Hotel Mopan, 55 Regent St., Belize City; tel. 501-227-7351, fax 227-5383; www.hotelmopan.com. Character is the Hotel Mopan's middle name. This hotel in an old wooden Colonial house on the South Side became a well-known meeting place for naturalists, archeologists and backpackers under pioneering tourism operator Jean Shaw, who died in 1999. Her daughter and son, Jeannie and Tomy, operate the hotel today. Don't expect luxury here, and the neighborhood isn't exactly grand (walking around at night is iffy at best), but the rooms are bigger than average, they've been upgraded, and there's still lots of atmosphere. All rooms have private baths with plenty of hot water, and A/C is available. Rates US$45 to $80 double.

Near International Airport and Between Airport and City Centre

D'Nest Inn. 475 Cedar St. tel. 501-223-5416; www.dnestinn.com. (Directions: from the Northern Hwy., turn west on Chetumal St., turn right at the police station, go 1 block and turn left, then turn right on Cedar St.) D'Nest Inn is a B&B run by Gaby and Oty Ake. Gaby is a retired Belize banker, and Oty is originally from Chetumal. The two-story, Caribbean-style house is on a canal 50 feet from the Belize River. It's in an area called Belama Phase 2, a safe, middle-class section between the international airport and downtown. Oty's gardens around the house are filled with hibiscus, roses, and other blossoming plants. The four guest rooms (the fourth was renovated and added to the roster in mid-2006) are furnished with antiques such as a hand-carved, four-poster bed, but they also have modcons like free wireless internet, air-conditioning, and cable TV. With a private entrance and your own key, you come and go as you like. Rates are US$65 to $75 double and include a delicious full breakfast. Highly recommended.

Global Village Hotel. Mile 8 1/2, Northern Hwy.; tel. 501-225-2555; www.globalhotel-bz.com. If you have an early morning flight out or you're overnighting en route somewhere else, the Global Village Hotel (actually it's more of a motel than a hotel) is a good choice near the international airport. The 40 rooms are sparkling clean and modern and are only US$50 double. This Chinese-owned place is located just south of the turnoff to the international airport, and the hotel has a free shuttle to and from the airport. You can also arrange to leave your car in the hotel's fenced parking lot with 24-hour security.

Black Orchid Resort. Burrell Boom Village; tel. 501-225-9029 or toll-free from U.S. and Canada 866-437-1301; www.blackorchidresort.com. This is a relaxing alternative to the crime and bustle of Belize City, and it's about the same distance from the international airport as the city centre. The small resort is on the Belize River, and you can launch a canoe, kayak, or powerboat from the hotel's dock, or just laze about the riverside swimming pool and thatch palapa. The air-conditioned riverview rooms (US$140 double in-season, US$120 off-season, plus tax) are large, with custom-made mahogany furnishings; garden-view rooms are US$20 a night less. A three-bedroom, two-bath house (US$340 plus tax for up to six, in-season) is a good choice for families; a guesthouse with shared bath is for those on a budget. The on-site restaurant serves good Belizean food (dinner US$18). Tours are available.

Dining in Belize City

In addition to the better choices listed below, greasy fried chicken is available as takeaway from small restaurants all over the city — a Belizean favorite known as "dollah chicken" whatever the price. The big hotels have their own restaurants, quite expensive but with varied menus and good service.

If you're shopping for food while in the city centre, **Brodies** is worth a look. It's on Albert Street, just past the park, and their selection of food is good if expensive, reflecting the fact that much is imported. Milk and dairy products, produced locally by Mennonite farmers, are delicious and good quality. Naturally enough, local fruit is cheap and plentiful, though highly seasonal — Belizean citrus fruits are among the best in the world. Fruits and vegetables are available at the Queen Square market near the Novelo's bus station. It has been newly renovated. Two modern supermarkets, a branch of **Brodies** and **Save-U**, are on the Northern Highway on the way to the international airport. This Brodies outpost has been remodeled and expanded, with dry goods as well as groceries, and is the largest and most modem supermarket in the country.

Most restaurants in Belize City are closed for lunch on Sunday, and many are closed all day. Some are also closed for lunch on Saturday.

The pricing system for restaurants in all areas is:

Inexpensive: Under US$7 per person for dinner, not including drinks or tip

Moderate: US$8-$15 for dinner, not including drinks or tip

Expensive: US$16-$29 for dinner, not including drinks or tip

Very Expensive: US$30 and up for dinner, not including drinks or tips

The Smokey Mermaid at The Great House. One of the best restaurants in the city, though not cheap. Try the coconut shrimp and banana chimichanga. 13 Cork Street in the Fort George area across from the Radisson, tel. 501-223-4759. Expensive.

Harbour View. On the Belize River, this is Belize City's most romantic restaurant. Fort St. next to the Tourist Village, tel. 501-223-6452. Expensive to Very Expensive.

Riverside Tavern. New in 2006, this Bowen family-owned restaurant has become very popular. It has the biggest and best burgers in Belize City (the 6-ounce burger with fries is US$8), and arguably in all of Belize, with a variety of other well prepared dishes, including steaks. You can dine outside overlooking Haulover Creek or inside in cold air-conditioning, with views of the large bar and its TV sets. Parking is safe, in a fenced, guarded lot right in front of the restaurant. 2 Mapp St. at N. Front St., tel. 501-223-5640. Recommended. Moderate.

Wet Lizard. Fun place with pretty good food. Gets lots of daytrippers from the cruise ships. 1 Fort St., next to Tourist Village, tel. 501-223-5973. Moderate.

Chon Saan Palace. This has been the best Chinese restaurant in Belize City for 30 years. It serves fresh seafood and is Hong Kong style. 1 Kelly St., tel. 501-223-3008. Moderate.

Neries. Very popular joint, serving Creole favorites. Corner of Queen and Daly streets, with another location at 124 Freetown Rd.

Mar's Belizean Restaurant. Clean place serving (as the name suggests) tasty Belizean food at easy prices. 118 N. Front St.; tel. 501-223-9046.

Dit's. Great pastries and inexpensive Creole food such as cowfoot soup. 50 King St.; tel. 501-227-3330.

Macy's. Long-established, reasonably priced Creole restaurant is popular with locals and very busy at lunch. It also serves traditional game such as armadillo, deer and gibnut ("the Royal Rat") but no longer turtle. 18 Bishop St.; tel. 501-227-3419.

Big Daddy's Diner. In the Commercial Center, just south of the Swing Bridge, Big Daddy's is a popular lunch spot for downtown workers. The large portions served cafeteria-style are cheap, and the clean, sunny surroundings including ceiling fans and views of Haulover Creek. Second level of Commercial Center, near Swing Bridge; tel. 501-227-0932.

Rural Belize District
CROOKED TREE

Crooked Tree is famous for the number and variety of birds that flock here, especially in the dry season (February to early June). You may even see the jabiru stork, the largest bird in the Americas. It stands nearly as tall as a human, with a wingspan of up to 12 feet. Even if you're not a birder, you'll appreciate the beauty of the Crooked Tree lagoon. Coming from the Northern Highway across the causeway toward Crooked Tree village, an old and predominantly Creole settlement, you'll see cattle cooling themselves in the lagoon, with their egret pals. Check in at the visitor center at the end of the causeway. You'll get a map and can walk or drive around the village, nearby bush trails and the lagoon front. Or ask about a local guide. Canoes are available for rent, too. Admission: US$4.

Crooked Tree Lodge. Crooked Tree Wildlife Sanctuary, tel. 501-626-3820; www.crookedtreelodgebelize.com. Formerly Paradise Lodge, this lodge has been rebuilt and redone by a Belizean-English couple. There are five nice cabañas (around US$75) on the shores of the Crooked Tree Lagoon. A new main lodge building houses a restaurant. A two-bedroom cabin is ideal for families.

Birds Eye View Lodge. Crooked Tree Wildlife Sanctuary, tel. 501-203-2040, fax 222-4869; www.birdseyeviewlodge.com. Birds Eye View Lodge is a modern two-story concrete hotel, just a few steps from the lagoon, covered with climbing vines and flowers. The hotel's 20 renovated rooms are clean as a pin, and the Belizean management is friendly. The hotel's dining room serves tasty Creole fare. Doubles US$80 to $120 Nov. 1-May 14, US$60 to $110 rest of year. Rates are plus hotel tax and 10% service. Continental breakfast is US$6, lunch is US$12, dinner US$15. The hotel can arrange birding, local tours, canoe rentals and such. A three-hour birding tour by boat is US$100 for up to four people. Canoe and bike rentals are each US$15 a day. Transfer from the international airport is US$75 for up to three people.

GALES POINT AREA

The Northern and Southern lagoons near Gales Point are excellent places to spot West Indian manatees. There is a "manatee hole" fed by warm under-water springs, about 200 yards off the peninsula point northeast, where manatees are commonly seen. Some of the manatees have been tagged with radio transmitters, which permit researchers to track their movements. Tours from hotels in Gales Point will take you on manatee watching trips, or you can arrange with someone in the Creole village of Gales Point to take you out. The village has a manatee guides association. When out manatee spotting, please be respectful of your fellow mammals. Responsible guides (and visitors) don't get too close to these huge, gentle creatures, nor do they try to swim with them or touch them. Gales Point is off the regular tourist track in Belize. There is no longer bus service to Gales Point from Dangriga or elsewhere, so you'll need a car or take a taxi from Dangriga. Very basic accommodations are available in local homes in Gales Point village. Near Gales Point are several miles of beach — not so good for swimming, but hawksbill turtles nest here.

Manatee Lodge. Gales Point (Mail: P.O. Box 1242, Belize City); tel./fax 501-220- 8040; www.manateelodge.com. If you like the British Honduras colonial atmosphere, with a truly lovely setting on a lagoon, this might be your cup of tea. There are eight rooms with polished hardwood floors, private baths, 24-hour electricity and jalousie windows in an old white frame building beside the Southern Lagoon. Doubles about US$85. Package plans including transportation from Belize City are available, as are meals. Breakfast and dinner daily is US$33. Canoes are complimentary. Among other tours, the hotel offers a half-day boat tour, which includes manatee watching and a visit to Ben Loman cave, US$137.50 for two persons.

Part of Barrier Reef Drive (Front Street) in San Pedro

CHAPTER 26:
CHECKING OUT AMBERGRIS CAYE

Getting to San Pedro

Getting to San Pedro is easy as caye lime pie, but it does require at least one stop along the way. There is no international air service direct to San Pedro's little airstrip.

From Belize City: You can either fly or take a water taxi to San Pedro (or to Caye Caulker). It's a 20-minute flight to San Pedro; the boat trip takes about 75 minutes. Two Belize airlines, Maya Island Air and Tropic Air, each have about one flight per hour every day to San Pedro, starting at around 7:30 a.m. and ending around 5:30 p.m. In peak visitor season, sometimes additional flights are added to accommodate demand.

Flights originate from both the International Airport in Ladyville about 9 miles north of Belize City, where your international flight arrives, and Municipal Airport, a small airstrip in Belize City. In many cases the same Maya Island and Tropic flight picks up passengers at both airports, making the short hop between the two in a few minutes.

Should you fly to San Pedro from International or Municipal? Depends on whether you'd rather save time or money. It's easier just to fly into International and walk over to the domestic terminal and catch your connecting puddle jumper.

But you'll save a little money, especially if traveling in a party of several people, by flying from Municipal. Adult and child one-way fares on both Maya Island and Tropic are approximately US$63 from International; from Municipal, adult one-way is US$35. Round-trip fares are just slightly less than twice one way. Only rarely are there any bargain fares or discounts for advance booking. Sometimes, mainly in the summer, the Belize airlines will offer deals if you pay cash, rather than use a credit card.

Transferring between the airports requires a 20-minute taxi ride. A taxi from International to Municipal is US$25 for up to four or five passengers. A tip isn't necessary unless the driver carries a lot of your luggage, in which case add a couple of bucks. Taxis – they have green license tags – are plentiful and await passengers just outside the main lobby.

party of four pays about US$480 round-trip to San Pedro via International, and US$318 round-trip from Municipal, even including the taxi transfers.

Do you need to make reservations for Maya Island or Tropic flights in advance? Off-season, it's not really necessary, though having a reservation won't hurt. In-season, a reservation might save a wait. Most hotels on Ambergris Caye will arrange for your air travel to the island at the time you make your hotel reservations, and there's usually no extra cost to you. The hotel gets a small commission from the airline. You also can book direct with the airlines by telephone or over the Internet. Here's contact information:

Maya Island Air: 800-225-6732 or 501-226-3838, fax 226-2192; schedules, fares and reservations at www.mayaregional.com.

Tropic Air: 800-422-3435 or 501-226-2012; schedules, fares and reservations at www.tropicair.com.

Astrum Helicopters (Western Highway near Belize City, tel. 501-222-9462, www.astrumhelicopters.com) offers VIP transfers of guests to selected hotels, including Cayo Espanto, Azul Resort, Isla Marisol, Chaa Creek and Maruba Jungle Lodge & Spa, all of which have heliports. Astrum also offers helicopter charters, tours, and aerial photography trips, plus medevac service.

If you are going to San Pedro or Caye Caulker, you have the option of taking a water taxi. Two water taxi companies, with fast boats that hold up to 100 passengers, connect Belize City with Ambergris Caye (US$12.50 one-way) and Caye Caulker (US$7.50 one-way), each with eight to ten departures a day. **Caye Caulker Water Taxi** (www.cayecaulkerwatertaxi.com) boats depart from the Marine Terminal near the Swing Bridge; **San Pedro-Belize Express** (www.sanpedrowatertaxi.com) boats leave from Brown Sugar building near the Tourism Village. Despite their names, both water taxi companies have service to both Caye Caulker and San Pedro. It's a 45-minute ride to Caulker and 75 minutes to San Pedro. Boats stop on demand at Caye Chapel. A cab to downtown Belize City from the International Airport is about 20-25 minutes and US$25.

Coming from Mexico or Northern Belize:

An option that became available in 2009 is to fly from Cancun to Belize City on **Maya Island Air** (www.mayaregional.com).

Another new option from Chetumal is a **San Pedro-Belize Express** ferry to San Pedro. As of this writing, there are two boats a day Friday to Monday each way. Boats depart Chetumal at 10 a.m. and 4 p.m. and depart San Pedro at 7 a.m. and 1:30 p.m. Fare is around US$35 one-way. Note that the schedule is very much subject to change.

Most travelers, however, will come through the border at Chetumal and Corozal Town. To get to San Pedro or Caye Caulker, you have several options:

1) Take **ADO** or another Mexican bus line from Playa del Carmen or Cancun to Chetumal (generally US$20 or less, depending on the class of service and the peso exchange rate). Many people prefer to hop a bus from the Cancun International Airport to Playa (about US$9 or less) and from there take ADO

or CCO to Chetumal. Most buses from Playa to Chetumal leave from the newer Playa bus station, not the older one near the waterfront. For information on Mexican bus schedules, visit Ticketbus (www.ticketbus.com.mx). To Chetumal, it is about five to six hours from Cancun and less than four and a half hours from

Playa. In Chetumal, you'll transfer to a Belize bus. With the breakup of Novelo's bus line, bus service in Belize is now fragmented among a number of small bus lines, and schedules and even the names of the bus lines can change. However, when you arrive in Chetumal just ask about a bus to Belize, and you'll have no problem finding one. Some buses -- typically they are old U.S. school buses -- leave from the main ADO terminal, but some leave from the Nuevo Mercado area, a short taxi ride from the ADO station. Cross the border - the bus waits as you go through both Mexican and Belizean customs and immigration. Cost to Corozal Town is US$1.50. Note: From Chetumal, you can also hire a taxi or transfer to take you across the border, instead of taking a bus, with the rate negotiable, but usually around US$30 per person, not including any border fees.

Then, from Corozal Town, continue down the Northern Highway (around US$6 - $8 and 3 to 3 1/2 hours) to Belize City, and from there take a water taxi *(see above)* or flight to San Pedro. Another bus option is to take a tourist bus, such as Linea Dorado, which runs from Chetumal to Flores, Guatemala, stopping at the Marine Terminal in Belize City. The fare from Chet to Belize City is around US$15,.

2) Transfer services in Corozal and elsewhere in Belize will also pick you up in Cancun or elsewhere in Mexico and bring you to Corozal or to Belize City. Belize **VIP Transfer Service,** formerly Menzies Tours (www.belizetransfers.com, tel. 501-422- 2725) is one of these. You'll pay US400 for up to four persons from Cancun to Corozal, US$350 from Playa del Carmen, US$300 from Tulum, US$45 from Bacalar and around US$30

from Chetumal. Other shuttle services also operate.

3) There is a water taxi from Corozal directly to San Pedro. There's one boat a day, operated by **San Pedro-Belize Express.** It departs Corozal from the pier near Reunion Park at 7 a.m. and returns from San Pedro at 3 p.m. It stops at Sarteneja on demand. Fare is US$22.50 one-way, US$40 round-trip. Check departure times locally, as they may change, and service may be reduced at times in the off-season. A second daily boat usually is added during high season. The trip takes around two hours, longer if it's bad weather or if there's a long stop at Sarteneja. It can be a buttbuster.

4) Have the bus from Chetumal drop you at the Corozal airstrip, or take a taxi to the airstrip and fly to San Pedro, a trip that takes about 25 minutes. Tropic Air has six flights a day to San Pedro, currently at 7:30, 9:30, 11:30, 1:30, 3:30, and 5:15 for US$47.50 one-way. **Maya Island Air** has several flights a day, for about the same price.

WHERE TO STAY: TOWN? NORTH? SOUTH?

Probably the biggest decision you'll make about Ambergris Caye is where to stay. We're not talking about a specific hotel but about the general area. The area you choose will determine to a great degree the experience you have on the island. You have four basic options:

1) in the town of San Pedro

2) just to the south of San Pedro near the airstrip, within walking distance of town

3) on the south end, beyond easy walking distance to town

4) on the north end of the island above the channel.

There is no one "best" place to stay. Each of these four areas has advantages and disadvantages. Which area you choose depends on what you want from your vacation. If you're looking for privacy and the feeling of being away from it all, consider the south end or the north end of the island. If you prefer easy access to restaurants, nightlife, shops and other activities, you'll likely be happier in San Pedro town or just to the south. There's little or no advantage to any one area in terms of beaches, although the beaches in town tend to be more crowded with boats than those outside of town.

HEART OF TOWN: Hotels in the town of San Pedro, with a few notable exceptions, are older spots, among them the original tourist hotels on the island. They are, again with a few exceptions, less expensive digs. If you're looking to save a buck or two, this may be the place for you. You also will be right in the heart of things, no more than a few sandy blocks from some of the best restaurants, bars, shops and dive operations on the island. Party animals will want to stay here or just the south of town. Accommodations here include Rubie's, Holiday Hotel, Spindrift, Lily's, Martha's, Sanpedrano, Mayan Princess, Hotel del Rio and The Tides. More expensive options in town include The Phoenix, SeaBreeze Suites and Paradise Villas.

AIRSTRIP SOUTH: If you want a larger variety of moderate and upscale lodging but still want to be within walking distance of the attractions of San Pedro Town, think about staying at the south edge of town and the area just to the south of town. The San Pedro airstrip is here, but you should have few or no problems with airport noise, since the planes are small one- and two-engine prop jobs, and there are no flights after dark. This is a good compromise between the activity of town and the remoteness of the north end and far south end. Among the hotels here are SunBreeze, The Palms, Belizean Reef Suites, Ramon's Village, Steve & Becky's Cute Little Hotel, Exotic Caye, Coconuts, Coral Bay Villas, Caribbean Villas, Belize Yacht Club and Changes in Latitudes.

SOUTH END: Although most of this area is beyond a quick walk to town, this a major growth area for tourism on the island. Some of the nicer upmarket hotels are located here, and more are on the way. An increasing number of restaurants and amenities also are located here. At the far end, you're two to three miles from San Pedro, so for visits to town you'll need to rent a golf cart (US$60 or $65 for 24 hours), ride a bike (some hotels offer them free to guests), take a taxi (about US$5 to town) or take a hotel shuttle, if available. Among the choices here are Villas at Banyan Bay, Grand Colony, Banana Beach, Mata Rocks, Royal Palm, Victoria House, Caribe Island Resort, Royal Caribbean, Sunset Beach and Pelican Reef Villas.

NORTH AMBERGRIS: By all accounts, the area north of "the River" – a narrow channel of water separating the south and north ends of the island – is where much of Ambergris Caye's growth will occur over the next decade or two. Houses, hotels, and even a restaurant or two are going up here. At present, though, access is limited by the fact that there are only two ways to get to the north end: One is by boat, usually a water taxi, either scheduled or on-demand. The other is via a bridge, new in early 2006, open only to pedestrians, bikes and golf carts, and then via a hike or ride on a narrow path to the various resorts and villas. Bring plenty of bug spray for use when you're away from the water. Crossing the bridge costs US$2.50 each way for a golf cart, US$1 for a pedestrian. Water taxis are US$5 to $20 per person for most destinations.

Accommodations on the north end include Cocotel Inn, Ak'Bol, Grand Caribe, El Pescador, Capricorn, Captain Morgan's, Belizean Shores, Coco Beach, Seascape Villas, Las Terrazas, Azul Resort, Mata Chica, Xamen Ek, La Perla del Caribe, Portofino, Costa Maya, Blue Reef, Salamander, Sueño del Mar and Tranquility Bay.

Not on Ambergris but close by, off the back side of the island, is Cayo Espanto and on Caye Chapel, the Caye Chapel Island Resort.

Here are approximate distances, in driving miles, of hotels and resorts from Central Park in San Pedro Town, roughly the center of town. Your mileage may vary.

SOUTH END

Pelican Reef	2.8 miles south
Miramar Villas	2.5 miles south
Sunset Beach Resort	2.5 miles south
Royal Caribbean Resort	1.9 miles south
Victoria House	1.8 miles south

Mata Rocks	1.4 miles south
Banana Beach Resort	1.4 miles south
Grand Colony	1.3 miles south
The Villas at Banyan Bay	1.2 miles south

AIRSTRIP SOUTH

Xanadu	1 mile south
Caribbean Villas	1 mile south
Coral Bay Villas	1 mile south
Coconuts Caribbean	.9 miles south
Corona del Mar	.9 miles south
Exotic Caye Beach Resort	.8 miles south
Belize Yacht Club	.7 miles south
Changes in Latitudes	.6 miles south
Pedro's Backpacker's Inn	.6 miles south
Ramon's Village	.4 miles south
Steve & Becky's	.4 miles south
The Palms	.4 miles south
Belizean Reef Suites	.3 miles south
Sunbreeze Hotel	.3 miles south

IN TOWN

Ruby's	.2 miles south
Holiday Hotel	.2 miles south
Coral Beach Hotel	.2 miles south
Spendrift Hotel	.1 miles south
Martha's Hotel	.1 miles south
Mayan Princess	.0 miles
Hotel Sanpedrano	.0 miles
Lily's	.0 miles
Conch Shell	.1 miles north
SeaBreeze Suites	.1 miles north
The Phoenix	.3 miles north
Paradise Villas	.3 miles north
Blue Tang Inn	.4 miles north
The Tides Beach Resort .	.5 miles north
Seven Seas	.6 miles north
Hotel del Rio	.7 miles north

NORTH AMBERGRIS

Ak'Bol	2.0 miles north
Grand Caribe	2.5 miles north
Cocotal Inn	2.5 miles north
El Pescador Lodge	2.9 miles north
Capricorn Resort	3.0 miles north
Capt. Morgan's Retreat	3.1 miles north

Coco Beach	3.1 miles north
Seascape Villas	3.2 miles north
Belizean Shores	3.3 miles north
Las Terrazas	3.8 miles north
Azul Resort	5.1 miles north
Mata Chica	5.2 miles north
Xaman Ek	5.6 miles north
Portofino Resort	6.0 miles north
Costa Maya Reef Resort	6.7 miles north
Blue Reef	8.1 miles north
Sueño del Mar	11.5 miles north
Tranquility Bay	12.0 miles north

HOW TO GET THE BEST HOTEL RATES

Ambergris Caye hotel rates are not cheap, averaging US$150-$200 double in high season, although rooms are available for under US$25, and you can pay US$500 or more a night. Rates in San Pedro, however, compare favorably with those in most resort areas of Mexico and Costa Rica and generally are far less than on Caribbean islands such as St. Maarten/St. Martin, Anguilla or St. Thomas.

There are several things you can do to enjoy lower prices. The most obvious is simply to go off-season, when most hotels drop rates 20 to 40%. Exact dates vary from hotel to hotel, but the low season generally starts just after Easter and runs until about mid-November. The island has more than 60 hotels and condotels. Occupancy rates on the island average less than 50%, so there are normally rooms available even in high season. Easter and Christmas/New Years are usually almost fully booked.

With most hotels having excess capacity, particularly in June, September and October and to a lesser degree also in the other off-season months, discounts of several types are available. In the off-season, many hotels have "walk-in" rates. These rates, typically 15 to 20% off the already discounted summer rates, can be real values.

Many hotels on Ambergris Caye also post special discounted rates for September and October, the two slowest months of the year for tourism.

Many hotels also offer sizable discounts for stays of a week or longer, or have a value package such as "stay seven nights/pay for five." Frequently, hotels offer discounts for Internet or other direct bookings, saving them travel agent or wholesaler commissions. These direct booking discounts usually range from 10 to 20%, and occasionally are as much as 30%.

When booking, always ask, "Is that your best rate?" or "Do you have a lower rate?" or "That's a little more than I was hoping to pay – is there a way I can get a better rate?" Keep probing to find out if you're getting the best price.

Most hotels require a deposit to hold reservations, usually nonrefundable or only partially refundable.

Nearly all hotels on the island accept Visa and MasterCard. Some accept American Express. Only a few accept Discover. If credit cards are not accepted, this is noted in the hotel reviews. Some hotels still surcharge credit cards by 5% or so, but this practice happily is declining.

OCCUPANCY RATES

Hotels in Belize generally do not enjoy high annual occupancy rates. In recent years, the country-wide occupancy rate has been in the low 40% range. The last year for which statistics from the Belize Tourism Board are available, 2008, it was 41.1%. This is at least 20 percentage points lower than annual occupancy rates in the U.S., Europe and the main Caribbean.

Ambergris Caye enjoys the highest hotel occupancy rate of any area of Belize, with occupancy rates in the mid-40s percent range. Some of the most popular properties have occupancy rates of over 70%, and near 100% at the height of the season. Many properties are virtually completely booked at Christmas, New Years, Easter and at times during the high season, especially March.

Caye Caulker's hotel occupancy rate in for the last year reported, 2008, was 40%, according to the BTB, and offshore islands had an occupancy rate of 29.1%.

Hotel occupancy rate by area, 2008:

Belize District	42.3%
Ambergris Caye	44.3%
Caye Caulker	40.0%
Cayo	39.4%
Corozal	19.7%
Orange Walk	38.6%
Stann Creek	43.6%
Placencia	39.2%
Toledo	27.5%
Other Islands	29.1%

Source: Belize Tourism Board, 2009

LODGING TYPES

You have several different types of lodging from which to choose on Ambergris Caye:

Condotels: These are condominiums run like a hotel. Units are individually owned and rented to visitors by on-site management that typical takes 40 to 60% of the gross. They have most of the same amenities as a regular hotel, except usually not a restaurant. Most condotels on Ambergris Caye are not the large sprawling condo complexes found in Florida or Hawaii. They are small, only two or three stories high, with from one to three dozen units. Typically they have a mix of one- and two-bedroom units; a few have three-bedroom suites. The advantage of a condotel is that you get a lot more space, including a kitchen, for a price not much more than for a regular hotel. The drawback is that most condotels do not offer the range of services

176

of a hotel, such as room service. Condotels range in price from under US$100 to over US$400 a night. Among the condotels on Ambergris Caye are Villas at Banyan Bay, Belizean Shores, Coral Bay Villas, Mayan Princess, Grand Colony, Grand Caribe, Pelican Reef and Xanadu.

Beachside cabañas and cottages: These come in two flavors – thatch and not. Thatch cabañas have thatch roofs and palapa-style walls, usually over concrete block or wood frames. Among resorts with thatch cabañas (in some cases, only some units are thatch) are Salamander Hideaway, Portofino, Captain Morgan's, Hotel del Rio, Ramon's Village, Exotic Caye, Xanadu and Victoria House. Other properties have more traditional wood-frame or concrete cottages or cabins. Beachside cabañas are available from around US$75 to more than US$600 a night.

Hotels: Nearly all hotels on the island are personality inns. Most are small, under 40 rooms, and all are three stories or lower. Hotels come in all price ranges, from US$15 to over US$400 a night. Nearly all the hotels, except for a few budget places, are on the water.

Privately owned houses for vacation rental: Dozens of private homes and villas are available on Ambergris Caye for weekly rental. Rates start at around US$700 a week and go up to US$6,000 or more.

Longer-term rentals: Monthly rentals of houses and apartments are available, starting at around US$300 for a small apartment, though most rentals are US$500 to $1,000 and up. The best way to find a rental is to ask around in person.

CAMPING

There are currently no campgrounds on Ambergris Caye, and camping, unless on your own land or on other private land with permission, is prohibited. Caye Caulker has a small private campground, and primitive camping is available on some outlying cayes, including Half Moon Caye.

Your Lodging Choices

These hotel reviews are candid and are not influenced by advertising (we accept none) or by comps. Keep in mind that hotel reviews, like movie reviews, are matters of opinion. Your mileage may vary.

Also, keep in mind that things change – rates, amenities, management. We routinely check with properties for current and projected rates. Note that rates for the Christmas, New Year's and Easter holidays may be higher than those shown here, and minimum stays may be required for those prime holiday periods.

SAN PEDRO TOWN

(Listed from the north to south. The hotels just north of town, including Hotel Del Rio, Seven Seas and The Tides, are about a 10 minute walk along the beach to town.)

Hotel Del Rio. Boca Del Rio Drive, tel./fax 501-226-2286; www.ambergriscaye.com/hoteldelrio/index.html. At this small seafront operation, you have the choice of a big cabaña, a small cabaña, less-expensive rooms in a Mexican-style building and even more modest rooms in a guesthouse. This is not a fancy resort, there's no air-conditioning, but it has personality some other places lack. In-season doubles are US$50 to $145, off-season US$40 to $105, plus 9% tax. Worth considering if you're watching your pennies and want a bit of thatch ambiance.

Seven Seas Resort. Boca Del Rio Drive, tel. 501-226-2382, or toll-free 866-438-1435; www.AmbergrisCaye.com/sevenseas/index.html. This long-established beachfront property has gone through a variety of incarnations over the years, including timeshare, but it remains a good value, though not an upscale one, at the north edge of town, within walking distance of downtown restaurants. In a small cluster of three-story pink and white buildings you'll find air-conditioned one-bedroom suites with tile floors and Belizean-made furniture. There's a small pool and a pier. Free wireless. Rates for direct booking in-season: US$101-$115, off-season, US$88-$102.

The Tides Beach Resort. Boca Del Rio Drive, tel. 501-226-2283, fax 226-3797; www.ambergriscaye.com/tides/. Owned and operated by San Pedranos Patojo and Sabrina Paz and with Patojo's Scuba Center on-site, this 12-unit hotel focuses on divers, and you'll often see wet suits and dive gear hanging over the balcony. Though built just a few years ago, with its wood construction and balconied verandahs, this three-story hotel has a vaguely colonial era appearance. The rooms are modern enough, though, with fans and pleasant furnishings. The hotel also offers two and three-bedroom suites with kitchens. No restaurant, but several good ones are nearby, and there's a tiny beach bar and a pool. Off-season rates are US$85 with A/C, and US$125 (suites US$205) in-season. Plus tax. Dive packages also available.

Blue Tang Inn. Barrier Reef Dr.; tel. 866-881-1020 or 501-226-2326, fax 226-2358; www.bluetanginn.com. The 14 studio-type suites with kitchens in this three-story blue hotel have been remodeled and upgraded, and there's a new "cozy" swimming pool. (For those who aren't divers, a Blue Tang is a colorful tropical fish seen around the barrier reef.) Rates US$120 to $180 off-season, US$150 to $210 November through April, including continental breakfast.

The Phoenix. Barrier Reef Dr.; tel. 501-226-3414; www.ambergriscaye.com/phoenix. This new beachfront condo resort is at the north end of town, on the site of what used to be a retreat for Catholic nuns and later the location of the Paradise Hotel. The 30 condo units are of nice size. The two-bedroom, two-bath units are around 1600 sq. ft., with kitchens, broadband internet and all the upscale amenities. There are two swimming pools, and an upscale restaurant, Red Ginger. Rates start at US$325 for a beautiful one-bedroom suite plus tax in-season.

Paradise Villas. Barrier Reef Drive, San Pedro. Paradise Villas is an attractive low-rise condo colony at the north end of town. In the past, a complication was that the units were managed and rented by several different companies, plus several owners of one or two units. However, we're told this confusing situation is improving. If you want to stay at Paradise Villas, just contact the agents and see what's available and compare prices. Choose from either one- or two-bedroom condos. The two-bedroom units are not as big as some other two-bedroom suites at island condotels. Though units vary in furnishings and amenities such as whether the air conditioning is just in the bedroom or throughout the units, they are basically similar. There's an attractive seaside pool area, and a small artificial reef at the end of the pier (built by the condo owners) to attract fish for snorkeling. Rates vary among the different agents, but most are in the range of US$135 to $200 in-season and US$90 to $150 off-season. Paradise Villas, tel. 877-331-9693 or 882-331-9693; www.belizevilla.com. Nellie Gomez Property Management, P. O. Box 143, Pescador Drive, San Pedro Town; tel. 501-226-2087, fax 226-2400; www.nelliesproperty.com. Tradewinds (this travel wholesaler manages 12 Paradise units and has a manager with an office across the street), tel. in the U.S. 800-451-7776, fax 414-258-5336, in Belize tel. 501-226-2822, fax 226-3746; www.tradewindsparadisevillas.com.

Conch Shell. Barrier Reef Drive, P.O. Box 43, San Pedro; tel. 501-226-2062; www.ambergriscaye.com/conchshell/. This center-of-town, waterfront two-story hotel, with its wood-frame construction, ceiling fans and linoleum floors, is an option for travelers who just want a clean, simple place to stay. Recently renovated. Rates around US$69 to $89 double mid-November to mid-April, plus tax, US$10 less the rest of the year. Free wireless available.

Tio Pil's Place (formerly Lily's Hotel). Barrier Reef Drive, San Pedro; tel. 501-226-2059, fax 226-2623; www.ambergriscaye.com/lilys/index.html. This family-run budget favorite has been around for more than 35 years, recently going upmarket a bit with air-conditioning and some remodeling. Regulars prefer the seafront rooms. Those on the second-floor have breezy verandahs with sea views, while the first-floor rooms are for the gregarious who like to gab with passersby. Rooms are smallish and simple, but all have fridges and comfortable beds. Doubles US$65 off-season, US$75 in-season, plus tax.

Sanpedrano. Barrier Reef Drive, San Pedro; tel. 501-226-2054, fax 226-2093. Six-room budget spot near the water. Bottom line: For the budget-minded.

Mayan Princess. Barrier Reef Drive, San Pedro; tel. 800-850-4101 or 501-226-2778, fax 226-2784; www.mayanprincesshotel.com. This three-story, seafront condotel, painted a distinctive coral pink, has 23 large and attractive one-bedroom suites (king or queen beds) with air conditioning, kitchenettes, phones and cable TV. Rates are a good value at US$120 double off-season, US$145 in-season, plus hotel tax and 10% service. Some further discounts may be available at certain times. Dive packages and long-term rates available. Amigos del Mar dive shop is nearby. No pool, but each suite has a balcony with wonderful views of the sea, and the whole atmosphere here is comfortable and homey. Long-time managers Rusty and Sheila Nale have moved on to Toledo, where they own Tranquility Lodge.

Martha's. Pescador Drive and Ambergris Street, (P.O. Box 27, San Pedro); tel. 501-226-2053; www.AmbergrisCaye.com/marthas/index.html. In the middle of town, not on the water, but a good budget choice with 12 clean rooms in a three-story wood building. No air conditioning and no phones in rooms. Rates US$27.50 double off-season, US$35 in-season, including tax. Monthly rates available off-season.

Spindrift. Barrier Reef Drive, San Pedro; tel. 800-688-0161 or 501-226-2174, fax 226-2251; www.AmbergrisCaye.com/spindrift/. This dominating three-story concrete hotel won't win any awards from Architectural Digest, but it is on the water in the center of town, with 22 rooms and 2 one-bedroom apartments. All but the cheapest rooms have air-conditioning. Caliente restaurant is on the first floor, and the Pier Lounge at the hotel hosts the "famous chicken drop" at which drinkers bet on where a chicken will poop. Doubles in-season US$53 to $110, apartment US$150, a little less off-season, all plus tax and 5% service.

Holiday Hotel. Barrier Reef Drive, San Pedro, tel. 501-226-2014, fax 226-2295; www.sanpedroholiday.com. This was one of the first hotels on the island, opening June 15, 1965. Built and owned by Celi McCorkle, an island native and near-legend in the hospitality industry, the three-story Holiday Hotel has been well-maintained and remains a pleasant spot convenient to most everything. All rooms have A/C and some have refrigerators. Celi's Restaurant and Celi's Deli are in the hotel. Bottom Time dive shop is located on the hotel's dock. Off-season doubles are US$80 to $110, US$110-$175 in-season. Rates plus 15% tax and service charge.

Rubie's (also known as Ruby's). Barrier Reef Drive, (P.O. Box 56, San Pedro); tel. 501-226-2063; www.AmbergrisCaye.com/rubys/index.html. This is the favorite of many value-conscious visitors. Rooms in the old wooden building are basic but clean, most with shared baths; those on the street side can be a little noisy. Year-round rates: older rooms with fans and en suite baths, US$40 double (cheaper single rooms at US$20 have shared baths); rooms in a new concrete addition on the ocean side sport A/C and private baths and go for around US$60 plus tax, still a good value. Good inexpensive breakfasts and light meals in the first-floor restaurant, which opens at 5 a.m. to catch the fishing crowd. The hotel is often full.

SOUTH EDGE OF TOWN/AIRSTRIP SOUTH:
(Listed from north to south, with those nearest town listed first.)
SunBreeze Beach Hotel. Coconut Drive (P.O. Box 14, San Pedro); tel. 800-688-0191 or 501-226-2191, fax 226-2346; www.sunbreeze.net. The SunBreeze always had a great location, just steps from the San Pedro airstrip (but you won't be bothered by airport noise) and within walking distance of most of what there is to do in town. SunBreeze has been upgraded and considerably improved. Most recently a number of the rooms have been refurbished. There's a freshwater pool, above ground but nice. The pool is just steps from the excellent Blue Water Grill, where you can charge your bar and restaurant tab to your room. Many other restaurants are within a few blocks.

SunBreeze has 39 large rooms, configured in a two-story motel-style U-shape. Five of them are billed as "premier" with amenities such as Jacuzzi tubs. All have strong air conditioners, telephones, color cable TV and tile floors. The best rooms are the deluxe rooms near the water. SunBreeze is directly on the water, with a dock and an independent dive shop, but there's a seawall and no real swimming beach. A good beach is at Ramon's nearby. The SunBreeze has handicap-accessible rooms, uncommon in Belize. Rates for doubles, in-season, US$170 to $225; off-season, US$140-$195, plus 9% tax and 6% service. Discounts for direct booking may be available. The same management also operates **SunBreeze Suites** north in town, formerly Aqua Marina Suites.

Belizean Reef Suites. Coconut Drive, San Pedro; tel. 330-544-4302 or 501-226-2582, fax 330-652-0026; www.belizeanreef.com. Bright white, spic 'n span one-bedroom, one-bath, two-bedroom, two-bath and three-bedroom, three-bath condos, on the sea. This is a popular spot for travelers who want a great location and lots of space. The first-floor units on the water are primo. In some units, there's air conditioning in bedrooms only. No pool, but there's a good beach close by at Ramon's. Rates (minimum four days) US$125 to $225 off-season, US$160 to $245 in-season, plus tax, no service charge. Lower rates for longer stays. Children under 10 not accepted.

The Palms. Coconut Drive (P.O. Box 88, San Pedro); tel. 501-226-3322, fax 226-3601; www.belizepalms.com. This three-story condotel on the water has a lot going for it: 12 attractive and well-decorated condominium apartments plus a small casita near the pool, which is small and on the back side but surrounded by tropical greenery, a sandy beach, and a convenient location at the south edge of town. Rates off-season: one-bedroom condo, US$148--$176, two-bedroom US$200 to $212, with discounts on week or longer stays; in-season: one-bedroom, US$204--$242, two-bedroom, US$275 to $292. Rates plus 9% hotel tax and 10% service charge. US$20 extra per person over two in the one-bedroom and four in the two-bedroom.

Ramon's Village. Coconut Drive, San Pedro; tel. 800-624-4415 or 601-649-1990, fax 601-649-1996; www.ramons.com. Anyone who has heard of San Pedro has probably heard of Ramon's Village, the creation of Ambergris native and pioneering hotel operator Ramon Nuñez. Now American-owned, over the years it has grown from a small, moderately priced collection of thatched cabañas on the beach into a much larger group of multiunit buildings and individual cabañas, with 61 rooms and suites. Rates also have gone up, for some units being near the top price point on the island, but Ramon's retains its sand-and-thatch ambiance. The resort has one of the better beaches on the island. Certainly, it's the best in or near town, part of the hotel's 500-foot water frontage. A small artificial reef near the 420-foot pier brings fish to snorkelers. The pool is gorgeous, but it's smaller than it looks in the brochures. Ramon's has a room service, a popular bar, a (fairly pricey, not particularly notable) restaurant called Pineapple and a big dive operation. Rooms vary from okay to gorgeous. They are divided into three basic categories: beach front, seaside and garden view. There also are one- and two-bedroom suites with kitchenettes, including the deluxe 600 square-foot Presidential suite, and several "honeymoon cabañas." All are now air conditioned. The location, just south of the airstrip, and a five-minute stroll from town, can't be beat. Ramon's does a first-rate job of marketing, especially to travel agents, and it enjoys one of the highest occupancy rates on the island. The crowd here is usually a little younger and more active than the average at island hotels. Rates vary depending on location and date. In-season, cabañas are US$180 to $255 double and suites are US$210 to $480. Off-season rates are only a few dollars less. Rates at **Steve & Becky's**, the cottage colony annex across the street, are US$145-150 double. All rates plus 9% tax and 10% service.

Corona Del Mar. Coconut Drive, San Pedro; tel. 501-226-2055, fax 226-2461; www.ambergriscaye.com/coronadelmar. This is a low profile lodging spot, also known as Woody's Wharf after the gregarious founder of the hotel, but regulars know it offers 12 pleasant rooms and four attractive apartments on the water, at moderate cost. It also has the island's first elevator, but no pool. Off-season rates US$70 to $120; in-season US$85 to $130, all plus tax and 10% service. Friendly, homey place and one of the best values on the island.

Pedro's Backpackers Inn. Seagrape Drive, San Pedro, tel. 501-226-3825; www.backpackersbelize.com. This hostel cum budget hotel south of town isn't on the beach, but it does offer affordable accommodations – single beds with share bath start at US$10 per person. New rooms in the annex with A/C, cable and private bath go for US$50 double in-season and less in low season. Free DSL internet, and there's a sports bar with pool table and projection TV. Also, a small swimming pool. The owner, inveterate Englishman Peter Lawrence, claims Pedro's has the best pizza in Belize.

Changes in Latitudes B&B. Coconut Drive, San Pedro, tel./fax 501-226-2986, www.AmbergrisCaye.com/latitudes/. With six small but pleasant and very clean rooms on the first level, and the helpful owners Renita and Cindy upstairs, this is a B&B with a tasty Belizean breakfast (hot entrees include breakfast tacos or Belizean eggs) served in the common room. Guests have 24-hour access to the common room and kitchen. Changes in Latitudes isn't directly on the water, but it's close. The owners have redecorated all the rooms (all have private bath, A/C and fan.) Rates US$95 double May to mid-December, US$115 rest of year, plus hotel tax (no service charge).

Exotic Caye Beach Resort. Coconut Drive, San Pedro; tel. 501-226-2870; www.belizeisfun.com. Formerly called Playador, this is another property that has gone through many changes over the years. Things seem to have settled down now, with the hotel offering thatch-style one- to three-bedroom units. There's a pool, a pleasant sandy beach, a dive shop and a café (open for breakfast and lunch). The bar, Crazy Canuck's, attracts a lively crowd, especially Canadians. Guests have complimentary use of the San Pedro Club's gym and outdoor tennis courts. The suites and rooms vary considerably in furnishings and amenities; in general you'll be happier in the pricier digs. Rack rates in-season are US$165 to $345, and US$150 to $335 in summer, plus tax.

Coral Bay Villas. Coconut Drive (P.O. Box 1, San Pedro); tel. 501-226-3003; www.coralbaybelize.com. One-bedroom beachfront condo suites in a white two-story concrete building with red tile roof. No pool, but there's a nice sandy beach. Offered through Southwind Realty, rates are US$120 double, off-season, US$150 in-season plus tax.

Caribbean Villas. Coconut Drive (P.O. Box 71, San Pedro); tel. 501-226-2715; www.caribbeanvillashotel.com. The folks who built and ran this place for many years, Wil and Susan Lala, sold out in 2004, and new management has added a beach bar and new swimming pool. There's a variety of accommodations in the two-level whitewashed buildings with tile roofs, from small studios to two-bedroom suites. You'll enjoy the nice beach area and pier, with a little artificial reef for snorkeling, and there are two outdoor hot tubs. There's no full-service restaurant (the beach bar serves continental breakfast and snacks) but several are nearby, as is a supermarket if you want to self-cater. A "people perch" is great for a bird's eye view of the island or for letting the birds see you. In this fast-changing island, this is one of the few hotels near town that still has a significant amount of undeveloped green space around it. Bikes are free for guests, and there are phones in rooms but no TV. Rates are US$105-$260 double mid-December through mid-April, and only a bit less, US$95 to $210, the rest of the year. All rates plus tax (no service charge).

Xanadu Island Resort. Coconut Drive, San Pedro; tel. 501-226-2814, fax 226-3409; www.xanaduresort-belize.com. Xanadu once billed itself as the "world's first monolithic dome resort," a description which might sound good to an engineer but doesn't exactly get our poetic juices flowing. Happily, these monolithic domes look much nicer than they sound. Owner Ivan Sheinbaum one day showed us a new unit that was under construction. The building process is costly, but the result is a masonry dome with foam insulation that, according to Ivan, a Canadian originally from South Africa, is fireproof and can withstand winds of up to 300 mph. The domes are covered with thatch palapa roofs, and inside the condo suites (studios, one-, two-, and three-bedroom) are attractively furnished in earth tone colors, with central air-conditioning, fans, phones and cable TV. Free wireless internet. You get the use of bikes, canoes and kayaks gratis. There's a nice little stretch of seaside sand, though with a seawall, a 350-foot pier and a lovely freshwater swimming pool. Rates US$190 (studio) to $600 (three-bedroom) in-season and US$150 to $495 May to mid-December, plus hotel tax and 8% service charge.

SOUTH END:
(This area begins about a mile south of town. Properties are listed from north to south, with those nearest town listed first.)

Villas at Banyan Bay. Coconut Drive (P.O. Box 91), San Pedro, tel. 866-352-1163 or 501-226-3739, fax 226-2766; www.banyanbay.com. At this

42-unit condotel, now taken over and operated by its lender, Belize Bank, there's all the pleasures of home ... if your home happens to be just steps from the Caribbean. Many of the guests here appear to be families, and a terrific family place this is. The kids love the big, two-section pool, and dad and mom go for the fully equipped kitchen and the whirlpool off the master bedroom. The beach here, about a mile and a half south of town, is one of the best on the island, though it does have some seagrass, and there's a dive and gift shop on the pier. The food at Rico's restaurant on-site doesn't always knock us out, but service is good, and it has a beautiful setting on the water for drinks or dinner; breakfast is handy and well done. We're impressed by the space at Banyan – these units with two full baths are significantly larger than most of the other two-bedroom condo on the island. And we're impressed by the high degree of maintenance. The apartments look just as good now as when they were built several years ago. The woodwork and cabinets are mahogany. The cathedral ceilings in the main living area sport a stunning array of tropical hardwoods. There's a fitness center, too. Rates: US$275-$475 for a two-bedroom condo in-season, depending on location and number of people, and US$195-$275 in the summer.

Grand Colony Villas. Coconut Dr.; tel. 501-226-3739, fax 226/2768; www.grandcolonyvillas.com. New in 2005, the Grand Colony Villas are among the most upscale condos on the island. The 21 two-bedroom, two-bath apartments, range from 1,100 to over 1,900 square feet and have 10-foot ceilings, marble and hardwood floors, mahogany doors and cabinets, and deluxe furnishings. There is also a three-bedroom presidential suite. Rates: US$350 to $775 in season. The beach here is one of the best on the island.

Banana Beach. Coconut Drive (P.O. Box 94, San Pedro); tel. 501-226-3890, toll-free 877-288-1011, fax 226-3891; www.bananabeach.com. Under new Canadian ownership since late 2009, this resort has just about everything to make your vacation a success – a genuinely friendly staff, spacious and furnished one- to four-bedroom suites, affordable rooms and a setting just steps from the sea. The 35 original one-bedroom units are in a single three-story building, designed in a style similar to Mexican hotels, around a courtyard with swimming pool, within watermelon seed spitting distance of the sea. A three-story addition, which went up in 2002, has a variety of "expandable" suites, regular rooms and also some one-bedroom efficiencies, which are rented for longer periods (one month or longer.) The suites have fully furnished kitchens. Also added was a second pool, an air-conditioned restaurant, El Divino, featuring excellent steaks and killer martinis. We recommend you spring for one of the seafront units, especially the second and third floor deluxe units in either the original or new building, all of which have fabulous views of the water. The hotel's tour office, Monkey Business, can set you up with tours, cart rentals and diving. Rates have risen with new management but are still a good value. Off-season, rates start at US$100 double for a room or US$125 for a courtyard suite, US$165 for a seafront one-bedroom suite and top out at US$465 for a four-bedroom seafront suite. In high season, rates range for US$115 to $530. All rates include breakfast.

Mata Rocks. Coconut Drive (P.O. Box 47, San Pedro); tel. 888-628-2757 or 501-226-2336, fax 226-2349; www.matarocks.com. Mata Rocks is a small beachfront hotel with 11 rooms and two junior suites, just south of Banana Beach. With its stucco and wood exterior in a distinctive white, turquoise and purple paint scheme, Mata Rocks has a comfortable, relaxed feel. The thatch beach bar hops, however, and if you want to pop into town, about 1 1/2 miles away, bikes are complimentary. All units have A/C and little fridges, and the junior suites have kitchenettes. In-season doubles US$145 to $170 for rooms and US$195 to $210 for junior suites. Summer rates US$110 to $170. Rates are plus tax but include continental breakfast and roundtrip transfers from the San Pedro airstrip.

Victoria House. Coconut Drive (P.O. Box 22, San Pedro); tel. 800-247-5159 or 713-344-2340, fax 713-224-3287; www.victoria-house.com. If what you want is an upscale but casual resort vacation, Victoria House is just about perfect. About 2 miles south of town, Victoria House is a quiet hideaway on 19 acres, with a variety of accommodations ranging from comfy motel-like rooms in two buildings at the back of the resort to rooms in the main lodge to thatch casitas (recently redone) to deluxe villas and gorgeous new condos. There has been lots of remodeling and upgrading of late, including a second fabulous pool, along with a new group of condo villas at the south edge of the resort. These new condo villas are our pick for some of the most beautiful beach accommodations in Belize. The hotel's restaurant, Palmilla, remains an asset. A full meal plan is US$75 per person per day, but many guests prefer not to be locked into a meal plan and dine around the island. A freestanding lounge cabaña on the beach is ideal for sipping rum drinks or Belikins. Head to the sandy beach area for relaxing, or swim off the pier. The hotel also has a gift shop and a dive operation. Service is top-notch everywhere. Victoria House is a popular place to get married, and the hotel has honeymoon packages. Rates for rooms in-season are June through mid-December, US$180 to $312, suites US$375 to $495; villas, condos and houses, US$595 to $1775. Rates a little lower off-season, all plus tax and 10% service. Rates higher during holiday periods.

Royal Caribbean Resort. 1 Seagrape St.., tel. 501-226-4220; www.ambergriscaye.com/royalcaribbean/. New in late 2005, the little yellow cabins lined up in rows at Royal Caribbean remind a lot of people of army barracks, or DFC by the Sea, but, inside, the 45 cabins are fairly spacious, with tile floors, wicker furniture, and kitchenettes, and all have cable TV and air conditioning. There's a pool and 400 feet of beach immediately next door (south) of Victoria House. The prices, US$125 double off-season and US$140 in-season, are attracting some guests. All rates plus tax. A restaurant is on-site.

Sunset Beach Resort. Coconut Drive, San Pedro; toll-free 866-527-8851 or tel. 501-226-3504; www.condosinbelize.com. This condotel is one of the last hotels on the South End (farther south are private homes and Pelican Reef), about a US$10 cab ride from town. There are one-, two- and three-bedroom units, and there's a nice pool. The beach has a seawall. Rates

US$165 to $195 in season, double, plus US$25 per additional person. Off-season rates are slightly less.

Pelican Reef Villas. Coconut Dr., 501-226-2352; 281-394-3739 in the U.S.; www.pelicanreefvillas.com. While listening to the pool's tinkling waterfall, it is easy to believe you've stumbled upon a hidden tropical treasure, when really the faux cave is a swim-up bar and Pelican Reef is only a little south of San Pedro's bustle. This condotel is one of the most popular on the island, despite relative spendy rates. Large alabaster buildings with butter-yellow trim house the 24 two-bedroom (US$436 including tax for up to four people) and three-bedroom (US$682 for up to six) units. Tastefully decorated, with fully equipped kitchens, mahogany cabinets, granite countertops and plush sleigh-beds, the units are gorgeous and the oceanfront views are stunning. No restaurant on site. The same owners operate **Athens Gate,** a new 12-unit condotel nearby that can be booked through Pelican Reef.

NORTH AMBERGRIS ABOVE THE RIVER CHANNEL:
These hotels are all north of the river channel. Depending on the golf cart trail condition, you can go by cart as far north as around Portofino. Most people, however, take a water taxi or the regularly scheduled Island Ferry or Coastal Xpress. Hotels are listed south to north, with those nearest town listed first.

Reef Village. North Ambergris, just north of the bridge, on the lagoon side; tel. 501-226-4311; www.reefvillagebelize.com. The first large complex you'll come to after crossing the bridge to North Ambergris, on the lagoon side, is this monument to unfortunate taste. Condos here start at around US$130,000, so quite a few of them have sold. If you're on a golf cart, you may be stopped by a time share tout trying to sell you a week or two. Vacation packages including lodging, three local dives and a snorkel trip are around US$1,500 for two. The same developer wants to do the giant South Beach project at the southern tip of the island. There is a new movie and a live performance theater at the resort -- it's called the Paradise Theater.

The Cloisters. North Ambergris, just north of the bridge, on the sea side; tel. 501-226-2816; www.ambergriscaye.com/cloisters/index.html. A cluster of condos, with rates from US$135 to $220 in-season, and US$85 to $145 off, plus tax.

Ak'bol Yoga Retreat & Eco-Resort. North Ambergris; tel. 501-226-2073; www.akbol.com. This hip little resort has seven simple thatch cabañas (US$135-$150 in-season), some with sea views, around a natural stone swimming pool. You'll love the outdoor showers in the cabañas. On the lagoon side is a three-story building with 30 single rooms (shared baths) for those attending yoga retreats. Rates for these rooms start at US$35 plus tax per person, and yoga lessons are US$15. Bean, the restaurant, serves local foods such as salbutes, panades, and pupusas at some of the lowest prices on the island, and it also offers pizzas and vegetarian dishes. Shade, the bar, has cold drinks at reasonable prices.

Grand Caribe Suites and Residences. Tres Cocos area of North Ambergris; tel. 501-226-4726; www.grandcaribe.com. Tim Jeffers' latest project on the island is a beaut! Set in an arc on a 5-acre beachfront site, Grand Caribe's 74 luxury condos, in eight four-story, red-tiled-roof clusters, face the sea and a 500-foot stretch of sandy beach. Grand Caribe debuted in 2008, with the last units opening in 2010. The one, two- and three-bedroom suites (US$365 to $695 in-season, US$275-$525 off-season, plus hotel tax) have Brazilian floor tiles, kitchens with granite countertops and mahogany countertops, and high-quality furnishings. Rare in Belize, some units have elevator access. An unusual feature is the long, curving pier with berths for a number of boats.

Cocotal Inn & Cabanas. North Ambergris, about 2 1/2 miles north of the center of town; tel. 501-226-2097; www.cocotalbelize.com. Looking for small, comfy, affordable spot on the beach? Cocotal could be it. There are only four units - two cottages and two suites in the main house. Our favorite is the casita, with vaulted hardwood ceiling and a four-poster queen bed. It's closest to the beach and also overlooks the pool. All have fully equipped kitchens, so you can cook your own meals, or hop on one of the complimentary bikes and ride to a nearby restaurant. The helpful owners are on-site. Rates are US$125 to $250 in-season, US$100 to $200 off. All rates plus 9% tax.

El Pescador. North Ambergris (P.O. Box 17, San Pedro); tel. 501-226-2398, fax 226-2977; www.elpescador.com. For more than a quarter century, El Pescador has been the island's leading fishing lodge. Today, it's bigger and more upmarket than it used to be, with a pool, villas and other resort amenities, but it's still devoted to anglers and angling. The focus here is on catching tarpon, bonefish, permit and jacks, but you can enjoy a fine meal, served family style in the dining room, or enjoy a drink and a cigar on the verandah. The lodge has 14 comfortable but hardly luxurious units in a rambling two-story colonial-style building with mahogany floors. Adjoining the lodge are new two- and three-bedroom villas, and these are deluxe, with prices to match. El Pescador's emphasis is on fishing packages, which include guide, boat, transfer from Belize City, meals and taxes, but there also are family and couples packages. About the only extras are drinks, tips for guides and purchases of any fishing gear. These packages start at US$1,495 per person for three nights (two persons per room and two per boat) and range up to over US$5,020 per person for a week (one person in a room and one per boat.

Capricorn. North Ambergris (P.O. Box 247, San Pedro); tel. 501-226-2809, fax 220-5091 www.ambergriscaye.com/capricorn/index.html. Under new ownership as of late 2006, the Capricorn restaurant has regained some of its lost luster. Capricorn the resort still has three cozy, hand-built wooden cabins, all with air conditioning. Double rates off-season US$155, in-season US$185, including continental breakfast, plus tax and 10% service. *(See review of restaurant, below.)*

Seascape Villas. North Ambergris; tel. toll-free 888-753-5164 or 501-226-2119; www.seascapebelize.com. This collection of six upscale homes on four beachfront acres, built by noted island developers Bob and Diane Campbell, opened in 2006. Each villa has around 3,000 square feet, with a sunken living room, slate floors, outdoor garden with hot tub, and unobstructed views of the sea. The homes are privately owned but managed by the developers, and available for rent when the owners aren't in residence. Expect to pay around US$450 to $750 per day, more for larger groups, less off-season.

Belizean Shores. North Ambergris (P.O. Box 1, San Pedro); tel. 800-319-9026 or 501-226-2355, fax 226-2931; www.belizeanshores.com. Belizean Shores is a popular condotel choice on North Ambergris (a US$7 water taxi ride to town, each way), with good rates and a lot of space in the units. The pool is a beaut, one of the best on the island, with a swim-up bar, and huge. The beach is small but fairly nice, and the seagrass is removed from some of the swimming area, and there's a 350-foot pier. There's free use of kayaks, so you can kayak out to the reef and snorkel. Rates US$139 to $199 double mid-April through November, US$239 to $299 in-season, plus tax. A sister resort nearby, **Coco Beach,** is even newer and nicer, though more expensive, with rates as high as US$649 for a two-bedroom seaview suite.

Las Terrazas. North Ambergris, 4 miles north of town; tel. 800-447-1553 or 501-226-4249; www.lasterrazasbelize.com. Las Terrazas, which opened in late 2007, is a luxury 39-unit condominium project with two- and three-bedroom suites. Rates are US$295 to $495 in-season, US$195 to $385 off-season. The condos have 9-foot ceilings, travertine tile floors, fully equipped kitchens with Brazilian granite countertops, and all the amenities including cable TV and high-speed Internet. A two-level pier sweeps out into the sea. A dive shop, White Sands Cove Dive Shop, is now on-site. When completed (originally set for late 2008 but now postponed), there will be a restaurant, fitness center and two pools (one pool is currently open).

Azul Resort. North Ambergris; tel. 501/226-4012; www.azulbelize.com. This is where we'd like to stay if we had the money — US$1,000 a day double all-inclusive (lodging, all meals, drinks, taxes, transfers), slightly higher at peak times. This resort has only two beach villas, but, man, they are nice. The two-level villas have 20-foot ceilings with beams of mylady wood. Custom kitchens feature Viking appliances, and the cabinets and most of the furniture are made of zericote wood. Each villa has a 50-inch plasma flat-screen TV, and Bose theater system. On the rooftop, you can relax in your own hot tub. The two beach houses share a beautiful pool, 400 feet of beach, and about 10 acres of prime property. Rojo Lounge, run by the same couple, Vivian and Jeff, is next door for drinks in a romantic beachside setting and some of the best food on the island. Bottom line: Hip, romantic and fabulous.

Mata Chica. North Ambergris, tel. 501-220-5010, fax 220-5012; www.matachica.com. When it opened in late 1997, Mata Chica raised the bar on what constitutes hip, deluxe lodging on Ambergris Caye. Mata Chica's original owners designed this resort to the hilt. Each of the 12 air-conditioned cabañas and 2 two-bedroom villas, has a fruit theme - mango, watermelon, banana, and so on - a theme that begins with the exterior color and is carried through down to the tiles in the baths. It all may be a little too much for some, but others say the colors remind them of Gauguin. New owners have made some much-needed renovations. The beach here is postcard lovely, though swimming isn't much, and a new pool opened in 2005. There's a mini-spa. Mambo, the hotel's expensive restaurant (entrees up to around US$30), offers an eclectic menu, albeit emphasizing Italian dishes and seafood. Like the lodging, Mambo is seaside monument to design, with dramatic lighting and little touches like salt and pepper shakers made from seashells. It's definitely a romantic spot for dinner. Doubles US$280 to US$415 in-season and US$215 to $295 off-season, plus tax and 10% service. Two-bedroom villas are US$725 in and US$525 off, for up to four persons. A 5,000 sq. ft. "beach mansion" is US$1,045 in-season. Rates include transfers from San Pedro and continental breakfast. Package rates also available. No children under 10.

Portofino. North Ambergris (P.O. Box 36, San Pedro); tel. 501-220-5096, fax 226-4272; www.portofinobelize.com. One of Portofino's drawing cards is that it has thatch cabañas, fairly rare on the island. The resort, which opened in 2001 on the site of another resort, the Green Parrot, has lushly landscaped grounds, a well-liked restaurant, dive shop, thatch units including beach cabañas, tree house suites and an 800-square-foot honeymoon suite with whirlpool. There's a new swimming pool. Rates: US$280 to $420 double in high season, US$220 to $375 in low, including continental breakfast but not taxes or 10% service. The Mansion (US$900 in-season) sleeps up to eight.

Blue Reef Island Resort. North Ambergris; tel. 866-825-8501; www.bluereefresort.com. About 8 miles north of San Pedro Town, Blue Reef, which opened in 2005, with construction continuing in 2006-2007, has one- and two-bedroom condo units in six three-story buildings, each with five or six units. The condo apartments are very attractive, with granite tile floors and 10-ft. ceilings, and all have sea views. The swimming pool also overlooks the water. They should be nice, as most sell for around half a million US. Each bedroom has a king bed. Guest rooms have satellite TV, air-conditioning and CD players. There's little within walking distance, so for company you'll have to depend on the hotel's shuttle boat into town, a 20 minute ride each way. According to all reports, the resort's restaurant has good food, or you can have groceries delivered and cook in your upscale kitchen. Rates: US$299 to $459 in-season, US$249 to $359 off-season, plus 9% hotel tax. All-inclusive packages available.

PRIVATE ISLANDS NEARBY

Cayo Espanto. tel. in U.S. 888-666-4282 or 910-323-8355; www.aprivateisland.com. Ready, willing and able to pay US$20,000 a couple for a week's pampering, not including airfare or tax? Then Cayo Espanto, a tiny private island on the back or bay side of Ambergris, about 3 miles west San Pedro, may be for you. At Cayo Espanto, the resort staff lines up, as on the old TV show "Fantasy Island" to greet you on arrival. Cayo Espanto's American owners quickly figured out that, in Belize's economy, it's not that expensive to hire a bunch of workers to keep the staff-to-guest ratio at two to one, especially given that the island has no more than 16 guests at one time. So if you like attentive service, you definitely will get it at Cayo Espanto, including your own "houseman" who cares for your every need day or night. Start with breakfast in bed and end the evening with pisco sours (all meals and most drinks, but not wine or champagne, are included in the price) on your private dock, before bundling off to your king-size bed with its luxurious Yves de Lorme sheets. Currently there are five villas, three one-bedroom and two two-bedroom. The villas are quite large – the smallest is 1,500 square feet – and all but one have small private "plunge" pools. We especially like the units with open-air design, with walls that fold out let the Caribbean in. Having said that, the villas are not as large or as deluxe as some other lodging in Belize, such as the condos at Victoria House, or the houses at Seascape or Azul Resort on North Ambergris. Meals are created by Cayo Espanto's crew of award-winning chefs and brought to your villa. Think dishes like Herbed Goat Cheese Mousse Atop Tomato Speckled Polenta Cakes with Balsamic Onion Compote. The resort offers a full range of tours, dive and snorkel trips, fishing and all the rest, but most guests seem to spend most of their time at their villas (and for the US$75 more per hour they're paying to stay here, who wouldn't?) The rates are like the money-is-no-object rates on villa rentals on St. Barths: US$1,195 to $2,295 double in winter, and US$1,195 to $1,995 off-season per night, including meals and most drinks, plus 9% tax and 15% service. There's a minimum stay of five nights (some exceptions to this may be made). Rates are higher during the Christmas season. Transfers from the International Airport by air are extra. Is it worth it? Obviously there are people who figure it is.

Caye Chapel Island Resort. Caye Chapel; tel. 501-226-8250; www.cayechapel.com. Caye Chapel is a privately owned island just south of Caye Caulker and about 12 miles from Belize City. The island resort was developed as a corporate retreat and deluxe golfing hideaway, but for some reason, perhaps weak marketing, it has never really taken off. The owner, Larry Addington, a Kentucky mining baron, having failed to sell the island in one chunk for a reported US$75 million, is trying to sell off the island piece by piece, with five villas and 14 building lots up for sale now. (Sunrise Realty in San Pedro is the sales agent.) The future of the island as a tourism destination is unclear. One thing's for sure, though: The island has Belize's only 18-hole golf course, a beautiful par-72, 7,000-yard seaside course. If golf is your game, this is the best Belize has to offer, with gorgeous views of the sea and the reef, and challenges provided by the brisk prevailing winds and the occasional crocodile. The clubhouse, between the front and back nines, rivals anything at a country club in the States. It has tile floors, high ceilings, imported fixtures and a bar that would knock the socks off Dean Martin's ghost. The island also is outfitted with a Olympic-size swimming pool, private airstrip and tennis courts. If you just want to visit and play golf, day rates for unlimited golf 9 am to 4 pm, golf cart and club rental, are US$150 per person, not including transport to the island -- US$20 roundtrip by water taxi from San Pedro. Day visitors who don't care to play golf are charged US$50, plus transportation.

AMBERGRIS CAYE DINING

Ambergris Caye has Belize's widest selection of restaurants, ranging from inexpensive local spots and pizza joints to a couple that will have you reaching for your Platinum Amex. The emphasis is on seafood, of course, but many restaurants also serve chicken and pork, and even steak. Lobster is usually the most-expensive item on the menu (in-season mid-June to mid-February), at around US$20 to $30. Pasta and Mexican-style dishes also are popular. After all that pricey seafood, an honest plate of Belizean beans and rice will taste real good. Vegetarians can get by okay in San Pedro, even if you don't eat seafood. Rice and beans are ubiquitous (but often these are seasoned with lard or meat). Many Mexican places do up vegetarian burritos, and of course pizza is available at many spots. Fruit plates, with mangos, pineapple, watermelon and other local fruits, are a part of breakfast at a lot of places. Many restaurants will do vegetarian versions of their specialties – just ask.

Dress on the island is very casual. Even at the spiffiest places, tee-shirt and shorts are okay, although some guests at the top restaurants will wear casual resort clothes – a light summer dress or a golf shirt with khakis.

Reservations are usually not necessary, except where noted. During the season, at popular dining spots, you may have to wait a few minutes, or longer. Grab a Belikin and relax while you wait.

Keep in mind that small restaurants on a resort island can change overnight, with the loss of a cook or a setback in the personal life of the owner. Always ask locally if the restaurant you're thinking about is still good.

Price ranges shown are for typical meals for one (usually dinner), not including tip, tax or alcoholic drinks. Price ranges:

Inexpensive: Under US$5
Moderate: US$6-$15
Expensive: US$16-30
Very Expensive: Over US$30

IN TOWN OR NEARBY:

Blue Water Grill. At SunBreeze Hotel, Coconut Drive; tel. 501-226-3347. Blue Water Grill aims high, and usually hits the spot. Try the mixed seafood grill or the local snapper dusted in cumin. The crispy Coconut Shrimp is a winner. Many dishes are Asian-influenced. One or two nights a week sushi is offered. Often jammed. Open for lunch and dinner. Expensive/Very Expensive.

Red Ginger. Barrier Reef Drive, at The Phoenix; tel. 501-226-4623. With its stylishly minimalist décor, this new restaurant could be in L.A., but it's actually at The Phoenix condos at the north end of San Pedro. No sea views here - you gaze at deep red and rich cream walls, with brown earth-toned accents, and tropical wild ginger plants in glass vases. The specialty is seafood. The service is a notch above most other places in San Pedro. Expensive/Very Expensive.

Wild Mango's. Barrier Reef Drive, south near the town library. Award-winning chef Amy Knox moved here from Victoria House, bringing her "New Wave Latin" cooking with her. She quickly made Wild Mango's one of the top restaurants on the island. One of the specialties is ceviche, not just one kind but a variety of different ceviches. You can try a sampler, the Three Amigos. Knox also delivers some great Mexican dishes and, of course, seafood. The snapper is particularly good. Open for lunch and dinner. Moderate/ Expensive.

Sunset Grill. On the lagoon side of town, tel. 501-226- 2600. Seafood is the specialty here, with the snapper dishes all very good, and after your meal you can feed the tarpon in the lagoon. Per the name, the sunset views are lovely. Open for lunch and dinner. Expensive/Very Expensive.

Elvi's Kitchen. Pescador Drive, tel. 501-226-2176, fax 226-3056. Yes, it's a little touristy, and yes, the waiters are a little hyper, and, yes, it's a little more expensive than some, but Elvi's does a fine job with fish and just about everything. Doña Elvia Staines began her restaurant as a take-out burger stand in 1974. It has grown in fame and fortune year after year, until today it is probably the best-known restaurant in Belize. There are still burgers on the lunch menu (around US$6) along with shrimp and fish burger versions. At dinner, you choose from large selection of seafood, chicken and other dishes, and almost all of it is good, with prices mostly under US$15 for entrees. We always enjoy our meals here. The sand floor and the frangipani tree around which the main dining room is built add atmosphere. Open for lunch and dinner. Moderate/Expensive.

JamBel Jerk Pit. Barrier Reef Drive, at the Coral Beach Hotel (there's also a location in Belize City). Take a fat Belizean grouper and jerk it Jamaica style and whattyagot? Some of the spiciest, tastiest food in San Pedro, that's what. The chicken wings, jerk-style pork, fish and chicken are all delicious. Open for lunch and dinner. Moderate.

Cocina Caramba. Pescador Drive; tel. 501-603-1652. Owner Rene Reyes has made a big success out of Caramba by simply serving good food in large portions at moderate prices. This spot is usually packed. Just about any of the seafood and Mexican dishes are tasty and well-prepared. Open for lunch and dinner. Moderate.

Caliente. Spindrift Hotel, Barrier Reef Drive. This restaurant, run by Jenny Staines and her partner, gets attention for its spicy versions of traditional favorites such as conch ceviche, its big variety of seafood and Mexican dishes and for its delicious soups. Locally popular for lunch, and open for dinner, too. Moderate/Expensive.

Estel's-by-the-Sea. Barrier Reef Drive, tel. 501-226- 2019. Charlie and Estella Worthington run this little seaside restaurant near Central Park. With its sand floor and piano (you ain't heard piano until you hear it played on a sand floor), this place reeks with atmosphere. It's a favorite spot for breakfast, with all the usual egg-and-bacon basics including fried potatoes, but you'll also enjoy the burritos and huevos rancheros. Opens early, closed Tuesdays. Free Wi-Fi, too. Moderate.

The Reef. Pescador Drive, tel. 501-226-3212. This local favorite serves tasty Belizean fare such as stew chicken with rice and beans in large portions at small prices. Open for lunch and dinner. At lunch, there's a daily special for a few dollahs. Inexpensive to Moderate.

Fido's. Barrier Reef Drive, tel. 501-226-3714. (Pronounced FEE-doh's.) Extremely popular, centrally located spot for a beer and a bite. Sit under the big palapa by the sea and enjoy burgers, fish and chips or lobster burrito. Live music many nights. Moderate.

Celi's Restaurant. San Pedro Holiday Hotel, Barrier Reef Drive, tel. 501-226-2014. Celi's, on the beach side of the Holiday Hotel, is one of the long-established, unpretentious eateries on the island. Fish is a specialty, and it won't cost you an arm and a leg. You can dine inside or in a screened area by the beach. Open for lunch and dinner. Moderate/Expensive. **Celi's Deli** (Inexpensive), for quick snacks, sandwiches, and meat pies, is nearby.

BC's Beach Bar. Tel. 501-226-3289. Named after the owners, Bruce and Charlene, BC's is on the beach just south of SunBreeze. Don't miss the Sunday afternoon barbecue here. On Tuesday evenings, they do burgers on the beach. Other times, it's popular with the drinking crowd. Moderate.

DandE's Frozen Custard. Pescador Dr. next to Cocina Caramba; tel. 501-608-9100. Dan and Eileen (DandE, get it?) Jamison, who used to run the local weekly paper, the *San Pedro Sun*, now operate this custard and sorbet shop. For something with an island flavor, try the mango sorbet or the soursop frozen custard. Inexpensive.

Rubie's (or Ruby's). Barrier Reef Drive, tel. 501-226-2063. If you can't sleep or are heading out for a day of fishing, get up early and grab a casual breakfast at Ruby's. For a few dollars, you can enjoy coffee, burritos and the best coconut tarts on the island. Later in the day, there are sandwiches and daily specials. It starts serving around 5 a.m., and usually stays open until just after lunch. Inexpensive.

Casa Pan Dulce Bakery. Boca del Rio area north, with a second location at the corner of Pescador Drive and Buccaneer; tel. 501-226-3242. Formerly La Popular, Pan Dulce has the best baked stuff on the island. It has a huge selection of more than 70 kinds of breads and pastries, all baked fresh locally. Inexpensive.

Street vendors offer food that is cheap, good and safe to eat. Most are in stalls at Central Park. You can get a whole plate full of delicious food for a few bucks. Don't worry – it won't upset your tummy. Also don't miss the Lions Club barbecue on Friday and Saturday nights. The barbecue is great and the flan is out of this world. The money also goes to a good cause – improved health care on the island. Inexpensive.

SOUTH OF TOWN

Hidden Treasure. Escalante area, tel. 501-226-4111.Hidden away on a back street in a residential neighborhood south of town, Hidden Treasure won Belize Restaurant of the Year from the Belize Tourism Board in 2009. At dinner, you dine by candlelight, in the sultry tropical air under a pitched roof set off by bamboo, mahogany and cabbage bark wood. The signature BBQ ribs are seasoned with traditional Garifuna spices and glazed with pineapple or papaya sauce. Mojarro a la Lamanai (US$20) is snapper seasoned with Mayan spices and cooked in a banana leaf. Expensive/Very Expensive. (Rather surprisingly, the restaurant is for sale.)

Palmilla, Victoria House Restaurant. Coconut Drive at Victoria House resort, tel. 501-226-2067. The main restaurant at Victoria House, Palmilla, once dependent on unexciting buffets, has had a marked change for the better under a succession of innovative chefs. For dinner, dine by romantic candlelight. Breakfast by the pool with views of the sea isn't to be missed. Expensive to Very Expensive.

Pinocchio Italian Restaurant & Pizzeria. Seagrape Dr., tel 501-226-4447. New in 2009, this trattoria imports rarities to San Pedro like gorgonzola cheese and Italian salami and provides a true taste of Italy. Covered seating that is open to the air gives an island ambience, while the brick pizza oven, homemade pasta and the staff's authentic accents are reminders that the owners hail from Rome. Expensive.

El Divino. Coconut Drive at Banana Beach; tel. 501-226-3890. This air-conditioned restaurant (there's also seating outside) has some of the best steaks around. Also try the wood fired pizza. The bar serves big, ice-cold martinis. Expensive.

Rico's Bar & Grill. Coconut Drive, at Villas at Banyan Bay. Food is only so-so, but no other restaurant on the island has a better seaside setting than Rico's. It's right on the beach. This is a fine place for breakfast or lunch on the water. After your lunch, you can feed your leftovers to the "pet" moray eels that hang out at waterside. Dinners are on the pricey side, but, again, the seaside setting is wonderful. Moderate/Expensive.

Ali Baba. Coconut Drive, on the east side near the airstrip. Excellent, high-value takeout roast chicken (whole chicken, US$8) and Middle Eastern dishes like hummus. Inexpensive/Moderate.

Antojitos San Telmo. Coconut Drive near Villas at Banyan Bay, tel. 501-226-2921. It's just a joint, but a good joint, with snacks like tacos and burritos for almost nothing. Inexpensive.

Tropical Cooking. Coconut Drive across from the Tropic Air terminal. Good local lunches at modest prices -- like four delicious chicken tacos for US$2.50. Inexpensive/Moderate.

NORTH AMBERGRIS

Rojo Lounge and Market. At Azul Resort; tel. 501- 226-4012. This may be is the hippest restaurant in Belize. It enjoys a romantic beachside setting, where you can watch the Caribbean change colors by day or the stars flicker at night. There's even a pool, if you feel like taking a dip. Try the conch pizza or grouper stuffed with cashew-crusted lobster. The guava-glazed ribs are a specialty. Killer mojitos, too. Rojo Market has groceries and prepared foods for takeout. You'll want to take a water taxi here. Expensive to Very Expensive.

Rendezvous. Next door to Journey's End, tel. 501-226- 3426. We'll meet you here! This may be the first Thai-French fusion restaurant in Central America and surely it's the best. Run by expats who formerly lived in Southeast Asia and elsewhere, with expert help from local cooks, Rendezvous has become one of the top restaurants on the island. With just 24 seats, the setting is intimate, on the second floor of a colonial-style house by the water. The menu changes from time to time, but you can expect dishes such as pad thai or chicken in a red curry coconut sauce. The restaurant even makes its own wines (from imported grape juice). Reservations suggested. Reached by water taxi. Expensive to Very Expensive.

Capricorn. About 3 miles north of San Pedro, tel. 501- 226-2809. After a brief downturn in quality, under new owners Capricorn has regained its sea legs and once again is one of the best restaurants on the island. If there's a weakness, it is that the chef stays with proven winners, such as filet mignon and grilled lobster (each US$38, plus tax and service) and rarely opts for innovation. The seaside setting is romantic. Reservations essential. Reached by water taxi. Very Expensive.

Mambo. Mata Chica Beach Resort; tel. 501-220-5010. Wow! If you'd visited the island a few years ago, you'd never have thought Ambergris Caye would get this kind of place. The restaurant space is open, appealing and upscale. Everything is designed to the hilt – even the menus show hours of design time. On those menus is a selection of sophisticated Italian dishes and seafood, along with daily specials. But you need to bring plenty of money or plastic. Prices are stratospheric, at least by Belizean standards. Open for lunch and dinner. Reached by water taxi. Very Expensive.

Aji Tapa Bar and Restaurant. Beachfront, Buena Vista area, North Ambergris (about 2 1/2 miles north of town centre), tel. 501-226-4047. Relax in a shady seaside patio, with views of the beach and barrier reef in the distance, and snack on delicious small plates of barbecue shrimp, bacon-wrapped dates, and a heavenly artichoke dip. For a special treat, try the seafood paella. Expensive.

Legends Burger House. Tres Cocos area, North Ambergris, on the golf cart path at the site of the former Sweet Basil, tel. 501-226-2113. Burgers and nothing but burgers, but they are excellent at this "American-style burger joint." New in late 2009, Legends already has a big following. Burgers, which come with crisp fries, are reasonably priced, from around US$6 to $10. Chili fries are US$6, and an ice-cold draft Belikin is US$2.50. Moderate

Lazy Croc BBQ. Just north of Grand Caribe, about 2 1/2 miles north of town centre, tel. 501-226-4015. As befits a BBQ joint, the menu here is short and sweet - pulled pork, BBQ chicken, ribs, Buffalo wings and chili, with sides of coleslaw, French fries, BBQ beans and macaroni and cheese. Barbecue platters with garlic toast and two sides are US$8-$15. Lazy Croc is only open only three days a week (11-6 Friday-Sunday). And, yes, there are real crocs in the lagoon near the restaurant, but don't give them leftovers. Moderate/Expensive.

WHERE TO PARTY

For visitors, San Pedro is the nightlife capital of Belize. Still, San Pedro is not exactly a world-class party town. Nightlife usually consists of drinks and dinner at a local restaurant, with perhaps a later visit to one of the "clubs" or hotel beach bars, a few of which rev up late and don't stop until 4 or 5 a.m. Quite a few expats on the island have made a career out of drinking.

Big Daddy's is probably the hottest spot on the island, and things sometimes go late and loud here. Across the street, **Jaguar's** hops, too, especially toward the weekend. The real action at these spots often doesn't get started until midnight. **Fido's** is always busy, with lots of people dropping in for a drink or to hear some music. **BC's, Wet Willy's** and the **Tackle Box** are popular bars where you can get a cold beer or something stronger. **Pedro's** is a local expat hangout, and some days there's a poker game going in the back room. Cholo's and a couple of other small bars have pool tables. Several hotels have popular beach-side bars, including the **Pier Lounge** at the Spindrift Hotel, (home of the chicken drop), Ramon's **Purple Parrot,** Exotic Caye's **Crazy Canucks, Coconut's** bar, Mata Rocks' **Squirrel's Nest** beach bar. You can stroll along the beach south of town and slake your thirst at a half dozen beach bars. If, after a long day in the sun, you're too pooped to pop a Belikin, you'll be glad that many of the island's hotels have cable TV, with about the same channels as you'd get in the U.S.

A long-time small casino on the island, the Palace Casino – where the slogan was "It Ain't Vegas" – has closed. A large casino is open at the **Belize Yacht Club,** but it still ain't Vegas. For more action, you can try the Princess Casino in Belize City. There also are three sizeable casinos in the Commercial Free Zone near Corozal Town (a 25-minute flight away), of which Las Vegas Casino is the largest and newest, and a small Princess casino in San Ignacio. A casino at the north end of the Placencia peninsula is under construction.

Shops on Front Street, Caye Caulker

CHAPTER 27:
CHECKING OUT CAYE CAULKER

Getting to Caulker

You can fly to Caulker's little airstrip on **Tropic Air** (www.tropicair.com) or **Maya Island Air** (www.mayaregional.com) from Belize City. Flights from either

International or Municipal to San Pedro will stop, on demand, at Caye Caulker. Fares are the same as to San Pedro – US$63 one-way from International and from Municipal US$35. Flights from San Pedro to Belize City also drop passengers at Caulker's airstrip, again for the same fare as to Belize City itself.

Most visitors to Caulker, however, come by boat. Two water taxi companies, with fast boats that hold up to 100 passengers, connect Belize City with Caye Caulker (US$7.50 one-way), each with eight to ten departures a day. The **Caye Caulker Water Taxi Association,** for a long time the main water taxi group, (www.cayecaulkerwatertaxi.com) boats depart from the Marine Terminal near the Swing Bridge in Belize City; **San Pedro-Belize Express** (www.sanpedrowatertaxi.com) boats leave from the nearby Brown Sugar dock near the Tourism Village. It's a 45-minute ride to Caulker.

GETTING ORIENTED

The Caye Caulker Water Taxi Association boats come in at the main public pier on the front side of the island, and the San Pedro-Belize Express boats dock at a pier nearby. If you come ashore at the main public pier, the pink and green Trends Beachfront hotel and behind it the Sandbox restaurant are on your right, and Seaside Cabañas are on your left. Walk a few sandy feet and you'll come to Front Street. Go right, or north, and in 10 minutes or so you'll pass several good hotels and end up at the Split, the main place to swim on the island. Go left or south and you'll find some of the island's better beachfront properties. Many of the island's restaurants, shops and hotels are on Front Street or on the beachfront.

If you come by air, the little airstrip is at the south end of the island. You can walk the 20 minutes or so back to the heart of the village, or you can get a golf cart taxi.

CAYE CAULKER HOTELS

This is not a complete list of island hotels, but these are among our favorites in all price ranges. They are arranged by location, either north or south of the main "front pier" where the Caye Caulker Water Taxi Association boats arrive, and then by price range, from most to least expensive.

North of the Main Front Pier:

Caye Reef Condos. Front St.; tel. 501-226-0381 or 610-0240; www.cayereef.com. Caye Reef Condos are the newest upscale accommodations on the island. The six two-bedroom condo apartments are on Front Street not far from the Split, with a small swimming pool at the front, hidden behind a wall. You can book either a two-bedroom entire unit or just one of the bedrooms. All units are fully air-conditioned, with tile floors, custom kitchens, private verandas with sea views (second and third floors), Belizean art on the walls and flat-screen TVs. There are great views of the reef from the fourth floor roof top patio, where there is a rooftop whirlpool. Rates for the full units are US$195 in-season, US$165 off. The penthouse is US$215 in-season and US$180 off. Rates plus tax and are higher at Christmas-New Years.

Iguana Reef Inn. Middle Street next to soccer field, (P.O. Box 31, Caye Caulker); tel. 501-226-0213, fax 226-0087; www.iguanareefinn.com. This is the Ritz-Carlton of Caye Caulker. The 12 suites have air-conditioning, Belizean furniture, queen beds and local artwork. A swimming pool was added in late 2006. Considering the size and amenities of the suites, the rates, US$135 to $165 in-season plus tax, are reasonable, and they include continental breakfast. A penthouse suite on the third level with two bedrooms and two baths is pricey at US$375. If there's a downside, it is that the hotel is on the back side of the island and not on the Caribbean, though from some suites you have a view of sunsets on the lagoon. The hotel's Web site is a good source of information about the island. No children under 10. The hotel currently is for sale.

Caye Caulker Condos. Front St., tel. 501-226-0072; www.cayecaulkercondos.com. Want a suite with a full kitchen to prepare

198

some of your own meals? Try these condo apartments. Each of the 8 cozy units, on the west side of Front Street, has a private verandah facing the water, less than 100 feet away; those on the second floor have the better views. All the units have tile floors and most have satellite TVs, but not phones. Bikes are free. There's now a swimming pool, too. Rates US$120 to $135 double in-season, US$110-$120 off-season, plus 9% hotel tax.

De Real Macaw. Front St.; tel. 501-226-0459, fax 226-0497; www.derealmacaw.biz. This friendly spot, which is on the west side of Front Street but still close enough to catch the breezes, has rooms and a two-bedroom self-catering apartment and beach house, some units with and some without air-conditioning. There's a porch with hammocks. In-season rates: US$25 to $70 for rooms, US$120-$130 for a two-bedroom unit, slightly lower off-season.

Trends Beachfront Hotel. Beachfront near public pier; tel. 501-226-0094, fax 226-0097; www.trendsbze.com. As you arrive on the water taxi, this tropically pink and green hotel is one of the first things you see, just to the right of the public pier. Thanks to its location and its seven bright clean rooms, each with a queen and a double bed, mini-fridge and private bath, it stays full much of the time. Rates around US$40 double, more if you need A/C. The same people operate the original Trends Guesthouse, around the corner. It's cheaper, but it's not on the water.

Tina's Bak Pak Hostel. Beachfront just north of public pier, tel. 501-226-0351; www.tinashostelbelize.com. For US$10 per person, you can grab a hammock or a bunk bed at this hostel on the beach. Though the original hostel dorms are very basic, you're right on the water, and the price and location mean this place is usually packed with young people. The "penthouse" dorm on the third floor has a view of the barrier reef. Tina's Hostel also now runs the former **Auxillou Suites** next door, which has been converted into upscale hostel space, with bunk beds in air-conditioned comfort at US$25 per person plus tax.

South of the Main Front Pier:

Seaside Cabanas. P.O. Box 39, Caye Caulker; tel. 501-226-0498, fax 501-226-0125; www.seasidecabanas.com. Rebuilt after a 2003 fire, this seafront hotel, with 15 rooms and a seafront suite, is now one of the top places on the island, and one of only a few hotels on the island with a swimming pool. Painted a deep mustard color, with a combination of tropical thatch and Moorish-influenced design, the buildings are in a U-shape. Four of the rooms have private roof-top terraces for sunning or watching the sea in privacy. The hotel now has in-room phones and free Wi-Fi. Rates around USS105 to $130 double most of the year, plus 9% tax. The hotel is currently for sale but is operating normally.

Tree Tops. P.O. Box 29, Caye Caulker, tel. 501-226-0240, fax 226-0115; www.treetopsbelize.com. Set back a little from the water, Tree Tops is run by Austrian-born Doris Creasy. All rooms have air-conditioning available, cable TV and a refrigerator. Two third-floor suites (US$98 plus tax),

Sunset and Sunrise, have king-size beds and private balconies with views of the sea. A small courtyard is a great place to read or just lounge in a hammock. Belize needs more places like this one – the guest rooms are clean as a pin, the entire place is meticulously maintained, the owner is helpful and rooms start around US$50 double. Highly recommended.

Barefoot Beach Belize. South of the public pier; tel. 501-226-0205; www.barefootbeachbelize.com Formerly the Seaview Guest House, the current owners, Kim and Susan Briggs, have turned this little seafront hotel into one of the most popular spots on Caulker. There are three rooms and a suite in a pastel blue, concrete building with pink and yellow trim and three cottages (US$97- $158 a day). Don't confuse this place with the similarly named Barefoot Caribe.

Lazy Iguana B&B. South of the public pier on the back side of the island, near airstrip, tel. 501-226-0350, fax 226-0320; www.lazyiguana.net. Owner Mo Miller says shoes are not required at this four-room B&B. The rooms are furnished with attractive wicker and tropical hardwood furniture. Views of the sunsets from the fourth-level rooftop terrace are terrific. The common room has TV and internet access. Rates US$95 to $105 double year-round, plus tax.

Pancho's Villas. Pasero St., tel. 501-226-0304; www.panchosvillasbelize.com. Pancho's Villas offers six attractive new one-bedroom suites in a yellow three-story building. Each suite has air-conditioning and ceiling fans, cable TV, Wi-Fi, fridge and microwave. It's not on the beach. Rates under US$100 including tax.

Maxhapan Cabañas. Tel. 501-226-0118. This little spot is in the center of the village and not on the water, but it's very popular because it's neat and clean and a good value. Set in a small, sandy and shady garden, there are rooms in a two-story cabaña and in a one-level building. They have tile floors and a veranda with hammocks. Complimentary bikes and snorkel gear. Rates around US$80.

Jaguar Morning Star. Middle St. south of the public pier, tel. 501-226-0347; www.jaguarmorningstar.com. This quiet little budget inn, just behind Treetops, is a good value. It's well run by a Belizean-Canadian couple. There are two rooms, way up on the third floor, with a verandah offering views of the island and the sea, plus a little cabin at the back in the garden. Rates US$45 to $65. Like many other places on Caulker, it's for sale.

Shirley's Guesthouse. South End near nature reserve, (P.O. Box 13, Caye Caulker); tel. 501-226-0145; www.shirleysguesthouse.com. Nine cabins and rooms, all clean and pleasant with sea views. Some with shared baths. US$50 to $90 December-May, US$40 to $65 rest of year, plus tax. Adults only.

Tom's Hotel. Beachfront, about 4 blocks south of the public pier, (P.O. Box 15, Caye Caulker); tel. 501-226-0102; e-mail toms@btl.net. This backpacker favorite, with 5 cabins and lots of rooms in a two-story concrete building, continues to attract a crowd. Many rooms are small, share baths and can be hot, but the seaside location, friendly management and low prices, starting at around US$15, keep regulars coming back. No credit cards.

Vacation Rentals

For small vacation rental house on Caulker, expect to pay around US$350 to $1,000 a week, or US$40 to $100 a night.

Caye Caulker Rentals. Front St., tel. 501-226-0029; www.cayecaulkerrentals.com. This rental agency has some two dozen houses for rent, some from as low as US$50 a night, and others, including beachfront houses, from under US$400 a week.

Heredia's Apartments & House Rentals. Calle del Sol, about a block from the public pier, tel. 501-226-0132. Offers several budget apartments and houses on the lagoon side, most under US$300 a week.

Caye Caulker Dining

Caye Caulker has more than 20 restaurants, mostly small spots with a few tables and sand or wood floors, where you can get a tasty meal for a few dollars. A few are more upmarket. Some don't accept credit cards.

Price ranges shown are for typical meals for one (usually dinner),
not including tip, tax or alcoholic drinks. Price ranges:
Inexpensive: Under US$5
Moderate: US$6-$15
Expensive: US$16-30
Very Expensive: Over US$30

Habaneros. Middle Street, tel. 501-226-0486. Caye Caulker's most upscale dining and arguably the best. Try the Snapper Santa Fe. Great fajitas. Mayan Pizza is a specialty for lunch. Moderate to Expensive.

Rose's Grill & Bar. On Center St., the street leading from the main public pier, just behind Haberneros; tel. 501-206-0407. This tiny restaurant is one of the best on the island, and the tables on the porch and inside are often packed. The specialty is seafood, and it's all fresh and delicious. Moderate to Expensive.

Rainbow Grill & Bar. On the beach about halfway between the public pier and the Split, tel. 501-226-0281. The Rainbow is the only eatery on Caye Caulker that's built out over the water, to catch the sea breezes. The grilled or fried seafood dishes are terrific. Inexpensive to Moderate.

Wish Willie's. You eat in the back yard of the owner, Maurice, and he will tell you what's on the menu today. It may be fresh fish, lamb or chicken. In most cases, the prices are low, and the rum drinks cost less here than anywhere else on the island. You may have to share a table with other guests and the service is sometimes slow, but keep in mind the money you're saving. Moderate.

Femi's. Beachfront; tel. 501-622-3469. Popular with younger travelers, Femi's is on the beach, with no walls to spoil the view. The food is pretty good, and the setting is excellent. Moderate.

Sandbox. Front St. at main public pier; tel. 501-226-0200. Whether outside under the palms or indoors under the ceiling fans, you'll always have your feet in the sand here. The Sandbox has a large menu, with tasty items such as lobster omelet with fry jacks for breakfast, lobster or conch fritters or barbecue chicken for lunch and red snapper for dinner. At night the bar gets lively. Moderate.

Syd's. Middle Street, south of the public pier, tel. 501-226-0294. Locals often recommend Syd's. It serves Belizean and Mexican faves like beans and rice, stew chicken, garnaches, tostadas along with lobster and conch, when in season, at prices lower than you'll pay at most other eateries. Moderate.

Glenda's. Come to Glenda's for a cinnamon roll, johnnycake and fresh-squeezed orange juice for breakfast, and come back at lunch for rice and beans. Closed for dinner. No credit cards. Inexpensive.

Amor y Cafe (formerly Cyndi's) is another good place for breakfast, along with love and coffee. Inexpensive.

Jolly Roger. Front Street near the Health Center. At little tables beside his house, Roger serves some of the best lobster on the island, at bargain prices. He barbecues delicious fish, too. Moderate.

WHERE TO PARTY

For Belikin and booze, the **Lazy Lizard** at the Split is among the most popular bars on the island. Its slogan is "A sunny place for shady people." For live music, your best bet is Oceanside on Front St. near the main public pier. **I&I,** near Tropical Paradise, a funky joint with rope swings and hammocks instead of chairs, blows reggae and other music. In the back is a tree house. **Popeye's** and **Sandbox** also are popular places to soothe a thirst. **Herbal Tribe** near the Split is a reggae bar.

Cabañas on Thatch Caye, off Dangriga

CHAPTER 28:
CHECKING OUT THE OTHER CAYES

Belize's two northern cayes, Ambergris and Caulker, are the two largest and by far the most popular of Belize's island, both by expats and visitors. However, Belize has more than 400 other islands in the Caribbean. Most are small, remote and unpopulated. They are wonderful if typically somewhat expensive to visit, and building and living on the islands also is expensive. Here, briefly, are some of the options for lodging.

NOTE ON FISHING LICENSES: If you plan to fish in Belize, whether around the cayes or even from a pier on the mainland, in most cases you now need a saltwater fishing license. Costs are US$10 per day, US$25 per week or US$50 per year. As of this writing, the rules and regulations on licenses are unclear (as are many things in Belize), but your fishing guide or hotel can assist in getting you a license, or, failing that, contact Belize Coastal Zone Management in Belize City (www.coastalzonebelize.org/, tel. 501-223-0719).

ST. GEORGE'S CAYE
Historical St. George's Caye is only about 8 miles or 20 minutes by boat from Belize City. It was the site of perhaps the most famous event in

203

Belize history, when, as the story goes, in September 1798 a ragtag group of Baymen defeated a larger Spanish fleet from Mexico. St. George's Caye Day on September 10 celebrates the culminating Belizean victory. Today, St. George's Caye is home to one dive resort and to a number of weekend and holiday homes of Belize City's economic elite.

St. George's Caye Resort. St. George's Caye; tel. 800-813-8498; www.gooddiving.com. This long-established resort, focused on diving and fishing, has 12 cabañas, including some that are set over the water, and a main lodge building. It's the exact opposite of a large resort. You get personal attention here and sometimes you may be the only guests at the hotel. However, prices are high – around US$500 a day or more per couple including taxes and service and not including high-cost items like fishing and diving -- and the new management does not always get positive feedback from guests. All-inclusive rates are US$197 to $279 per person in-season and US$197 to $246 per person off-season. Rates are plus tax and 10% service charge, and do NOT include diving or fishing, but do include lodging, all meals, transfers from the international airport (with 4-night booking), domestic bar beverages and alcohol, unlimited use of kayaks, hobie cats, windsurfers and snorkeling equipment and wireless internet in the main lodge.

SPANISH LOOKOUT CAYE

Hugh Parkey's Belize Adventure Lodge. Spanish Lookout Caye (P.O. Box 1818, Belize City); tel. 501-223-452; www.belizeadventurelodge.com. Named after a well-known dive and hotel operator who with his wife Therese for many years ran the famous Fort Street Guesthouse in Belize City. He died of a heart attack in 2002, while diving in Mexico. This lodge formerly featured a swim-with-dolphins program. Now it has 12 cabañas on a 186-acre island about 25 minutes from Belize City. Some of the cabañas are built over water. Rates are attractive, US$200 double year-round, including meals. Transfer from Belize City is US$38.50. Four-night dive packages, including transfers, lodging in an over-the-water cabaña, meals and four dives is US$1,249 per person in winter and US$1,099 per person in summer.

TOBACCO CAYE

About 10 miles east of Dangriga, Tobacco Caye is a tiny 5-acre coral island. It is getting more attention these days because it offers snorkeling off the shore. As so often happens in Belize, though, rates have shot up at some of the hotels here. There's no scheduled water taxi service, but you can hook a boat at Dangriga to take you out – around US$17.50 one-way. Captain Buck is reliable. Check at the Riverside Café.

Tobacco Caye Lodge. Tel. 501-520-5033; www.tclodgebelize.com. About the best the island has to offer, with tropically blue duplex cabins. Double rooms are around US$80.

Gaviota Coral Reef Resort. Tel. 501-509-5032. The food here, served family-style at fixed times, is very good. You'll enjoy fresh fish, beans and rice, and even salads. The clapboard rooms and cabins are tiny, but the location on the east side of the caye provides cooling breezes. A new cabin is built over the water. At under US$40 per person, plus tax, including all meals, it's a good value. Gaviota is for sale.

Other choices: **Reef's End, Lana's on the Reef, Paradise** and **Ocean's End.**

RAGGED CAYE RANGE

Royal Belize. Ragged Caye Range; tel. 305-675-4660; www.royalbelize.com. This new private resort on a 7-acre caye is a 30-minute boat ride from Dangriga. There are just four cottages on the island, which rent from US$350 a night, but at that rate there may be other guests on the island, or from US$600 to $1150 a night on an exclusive basis, if you want the island to yourself (even if you just rent one house). Minimum three-day stays, and taxes are additional. All on-island activities are included in the rates, including use of a Wave Runner, kayaks and snorkeling equipment. Diving, fishing and land tours are not included, nor are meals or drinks. Custom meals (US$50 per person per day) are prepared according to the guests' preferences. Booze is at cost plus 20%. Island is offered for sale for US$2,775,000.

SOUTHWATER CAYE MARINE RESERVE

Southwater Caye, about 15 acres in size, is one of the most beautiful small islands off Belize. The south end of the caye, where Pelican Beach's cottages are located, has a nice little beach and snorkeling right off the shore.

Pelican Pouch. P.O. Box 2, Dangriga; tel. 501-522-2044, fax 522-2570; www.southwatercaye.com. Three charming but simple cottages plus five budget rooms in the main building. In-season, cottages are US$220 double including three meals; rooms are US$165 with all meals. Rates include tax. For around US$500 a person, Pelican Beach also has a four night package – three nights at South Water and one night at its hotel in Dangriga, including meals, boat to South Water and taxes.

Other choices on the island is the expensive **Blue Marlin Lodge** (501-520-2243, www.bluemarlinlodge.com), with good dive and fishing options, and the budget-level **International Zoological Expeditions Cottages** (501-520-5030, www.ize2belize.com), which caters to student groups. Note: Visitors to Southwater Caye Marine Reserve (including those staying on Tobacco Caye and Southwater Caye) pay US$5 a day per person marine reserve fee, or US$15 for up to a week's stay.

COCOPLUM RANGE

These islands are about 9 miles off Dangriga. They are not directly on the reef.

Thatch Caye. P.O. Box 143, Dangriga; tel. 501-603-2414 or toll-free 800-435-3145; www.thatchcayebelize.com. There are 11 guest cottages on this "hand built" island. (The owners spent years putting up bamboo sea walls and raised boardwalks.) You can head out for a day of fishing, diving, sea kayaking, or snorkeling, then enjoy a delicious meal in the thatched-roof dining room, sip an ice-cold drink and surf the web on the free Wi-Fi in the bar before heading to your seaside cabaña or casita where you'll be lulled asleep by the trade winds (air conditioning is available in some units for US$50 a day extra). Some of the cabañas are built partly over water, while the slightly more expensive casitas have third-level "widow walks" where you can gaze for hours at the sea. In-season weekly packages including lodging, all meals, snorkel and mainland trips and transportation from Dangriga are around US$2,800 to $3,600 double. Thatch Caye strives for sustainability, with solar and wind power.

Coco Plum Caye. www.cocoplumcay.com. This 16-acre island has five cottages, all air-conditioned and painted in bright tropical colors. All-inclusive rates include meals, drinks and use of snorkeling equipment and kayaks, with a minimum four-night stay. The snorkeling off the shore is only so-so, but most rates include snorkel trips to the reef a few miles farther out. Diving and fishing packages also available. Rates: Around US$500 a night double, all-inclusive.

WHIPRAY CAYE

Whipray Caye, about 11 miles off Placencia, is a great spot for anglers, as you can wade out about 50 yards in the flats and fish for tarpon, permit and other game fish. Julian Cabral, a well known Placencia fishing guide, owns the island and with American wife Beverly Montgomery-Cabral operates **Whipray Lodge** and the **Sea Urchin** bar and restaurant (tel. 501-610-1068, www.whipraycayelodge.com.) The three basic cabins can accommodate up to eight people. There's also good snorkeling here.

THE ATOLLS

Atolls are characterized by a large lagoon surrounded by coral reefs. While atolls are common in the South Pacific, they are rare in the Western Hemisphere. Of the four known atolls in the Western Hemisphere, three are in Belize – Glovers, Turneffe and Lighthouse. (The fourth, Chinchorra, is in southern Mexico.)

GLOVERS ATOLL

Glovers Atoll is the smallest of the three atolls in Belize, with an area of about 140 square miles. Some 45 miles from the mainland, Glovers offers some of the best diving and snorkeling in the Caribbean. The atoll has hundreds of coral patches in the lagoon. Around the atoll are 50 miles of walls dropping from 40 to 2500 feet or more. Fishing is restricted in this marine reserve – if you are fishing, reserve rangers will collect a fee of US$10 per person per day.

Isla Marisol. 189A Rear Ghans Ave., Dangriga; el. 501-615-1485 or 501-520-2056; www.islamarisol.com. Southwest Caye, where Isla Marisol is located, is owned by the Usher family, which obtained the island in the 1940s. Lodging at this resort is mostly in small wood cabins with zinc roofs.

There's a restaurant and bar. Three-night beachcomber packages, including lodging, meals and transport from Belize City, start at about US$2,000 per couple from November to June and US$1,900 the rest of the year. Fishing and dive packages are higher.

Off the Wall Dive Center and Resort. Long Caye, tel. 501-614-6348; www.offthewallbelize.com. Run by Kendra and Jim Schofield, Off the Wall focuses on diving, but there's excellent snorkeling and fishing as well. Facilities are rustic — small wood cabins, composting toilets, and outdoor rainwater showers. Meals are served in a beachfront thatch palapa with sand floor. There is no a/c, no room phones, no room TVs, which many find just about perfect. Rates US$1,395 to $2,095 per person weekly, depending on activities.

Glovers Atoll Resort. Northeast Caye (P.O. Box 563, Belize City); tel. 501-520-5016, fax 501-223-6087; www.glovers.com.bz. Don't let the name mislead you – this isn't your typical resort. The Lomont family, who came to Belize in the 1960s, offer very basic accommodations on Northeast Caye, about 45 miles out in the Caribbean at a reasonable price in a beautiful setting. You won't get running water or electricity here, but you can enjoy one of the most stunning parts of the Caribbean Sea. Around the 9-acre island you can dive or snorkel right from the shore. Weekly per-person rates year-round: Simple palmetto thatch cabañas are US$249 and those built over the water are US$299; thatch cabañas on beach, US$249; dorm room or tent, US$199; camping, US$149. Children under 12 are half price. Rates include transportation by boat to and from Sittee River near Hopkins but not 9% hotel tax. The weekly boat from Sittee River leaves Sundays. You'll need to bring most everything you need, including toilet paper, food, beer, cooler with ice and other supplies. Bottled water (US$1.50 a gallon) and kerosene (US$1 a pint) and a few grocery items are usually available on the island. Simple meals are offered, but they're fairly expensive – breakfast US$9, lunch US$12, dinner US$18-22. You can rent kayaks, canoes, and dive and snorkel gear. All in all Glovers Atoll Resort is quite a remarkable place, but not for everyone.

LIGHTHOUSE REEF ATOLL

Lighthouse Atoll is about 45 miles off the mainland coast, east of Belize City. The atoll is famous (thanks to Jacques Cousteau) for the Blue Hole inside the lagoon. The Blue Hole, an underwater sinkhole or cenote, is about one-quarter mile across and about 500 feet deep. Divers usually find the Blue Hole less interesting than they expected it would be, with very little sea life other than some sharks, but it's worth doing once. Several divers have died here, and it is not for novice divers. Half Moon Caye, a 45-acre coral island, is one of the most beautiful of all the Belize cayes, and it was part of Belize's first marine reserve. There's a daily fee of US$40 per person to visit the reserve.

Lighthouse Reef Resort is closed for renovation and may eventually reopen under a new name. You may be able to arrange accommodations at

Long Caye. Try **Calypso Beach Retreat** (tel. 303-523-8165; www.calypsobeachretreat.com), which is open when there is demand from dive groups.

TURNEFFE ATOLL

Turneffe Atoll is about 25 miles from the mainland, to the east of Belize City. The central lagoon, which has some 200 small mangrove islands, is about 240 square miles in area. There is also a smaller northern lagoon. Like Belize's other atolls, Turneffe offers magnificent diving and great fishing. The eastern and southern side of the atoll offers the best diving. Probably the most famous site is The Elbow, on the southern tip. Spur and groove diving is here only for experienced divers.

Turneffe Flats. U.S. office: P.O. Box 36, Deadwood, SD 57732; tel. 800-815-1304 or 605-578-1304, fax 605-578-7540; www.tflats.com. It's remote, it's beautiful and it's air-conditioned. The lodge, on the northeast side of the atoll, provides boat transport from Belize City to Turneffe on Saturdays. The trip takes about 90 minutes. Dive packages are around US$2,250-$2,500 per person for a week, depending on the time of year inclusive of lodging, meals, three dives a day and transport to the island but not booze, tips or taxes. Weekly fishing packages are more, around US$3,500 to $4,000 per person. Shorter packages are available at some times.

Blackbird Caye. Tel. 888-271-3483; www.blackbirdresort.com. Owned by a well-connected Belizean family, Blackbird Caye (currently for sale) , on the eastern side of the atoll, is another option on beautiful Turneffe. All units have air-conditioning. The newer deluxe cabins are more spacious, with king beds. Dinner is served in a large thatch palapa. Dive packages from around US$1,100 per person for three days, US$2,300 per person weekly, per person, in high season, slightly less off-season. The resort is for sale.

Turneffe Island Resort. U.S. office: 440 Louisiana, Ste. 300, Houston, TX 77002; tel. 800-874-0118; www.turnefferesort.com. Accommodations are in eight private cabañas or in 20 rooms in four buildings on Big Caye Bokel at the southern end of the central lagoon. Three-night packages range from US$800 to $2,500 per person, depending on the time of year, level of accommodations and the type of activities.

Serenity Sands B&B near Consejo, Corozal District

CHAPTER 29:
CHECKING OUT COROZAL

How to Get There

From Mexico: ADO (tel. in Mexico 525-133-2424), Riviera and other Mexican bus lines serve Chetumal, capital of the Mexican state of Quintana Roo and, with a population of more than 200,000, far larger than any city in Belize. Buses run frequently from various towns and cities in the Yucatán, including Cancun, Mérida and Playa del Carmen. Fares. First class and deluxe buses — with reserved seats, videos, and bathrooms — are around US$16 to $20 depending on the origin and class of service and the peso exchange rate. It's about five hours from Cancun, a little over four from Playa del Carmen and six from Mérida. At the Chetumal bus station, you change to a Belize bus to Corozal Town (fare US$1.50), or take a taxi to the border or use a transfer service. Buses leave Chetumal for Corozal Town and points south beginning at 4 a.m., and currently the last bus is at 6:30 p.m. At the border, which sports a new Belize customs and immigration office, marked by a bridge over the Rio Hondo, you get off the bus to go through customs and immigration and then reboard for the 15-minute ride into Corozal Town. A taxi into Corozal Town from the border is less than US$10.

Transfer services in Corozal and elsewhere in Belize will also pick you up in Cancun or elsewhere in Mexico and bring you to Corozal. **Belize VIP Transfer Service,** formerly Menzies Tours (www.belizetransfers.com, tel. 501-422-2725) is one of these. You'll pay US400 for up to four persons from Cancun to Corozal, US$350 from Playa del Carmen, US$300 from Tulum, and US$45 from Bacalar or US$30 from Chetumal. Other shuttle services also operate.

From points south in Belize: Corozal Town is about 83 miles by road from the International Airport in Ladyville and 9 miles from the Mexican border. Figure about two hours by car on the Northern Highway from Belize City. Northern Transport, Gil Harry, Tillett's, Belize Bus Owners Cooperative (BBOC), Chell, Russell, Venus and T-Line are among bus lines on the Northern Highway, with frequent service in both directions. Fares are about US$6 to $8 to Belize City, depending on the type of bus, and by regular (local) bus the trip takes about three to four hours. Most buses on this route are retired school buses or other older equipment, but a few express air-conditioned buses also serve it.

Maya Island Air and **Tropic Air** each fly five or six times daily between Corozal's tiny airstrip and San Pedro, Ambergris Caye (25 minutes, US$46 one-way). The airstrip is about 2 miles south of town, a US$5 cab ride. Purchase tickets at most local hotels. A water taxi, operated by **San Pedro-Belize Express,** also connects San Pedro and Corozal Town. Daily it leaves Corozal at 7 a.m. and San Pedro at 3 p.m. for the 1 1/2 hour trip. In the winter a second trip usually is added. Fare is US$22.50 one-way. On demand the ferry stops at Sarteneja.

Where to Stay

Serenity Sands B&B. Mile 3, Consejo Rd. (P.O. Box 88, Corozal Town), 501-669-2394; www.serenitysands.com. This new B&B is hidden away off the Consejo Road north of Corozal Town. On the second floor of a large home, there are four tastefully decorated rooms with private balconies, Belizean art and locally made hardwood furniture. Although not directly on the water, Serenity has a private beach on the bay a few hundred feet away. Rates are an excellent value for the high quality you enjoy, from US$75 plus tax. Full breakfasts, mostly organic, are included. For families, there's a 2-bedroom cottage near the B&B. Best visited with a rental car.

Almond Tree Resort. 425 Bayshore Dr., South End; tel. 501-628-9224; www.almondtreeresort.com. New small inn is a fine upscale choice at reasonable rates. Almond Tree has a fresh water pool and a sandy beach. There are six rooms all with queen beds, 1 large suite with separate living room and panoramic views of Corozal Bay, 2 smaller suites. Room rates range from US$75 and $125 in season, double occupancy. This includes morning coffee, tea, juice, yogurt and fruit. There is air conditioning in rooms, hot water, cable TV, laundry services, bikes and wireless access throughout premises. Restaurant and bar coming.

Casablanca by the Sea. Consejo Village; tel. 501-423-1018; www.casablanca-bythesea.com. This little inn out Consejo way doesn't get as many guests as it deserves, but it's a fine getaway. It's a great place to just relax and do nothing. The views of Chetumal across Corozal Bay are terrific.

Rooms are around US$75 double.

Corozal Bay Resort. Almond Dr., South end of Corozal Town, next to Tony's Inn; tel. 501/422-2691; www.corozalbayinn.com . Doug and Maria — she's originally from Mexico, and he's a Canadian by birth of German heritage who moved to Belize with his family when he was a youngster — have built 10 attractive cabañas on the water. The cabañas, painted in colorful tropical pastels, are surprisingly spacious and have bay thatch roofs. While most of them are situated to catch the breeze from the bay, they do have air-conditioning, tile baths, two comfortable beds in each cabaña, and 27" TVs with cable. Two units at the back connect, making them ideal for families. Doug had several hundred dump truck loads of sand brought in and created a tropical beach on the bay. There is a seawall, but you'll love the water view and the concrete pier. You can sit by the pool, sip something cold in the re-done outdoor restaurant and bar and, if you have a wireless laptop, check your e-mail. Rates are US$60 to $70 double. New budget rooms are under construction.

Tony's Inn. South End, Corozal Town; tel. 501-422-2055 or 800-447-2931; fax 422-2829; www.tonysinn.com. A longtime favorite of travelers to Corozal, Tony's has 24 motel-like rooms with tile floors, cable TV and A/C. The breezy bayside palapa restaurant, Y Not Grill, is one of the best in town. Rates: US$80 double January-April, US$70 rest of the year.

Copa Banana Guesthouse. 409 Bay Shore Drive., South End, Corozal Town, tel. 501-422-0284, fax 422-2710; www.copabanana.bz. Whether you're just passing through or in town shopping for property around Corozal, you couldn't do much better than this guesthouse. The rates are affordable, you can cook meals in the common kitchen, complete with dishware, stove, coffeemaker, microwave and fridge, and the owners even run a real estate business, Belize North Real Estate Ltd. Connie and her partner, Gregg, have done up two banana-yellow one story, ranch-style concrete houses, with a to-tal of five rooms (some with queen beds, some with two twins). Guests have private bedrooms but share the common space. The owners have added a long-term rental apartment with a view of the bay. Rates: US$55 dou-ble/US$350 week.

Las Palmas. 123 5th Ave., Corozal Town; tel. 501-422-0196; www.laspalmashotelbelize.com. This was formerly the budget-level Nestor's Hotel. It has been totally renovated and rebuilt, moving the whole property upmarket. Rooms go for about US$40 to $50 a night, double. Las Palmas is currently for sale.

Sea Breeze Hotel. 23 1st Ave., tel. 501-422-3051; www.theseabreezehotel.com. The Sea Breeze is your best budget choice in Corozal, with rooms starting at US$20 plus tax. The green-and-white painted building, formerly a Catholic nunnery, is across the street from the bay, be-hind a concrete wall. Inside, you'll find comfortable, no-frills guest rooms and a well-stocked bar (for guests and friends of guests only). Breakfast, at one of the lowest prices in Corozal, is served, also for guests only. Rooms, especially those in back, are simple and can be hot. The hotel is currently for sale.

Dining in Corozal Town

Y Not Grill at Tony's Inn in Corozal Town (Tony's spelled backwards, get it?) Always the best fajitas in Belize, in a pleasant, breezy bayside setting.

Patty's Bistro 2nd Street North, Corozal Town. You can eat your fill of fried chicken, pork chops, stew chicken and other local dishes for literally almost nothing. What a bargain! It moved in 2009 to 2nd Street North, around the corner from Mark's Fried Chicken.

Cactus Plaza. Grab a seat and order a plateful of tacos, tostadas, salbutes and other Mexican items. You won't be stuck with a big check -- most dishes are less than US$4. On weekends, this becomes a nightclub, and it can be noisy. 6 6th St., 2 blocks west of bay; tel. 501-442-0394.

Venky's. For takeout curries and other Indian food at modest prices, Venky's is the place. It's on 5th Avenue, across from the Immigration office. Tel. 501-402-0536

Other favorites in Corozal include **Vamps, Miss June's** and **Purple Toucan.** Purple Toucan on 4th Street is home to monthly expat luncheons, usually the second Tuesday of the month, starting at around 1:30 p.m.

Rural Corozal District

COPPER BANK/CERROS AREA

Getting Here from Corozal Town: You can drive from Corozal Town, crossing the New River on the hand-pulled ferry. To get to the ferry from Corozal, take the Northern Highway south toward Orange Walk Town and watch for ferry sign. Turn left and follow this unpaved road for 2½ miles to the ferry landing. At a T-intersection, turn left for Copper Bank. The trip to Copper Bank takes about a half hour, but longer after heavy rains, as the dirt road can become very bad. As you enter Copper Bank, watch for signs directing you to Cerros Maya.

Where to Stay

Cerros Beach Resort. Near Cerros Maya site on north side of Cerros peninsula; entering Copper Bank village, watch for signs to Cerros Beach Resort; tel. 501-623-9766; www.cerrosbeachresort.com. This is an off-the-grid option for good food and simple lodging on Corozal Bay, near the Cerros ruins. Expat owners Bill and Jen offer expertly made local and American food. For overnight stays, four small solar-powered cabañas go for as little as US$40 plus tax off-season.

SARTENEJA

This small Mestizo and Creole community enjoys waterside setting that makes it one of the most relaxed and appealing in all of Belize. Lobster fishing and pineapple farming are the town's two main industries, and Sarteneja is also a center for building wooden boats. Most residents speak Spanish as a first language, but many also speak English. Real estate investors are beginning to discover Sarteneja.

How to Get There: Driving to Sarteneja from Corozal Town takes about 1½ hours via the New River ferry and a second ferry across the mouth of Laguna Seca. The road is unpaved and can be very muddy after heavy rains. On the way here you'll pass several developments, including Orchid Bay. You also can drive to Sarteneja from Orange Walk Town, a trip of about 40 miles and 1½ hours. There are several buses a day, except Sunday, from Belize City via Orange Walk Town. The daily water taxi between Corozal Town and San Pedro will drop you at Sarteneja, on request. Sarteneja has an airstrip, with two flights daily on Tropic Air from San Pedro (US$46 one-way).

Where to Stay

Candelie's Seaside Cabañas. North Front St., Sarteneja Village, on the seafront at the west end of the village; tel. 501-423-2005. Candelie's has two charming cottages by the sea -- Wood Stork and Brown Pelican. Wood Stork, closer to the water and with a large mural of the stork on the side, has air-conditioning, while Brown Pelican has a fan. Both are good values, at US$50 plus tax. There is a restaurant, where meals must be ordered in advance. For US$10, you get a home-cooked meal, such as conch fritters and rice, plus pineapple juice and lime pie.

Backpackers Paradise. Bandera Rd., Sarteneja Village, tel. 501-403-205; www.bluegreenbelize.org. This is basically a hostel. Rates are US$11 double for a small cabaña with share outside bathrooms or US$3.25 per person for camping. A "honeymoon cabaña" with private bath is US$19 double. The cabañas are barely large enough for a double bed, lacking chairs, closet and frills. There's a restaurant with low prices. A common kitchen is for those who want to cook their own meals. Free Wi-Fi.

CHAPTER 30:
CHECKING OUT ORANGE WALK DISTRICT

Your first introduction to Orange Walk District likely will be the sugar cane fields — and concomitant hulking sugar cane trucks — near Orange Walk Town on the Northern Highway. Orange Walk Town itself is a somewhat scruffy, bustling place with more of a Mexican than Belizean ambiance, having not a great deal of interest for the visitor. There's a formal plaza, and the town hall is called the Palacio Municipal. The businesses and houses along the main drag — Queen Victoria Avenue or the Belize-Corozal Road — have barred windows, and some of the hotels and bars are in fact brothels.

The real Orange Walk is the big, wide and lightly populated area to the southwest of Orange Walk Town, up against the Guatemala border. Here you'll find large tracts of public and private land, teeming with deer, oscellated turkey, toucans and all manner of other wildlife. A handful of remote jungle lodges offers you the chance to see crocodiles, howler monkeys and even the illusive jaguar. Maya sites, discovered and undiscovered, are everywhere, including one of the most impressive and beautifully situated ones in the region, Lamanai. Mennonites are a potent agricultural and economic force in Orange Walk, especially in the Shipyard area. Farmland and a rural acre or two would be the appeal for expats in this part of Belize.

Getting There: By car via the Northern Highway, Orange Walk Town is about 55 miles north of Belize City and 35 miles south of Corozal Town. From Belize City or Corozal Town to Orange Walk Town, Northern Transport, Gil Harry, Tillett's and T-Line offer frequent bus service — every hour or so — on the Northern Highway. There is no air service to Orange Walk Town.

To Lamanai: By road from Orange Walk Town, take the all-weather road west to Yo Creek, then southwest to August Pine Ridge and San Felipe, bearing left (southeast) at San Felipe to Indian Church Village near the Lamanai ruins, a total distance of about 36 miles from Orange Walk. Alternatively, you can go from near Orange Walk Town through the village of Guinea Grass to Shipyard. Figure about 3 hours by car from Belize City. There's limited non-daily bus service to Indian Church from Orange Walk. A more scenic option is a boat trip up the New River to the New River Lagoon, about 1 1/2 hours and around US$40-$45 per person. If you are staying at Lamanai Outpost, the hotel will arrange your transportation. If not, boat trips can be arranged at the New River bridge or in Orange Walk Town.

To Gallon Jug: You follow the same route as to Lamanai, but at San Felipe you turn right and go west to Blue Creek Village, a Mennonite settlement. The Mennonites have paved part of the road here. From Blue Creek, it's about 35 miles to Gallon Jug. Figure about 4 hours by car from Belize City. Charter flights are available from Belize City to Gallon Jug's modern little airstrip.

Orange Walk District Lodging

Chan Chich Lodge. Gallon Jug (Mail: P.O. Box 37, Belize City); tel./fax 501- 223-4419; or P.O. Box 1088, Vineyard Haven, MA 02568, tel. 800-343-8009, fax 508-693-6311; www.chanchich.com. Very simply, this is one of the classic jungle lodges of the world. It's owned by Barry Bowen, a fifth-generation Belizean who also has the Coca-Cola bottling franchise in Belize and who brews Belikin beer, among many other endeavors. The trip here by car from Orange Walk Town is an incredible experience, although if you want to get here more quickly, you can come by charter plane. The drive takes you through deep bush, including the 262,000 acres of Programme for Belize lands next door, and around every curve you might encounter anything but another vehicle — deer, a quash, a snake sliding across the road, one of Belize's cats, a flock of oscellated turkeys, a dense shower of butterflies. Closer to the lodge, which is on a quarter million acres of private land, you'll spy the neatly fenced fields of Bowen's 2,500-acre Gallon Jug farm, which raises cattle, corn, soybeans, cacao, cardamon and coffee. Gallon Jug is the only place in Belize that produces coffee in any commercial amount. The lodge, across a suspension bridge at the end of a short paved road, enjoys an astounding setting. It was built literally on top of a Maya plaza. Around the lodge are tall, unexcavated mounds. There are 12 thatch-roof cabañas, re-cently upgraded, comfortable rather than luxurious, each with two queen beds, 24-hour electricity (but not air-conditioning), bath with hot and cold water shower, and a wrap-around verandah. The cabins fartherest from the restaurant kitchen and on the edge of the lodge grounds, such as number 2 and 9, are most desirable. There also is a two-bedroom villa with A/C. Americans Tom and Josie Harding supervised the construction of the lodge in the early 90s and stayed on as managers until 2001, when they moved on to San Pedro. New management appears to be doing a very good job. Meals are served in a large thatch cabaña, which also houses a gift shop, and the bar is next door — guests congregate there for a social hour before dinner. A beau-tiful swimming pool, located at the edge of the jungle is screened to keep out bugs. Around the lodge grounds is a series of cut and raked trails, ideal for wildlife spotting and birding. You can enjoy the jungle setting without having to wrestle snakes and briars. Will you see a jaguar? There's a better chance here than at most other places in Belize. The lodge has been averaging about one jaguar sighting a week. Even if you don't see the elusive big cat, you'll definitely see plenty of other wildlife including howler monkeys, whether you walk the trails on your own or go on one of the nature tours offered by the lodge. Guides at Chan Chich are extraordinarily knowledgeable, and you should take at least one guided nature tour while at the lodge. Birding is terri-fic here, with more than 350 species identified; often 40% or more of guests are birders. Canoeing, horseback riding, birdwatching and nature tours, and trips to Maya sites are available. Rates: Doubles, room only, are US$250 to $300 Nov. 1-Apr. 30, US$205 to $235 the rest of the year. The villa (for 2 to 5 people) is US$895 in-season, US$795 off-season. Meal packages, which are necessary since there are no other dining choices nearby, are US$70 adults, US$30 for children under 12. The lodge also offers an all inclusive package (room, meals, taxes, most tours and activities, Belikin beer and soft drinks). Rates are plus the usual 9% hotel tax and 10% GST on meals but do not include a service charge. Chan Chich's approach, which we like, is to tip what you feel is fair (tips are divided among all staff) and only once, at the end of your stay.

Lamanai Outpost Lodge. Indian Church Village; tel. 888-733-7864 or 501- 223-3578; www.lamanai.com. Lamanai Outpost is another extraordinary jungle lodge. One of the reasons it's so special is the setting. Built by the late Colin Howells, a legend in hospitality circles in Belize, Lamanai Outpost perches on a low hillside with a view of the beautiful New River Lagoon. The lodge has 17 rooms, recently refurbished, in thatch cabañas set among hillside gardens. The lodge is closely involved with archeological and nature study programs through the Lamanai Field Research Center. The center has resident naturalists, archeologists, ornithologists and biologists. On one visit here, my family enjoyed meeting grad students from the University of Texas who were doing crocodile research in the New River Lagoon. We went along on a night trip to catch crocs (fortunately, that night they didn't catch any.) Manager Mark Howells, Colin Howells' son, does a good job with the lodge, in everything from supervising the housekeeping to providing security. Kids love Lamanai, as there always seem to be monkeys, parrots and other creatures around. For adults, next to the new open-air dining room, in what was the former restaurant, there's now a bar and lounge, The Digger's Roost, with archaeological memorabilia and a full-size reproduction of a Lamanai stela showing Lord Smoking Shell. A dock extends 130 feet into the lagoon and is good place for stargazing and swimming — just keep an eye out for Ol' Mister Croc. Birding is superb in this area, with at least 375 species identified nearby. Winners of a recent one-day "bird-a-thon" at Lamanai spotted 172 species in 24 hours. The Lamanai ruins and archeological reserve are within walking distance. Indian Church village is also within walking distance, and near the village are the ruins of two Spanish churches. Don't miss taking a nightspotting tour — the New River Lagoon and New River are fascinating at night. Package rates include lodging, meals and tours and are not cheap. They start at over US$500 a night. Per person. Room only rates are more affordable.

ORANGE WALK TOWN AREA LODGING

Few tourists linger in Orange Walk Town, and hotels cater mostly to visiting Belizeans and Mexicans.

Hotel de la Fuente. 14 Main St., Orange Walk Town; tel. 501/322-2290; www.hoteldelafuente.com. Orlando de la Fuente and his wife have opened this nice addition to the limited hotel scene in Orange Walk Town. The low rates (around US$25 to $50) put it among the best values in Northern Belize. All 8 rooms have air conditioning and DSL broadband, and there are also 2 suites with kitchenettes.

St. Christopher's. 10 Main St., Orange Walk Town; tel. 501-322-2420, fax 302- 1064; e-mail rowbze@btl.net. This hotel on the New River has attractive rooms, some air-conditioned. Rates for doubles with A/C the rate are about US$45.

For **dining,** check out the new **Nahil Mayab** in Orange Walk Town. Lovely and not overdone Maya-themed decor, good service and the best ceviche we've had in years, only US$3 for an appetizer serving of shrimp ceviche, beautifully presented and really big enough for two.

Partially excavated Maya site at Pook's Hill

CHAPTER 31:
CHECKING OUT CAYO DISTRICT

How to Get There

San Ignacio is about 67 miles, or about 1 3/4 to 2 hours by car, west of Belize City, and the Guatemala border is another 9 miles west. The Western Highway is a good paved two-lane road. However, after a rain parts of the road can be extremely slick, with accidents common.

Several bus lines run from Belize City to Belmopan, San Ignacio and the Guatemala border, with frequent, inexpensive service (US$3 to $4) from Belize City. The buses run from the main terminal (the old Novelo's terminal, and most people still refer to it as Novelo's) in Belize City, not from the international airport. From the international airport, you'll have to take a taxi into town (US$25) or lug your bags by foot about 2 miles to the Northern Highway, where you can catch a bus into Belize City and connect with a San Ignacio bus there.

In addition, several operators in San Ignacio, including PACZ Tours and Aguada Hotel have vans running from the airports in Belize City to San Ignacio. Fare is about US$40 to $60 per person one-way. You need to book ahead. Even if your hotel doesn't have a set van schedule, it can arrange a transfer from Belize City, typically for US$110 to $185 for a party of up to four or five. Service by Guatemalan transportation services Linea Dorado and San Juan from the Belize City Marine Terminal near the Swing Bridge to

Flores, Guatemala, near Tikal, is usually available, for around US$25. These vans are not supposed to pick up or drop off passengers in Belize (except in Belize City), but you can get off at the Belize-Guatemala border.

Finally, some taxis at the international airport will drive you to San Ignacio. Bargain, but expect to pay around US$100-$125 for up to four or five people.

To explore the Mountain Pine Ridge on your own, you must have a car. Two roads lead to the Mountain Pine Ridge reserve. The first, the Pine Ridge Road (also known as the Chiquibul Road) turns off the Western Highway at Georgeville, at about Mile 63. This road, unpaved and very rough in places, depending on when it has rained and when it was last scraped, runs past the Barton Creek area, large farms and the Slate Creek preserve, leading to the entrance of the Mountain Pine Ridge reserve. It's about 10 miles from Georgeville to the reserve gate, where you must stop and register with the guard, who will take your name, vehicle information and destination, but there is no entrance fee. The other route to the Pine Ridge is the Cristo Rey Road, which turns off the Western Highway at about Mile 68 1/2, at Santa Elena just before you enter San Ignacio. The mostly unpaved road runs through Cristo Rey and San Antonio villages. It is about 12 1/2 miles by this route to the junction with he Pine Ridge Road, and then another 1 1/2 miles to the reserve gate, the same gate you would reach from Georgeville. From the Pine Ridge gate, you continue on an unpaved road. At some points the roadbed is sandy, and at others red clay. If you are going to Hidden Valley Inn or Hidden Valley Falls, about 4 miles into the reserve you turn left (watch for a sign) and go a few miles to the lodge or falls. If, instead of turning, you go on, you'll soon see the Pine Ridge Lodge, on the right, a little more than 4 miles past the entrance gate. About 1/2 mile farther, there's a turn to the right to Blancaneaux Lodge; Five Sisters Lodge is a little farther on the same spur road. If you continue on the "main road" rather than turning on the spur road to Blancaneaux and Five Sisters, you will pass near the Rio On, a popular swimming area, and the Rio Frio cave. At about 14 miles into the reserve, you'll reach Douglas De Silva (formerly called Augustine), a village of small white frame houses with tin roofs. Turn left here and you'll be on your way to Caracol. Ten miles from Douglas De Silva, you cross the Macal River and are in the Chiquibul wilderness. Caracol is about 50 miles from the reserve entrance gate.

Note that due to occasional bandit attacks in the Mountain Pine Ridge, you can no longer drive on your own to Caracol. You have to go in a convoy guarded by Belize Defence Forces troops. Check locally for times to meet up with the convoy. You can drive alone to the four lodges in the Pine Ridge, but not all the way to Caracol.

Keep in mind that all of the roads in this region are logging roads. After heavy rains, the clay sections in particular can become extremely slick and difficult to negotiate, even with a four-wheel drive vehicle. If you do not have your own vehicle, you can take a taxi from San Ignacio to the lodges in the Pine Ridge (perhaps US$75 for up to four or five people). A Mesh bus makes trips daily except Sunday from San Ignacio to Cristo Rey and San Antonio villages (about US$1.50, ask at Eva's for exact schedule). It gets within about 1 1/2 miles of the Mountain Pine Ridge entrance gate. The four lodges in the Pine Ridge also provide transfers from Belize City to the Pine Ridge (about US $150 to $185 per party, one-way). Hotel packages usually include transfers from Belize City. You also take a charter flight to Blancaneaux's airstrip.

BELMOPAN LODGING

The lodging choices in Belmopan proper are small motels and hotels, geared more toward the needs of government bureaucrats and others on government business than of tourists. Jungle lodges and other more interesting lodging choices are located outside of Belmopan along the Western and Hummingbird highways.

Yim Saan Hotel & Restaurant. 4253 Hummingbird Hwy., Belmopan City; tel. 501-822-1356. This Chinese-owned property is the nicest lodging in Belmopan. Rooms are modern and clean. There's a good restaurant on the first floor. Rates around US$50 double.

Bull Frog Inn. 25 Half Moon Ave. (P.O. Box 28), Belmopan; tel. 501-822-2111, fax 822-3155; www.bullfroginn.com. This will remind you of a small mom 'n pop motel in the U.S. or Canada. The 25 rooms have air-conditioning, cable TV and are clean and comfortable enough, though your bed may not be quite as new as you'd like and the TV picture may roll. Rates, geared to the business people and government officials who make up 70% of the guests here, are US$75 double.

BELMOPAN AREA JUNGLE LODGES

Pook's Hill. Off Mile 52 1/2, Teakettle Village (Mail: P.O. Box 14, Belmopan); tel. 501-820-2017, fax 822-3361; www.pookshillbelize.com. Directions: Turn south off the Western Hwy. at Mile 52 1/2 at Teakettle village. Go about 4 miles on a dirt road, then turn right and go another 1 1/2 miles to the lodge (the route is well-signed.) How about a remote lodge in deep jungle, next to a river, near Actun Tunichil Muknal and on the site of a Maya plaza, run by an engaging international staff where meals and drinks are by lantern-light and you're isolated from the cares of civilization? That pretty much describes Pook's Hill, a collection of thatched, Maya-style cabañas on 300 acres next to Tapir Mountain Reserve and the Roaring River. There is a partially excavated Maya site at Pook's Hill. There's hiking (free guide), tubing and river swimming in the Roaring River and excellent birding. Actun Tunichil Muknal tours from the lodge are US$99 per person. Rates US$203 to $236 plus tax double in high season, US$165 to $197 May to October. Meals, served buffet-style with a common table sure to get everyone talking, are tasty and filling -- US$12 breakfast, $15 lunch and $25 dinner. Transfers for up to four persons from the international airport are US$110. Pook's Hill, by the way, is named after Rudyard Kipling's Puck of Pook's Hill. The lodge is for sale.

Belize Jungle Dome. Off Mile 47, Western Hwy., Belmopan, tel. 501-822- 2124, fax 822-2155, www.belizejungledome.com. Directions: From Western Hwy., turn north at Mile 49 and cross bridge over Belize River. Follow gravel road 3 miles until you see Banana Bank sign. Turn right and follow dirt road 2 miles. The owners, Andrew, a former pro soccer player with Newcastle in England, and Simone, Dutch and formerly a veejay for MTV Europe, moved to Belize in 2001 and built this inn in the bush, topped with a geodesic dome, next door to Banana Bank Lodge. The owners have since moved on to Barbados, and the lodge is for sale, but capable management is on site. The four suites and standard room here have tile floors, lots of windows, air-conditioning and an uncluttered look. You can check your email at the wireless hotspot by the swimming pool, take a yoga or pilates class or eat an organic meal (breakfast US$10, dinner US$20) on the terrace. Rates: US$105 to $200 in-season, double; US$95 to $160 off-season. Rates plus tax. For large groups, the owners' three-bedroom house is available.

Banana Bank. Off Mile 49, Western Hwy. (P.O. Box 48, Belmopan); tel. 501-820-2020, fax 820-2026; www.bananabank.com. Directions: From Western Hwy., turn north at Mile 49 and cross bridge over Belize River. Follow gravel road 3 miles until you see Banana Bank sign. Turn right and follow dirt road 2 miles. You're guaranteed to see a jaguar at this lodge. A spotted jaguar called Tika lived here for 26 years and after her death was replaced by Tika 2. The Belize government has granted permission for the lodge to have the jaguar. John Carr, who in his youth was a real Montana cowboy and rodeo star, in 1973 with a partner bought Banana Bank, then a 4,000-acre ranch with 1,500 head of cattle. At one time the ranch was headquarters for Belize Estates, one of the large companies that in colonial days logged huge tracts of land granted them by the Crown. John Carr and his wife, Carolyn, have lived on the ranch since 1977, one of a small group of pioneering American expats who adopted Belize as their home. Carolyn is a noted artist; her paintings of Belize street scenes and wild creatures have been widely exhibited, and her work has appeared on the cover the Belize telephone book twice, most recently in 2009. She has a studio at the lodge. Our favorite is her painting titled "Jimmy Hines," which shows the old market in Belize City where fishermen are cleaning lobster, snapper and jimmy hines, the local name for a type of sea bass or grouper. Anyway, back to the lodge. It's a family-oriented spot, a great place for kids. Daughter Leisa now helps run the lodge. The lodge has five cabañas, with bay leaf thatch, on a bank above the Belize River. The cabañas are spacious, with curving internal walls and 24-hour electricity, but no air-conditioning. Rooms are also available in the Gallery, Chateau Brio and Chalet building. Some rooms have air-conditioned. You can hear howler monkeys calling, and besides Tika 2, on the grounds of the lodge are toucans, parrots and a spider monkey named Simon. (Note that some wildlife rescue organizations and other groups in Belize strongly oppose the practice of keeping wild animals and birds in captivity, even with government permission.) The food is filling and tasty, served family-style. Banana Bank is especially good for those who like to ride, as the lodge keeps about 100 horses. The horses are mixed breeds, mostly quarter horses. There's a large stable, a round pen to hone your riding skills and a larger arena. New in 2006 was an on-site swimming pool, with a bar and dining area added in 2009-2010. Free Wi-Fi is available at the pool. Rates: US$77 to $175 double, breakfast included. Lunch is US$10 and dinner, US$15. Rates are plus tax. Meals are well prepared and served family style. Note that there is something of a Christian atmosphere here, with prayers sometimes offered at meals. The lodge also offers many packages, including tours, all meals and horseback riding. Transfers from the international airport are US$120 one-way.

Caves Branch Adventure Co. & Jungle Lodge. Hummingbird Hwy. (P.O. Box 356), Belmopan; tel. (radio phone) 501-822-2800; www.cavesbranch.com. Directions: About 14 miles from Belmopan at Mile 41 1/2 of the Hummingbird Hwy. (mile markers on the Hummingbird from Belmopan run backwards, starting at Mile 55 at the Western Hwy.), turn left and follow a dirt road less than a mile to the lodge grounds. Then, get ready to sweat! Set in a 58,000-acre chunk of private land on the Caves Branch river, this is Belize's premier jungle lodge for travelers who like to do things outdoors. Ian Anderson, a Canadian, and his teams run strenuous caving, hiking and river trips, and they do a top-flight job. They call them adventure trips, not sightseeing. In short, this is not a place for couch potatoes. More than a dozen adventure tours are offered, open to non-guests as well as guests. Each Caves Branch guide has been trained in first aid and in cave and wilderness rescue. However, the lodge is going more upscale, with a new swimming pool, botanical garden and tony treehouse suites. It is now owned by the same people who own Jaguar Reef Lodge and Spa in Hopkins. The lodge has six types of accommodations: Rates: The four new hillside, split level treehouse suites are the most upmarket, at US$225 to $285 year-round. The jungle suites are also fairly luxe, with a master bedroom with king-size bed, inside bathroom with hot and cold shower and toilet, wicker-furnished living room with pull out bed, at US$185 double. Three jungle bungalows with queen beds are US$165 double. Six jungle cabañas are more basic, with outside washroom facilities, for US$98 double. The camp also has budget accommodations in a co-ed bunkhouse, for US$15 per person. Buffet meals are delicious and healthful, though not bargain-priced, at US$12 for breakfast or lunch, US$24 for dinner. Caves Branch also has a variety of packages, including a one-week "Bad Ass" trip which takes you to some of Belize's least visited caves, waterfalls and cenotes, for around US$1,200 a person, plus 19% tax and service charge. Cave tubing is US$95 per person, and the Black Hole Drop is US$105. Transfers from Belize City are US$130 for up to four persons. Note that in late spring and early summer the river that runs by the lodge may be completely dry.

SAN IGNACIO AND SANTA ELENA LODGING: IN OR NEAR TOWN

Ka'ana Boutique Resort and Spa. Mile 69¼, Western Hwy.; 501-824-3350, 877-522–6221 in U.S.; www.kaanabelize.com. Owned by the people who have Belize's oil company, Belize Natural Energy, Ka'ana is your most upscale option in or near San Ignacio. It has a wine cellar, spacious rooms outfitted with extras like iPod docks and espresso machines, and flat-screen TVs. Rates are US$250 to $350 a night (plus tax and 10% service) for a double, higher at Christmas. The infinity swimming pool with waterfall uses a new saltwater filtration system. La Ceiba restaurant, while attractive, is expensive.

San Ignacio Resort Hotel. 18 Buena Vista St., (P.O. Box 33), San Ignacio; tel. 501-824-2034, fax 824-2134; www.sanignaciobelize.com. This is the closest thing to an international-style hotel in San Ignacio Town. But, in Belize, that can mean anything, and in this case it means cinderblock walls in the hall and a green iguana project out back, with 14 acres of bush, and a casino next door. The location is convenient, the deluxe rooms are comfortable, the pool relaxing, the Running W Steakhouse satisfying, the Stork Club bar a good place to grab a cool one and watch a big-screen TV, and the management and staff accommodating. Unfortunately, rates are on the high side. A branch of the Princess Casino adjoins the hotel. Rates: US$170 to $300 in-season, US$153 to $300 off-season, plus 9% hotel tax and 5% service.

Cahal Pech Village. Cahal Pech Rd., 1 mi west of town off Western Hwy., San Ignacio; tel. 501-824-3740, fax 824-2225; www.cahalvillageresort.com. This resort is set on a high hill at the western edge of San Ignacio, near the Cahal Pech Maya site. Ever-growing and improving, the latest additions are new cottages and rooms and a two-level swimming pool, guarded by a giant statue of a pteryldactl. The restaurant serves Belizean and American fare such as grilled fish, pork chops, spaghetti and steaks in an open-air space with views of the valley below. Dinner is around US$12. Rates US$99 to $119 double, plus tax and US$5 per couple per day service charge.

Casa Blanca Guest House. 10 Burns Ave., San Ignacio; tel. 501-824-2080; www.casablancaguesthouse.com. While it's in the center of busy San Ignacio, this small hotel, winner of the Belize Tourism Board's "best small hotel award" a few years ago, is quiet and a great choice if you want to save money. The rooms, with white walls trimmed in mahogany and locally made wood furniture, are a big step above typical budget lodging. Some rooms have air-conditioning. You can prepare snacks or full meals in the shared kitchen. Casa Blanca is often fully booked. Rates: US$20 to $50.

Aguada Hotel & Restaurant. Aguada St., Santa Elena; tel. 501-804-3609; www.aguadahotel.com. Across the highway from La Loma Luz hospital. This motel — just east of San Ignacio in Santa Elena — is a real find. You can stay here in a clean, modern room with air-conditioning for around US$40-$65 double. The 18 rooms — some were added on the second floor and in a new building in the back — are not overly large, but there is a swimming pool. The café is a friendly, casual place serving Belizean and American dishes at around US$5 to $10 for a full meal.

BENQUE VIEJO AREA

Mopan River Resort. Benque Viejo del Carmen, Cayo; tel. 501-823-2047, fax 823-3272; www.mopanriverresort.com. Closed September-October. The valu-o-meter got turned up to wow in Cayo when this all-inclusive opened in 1999. Some visitors complain that Belize hotel rates seem reasonable enough, but at checkout the total tab is lot higher than expected, after adding the price of meals, drinks, transfers, tours, tax and service charges. But here, the original owners Jay and Pamella Picon delivered almost everything for one price: transfers from your arrival flight in Belize City, room, all meals, daily tours (including trips to Tikal, Caracol and Barton Creek cave, plus kayaking on the Macal River), local beer and drinks, and even tips and taxes. And that one price wasn't a budget-breaker. Now, under new management, the all-inclusive is still an excellent value, starting about US$241 per person per day (based on a 7-day stay.) No tipping is allowed. Virtually everything is included in the AI price. Guests are responsible only for site admission fees, border fees and departure taxes, usually adding up to about US$150 per person a week. Fact is, it may be the best upmarket deal on the mainland. The location is a bit, well, unexpected, across the Mopan River from the back streets of old Benque, but once you've taken the short ferry ride to the resort's coconut palm-studded grounds, you're in your own private paradise. The 12 thatch cabañas are done up in high Belizean style, with cabbage bark wood floors and mahogany cabinets, and they come with most of the modcons, including cable TV, VCR, 24-hour electricity, A/C, some of the best beds in Belize and refrigerators stocked with complimentary soft drinks and Belikin. Three of the cabañas are larger suites, with full kitchens. Buffet dinners are tasty and served family-style. The resort has good security: Guards with Rottweilers patrol after dark. So what's the down side? The location will be a turn-off for those expecting to be in the jungle — this is not a jungle lodge. And it's not for those who want to do things entirely on their own, trying different restaurants, heading out on a whim, and staying up late to sample local nightlife. As at many small lodges, the particular mix of guests when you're there has a lot to do with your total experience. There's a swimming pool and a wedding chapel. We recommend you do not swim in the Mopan River here.

Trek Stop. Benque Rd., San José Succotz Village, Cayo; tel. 501-823-2265; www.thetrekstop.com. 6 miles west of San Ignacio, on the south side of Western Hwy. (Benque Rd.). American expats Judy and John Yaeger and their Belizean partner opened this spot in 1998. They own 22 acres, perched beside the highway on a hillside near San José Succotz Village and the Xunantunich Maya ruins. Budget travelers will find cheap sleeps in cozy, neat-as-a-pin cabins (US$15 single, US$24 double), with screened windows, outdoor composting toilets and solar-heated showers. Larger cabins run US$28 to US$35 double, and the more expensive one has a private bath. A small butterfly farm and nature center, Tropical Wings, a disc golf course and a small restaurant with inexpensive Mexican and Belizean dishes are also here. Camping is permitted; US$5 per night per person. There's also a common kitchen, and free Wi-Fi. Bikes, kayaks and inner tubes are available for rent. Highly recommended for those seeking quality budget accommodations.

JUNGLE LODGES ON MACAL RIVER

Most of Cayo's lodges are on either the Macal or Mopan rivers. In general, the lodges on the Macal are more upmarket. With some exceptions don't expect to be in a "movie jungle" or rainforest. Most lodges share their locations with cattle ranches or citrus farms and second-growth bush, though the jungle is seldom far away.

The Lodge at Chaa Creek. Chial Rd., (P.O. Box 53, San Ignacio); tel. 501-824-2037, fax 824-2501; www.chaacreek.com. Directions: From San Ignacio, go 4 3/4 miles west on Benque Rd. (Western Hwy.) and turn left on Chial Rd. (look for signs to Chaa Creek, duPlooy's and Black Rock lodges). Follow signs on this unpaved road 3 1/2 miles to Chaa Creek. Mick and Lucy Fleming started Chaa Creek in 1980 when tourists were almost unknown in Cayo. Over the years, they've expanded, improved and fine-tuned their operation until it has become one of the best run, most-professional operations in all of Central America. Everything works here: The grounds, comprising a total of 365 acres on the Macal River, are beautifully planted and maintained. A gorgeous swimming pool was added in 2009. The 23 large rooms and suites are mostly in thatch cottages, and all have high-quality furnishings set off with Guatemalan wall hangings and bedspreads, the perfect marriage of comfort and exoticism. The honeymoon Treetop Suites, Garden Suites, Orchid Villa, Spa Villa, Macal Cottage and Sky Room offer more privacy and extra room. Staffers are friendly, not fawning, and move quickly to solve any problem. There's electricity, plenty of hot water and cold beer, and, if you like, Chaa Creek will sell you a good cigar to enjoy after dinner with your cognac. Recent additions are a fully equipped, modern spa, by far the best in Belize, offering everything from aromatherapy to seaweed wraps, and a conference and meeting center. You won't run out of things to do here, either. You can visit the Chaa Creek Natural History Centre and Blue Morpho Butterfly Breeding Centre, tour the Rainforest Medicine Trail (formerly Panti Trail) next door, now owned by Chaa Creek, visit a Maya-style cacao plantation and other farming projects, go horseback riding or canoeing, or take one of the many top-notch tours offered by Chaa Creek Expeditions. Chaa Creek helped reintroduce howler monkeys to the Macal River Valley. Birding is excellent, with some 250 species spotted on the grounds. Chaa Creek has won a number of environmental and other awards. For all this, you pay a premium price. Rates: Rooms are US$300 to $350 double in-season, and suites US$450 to $575, with small reductions off-season. Rates include breakfast but are plus 9% tax and 10% service. Dinner is US$32 plus 10% tax and 10% service. Packages and summer specials are available. Transfers from the international airport are US$135 one-way for up to four persons. For those who want the Chaa Creek experience at a Filene's Basement price (US$110 double including breakfast and dinner, plus hotel tax and 10% service), the

Macal River Safari Camp has 10 small "cabinettes" on platforms and very good Belizean-style meals.

Mystic River Resort. Mile 6, Cristo Rey Rd., San Antonio Village; tel. 501-678-6800; www.mysticriverbelize.com. Operated by a couple who were formerly Ambergris Caye residents (he's American, she's French), this new jungle lodge helps raise the bar on dining and stylish luxury on the Macal. Mystic River has five cottages, all with views of the river from covered porches, stone fireplaces, king beds and designer furnishings. At the lodge's restaurant, La Ranita (Little Frog), in a high-ceiling thatch palapa set about 100 feet above the river, a talented Belizean chef serves Belizean, American, Thai and other dishes, while you enjoy the views and sounds of the jungle up close and personal. Rates US$175 double, plus 9% tax and 10% service.

Table Rock Lodge. Cristo Rey Rd., San Antonio Village; 501-670-4910; www.tablerockbelize.com. Though open for only a short time, this small ecolodge has already made a big name for itself, rating highly on TripAdvisor.com. The lodge has only three thatch cottages, all with tile floors and four-poster beds. It is part of a small working farm, perched just above the Macal River. You can explore winding pathways and cut trails down to the river, or visit with the donkeys, Napoleon and Josephine. Rates are US$135 to $155 double in-season, US$95-$115 May-October, plus tax. Small as it is, Table Rock has its own chef, and meals here are excellent. A meal package including breakfast and dinner is only US$29 per person plus 10% service and 10% tax. Riverside camping also is available for around US$30, including tent, set up and break down, and firewood.

duPlooy's Lodge, San Ignacio, Cayo; tel. 501-824-3101, fax 824-3301; www.duplooys.com. Directions: From San Ignacio, go 4 3/4 miles west on Benque Rd. (Western Hwy.) and turn left on Chial Rd. (look for signs to Chaa Creek, duPlooy's and Black Rock lodges). Follow signs on this unpaved road about 4 miles to duPlooy's. Since it opened in the late 1980s, duPlooy's has been seen by some to play second fiddle to its Macal River neighbor, Chaa Creek. But that's unfair, because duPlooy's has its own style — a little more casual, a little more oriented to birders and tree-huggers and nature lovers. On part of the lodge's 60 acres about 10 miles from San Ignacio, Judy and the late Ken duPlooy created something very special: the Belize Botanic Gardens, with plantings of some 2,500 trees from all over Belize and Central America. An orchid house, with some 120 species of orchids from all over Belize, is also on the grounds. For most guests, the focus of the lodge is the remarkable deck, which rambles 200 feet off from the bar. From vantage points on the long walkway beside the Macal River, you're sure to see a variety of birds, iguanas and other wildlife. Bring your camera and binoculars. About 300 species of birds have been identified within 5 miles of the lodge. In accommodations, duPlooy's offers something for anyone. For the top-of-the-market segment, duPlooy's has three large detached bungalows, each with king-size bed, fridge and delicious hammock with a view down the hill to the Macal River, for US$225 double. Also for families or groups, there's the casita, a two-story house for US$290. There are also nice lodge rooms with two queen-sized beds, US$180 double. The River House has three and four bedroom family suites for US$280 to $290; the entire seven-bedroom house is US$475. Rates include continental breakfast and are plus 9% hotel tax and 10% service. Room rates are discounted 20% in the off-season. Regardless of lodging, a full meal plan is extra. Note that duPlooy's does not serve beef, due to what the owners consider is rainforest deforestation associated with cattle ranching, but it does serve pork, chicken and seafood, along with vegetarian dishes. The lodge also has a good selection of tours to Cayo and Petén sites. Package plans including meals, transfers from Belize City and tours are available. duPlooy's is trying to sell some of its hotel units as residences.

Crystal Paradise. Crysto Rey Village (Mail: P.O. Box 126, San Ignacio, Cayo); tel/fax 501-824-2772; www.crystalparadise.com. Directions: From San Ignacio, take the Cristo Rey Rd. about 4 miles to Crystal Paradise. This is one of the few lodges in Cayo owned and operated by native-born Belizeans, in this case by the Tut family (pronounced Toot). Many of the numerous Tut family pitch in and help at the lodge, which is located near the village of Cristo Rey on the Macal River. You likely will be greeted by one of the junior Tuts. Mama and daughters do the cooking. Several of the sons are guides. With, or without? That's the question: Do you want a cabaña with a thatch roof, or a simpler and cheaper room without? Either way, you get a private bath with hot and cold water, ceiling fan and 24-hour electricity. The Tuts offer horseback riding (US$35 per person for a half day), mountain bikes to rent and a variety of tours. Rates US$105 to $129 double, plus tax, including breakfast and dinner.

LODGES ON THE MOPAN RIVER

Clarissa Falls Resort. Mile 70, Western Hwy. (Benque Rd.) 5 ½ miles west of San Ignacio; tel. 501-824-3916; www.clarissafalls.com. Friendly owner Chena Galvez has spent her life on a cattle ranch here, on a rolling 800-acre expanse of grassy pasture. Chena and family have built these pleasant though simple thatch cabañas. Rates US$75 double plus tax for a cabaña. If you're on a tight budget, there's camping at US$7.50 per person and, for students only, rooms in a bunkhouse and three meals daily for US$45. You can swim or tube on the river, or play golf on the 5-hole course.

Camping/RV Campgrounds

Cayo has more camping options than any other area of Belize. Here is a sampling. For other places that allow camping, ask locally. A number of the hotels and lodges in the area will permit overnight camping or RV parking.

227

Caesar's Place. Mile 60, Western Hwy.; tel. 501-824-2341, fax 824-3449; . Tent and RV camping available. Caesar's Place also has hotel rooms.

Clarissa Falls. Mile 70 1/2, Western Hwy. (Mail: P.O. Box 44, San Ignacio); tel. 501-824-3916; www.clarissafalls.com. This popular Belizean-owned cabaña colony on the Mopan River (see above) also allows camping, at US7.50 per person. RVs and trailers permitted, too.

Inglewood Camping Grounds. Mile 68 1/4, Western Hwy. (Benque Rd.), tel. 501-824-3555; www.inglewoodcampinggrounds.com. A newer, more complete camping option with water and electric hook-ups and a dump station is on the Western Highway just west of San Ignacio. Inglewood offers tent camping with hot and cold showers, rustic cabañas and hook-ups for RVs. US$7 per person for tent camping space, US$15 for RV camping with water, plus BZ$0.50 per kilowatt for electricity. Hot showers and sanitary dumping, no charge.

MOUNTAIN PINE RIDGE LODGING

Blancaneaux Lodge. Mountain Pine Ridge (P.O. Box B, Central Farm, Cayo); tel. 501-824-3878, fax 824-3919, or in the U.S., tel. 800-746-3743; www.coppolaresorts.com/blancaneaux. Directions: From San Ignacio, go 12 1/2 miles to the entrance to the Mountain Pine Ridge reserve or go by way of the Pine Ridge Rd. from Georgeville, then 4 1/2 miles (watch for sign) and turn on dirt road, approx. 1/2 mile to the lodge. You also can fly here via a charter, as the lodge has an airstrip. Francis Ford Coppola ought to win a sixth Oscar for his incredible lodge, to add to the collection he won for the Godfather movies and other parts of his oeuvre. Coppola has said Belize reminds him of the verdant jungles of the Philippines, where he filmed *Apocalypse Now,* the movie that best caught the crazed atmosphere of the Vietnam war. In 1981, he bought an abandoned lodge, spent a fortune on fixing it up and reopened it in 1993. Mexican architect Manolo Mestre created the jungle chic look, and Francis and Eleanor Coppola themselves chose the Mexican and Guatemalan furnishings for the villas and cabañas. The result is simply one of the most extraordinary lodges in the world. It seems impossible, but Blancaneaux looks better and better each time we visit, even considering the loss of a number of pine trees due to Southern Pine Beetle blight. The grounds are beautifully maintained, with native flowers accenting pathways, grass areas are manicured. On our last three stopovers, we stayed in the villas, where we dreamed about selling that screenplay to Hollywood. The villas have two huge bedrooms. They look even larger than they are, because the thatch roofs soar more than two stories high. Each has a screen deck area with views of the Privassion River. The tiled Japanese-style baths are large and special soaps and lotions are complimentary. Between the two bedrooms is a great room with kitchen and an unscreened deck (mosquitoes are only rarely a problem in the Pine Ridge.) Note that getting about Blancaneaux's hilly grounds requires climbing many steps up and down. The regular cabañas, though far less spacious and luxurious than the villas, are pleasant for a couple, especially with their new decks and remodeled bathrooms. They're also less of a burden on your credit card, at US$280 to $550 in-season (US$230 to $500 May-November) as opposed to US$540, double occupancy, or US$600 for four people, for the villas in-season (US$475-$575 offseason). Mr. Coppola's personal villa is US$725 double (US$625 off-season). The new Enchanted Cottage ($1,400 in-season, $800 off) sits on a hill away from the main lodge grounds. The cottage has a private pool, a bedroom with king bed and fireplace, a kitchen with wine cooler, espresso machine and heated slate floor, and a bath house with Japanese tub and steam room. All rates are plus 9% hotel tax and 10% service. Included is a continental breakfast. The lodge has 24-hour electricity provided by a hydroelectric plant. Staffers can enjoy satellite TV in their rooms, but nothing so pedestrian is available in the guest lodging. The dining room in the main lodge building is comfortably up-scale. The Italian dishes in the restaurant are excellent, if a little pricey, and gradually a wider variety of choices has been added, a boon to those staying for more than a few days. You can even get real espresso and pizza from a wood-burning pizza oven. Most of the fruits and vegetables served are grown in the lodge's organic gardens. Wines from the Niebaum Coppola Estate Winery in Napa Valley are available. When you're in the bar, just off the lobby, note the slate bar top carved by the Garcia sisters, and the ceiling fan, which was used in *Apocalypse Now*. A restaurant serving Guatemalan food is at the far end of the new pool, where the croquet pitch used to be. In the winter, the fireplace in the bar adds a cozy touch when nights drop into the low 50s. The hotel and restaurant service is excellent. Many tours are available. Coppola also operates the Turtle Inn in Placencia and La Lancha near Tikal in Guatemala.

Hidden Valley Inn. Mountain Pine Ridge, (P.O. Box 170, Belmopan); tel. 501-822-3320, fax 822-3334; www.hiddenvalleyinn.com. Directions: From San Ignacio, go 12 1/2 miles on Cristo Rey Rd. to the entrance to the Mountain Pine Ridge reserve, (or go by way of the Pine Ridge Rd. from Georgeville), then 4 miles (watch for sign to Hidden Valley Falls and Inn) and turn left on dirt road to the lodge. With its thousands of acres of surrounding property, private waterfalls and great birding, Hidden Valley Inn always has had the potential to be one of the best lodges in Belize. Now, with new ownership (the Roe family, who also are involved in the SunBreeze in San Pedro and the Biltmore in Belize City and who have many other interests in Belize) and new management, Hidden Valley is moving back to top form. The 12 private cottages, each with a bedroom (queens or two doubles), living room and tiled bath, are not your traditional thatch but marl daub with zinc roofs. They've been spruced up, and two are billed as deluxe units. All have salt tile floors and comfortable furnishings, and the fireplaces come in handy in the winter. There's a beautiful swimming pool and a hot tub, in a grand setting by the side of the main lodge building. On recent visits, we had several delicious meals in the comfortable lodge dining room. It's wonderful to wake up early in the invigorating air of the Pine Ridge and walk some of the trails around the lodge. I'm told there are 90 miles of trails, several leading to waterfalls that are open only to Hidden Valley guests. Honeymooners or even old married folks can reserve Butterfly Falls or other falls for your own private day at a waterfall, complete with champagne. You can also walk through a small coffee finca — the lodge grows and roasts its own coffee. Yes, many of the Mountain Pines in this area have succumbed to the beetle infestation, but the pines are quickly regenerating. I saw many that are already 10 or 12 feet tall. The birding is actually better than ever here, as it's now much easier to spot the little feathered friends. A sizable percentage of Hidden Valley Inn guests are birders, who want to add to their life lists rare birds such as the Orange-breasted Falcon, King Vulture and Keel-billed Motmot. Rates at Hidden Valley: US$195-$250 double Nov.-April, US$155-$213 rest of year (higher rates during Christmas), plus 9% tax and 10% service. The full meal plan is US$60 per day per person. Transfers for up to four from Belize City are US$185, or US$85 from San Ignacio. Packages are available, and the hotel offers many tours and trips.

Moonracer Farm. Mountain Pine Ridge Rd. 600 ft south of the junction with Cristo Rey Rd.; tel. 501-667-5748 or 585-200-5748 in the U.S.; www.moonracerfarm.com. This new lodge, not in but near the entrance to the Mountain Pine Ridge, offers a comfortable rustic setting and lots of activities at a modest price. Owners Tom and Marge Gallagher, refugees from New York, bought this 50-acre farm in 2007 and have been working to turn it into a place to enjoy nature. Rates US$65 to $120, plus tax. A full meal plan is US$30 per person per day.

Dining in Cayo

If you're staying at a jungle lodge, you'll probably take most of your meals there. Chaa Creek, Blancaneaux, Hidden Valley Inn, duPlooy's, Caves Branch and other lodges have excellent, if somewhat pricey, meals. San Ignacio is the center for dining in Cayo, with a host of small, generally inexpensive restaurants.

Sanny's Grill. On a good night, this is one of the best restaurants in Cayo. With a hot grill and sizzling spices, this restaurant transforms Belizean basics, like chicken or pork chops, beyond standard fare. Try the lime-thyme red snapper, along with the tastiest, spiciest rice and beans in the Cayo. Eat them in the casual dining room or out on the covered deck. In a residential area off Benque Road, the place can be hard to find after dark. 23rd St., heading west of San Ignacio, look for sign just beyond the Texaco station. Tel. 501-824-2988. Moderate to Expensive. Open for dinner only.

Ko-Ox Han-Nah. Formerly Hannah's (the new name in the Maya language means "Let's go eat"), this is probably San Ignacio's most popular restaurant, and deservedly so. It's not fancy—you eat on simple tables in a room opening on busy Burns Avenue—but the food is inexpensive and well-prepared. In addition to beans-and-rice dishes, Hannah's serves salads, sandwiches and curries. 5 Burns Ave., tel. 501-824-3014. Moderate.

Serendib. In 2006 Belize's only Sri Lankan restaurant changed owners, but you can still get authentic curries. 27 Burns Ave. Closed Sunday. Inexpensive to Moderate.

Mom's Place. Old Belize hands will recall the original Mom's, a famous hangout for travelers and expats in Belize City. A daughter of the original owner of Mom's in Belize City is involved with this restaurant. The cheeseburger and chicken-fried steak will bring back memories. Prices are affordable, with most dishes under US$7. Joseph Andrews Dr., near Sacred Heart College, San Ignacio. Inexpensive to Moderate.

Eva's. Long-time owner Bob Jones sold Eva's, but this San Ignacio institution serves as a restaurant (food is okay), internet café, information center, trading post, tour office and meeting hall. 22 Burns Ave., tel. 501-824-2267. Inexpensive.

Hode's Place Bar & Grill. Bigger than it looks from the outside, with a large shaded patio and swings and slides for the kids at the back, plus an ice cream stand, Hode's is also popular for cold beers, karaoke and billiards. It has good food in large portions and at modest prices. Savannah Rd. in San Ignacio, next to soccer stadium. Inexpensive to Moderate.

Mr. Greedy's Pizzeria. This has the best pizza in Cayo. In the afternoons, a cheap happy hour (US$1 rum drinks) draws a crowd. Free wireless, too. Downtown San Ignacio at 34 Burns Ave., across from Venus Hotel; tel. 501- 804-4688.

Benny's Kitchen. This little open-air restaurant near Xunantunich is a local find. Most items on the menu are US$5 or less, including chilimole (chicken with mole sauce) and escabeche (onion soup with chicken). San José Succotz Village, across Benque Rd., from ferry to Xunantunich, tel. 501-823-2541. Inexpensive.

Ristorante Puccini's. One of Belmopan's best places to eat, with good pasta dishes, fajitas and steaks. You can dining inside in the air-conditioned dining room or at the small bar. Constitution Dr., Belmopan; tel. 501-822-1366.

CHAPTER 32:
CHECKING OUT DANGRIGA AND HOPKINS
Getting There

Dangriga is connected with the north by the Hummingbird Highway and by the Coastal Highway, which is also known as the Manatee Highway. Running south from Dangriga to Punta Gorda, a distance of about 100 miles, is the Southern Highway. Once this was widely considered the worst "main" road in Belize, with cars and big trucks raising thick clouds of dust in dry weather and bogging down in the mud in wet. Things have improved. It's now completely paved except for a 5-mile section near Golden Stream. James buses connect Dangriga with Belize City (US$8). Dangriga has an airstrip, with regular service on Maya Island Air and Tropic Air from Belize City. One-way fares from the international airport are around US$63, and from municipal about US$42.

The road into Dangriga is completely paved. The access roads to Hopkins from the Southern Highway is partly paved, but it was a lousy paving job and the road is now badly potholed, and that to Sittee River is completely paved (though the paving ends before you get to Hopkins).

You'll probably get wet, you'll probably get eaten up by mosquitoes, but you'll get to experience the "real jungle" at **Cockscomb Basin Wildlife Sanctuary** and Jaguar Preserve. This preserve covers 150 square miles of broadleaf rainforest. Much of it has been selectively logged for mahogany and other valuable trees, and some of it was affected by hurricanes, but to the novice bushwalker the rainforest canopy, up to 130 feet high, and the exotic plants and trees are nothing at all like back home. Parts of the preserve get up to 180 inches of rain a year, and the preserve includes the two highest peaks in Belize, Doyle's Delight at 3,688 feet and Victoria Peak at 3,675 feet. Cockscomb has the most extensive trail network of any park in Belize. Trails at the preserve vary from short self-guided hikes near the visitor center to a 17-mile multi-day trek to Victoria Peak, only for the physically fit and best done with a local guide during the dry season. While it's unlikely that you will see one of the 200 or so jaguars in the preserve, you may well see tracks or scat, as the jaguars do frequent the trails and entrance road at night. If you hike long enough, however, you will run into quite a few other wild creatures. The preserve is home to some 300 species of birds, along with all five types of Belize's wild cats, black howler monkeys, peccaries and snakes of all types and biting abilities. The best time to see wildlife is at the start of the rainy season, usually mid-June to early August, although with luck you will see wild creatures anytime you are in the preserve. Animals are most active on cooler, cloudy days.

Mayflower is a smaller park, but perhaps more interesting to the casual visitor than Cockscomb, as it has several beautiful waterfalls and some Maya sites.

Dangriga, with a population of around 9,000, is the largest town in Belize south of Belize City. Until the 1980s it was known as Stann Creek, when it was renamed Dangriga, meaning "sweet waters" in the Garifuna language. Dangriga, like Orange Walk Town, is not at all a visitor destination, though it is a useful jumping off spot for some of the central and southern cayes. Physically, it slightly resembles the older sections of Belize City, although it is much smaller.

DANGRIGA LODGING

Pelican Beach Resort. Scotchman Town, on the sea near the airstrip, (P.O. Box 2, Dangriga); tel. 501-522-2044; www.pelicanbeachbelize.com. The rambling white wood-frame main building at Pelican Beach, reportedly once a dance hall, always reminds us of boarding houses of our youth in Florida; others say it reminds them of old hotels on the coast of Maine. Inside, though, it's vintage Belize, with simple wood paneling and furniture that wasn't selected by any interior designer. There are about a dozen rooms in the main building and others in a separate structure. All rooms have fans, and some have air conditioning. In any event, this is the best hotel in Dangriga. It's on the water at the north edge of town, and there's a beach area and a breeze-swept pier. Some people swim here, but it's not exactly Cane Garden Beach in the British Virgin Islands. The restaurant is quite good, if a bit expensive (US$15 to $30 for dinner) and if you're a French fries lover as I am, try a basket of fries, as they are just about the best in Belize. Originally opened in 1971, Pelican Beach is operated by Tony and Therese Rath and family. Therese's family, the Bowmans, were prominent in colonial days, and she is prominent today in Belize's conservation organizations. Tony, a noted photographer, is among Belize's new breed of Internet entrepreneurs, running the Belize by Naturalight web sites and doing web design for many Belize businesses. Rates: Doubles range from around US$125-$135 double in-season (mid-November thru mid-May), with modest discounts off-season. Prices are plus 9% hotel tax and 10% service. Packages are available. Pelican Beach is associated with the delightful Pelican Beach cottages on Southwater Caye.

Chaleanor Hotel. 35 Magoon St.; tel. 501-522-2587; e-mail chaleanor@btl.net. This is a decent budget/low moderate choice in Dangriga. It's well-run and a good value. The 18 rooms in this tall, three-story hotel are larger than at many budget hotels, and all have private baths. Some rooms with TV and air-conditioning. Rates start around US$35.

HOPKINS LODGING

A seaside Garifuna village of about 1,400 people living in unpreten-tious frame houses, Hopkins was first settled in1942 after a hurricane devas-tated New Town, a Garifuna community just north of present-day Hopkins. The village gets its name from Frederick Charles Hopkins, a Catholic bishop of the early part of the 20th century. Hopkins was itself leveled by Hurricane Hattie in 1961. The village only got electricity and telephones in the mid-1990s. If "poor but proud" fits anywhere, it fits here. Villagers have gotten by on subsistence fishing and farming, and some are now earning cash money from tourism. You'll find most folks friendly. Many are eager to share their thoughts with visitors, and it's safe to walk around the village most anytime. The beach is nice, though many coco palms have died. Just south of Hopkins is the Sittee Point and False Sittee Point area, where hotel and real estate de-velopment are starting to take off. Many lots have been sold to expats looking for their little piece of the Caribbean, though only a few homes have so far been built.

You may have heard about the ferocious sand flies in this area, and, yes, they can be pretty bad. At times. At other times, they're hardly to be no-ticed. Sorry, but we're not able to predict exactly when they are at their worst. The hotels here do their best to control the little devils, without resort-ing to hydrogen bombs, but at times the sandflies can be a pain in the neck, and also the foot, leg and everywhere else. An oily lotion such as baby oil and a bug spray with DEET helps.

Hamanasi. Sittee Point, Stann Creek District (P.O. Box 265, Dan-griga); tel. 501-520-7073 or in U.S. 877-552-3483; www.hamanasi.com. Opened in late 2000, Hamanasi quickly became one of the top beach and dive resorts in southern Belize. It was named the Hotel of the Year in 2009 by the Belize Tourism Board and gets high ratings on TripAdvisor.com. On about 22 acres with 400 feet of beach frontage, the resort is south of Hopkins vil-lage, about 500 feet north of Jaguar Reef. The restaurant and lobby are attrac-tive, graced with local art, the grounds well kept and the pool, with a "zero effect," is one of the nicest we've seen in Belize. There are several types of accommodations — 12 rooms in the main seafront building, beachfront suites and 9 "tree houses" (actually just units raised on stilts and set in the trees in the back). All the accommodations are really nice, though we like the beach-front suites best. The owners, Americans Dana and David Krauskopf, who look like they just stepped out of a *Travel & Leisure* magazine spread, seem to know what they are doing. Certainly their cats, furry grey émigrés from Russia, where the owners lived for awhile, know exactly what they're up to. Hamanasi's dive operation provides full diving services. Hamanasi has three dive boats, including a 43-footer with twin 200-horsepower Yamaha outboards. A two-tank dive on the southern barrier reef, about 30 minutes out, is US$115, and a three-tank, full-day dive trip to Turneffe is US$185, and to Glover's atoll US$195. A half-day reef snorkeling trip is US$75. The resort also offers inland trips. Tours to Cockscomb are US$75. Room rates: US$295 to $440 double in high season (Christmas/New Years and mid-February to mid-April), US$245 to $385 in the shoulder season (most of January, mid-April to early June and U.S. Thanksgiving) and US$195 to $325 early June to mid-December, except Thanksgiving. Rates plus 9% hotel tax and 8% service. Continental breakfast included in room rates. Packages are available, and there are minimum-stay requirements of three to five days, depending on the season. The hotel's restaurant is very good, if expensive, with a fixed-price dinner at US$40.

Jaguar Reef Lodge & Spa. Sittee Point, Stann Creek District; tel. 501- 523-7365, or 866-910-7373 in the U.S. and Canada; www.jaguarreef.com. Jaguar Reef is now jointly operated with Almond Beach next door. The resort has many different types of accommodations. The attractive main lodge building (rebuilt after a fire in early 2003) houses the beachfront restaurant, bar, gift shop and front desk. The beach here is beautiful. Jaguar Reef runs a variety of tours, both on land and sea. Rates: US$200 to $325 double, January– through mid-April, US$150 to $275 rest of the year except Christmas/New Years. Rates are plus 19% for tax and service. Packages and specials are available. The full meal plan is US$53, or $31 for dinner only.

Kanantik Reef & Jungle Resort. Between Hopkins and Placencia (P.O. Box 150, Dangriga); tel. toll-free 877-759-8834 or 501-520-8048, fax 520-8089; www.kanantik.com. Want to do both the barrier reef and the jungle without having to decide anything, except whether to have the fish or the beef for dinner? Care to relax on a deserted, coco palm-lined private beach the length of four football fields? Enjoy an active seaside vacation, with all the snorkeling, kayaking and touring you can handle? Don't mind paying top dollar? Then Kanantik, a luxury all-inclusive that opened in 2002, may be your place. Kanantik — it's a Mopan Maya word meaning "to take care"— has 25 cabañas hidden away on 300 acres just north of Hopkins. The thatch cabañas, echoing African designs, are striking round structures with conical roofs. They are air-conditioned, luxuriously outfitted and large, about 525 sq ft. The resort took years to plan and build; construction included bulldozing a lengthy road and building an airstrip. When we were there, the food was excellent, and the dinner conversation, led by co-owner Roberto Fabbri, an Italian by way of San Francisco, was equally so. This is not a place for you if you like a lot of active nightlife (it's miles from the nearest village) but if you're an all-inclusive type, this is one of Belize's few options in that category. The all-inclusive rate of US$804 per day per couple, including tax and service, covers lodging, tours, meals and local drinks and beer. The room-only rate is US$300 a day, single or double. Other packages, including five-day dive packages at US$3,750 double, are available. Kanatik is on the market for around US$8 million.

Belizean Dreams. Hopkins; tel. 501-523-7272 or 800-456-7150; www.belizeandreams.com. This condo colony just north of Jaguar Reef is among the most upscale accommodation choices on the Southern Coast. All villas have the same floor plans and furnishings, but some are directly on the beach, and the others have sea views. The units can be reserved as a complete villa, or choose a single bedroom or two-bedroom suite. The bedrooms have vaulted ceilings with exposed beams and four-poster king beds. Rates: US$239 to $499 in high season, US$169 to $439in summer. The same developer has built a group of new, similar condos called **Hopkins Bay,** at the north end of Hopkins village.

Beaches and Dreams Seafront Inn and Barracuda Bar & Grill. Sittee Point, tel. 501-523-7259; www.beachesanddreams.com. Owners Tony and Angela Marsico traded running a restaurant in Alaska for operating a beachside inn and restaurant in Belize. They've spruced up the inn's two octagonal cottages, each with two units with vaulted ceilings and rattan furniture. They've also turned the restaurant into one of the best eateries on the southern coast, with delicious dishes like fig-stuffed pork chops and Gibnut gumbo. Rates US$125 in-season, US$95 mid-April to mid-November, plus 9% hotel tax.

Jungle Jeanie's/Jungle by the Sea. Hopkins; tel. 501-523-7047; www.junglebythesea. Nope, it's not in the jungle, but the six cabañas are on a nicely shaded stretch of beach a little south of Hopkins village. Owners "Jungle Jeanie" Barkman and husband are Canadians who have lived in Belize for years. Rates for cabañas are US$90-$120 double, plus hotel tax.

Hopkins Inn. Hopkins (P.O. Box 121, Dangriga); tel. 501-523-7283; www.hopkinsinn.com. Attractive cottages on the beach, with full bath, fridge, fan and private verandah with sea views. The hotel is well run by Greg and Rita Duke, who are knowledgeable about the area. Rates US$49 to $99 double, including continental breakfast, plus tax. German spoken.

Tipple Tree Beya Inn. Hopkins; tel. 501-520-7006; www.tippletree.com. If you're looking for an inexpensive, simple little place on the beach, this is a great choice. The hotel is popular, so reserve in advance. Rates range from US$30 to $75 double, plus tax. German spoken.

Dining in Hopkins

Besides the hotel restaurants, of which the one at **Beaches and Dreams** is the best, a number of small restaurants are run by local people, often in their homes. Try **Innie's, Iris's** or **Yugadah Café.** You'll pay around US$4 or $5 for fish or chicken and beans and rice, up to US$10 to $13 for a lobster dinner. A new, European-owned café is **Thongs.**

CHAPTER 33:
CHECKING OUT PLACENCIA
Getting There

By car, from the intersection of the Hummingbird Highway (also known as the Stann Creek Valley Highway) and the Southern Highway, it is about 22 miles to the turn-off to Placencia. Then, from the Southern Highway, it is about 9 miles to Riversdale, the elbow point at which you begin to see the blue Caribbean. From here, it is another 16 miles or so to the south end of Placencia village.

Glory be! Paving of the road is at long last well under way. As of this writing the road is paved from Placencia village to past Maya Beach. Completion is expected by 2011. It's an excellent road, too; the only problem is that there are way too many huge speed bumps.

Maya Island Air and Tropic Air each have 10 or 11 flights daily from Belize City. Fares from the International Airport are about US$95 one-way and from the Municipal Airport, about US$80.

By bus, there are at least two departures daily from Dangriga. You can make connections in Dangriga from various points north, including Belize City, Belmopan and San Ignacio. Cost from Dangriga is about US$4.

If you are arriving by bus from the mainland across the lagoon at Independence/Mango Creek, a little water taxi — the Hokey Pokey — costs US$3 and runs eight trips daily in each direction. Currently, the first trip from Independence/Mango Creek is at 6:30 a.m. and the last one at 5:30 p.m. For updates, check www.aguallos.com/hokeypokey/ or telephone 501-523-2376.

The main reason to come to Placencia is for activities on the water, primarily fishing, diving and snorkeling. While you can make trips from Placencia to Maya ruins and other mainland sites, doing so is not quite as easy as it might seem when you look at a map. Just getting back to the Southern Highway is a 25-mile, 35+-minute trip.

Placencia Peninsula Lodging

You have a choice to make about where to stay on the Placencia peninsula. You have to decide whether you want to stay in Placencia village, the main "population center" for the area, or north of the village. Placencia village is a Creole village at the southern tip of the peninsula. It's a bit funky, and nearly all of the lodging choices here are in the budget or moderate categories, but it is the focus for restaurants and what shopping there is.

By contrast, the area north of Placencia village has most of the peninsula's upmarket resorts. It's less jammed up, and the beaches are generally prettier. If you're a budget traveler, or if you don't have a car (and don't want to bike or take a taxi back and forth between your hotel and the village) you may want to stay in or near Placencia village. If you decide you want something more upscale and with fewer people around, then your decision becomes: Where north of Placencia village do you want to stay? There are two "addresses" north of Placencia village: Seine Bight, a Garifuna village about 5 miles north of Placencia village, and Maya Beach, about 7 miles north of Placencia village. Maya Beach isn't a village but a small collection of houses and hotels. (Another small collection of houses and hotels is farther north, between Maya Beach and Riversdale, the elbow point where the road from the Southern Highway comes to the Caribbean Sea and turns south down the peninsula.) A primary consideration is how far north of the "action" in Placencia village you want to be. Unless you have a car, you're at the mercy of your hotel shuttle, if there is one, taxis (which cost as much as US$20 one-way to go from Placencia village to the north end of Maya Beach). Some hotels do offer guests the complimentary use of bicycles, which is another option for getting back and forth, though not a very good one after dark.

Turtle Inn. Placencia; tel. 501-824-4912; www.coppolaresorts.com. The original Turtle Inn was a fixture for many years in Placencia, when the late Skip White ran it. A few years ago, it was bought by Francis Ford Coppola and reopened as Blancaneaux's Turtle Inn. Then, in October 2001, a nasty lady named Iris paid a visit to Placencia, and Turtle Inn was virtually blown away. After a complete rebuild, Turtle Inn reopened in early 2003. On a recent stay, Turtle Inn knocked me out. My family and I had a two-bedroom sea front villa, and you couldn't ask for anything nicer or more stylish. The villas and many of the single cabañas sit just feet from the sea, so the gentle lap-lap of the Caribbean soothes you, and the prevailing offshore breeze keeps you cool. (There is no air-conditioning, so on a calm summer day it can get pretty warm.) Our villa was a pure delight. In some ways, the villas at Turtle Inn remind me of those at Blancaneaux Lodge: The bay-thatch

239

ceiling soars high, there's a wide screened porch across the front, and the main living area has comfy seating and a fridge. The two bathrooms are in the Japanese-style, with both showers and tiled square tubs (there also are outdoor garden showers, which are more fun than you'd think.) But, unlike Blancaneaux, the villas and cabanas at Turtle Inn are Balinese in inspiration, with wonderful art and furnishing, and even the doors, picked out personally, I'm told, in Indonesia by Mr. Coppola and his wife, and imported in 14 container loads. We also got a tour of Mr. Coppola's personal villa, the Pavilion, which is available for hotel guests when the director isn't there. It has several extra touches, such as saunas in the bathrooms. Pavilion also comes with its own private pool. We sneaked a swim in the Coppola pool, though normally it is reserved for use by the party in the Pavilion villa. But even if you don't stay in the Pavilion villa and stay in one of the other 24 units, you'll be very happy with the other pools, a large turtle-shaped, zero-effect pool, between the restaurant and the attractive sandy beach, and another one infinity pool in the triangular shape of the Coppola Resorts logo. Turtle Inn has a small marina on the lagoon side. There are several choices for dining, including the main restaurant, Mare, which features Italian and seafood dishes; the Gauguin Grill, a beachfront seafood eatery; and Auntie Luba's Kitchen, a faux Belizean diner. There are two bars, including the Skip White Bar. I found the food, service, amenities and staff responsiveness all very accommodating. The upscale made-in-Belize bath soaps, shampoos and lotions delighted my wife and daughter, who also were given Balinese sarongs. We had a walk-talkie to hail our "houseman" should we need anything. The open-air restaurant with a sunken sand floor is as tropical as you could want. Like Blancaneaux, Turtle Inn has a wood-burning pizza oven and serves excellent wines from the Niebaum-Coppola winery. A continental breakfast of fresh-baked breads and fruits is included in the room rate. Rates: In-season, Turtle Inn cottages are US$375 to $450 double, and villas US$650 to $750 for four persons (the Pavilion Villa is US$1,850.) Summer rates are slightly lower, Christmas rates higher. Rates are plus 9% hotel tax and 10% service.

Inn at Robert's Grove. Seine Bight; tel. 501-523-3565; fax 501-523-3567 or, in the US., 800-565-9757; www.robertsgrove.com. This 52-unit luxury property on 22 seaside acres, which opened in 1997, raised the standard on what visitors to this part of Belize can expect in a beach resort. It is owned and operated by ex-New Yorkers Risa Frackman, svelte and charming, and Robert Frackman, gruff but gracious. I've stayed several times in one of the "deluxe suites" that come in one- and two-bedroom versions. These suites are a delight, with a large, strikingly decorated living room — a happy mélange of Mexican tile, Guatemalan fabrics and African art — with cable TV, veranda with a sea view, a master bedroom with king-size bed with a luxuriously firm new U.S.-made mattress and a jumbo bathroom with big, tiled combination bath and shower. The resort has facilities still missing at some other Belize resorts — not one but three swimming pools, roof-top whirlpools, tennis courts, work-out room and complimentary use of small sailboats, kayaks, bikes and other equipment. The main restaurant, under the hand of chef Frank DaSilva, is excellent. Don't miss the weekly Saturday night poolside barbecue, featuring all-you-care-to-eat lobster (in-season), shrimp, fish, chicken and other items. A casual restaurant on the lagoon side, at the marina and near the dive shop, is open seasonally. There's a tour desk, PADI dive center and a sandy beach where you can actually swim. Rates, while not cheap, do not leave you with the impression that you are being held up at Amex-point. In-season, rates for doubles are US$189 to $460; off-season, US$155 to $375. All rates plus 19% tax and service. Robert's Grove also offers day and all-inclusive overnight trips to a private island, Ranguana Caye, and to tiny Robert's Caye. In 2008, Robert's Grove was named Hotel of the Year by the Belize Tourism Board and is highly rated by TripAdvisor.com.

Chabil Mar Villas. Placencia; tel. 501-523-3606 or 866-417-2377; www.chabilmarvillas.com. This gated condotel s one of the most upscale on the peninsula. Chabil Mar means "beautiful sea" in Ketchi Mayan, and the sea and 400 feet of beach here are indeed beautiful at this Canadian-developed property. The one- and two-bedroom villas are tastefully designed and luxuriously furnished, down to wine corkscrews and service for eight. They have features such as marble floors, original art and four-poster king beds. Every comfort is at hand, from broadband Internet to DVD players to washers and dryers in each unit. Rates: US$375 to $575 in winter, US$350 to $495 in summer, plus 9% tax and 10% service.

Maya Beach Hotel and Bistro. Maya Beach, tel./fax 501-520-8040 or 800- 503-5124; www.mayabeachhotel.com. Before ending up here, owners John and Ellen Lee (he's Australian, she's American) traveled and worked in 20 countries. They must have figured out what travelers like, because their Bistro by the beach (see below) is one of the best restaurants in Belize, and the hotel is a classic beachy inn. A new swimming pool is beside the restaurant. The Bistro menu changes from time to time, but among the standards are the gazpacho with grilled shrimp, snapper stack and cocoa-dusted pork chop on a risotto cake. In addition to the simple but pleasant hotel rooms with views of False Caye and the sea, the hotel rents apartments and houses nearby. Rates: US$65 to $139 in-season, US$55 to $99 off-season, with rental apartments/houses US$111 to $300. Rates plus tax and 10% service charge. Highly recommended.

Maine Stay. Seine Bight; tel. 501-523-3507 or 207-512-2381 in the U.S.; www.traversbelize.com. This is a good spot for families to stay for a week or longer. Two units each have a pair of wooden cabañas, connected by a covered breezeway and deck, with two bedrooms and two baths. Both have kitchen, washer and dryer and Wi-Fi. There's 400 feet of beach and a 100-foot pier. Rates in-season (Nov.–May) for four persons is US$1,395 per week and US$1,095 off-season, plus tax (no service charge). Owners, from Maine of course, live across the street.

Barnacle Bill's. Maya Beach; tel. 501-523-8110; www.barnaclebills-belize.com/. The opening of this little place in Maya Beach in 2000 marked a welcome trend toward moderately priced self-catering cottages on the beach.

241

American owners Barnacle Bill (known as the wit of Maya Beach) and Adriane Taylor put up two one-bedroom Mennonite cottages about 60 feet from the beach. The bungalows are on stilts, cooled by fans and sea breezes, and each has a full kitchen with fridge, microwave, two-burner stove and cooking utensils. They'll sleep up to three. The bedroom has a queen bed, and there's a sofa sleeper in the living/dining area. For groceries, a small market is not far away, and there are several restaurants and bars nearby. Doubles are US$110 Nov.-May, US$95 rest of year, plus 9% hotel tax. Minimum stay 5 nights, 7 at Christmas.

Westwind. Placencia; tel. 501-523-3255; www.westwindhotel.com. George Westby's Westwind Hotel is a dependable spot to rest your head. The rooms are spotlessly clean. All rooms have a balcony, patio or terrace with at least a partial view of the sea. Rates: US$75 to $90 double.

Tradewinds. Placencia; tel. 501-523-3122; If you want a beachfront cottage but don't want to pay the higher prices north of the village, Tradewinds is your best bet. The pastel-colored cabins on the beach at the south end of Placencia village are cute as a bug's ear. They're not large, but at about US$78 to $102 in-season, and as low as US$65 off-season, they're a decent value. Fridges, fans and two double beds are standard. There have been some thefts reported from the cabins here, as at some other hotels in the village without security guards.

Lydia's Guest House. Placencia Village; tel. 501-523-3117; e-mail lydias@btl.net This is a top budget choice, at the north end of the village. It's run by Lydia Villanueva and offers 8 basic but clean rooms, with fans, shared bath, shared kitchen, refrigerators, and, on the second floor of the wood-frame house, a veranda with hammocks. Rates: around US$25 double in-season, a little less in summer.

Dining in Placencia

Robert's Grove and **Turtle Inn** (both in the Expensive/Very Expensive category) have worthy restaurants. In addition, try these local places:

Maya Beach Hotel Bistro. Opened in 2004, the restaurant at this small hotel has quickly become one of the most talked about in Southern Belize. It was expanded in 2008-2009. You'll enjoy the interesting presentations and sophisticated dishes such as five-onion cioppino and cocoa-dusted pork on risotto (US$23). The Bistro has added a selection of small plates and appetizers including fish cakes, a shrimp corn dog, and honey-coconut ribs, starting at US$5. Maya Beach, tel. 501-520-8040. Closed Mondays except to hotel guests. Moderate to Very Expensive.

French Connection. A young European couple is working hard to bring French and other continental food to Placencia village. Main courses change frequently, but are along the lines of grilled pork chop with wild mushrooms and brandy sauce (US$20) or baked grouper with a ragout of chickpeas (US$21). The setting, in a new location near the police station, and service are charming. Tel. 501-523-3656. Tha...nk you! Expensive to Very Expensive.

De Tatch. Laidback and tropical, De Tatch is popular for its beer and simple but delicious food. In the village at the Sea Spray Hotel. Inexpensive to Moderate.

Yoli's. On a pier at the south end of the peninsula, this bar and restaurant (the food is from Marlene's kitchen nearby) has the peninsula's most tropical setting. Inexpensive to Moderate.

Tutti-Frutti. Great place for amazingly delicious and authentic gelati in a variety of tropical fruit and other flavors. In Placencia village near the BTIA office. Highly, highly recommended! Inexpensive.

Rumfish y Vino. This new place run by expat New Yorkers, in a breezy second-story location in Placencia village, is a good spot to have drinks and tapas. Try the small plates, such as Thai curry shrimp (US$14.) Bigger dishes include grilled fish, shrimp and also lobster stew (US$22). Nice selection of Italian wines. Placencia village, near BTIA office; tel. 501-523/3293. Expensive.

Danube. Wiener schnitzel in the tropics? That may not be what you were expecting, but the Austrian and Hungarian dishes are excellent at this new restaurant. In its own blue building, Danube has a relaxed atmosphere with art on the walls by the co-owner, Simone Gareis. On main road 2½ miles north of the Placencia airstrip; tel. 501-610-0132.

Rio Grande in Toledo District

CHAPTER 34:
CHECKING OUT PUNTA GORDA
Getting There

Via the Southern Highway, PG is about 100 miles from the junction with the Hummingbird/Stann Creek Valley Highway near Dangriga. Since the Southern Highway is now almost completely paved, except for about 5 miles near Golden Stream by car from Dangriga if you push it a little you can make the trip in about 2 hours. Add 3 hours or more if leaving from Belize City, depending on your route and driving habits.

By bus from Belize City (James Line is your best choice), figure about 6 hours minimum. Both Tropic Air and Maya Island Air have about half a dozen flights a day from Belize City to PG; from the International Airport to Punta Gorda, the fare is about US$120 one-way and from Municipal, US$102.

There is regularly scheduled daily water taxi service between PG and Puerto Barrios Guatemala. Currently, there are three boats daily to Puerto Barrios and limited service a couple of times a week to Livingston. One-way fare is US$20 to $22.

Punta Gorda Area Lodging
Machaca Hill Rainforest Canopy Lodge. 5 miles north of PG (P.O. Box 135, Punta Gorda); tel. 501-722-0050 or 800-242-2017; www.machacahill.com. Formerly the fishing lodge known as El Pescador

PG, under new owners Machaca Hill now focuses on more traditional jungle lodge activities, such as trips and tours in the Laughing Falcon Reserve, an 12,000-acre private nature reserve. The new manager, Brian Gardiner, formerly ran safaris in Africa. He and the owners have taken the lodge far upscale, redoing the main lodge and adding a gorgeous spa. The rates are now among the highest in Belize, at almost US$1,300 a day per couple, all-inclusive. The lodge is set on a steep hill, called Big Hill for the farm that was originally here, on 470 acres above the Rio Grande. A small tram takes guests down to the boats docked on the river at the base of the hill. Up top, on a clear day, you have views of the Gulf of Honduras, with Guatemala and Honduras in the distance. Troops of howler monkeys come by frequently. After a day exploring the Toledo rain forest, dive into the pool, then dine on fish and fresh vegetables from the lodge's organic garden. The cottages (totally renovated in 2009-2010) have vaulted ceilings, tile floors and air-conditioning. All-inclusive rates, including meals and tours, are US$540 per person in high season, US$460 off-season, plus tax and 10% service. Bed-and-breakfast rates are much lower, US$400 double in-season and US$280 off-season.

Lodge at Big Falls. Big Falls (P.O. Box 103, Punta Gorda); tel. 888-865-3369 in U.S. and Canada; www.thelodgeatbigfalls. This lodge, on about 30 acres on the banks of the Rio Grande River near the village of Big Falls, opened in 2003. The owners, Americans who lived for years in England, are Rob and Marta Hirons. They've done a good job developing the lodge property. The accommodations are what most visitors are looking for in a lodge — thatch cabañas, but nice ones, with tile floors and private baths. A new pool opened in late 2005. The main lodge building has a restaurant, library and computer with satellite Internet access. Kerosene lamps provide the light. Current rates: May to October, US$140 double; rest of year, US$180, plus tax and service. Higher rates at Christmas/New Years. Breakfast is US$11, dinner US$32.

Cotton Tree Lodge. San Felipe village; tel. 501-670-0557 or 866/480–4534 in U.S.; www.cottontreelodge.com. Named after the silk cotton tree, aka kapok or ceiba, a giant example of which stands near the main lodge building, Cotton Tree Lodge sits beside the Moho River about 15 miles from Punta Gorda. The lodge has raised wooden walkways; in the summer rainy season the Moho often floods, and at times the grounds become a large lake. Good meals (dinner US$24) are served in a huge thatch palapa. All-inclusive rates in-season are US$390 to $550 for two persons per day, just a little less in summer, and include accommodations, meals, tours, taxes, and transfers, but not alcoholic beverages. Room-only rates also available, at US$169-$239 double in-season, and US$139-$229 off-season. All rates plus tax.

Tranquility Lodge. San Felipe Rd, Jacintoville, about 9 miles north of Punta Gorda; tel. 501-677-9921 or 800-819–9088; www.tranquility-lodge.com. Owners Sheila and Rusty Nale, who for many years ran the Mayan Princess on Ambergris Caye, have upgraded the rooms at this small

245

lodge on Jacinto Creek. All four rooms have air-conditioning, flat-screen TVs, Wi-Fi and iPod docks. Meals (for guests only) are served in a thatched dining room on the second floor, above the guest rooms. Dinner is US$25. Rates are US$100 to $125 in-season, US$80 to $100 off-season, plus 9% tax and 10% service.

Sun Creek Lodge. Off Mile 86, Southern Hwy.; tel. 501-614-2080; www.suncreeklodge.de. This lodge is run by Bruno Kuppinger, a German, and his beautiful Belizean wife, Melissa. Bruno offers tours, including a new high-adventure tour to the remote Columbia River Forest Reserve, called Maya Divide. Melissa focuses on the lodge and does the cooking, and I'm told she's an excellent chef. The round thatch cabanas at this lodge are simple but look comfortable, with outdoor showers surrounded by plants. There also are new more upscale villas across the road. The grounds are nicely landscaped. Car rentals available. It's 14 miles from Punta Gorda. Rates are US$40 to $100 plus 9% tax, year-round.

Coral House Inn. 151 Main St., Punta Gorda; tel. 501-722-2878; www.coralhouseinn.net. Americans Rick and Darla Mallory bought and renovated a 1938 colonial-era house and turned it into one of the coolest guesthouses in Belize. You'll recognize it by the coral color and the vintage red and white VW van parked in front. There's a small swimming pool, recently upgraded. Nearby are Confederate graves in a cemetery, a legacy of the Confederate immigration to Toledo after the U.S. Civil War. The four guest rooms, US$83 to $100 double, plus tax, have tile floors, good beds, air-conditioning and free wireless Internet. The Mallorys also manage a nearby cottage, with one bedroom and a full kitchen, which goes for US$125 a night.

Hickatee Cottages Lodge. Ex-Servicemen Rd. about 1 mile south of Punta Gorda; tel. 501-662- 4475; www.hickatee.com. A charming and down-to-earth British couple, Ian and Kate Morton, created Hickatee Cottages. It opened in late 2005 and quickly became one of the best little inns in Belize. We *highly* recommend it. The three rooms and one suite in Caribbean-style cottages, with zinc roofs and private porches, are nestled in lush foliage. Rates are an affordable US$75 to $110 double or triple, including continental breakfast. Delicious meals are available every day but Wednesday (dinner is US$17.50), with fruits and vegetables from the owners' organic nursery next door. There's a small but well-stocked bar. Free Wi-Fi. Guests can cool off in the plunge pool after a ride on complimentary bikes. On certain days, the lodge offers guests free visits to Fallen Stones butterfly farms. A hickatee, by the way, is a river turtle, *Dermatemys mawii*.

Blue Belize Guest House. 139 Front St., Punta Gorda; 501-722-2678; www.bluebelize.com. You can do your own thing in one of the four attractive self-catering flats, with kitchenettes, large bedrooms and verandas with hammocks. The guest house is set on a bluff overlooking the water. Co-owner Rachel Graham is a PhD marine biologist whose specialty is sharks, and the other owner, Dan Castellanos, is a local fishing and tour guide. A continental breakfast is included. Rates US$70 to $135 plus 9% tax.

Tate's Guest House. 34 José Maria Nuñez St., Punta Gorda; tel. 501-722-0147. Run by William Tate, a long-time post office worker in PG, and his family, this guest house on a quiet residential street is a good value. The rooms are clean, and the atmosphere friendly. There's a small common kitchen with refrigerator and microwave for guest use. Rates US$25 to $40.

Nature's Way Guesthouse. 65 Front St., Punta Gorda; tel. 501-702-2119; e-mail natureswayguesthouse@hotmail.com. This rambling, funky old guest house appeals to the hippy backpacker in us. It has a nice location, on the water toward the south end of town, and guests here are often well traveled, with stories to tell. At these prices — starting at around US$15 — don't expect a Hampton Inn.

Dining in Toledo

In addition to the restaurants listed below, **Hickatee Cottages** (Moderate) and **Machaca Hill Lodge** (Expensive to Very Expensive) both have excellent restaurants, open to the public by reservation. Note that restaurants in PG may close for a month or two, then reopen unexpectedly.

Emery's. Despite changes of management, Emery's has consistently good food, served in an open-air palapa. Inexpensive to Moderate. North Street near the gas station. Inexpensive to Moderate.

Marian's Bayview. Here you choose from one or two dishes owner Marian prepares for the day, perhaps local fish or Indian dish. The restaurant is on the third floor of a concrete building, with views of the water. It has bare light bulbs and rough cement floors, but you come here for the food, not the atmosphere. Front and Vernon Sts., Punta Gorda, tel. 501-722-0129. Inexpensive to Moderate.

Gomier's Restaurant and Soy Centre. This restaurant opens only if the St. Lucia-born owner, Ingnatius "Gomier" Longville, feels like cooking, and you won't know that until about the time the restaurant is supposed to open. If open Gomier's does excellent vegetarian meals, from organic ingredients grown by the owner. The owner also offers cooking classes, for US$50 a day. Alejandro Vernon St., Punta Gorda. Closed Sunday and some other days. Inexpensive to Moderate.

Earth Runnins Café and Bakut Bar. This is a laid-back, Rasta spot for a beer and good food at moderate prices. Runnins is a Rasta word for happenings, and Bakut is a tree with long seed pods with edible but smelly beans. Local seafood is the specialty here. Check out the bar, which was made from a large rosewood tree that was felled by Hurricane Iris in 2001. There's live music some nights. Main Middle St., tel. 501-702-2007. Closed Monday and Tuesday. Inexpensive to Moderate.

Mangrove Inn at Casa Bonita. The cook and co-owner of this little restaurant, Iconie Williams, formerly operated one of PG's best eateries, also called Mangrove Inn, and she has reopened it here in the B&B in her home. Iconie cooks different dishes every evening, but you'll usually have a choice of seafood (snapper, snook, or shrimp, less than US$10) or hearty fare like roasted chicken (US$5). Open daily for dinner only. Front St. in Cattle Landing area, tel. 501-722-2270. Inexpensive to Moderate.

Coleman's Café. This restaurant in Big Falls village serves simple but tasty Belizean dishes such as stew chicken with beans and rice. Sit at tables with under a covered patio, open to the breezes, and enjoy real Belizean hospitality. Big Falls Village, near the rice mill; tel. 501-720-2017.Inexpensive to Moderate.

"Hello, how are you today?"

CHAPTER 35:
QUESTIONS AND ANSWERS ON LIVING IN BELIZE

Here are some of the questions on living, working and buying property in Belize folks have posed to me, together with my answers. Names of the people who posed the questions have been expunged to protect the innocent. Other Q&As are on my Website at www.belizefirst.com.

Q. Is Belize a place where a 36-year-old Californian (with no kids who's tired of the rat race) could move and live permanently? Are there any decent jobs...even at any of the resorts? Is it safe?

A. I guess the answer is: Possibly. Belize is a small, developing country, with high unemployment especially in rural areas, a population of only a little over 330,000 and the economy of a small town of 40,000 people in the U.S. Pay scales are much lower than in the U.S., roughly one-sixth to one-fourth of those in the U.S. for similar jobs. To work in Belize you need a work permit, and, unless self-employed or hired by a Belize company that cannot fill the position with a Belizean, you also need official residency status, which requires you to live in Belize for a full year, leaving for no more than14 days. The Belize government encourages immigration by people who have money to invest and who can create jobs for Belizeans; it makes it more difficult for others. Having said all that, there are Americans who have come to Belize and have found work fairly easily, mainly in the hotel industry or in real estate sales. And quite a few Americans have come to Belize and started businesses with some success.

Q. We have purchased a commercial lot on Long Caye in the Lighthouse Reef Atoll. We are planning on building a Bed & Breakfast with four units to rent, an office, and a shared kitchen/living area which we will serve breakfast. We are not planning on moving to Belize, but hiring Belizean workers to manage, clean, cook breakfast, work the office, etc. We may rent out canoes, bikes etc. from the office and may have a small gift shop. What licenses are required to operate this bed and breakfast? Do we need work permits even though we will not be doing the work? Do we need a hotel license and do we need to form a Belizean corporation? If we need to do these, whom do we contact to get the paperwork? Do we need a Belize bank account?

A. First, I have some unsolicited advice: Your idea about operating a B&B using hired help is a prescription for trouble. I have visited or stayed at more than 150 hotels in Belize, and I don't think I have found more than two or three where it was operated successfully by an absentee owner. (The exceptions of course are a few of the large hotels or resorts such as the Radisson, which can afford to hire a professional GM and staff.) In general, if you are going to be operating a business in Belize, even if you are not there full-time, you likely will need a work permit, in this case a self-employed work permit and residency status which in most cases are fairly easy to get, assuming that you are making an investment and hiring Belizeans. You will also need a permit, administered through the Belize Tourist Board, to operate a guesthouse or hotel. Often also you need a local approval from the village or town council to operate, but in the case of Long Caye where there is no village I doubt you will need anything. You will probably want to have a Belize bank account so you can pay local bills, wages, etc. However, you should avoid putting much money in this account and instead use a bank account in the U.S. for most transactions. As to the form of business, corporation or whatever, that is up to you. You will probably want to have a Belize attorney. I would suggest starting by contacting the Belize Tourism Industry Association (also joining it) and the Belize Tourism Board and seeking their advice. The BTIA has a Belize Hotel Association division for members who operate hotels. It's difficult to know how to respond to your specific questions because to me it is still unclear what will happen with Long Caye. There are plans, dreams, some lots sold, but it will be years before it's clear what kind of a development it will really be, what actually will get built, how transport to the island will be set up, and how owners and visitors will respond to the island as it evolves. I don't mean to be negative. It may be that your idea will work great. As I say, I think Long Caye and what it becomes is still a question mark, but it's a unique place and it could be something special. Someday. Maybe 50 years from now. But I have seen so many people come to Belize, spend a lot of money on their hotel dream and end up with a failure. As you doubtless know, outside of San Pedro, Belize City and a couple of other areas, hotel occupancy rates in Belize are very low, averaging only a little over 40%. And in remote areas they are much lower than that. Good luck.

Q. *My wife and I are both 55 and would like to retire but work in Belize. She is a teacher. I am in management. Are there any opportunities? Do I need to start a business, i.e. refrigeration repair or like type? Most importantly, my wife is a diabetic. How is the available care? My thoughts are to settle in the Dangriga area.*

A. Under the Qualified Retired Persons program, which offers some tax and other incentives for retiring in Belize, you cannot work for pay in Belize (although you can have income from businesses outside Belize and from investments in Belize.) To work in Belize, you would need a work permit, either a regular one if working for someone else, or a self-employed work permit if you run your own business. You would also need regular residency, which in some cases requires that you live in Belize for a year before applying. While expats in Belize can and do find work, jobs other than those in tourism are fairly scarce and pay is much lower than in the U.S. More than 100,000 Belizeans have left Belize, mostly going to the U.S. to find better paying jobs. Teaching jobs are pretty hard to find in Belize, as there are many Belizeans who are qualified. Pay is low, under US$1,000 a month for a degreed high school teacher. Your best bet probably would be to start a business in Belize, one that employs Belizeans. The government encourages that kind of investment. Belize has a mixed public and private medical system. Care is inexpensive but certainly is not up to the standards of the U.S. or Canada. There is a regional hospital in Dangriga. I don't know the specifics about diabetes care in Dangriga, but since there are many few diabetics in Belize there is local care. However, don't expect the high-quality, evidence-based medicine that you find in the U.S. or Canada.

Q. *Where would be the best place to live in Belize if we should decide to move there? We would prefer something coastal. But as far as economy, away from the crime. And how hard would it be to move there from the U.S.?*

A. I recommend you look at the Corozal Town/Consejo Shores area in northern Belize. It is not on the Caribbean, but it is on Chetumal Bay. This is a fairly safe, friendly area, close to Mexico for more extensive shopping and medical care, and it is one of the lowest cost places in Belize. I would also suggest you look at the Punta Gorda area in Toledo District.

Q. We bought a piece of property a little north of the airstrip in Placencia. We have just been informed by the lawyer that handled it that the area has been declared a compulsory registration area under the Registered Land Act and that we must convert our deed to registered land and be issued a new title by the government. I've been searching different web sites including the government one and really can't find any information about this land act. Do you have any info on it or an idea about where I can find out more? Also, the lawyer says he can handle the matter for US$200 but as I'm going to be in Belize in September, do you know where I can go to take care of it?

A. Yes, Belize is gradually moving to a new (and better) system of title registration. Right now, there are at least three systems in effect in Belize: the conveyance system, which requires a new title search each time a property is sold, a version of what is called the Torrens system which provides for a property transfer certificate, and the Registered Land Act system, whereby the owner has a title certificate and the whole system is computerized. Which system you use depends on where the land is. Eventually the whole country will be on this system. Obviously your property is one that is coming under the new Registered Land Act system, which is a good thing. I recommend you check with the Lands office in Independence or Dangriga, but you could call the Department of Lands & Survey in Belmopan (501-822-2333) and find out.

Q. *Recently, I saw an advertisement in a magazine offering Belize passports. Is this real or a scam of some kind? I am a Canadian with a valid Canadian passport, presently living and working at Nigeria in the offshore exploration business.*

A. The Belize Economic Citizenship ("buy-a-passport") program was controversial and was discontinued as of January 2002. The ad you saw is a scam.

Q. *I have just finished reading your Living Abroad in Belize. My wife and I have made the decision to move to Corozal Town area. I do have a couple of questions that I am having a hard time getting a definitive answer to. The first question is how do my wife and I enter the country as tourists and bring in our personal belongings (we intend to apply for a self-employment work permit after we are in the country). The second question is how do we get government departments to return e-mails about these inquiries. Thanks for your help with our questions and congratulations on a job well done with your book.*

A. Thank you for buying my book. I appreciate it! As to your questions, the letter of the law is that you will not be able to bring in your household goods and such without paying import duties and taxes on them. Of course as a visitor you can bring in items for personal use and can bring in a vehicle for temporary use (it will be entered on your passport). As to government officials not answering your questions, welcome to Belize! You will find that as a non-voter, non-Belizean you will often run into this problem, especially if you are working via e-mail or even by phone. In person, things work a little more smoothly. One of the points I make in my books is that expats are not so much at the bottom of the social ladder as beside it — government officials (there are exceptions, of course) are much more responsive to their political constituencies. In Belize, I am afraid, you are a "nobody" at least until you become an official resident or a citizen. In the meantime, I'd suggest you telephone government offices, or better yet, visit in person. It's easier to ignore e-mail than a persistent, but polite, voice on the phone or in person. If you are investing in Belize, you may get a more attentive hearing, but that depends in part on how much you are investing and how you "work" with the government officials. Those who decide to enter Belize under the Qualified Retired Persons Program generally find that the Belize Tourism Board, which administers that program, is more responsive. Of course, retired persons under this program cannot work.

Q. *I have been researching Belize with the intent of relocating there. I have been interested by properties having some type of fruit or nut plantations. I would like to know if I owned one of these properties could I benefit from the sale of the fruit? Can one make enough money to live without having to get a job? What about raising geese or chickens? Could they be sold to a market? Is this line of thinking feasible or am I wasting my time?*

A. Of course there are many sides to the issue, but there's no reason why one couldn't make a living from small farming operations, truck gardening, fruit and such. Certainly there are Mennonites and others who do. You have to keep in mind that the Belize market is small and spread out, so export operations, for cacao, citrus or for high-value niche products such as herbs or organic produce, are often more feasible than selling to domestic markets. However, it may also be possible to generate good income from well-run truck farming, raising fowl or livestock, especially if you can serve a specialty market such as local tourist hotels and restaurants. I recommend that you spend as much time in Belize as possible, talking to other farm and ranch owners to see the special problems faced in Belize. Remember, Belize is a sub-tropical area with a lot of bugs that love to feast on tender plants and fruits. Farming in Belize is not easy!

Q. *Like probably everybody who contacts you, I am thinking about relocating to Belize. I am 53. I have built up a pretty decent nest egg. Not decent enough to retire yet in the USA, but possibly in Belize if what I am thinking about is realistic. Two questions:*

1) Why do you suggest keeping most of one's money out of Belize - is there really significant risk of one of the major banks defaulting, or somehow stealing depositor funds?

2) If I came to Belize, as a tourist, opened a bank account, purchased a CD at the same bank, would the interest on that CD be taxable?

The big picture is I am mulling the possibility of permanently relocating to Belize. I would purchase a very large CD, and live off of the interest. I would work towards becoming a permanent resident, not via the QRP be-

cause I have been self employed all my working life and have no pension and can't start collecting social security for another 12 years. So the CD interest would be my sole income. Would that income be taxable? Based on the general approach I have laid out, would I be able to attain the non-QRP permanent residency? I hope I have clearly described what I am thinking about.

A. On the safety of Belize banks, I think most people would say that the chance of a Belize-based bank going bankrupt, defaulting on payments to depositors or otherwise losing the money of its customers is quite low. Banks in Belize are small, typically with assets of less than a few hundred million U.S. dollars (about the size of a small hometown bank or savings bank in the U.S.), but they generally are conservative and well-capitalized. However, you should know that there is no deposit insurance in Belize, so all your money on deposit is 100% at risk, however slight the risk may be. In addition, there is also the risk of a devaluation of the Belize dollar -- that risk, again while slight is probably higher than the risk of bank default or bankruptcy. Belize has a high external debt relative to GDP, and government finances are not in good shape. If the Belize dollar were devalued, say by 25%, then the value of your nest egg would also be reduced by 25% when measured in a hard currency such as the U.S. dollar or euro.

I guess it comes down to what level of risk you are willing to accept on your life savings in return for what will probably be a significantly higher interest rate on savings and CDs in Belize as compared with the U.S. Personally, I would be reluctant to keep a large proportion of my nest egg in a local Belize bank, or a small bank in any country that does not offer some kind of deposit protection.

As to taxes on interest and dividends, this is a fairly complicated question and I do not have the expertise to provide tax or investment advice. You should consult a competent tax attorney, CPS or investment adviser. However, in general, there are several different situations that may apply:

One is if you are officially a resident of another country, not Belize. In that case, you can open an "offshore" account in Belize, whether through the establishment of an International Business Company or simply by opening a savings or time deposit account with the international division of a Belize bank. This account could be in U.S. dollars, euros or many other currencies. In this case, you would not pay Belize income tax on your savings. However, you may be and probably are subject to tax on the interest in the U.S. assuming you are a U.S. citizen.

The second situation is if you are depositing money in a "local" Belize bank in Belize dollars. In this case you would be subject to a Belize withholding tax of 15% of the interest paid. However, I believe that it is still the case that if your total interest is less than BZ$25,000 annually the withholding tax rate is 5%, but I have not checked that recently. You may also be subject to U.S. income taxes on the interest, as the U.S. taxes its citizens on their worldwide income. The U.S. foreign earned income tax exclusion for expatriates resident abroad does NOT apply to dividends and interest.

As a Belize permanent resident or Belize citizen, you are subject to Belize income taxes on all income derived in Belize, including interest income. However, there is an exclusion on the first BZ$20,000 in income -- that is not taxable. Income derived outside Belize is not taxable in Belize.

In general, without knowing anything about your personal situation, I would say you would have a good chance of getting permanent residency in Belize, assuming you pass the health exam, background check, etc. As you may know, this requires living in Belize for one year, at which time you can apply for residency. Approval can take up to a year, sometimes even longer. Among several other things, you have to demonstrate that you have adequate financial resources, and your savings in the U.S. or Belize would likely satisfy that requirement. Good luck.

Q. *I have a few questions about some "logistics" of living in Belize: What is veterinary availability like in Belize? (Based on government website, it appears it is possible to bring small domestic pets.) I gather there are not a lot of bookstores and/or newsstands in Belize. How's the library? I hesitate to ask this for fear of sounding snooty, but might as well: What does Belize offer in the way of the arts? How easy/difficult is it to get things to Belize.... like mail order items, etc. on an occasional basis (I'm not talking about huge stuff that requires a container.)*

A. There are vets in Belize City, Corozal Town, San Pedro, Cayo and elsewhere. Expats with dogs or cats don't seem to have trouble getting care for their animals. Some pets don't adapt well to the hot, humid Belize climate, however, and may suffer from diseases they pick up from stray animals. But it seems to me that most expats in Belize do have a dog and generally they report no big problems. Yes, it's simple to bring pets into Belize. *See detailed information on bringing in your pets in Chapter 21 of this book, Mechanics of Moving to Belize.* Right, there are not a lot of bookstores in Belize. There are small bookshops in Belize City, San Pedro and San Ignacio, but the inventory is limited at best. There are public libraries in all towns. Don't expect the New York Public Library but at least you can find some reading matter. If fine arts — opera, dance, symphony, theater, galleries — are a priority, Belize is not for you. There are only three movie theaters in the entire country, at Reef Village near San Pedro, at the Princess Hotel & Casino in Belize City, and a tiny one in downtown San Ignacio. There are some talented artists working and several galleries in Belize City and San Pedro have interesting work. There are a couple of dance troupes. Belize is a lot like a small town in the U.S. There aren't a lot of public venues for the arts, but artists, writers and musicians find each other and there are small groups that support the arts and hold meetings and such. As to ordering items from abroad, yes you can do that. Amazon.com gets a bit of business from Belize. You will have to pay import duty on a lot of items, which can be substantial, and shipping charges (especially for heavy items like books) are high.

Q. *We are moving to Belize and want to buy a car when we get there. I'm 55 yrs old and qualify as a retired person. Are there used cars for sale in Belize? What are the price ranges for say a ten-year-old car or truck? Could one buy a Volkswagen in Mexico, say in Chetumal or Cancun, and drive it into Belize? Or would it be better to buy it in Miami and ship it to Belize?*

A: Yes, there are used cars for sale in Belize, mostly at dealerships in Belmopan and Belize City, though some are by private owners. It's possible you could find a good deal, but in general the relatively small market for used cars and lack of competition mean that prices are usually higher, 10 to 20% higher, than in the highly competitive U.S. market, and the selection is much smaller. Also, many used cars in Belize have had a hard life, due to the bad roads. In some cases flooded or wrecked cars are brought into Belize and re-sold there without disclosure of their past history. If possible, get the Vehicle Identification Number (VIN) and check its history online. There are no laws to protect consumers if you get a lemon. Under the Qualified Retired Persons Incentive Act, any car you bring into Belize (including one you buy from Mexico) is supposed to be three years old or less. If it is older, in theory (and probably in practice) you will have to pay duty on it. Duty varies by number of cylinders, type of vehicle and the value of the car, but with duty and tax figure 65 to 75% of book value. Pick-up trucks (not SUVs) are taxed at a lower rate, around 20% including GST. Overall, if you are going to be in Belize long-term under the QRP I think you would be better off bringing in an almost new vehicle from the U.S., even with the cost of shipping from Miami or wherever, you'll likely come out ahead. There's a glut of quality used cars now in the U.S., prices are low and selection is huge. As a Qualified Retired Person, your vehicle would be entered duty-free.

Q. *I am a builder in Arizona with many years in commercial and residential development and interested in relocating to Belize. What is the demand for a person with my expertise in Belize?*

A. There is certainly demand for qualified builders in Belize. That said, whether you can successfully enter the market or not is another matter. As in many places, well-established local firms dominate the market. Mennonite builders in particular are well-established and in demand. Further, you face competition from many individual builders and contractors, most of whom work for rates that are much lower than you are probably accustomed. You also face a number of obstacles in terms of getting residency and work permits. Working, and specifically building, in Belize is quite different from the U.S. The materials are different, the way people do things are different, there are shortages of many materials and of skilled or semi-skilled workers in some cases. Theft and shrinkage is a problem, and many expat business people have problems dealing with local politicians and ways of doing things. Keep hammering away!

Q. *Are there ophthalmologists (medical eye doctors) or optometrists (nonmedical practitioners) in Belize? How many of each and where are they located? How many people are thought to be retired in Belize?*

A: There are ophthalmologists and optometrists in Belize, mostly located in Belize City but some have offices elsewhere including San Pedro. I do not know the exact number, but there are at least five ophthalmologists in practice in Belize City alone, and several opticians and optometrists. The ophthalmologists offer the usual range of services including cataract surgery, intraocular lens implant, radial keratomy, etc. There also are a number of eye surgeons and other eye specialists just across the border in Chetumal, Mexico. I am not sure if you are asking about how many expats are retired or otherwise living in Belize, but if so the answer is, no one knows for certain. My estimate is in the range of only around 3,000 to 4,000, but many Americans, Canadians and others have bought property in Belize but do not live there year-round. Keep your eyes open!

Q. *I have a few questions about living in Belize. I am coming to visit for 20 days to scout out property. My questions are: 1) What is the bank interest rate currently on CD's? 2) Do we need to bring our daily medications? 3) Do we need a prescription at the drug store to get medications such as blood pressure medication? 4) What can we expect to pay for rent on a two bedroom living quarters?*

A. CD and savings rates in Belize (Belize currency accounts) currently range from around 6% to 9% depending on the amount and term and the bank. Rates are higher than in the U.S. Keep in mind that most expats and retirees keep most of their funds in a U.S. or other hard-currency bank and only deposit in Belize what is necessary for routine transactions (or in the case of people in Belize under the Qualified Retired Persons Incentive Act the minimum US$2,000 required by that Act.) Belize banks do not have deposit insurance, so if a bank fails you could lose all your funds. The Belize dollar is not a currency that can be easily exchanged outside Belize. I would bring your regular medications. They probably are available in Belize, but they might not be, or not be in the same size or strength as what you are used to. Outside of Belize City, they might not be available at all. Many medications are available in Belize without a prescription (you may need to show an empty bottle). Doctors often own pharmacies in Belize. Costs for medications are generally less in Belize than in the U.S. You may be able to order your prescriptions from India or elsewhere at lower cost than you would pay in either the U.S. or Belize. As in the U.S. or anywhere rent varies tremendously based on location. In a less expensive area such as Corozal Town or in a remote village you might pay US$300 to $800. On Ambergris Caye or in Belize City you would pay US$700 to $1,500 a month, or more. The more time you spend in Belize, the less you will pay.

Q. *I saw an ad for a house in Corozal for $25K looks too good to be true. Just wondering if you knew of it or another cheap place. I have a limited trust fund income. Do you know of any communities that I could live at on say $1000/month? I would not want to buy at first. Have had some big* *personal problems here (like anybody cares about a divorced guy) and need someplace with a supportive environment.*

A. You can live in Corozal Town or Cayo or Toledo for US$1000 a month, or less, but that would be a basic kind of lifestyle. Rental houses start at under US$250 a month for something Belizean and basic but you'd probably pay more in the range of US$350 and can go up a long way from there. Belizeans are among the most friendly folks you'll ever meet.

Q. *I am a citizen of Houston, Texas, and I'm thinking of possibly moving to Belize in the future because I'm afraid that the laws on identification are going to start to chafe me pretty soon because of the so-called "war on terrorism" here. I'm as hurt by the attack on us as much as anybody but there's a limit to what I'm going to be able to take in the name of increased national security. My concerns about Belize may seem unreasonable, but I believe you'll see that they are also typically Texan. First on my mind are the regulations on firearms. Here in Texas we're free to own guns and we don't even have to put up with those stupid 3-day waiting periods for handguns as I hear they do in Florida. We're also allowed to carry concealed handguns provided we take tests and get a license from the state of Texas. Businesses can prohibit them on their premises by posting a sign. So I'm curious about whether it's legal to own a gun in Belize, whether they have registration or licenses or whether you can just own one. And if the situation is so bad that people aren't allowed to protect themselves, even in rural areas what the penalty might be for illegally possessing firearms. Contrariwise, what might be the easiest way to bring my gun or guns with me to Belize?*

A. Gun laws in Belize are much more restrictive than in Texas. Tourists and nonresidents may not import or possess guns at all. Citizens and official residents with a need for them – farmers in rural areas, for example — may own guns legally if they obtain a license from the government and pay a fee. However, gun permits are getting more difficult to obtain. Even the possession of a single 22 rifle or shotgun shell without a license can land you jail.

Q. *Are there any chiropractors in Belize? In your opinion is there a need for more?*

A. Yes, there are chiropractors in Belize City, San Pedro and Placencia and one or two elsewhere. Local bush doctors with chiropractic skills are called "bonesetters" in Belize. Belize is a country with just 330,000 people and with per-capita GDP only about one-tenth that of the U.S. Thus, total demand for chiropractic services in all of Belize is probably no more than in an American town of 40,000 people.

Q. *If I have $5,000 in my pocket, a college degree, scuba diving certification, how hard would it be for me to come to Belize and get a job?*

A. Fairly difficult. The unemployment rate in Belize is higher than that in the U.S. Pay scales vary, but in general are one-fourth that in the U.S.

To work in Belize you have to have a work permit, which is not easy to get and costs US$1,500 a year for most positions. Since 2002, it has been illegal for an employer to hire or employ a worker without a Belize Social Security card. It's not impossible to find work in Belize, and quite a number of expats have done it successfully, but it won't be easy, and you probably won't make much money.

Q. *I am writing to inquire about a business venture I am considering in San Pedro. I spent some time in San Pedro recently and saw an opportunity to start a business that would not compete with the locals, at least it appeared so to me, and would like to get your input. I will be taking a huge risk to leave my current job and start new at 41, but I feel it could be the opportunity of a lifetime, as well as assist some Belizeans in fulfilling their dreams as well. I am considering opening a tattoo shop in San Pedro and know that I could employ Belizeans to work there as well. What do you think of this idea? Am I way off track? I have investigated the business side and am aware of all the licensing, etc, that I will need. I don't want to overload you with information on my research. So, can you share your thoughts on this idea with me? I would really appreciate it.*

A: You would just as well ask the Man in the Moon his opinion on a tattoo parlor in San Pedro, as I know absolutely nothing about the tattoo business and in general don't understand the appeal of tattoos. I have no idea whether it would work in San Pedro. I would only be able to make two comments: One, over the years I have noticed that expats opening a business in Belize have a tougher time than they think they will. Almost everything takes longer and is more expensive and more difficult to execute than they had anticipated. My advice is always to take the revenue figures in your pro forma and cut them by half and then double your expense figures, and you may have a good idea of what your business in Belize will actually do. Two, if you are going to open a business in Belize, I think San Pedro is the place to do it, at least for the next five years or ten years. Tourism is fairly healthy in San Pedro, although it has been hit by the global recession and a few hotels have closed. it is more or less year-round rather than being highly seasonal as in some other areas, and there is enough money running through the economy that a well-run business can get a piece of it.

Q. *Does Belize use the metric system?*

A. As with the English language, refugees from the U.S. will not have to learn a new measurement system in Belize. No Krazy Kilometers here. The metric system, regardless of its merits, hasn't made much of an inroad in Belize. Distance is measured in miles, feet, yards and inches. Road signs say 55 mph. Liquids are measured in quarts and ounces, not liters. You buy gasoline by the U.S. gallon. And speaking of inroads, yes, you drive on the right in Belize, despite its British heritage. Electrical current and outlets in Belize are the same as in the U.S. and Canada.

Q. *What time is it in Belize?*

A. Belize Time. No, seriously, local time is the same as U.S. Central Standard Time. Belize does not observe Daylight Savings Time.

Q. *What job opportunities are there in Belize in the hospitality industry?*

A. Most hotels in Belize are small and owner-operated. The largest property in the country has only about 160 rooms, and most have fewer than 20, so opportunities for management level work are somewhat limited. In the restaurant and bar field, it is almost impossible for a non-Belizean to get a work permit, unless you are investing in business and operating it. Having said that, there are always opportunities for hardworking people who have a variety of skills and experience in operating in developing countries. If you are interested in working in Belize, I'd suggest you e-mail your resume to the larger properties and also come to Belize and try to meet as many resort and hotel owners as you can.

Q. *My wife and I are just over 50 years old, and we are looking to retire in Belize. We are wondering what kind of job opportunities there are in Belize. I am a pilot and my wife is in computer technology. Can Belize use our skills? Who would we contact?*

A. While your skills are in some demand in Belize, whether you can find work there or not depends on a variety of factors — your willingness to work for a fraction of U.S. salaries, whether you can get a work permit and whether you are willing to spend some time in the country to explore opportunities, among others. It is highly unlikely that you can find work without being in the country. There are two small airlines in Belize — Maya Island Air and Tropic Air, plus several charter operators. Computer work is limited, but a few larger companies such as Belize Telecommunications Ltd. do have a need for those with computer skills. Since you are over 45, you likely qualify for the incentives available under the Qualified Retired Persons Incentive Act. However, residents under that program cannot work for pay in Belize; you would need to get regular residency.

Q. *I was recently in Belize and looked at a piece of property for sale in a "development" about 8 miles east of San Ignacio. It was a absolutely beautiful lot of around 5 acres on top of a mountain with an incredible 200 degree view of the surrounding country side. The owner will provide electricity but there is no water. It's one of the most beautiful properties and view I have ever seen. There are 8 lots for sale, all between 3 and 5 acres, costing between US$40,000 to $70,000. The lot I'm considering is US$60,000. The owner will finance at 10% down for 10 years at 10%. My question is do you think that this price range is considered extravagant in Belize for this type of property? Or is that about right for this area?*

A. I'm not an expert on real estate. I would think, though, that the prices being asked for the property you are considering are more than the average in Cayo, even for prime property. US$2,000 to $3,000 an acre is considered fairly pricey for accessible land in small tracts in Cayo, and the tracts you are talking about are in the range of US$10,000 an acre. It is unlikely you could sell the land for anything like the price you are paying. Or you might sell it but it could take 30 years. It's one thing to buy land in Belize. It's another thing to sell it. However, all real estate is unique, and if you love the property and don't expect it to sell it at a profit anytime soon, then who is to tell you that you shouldn't buy it?

Q. *I have read much of your writings about Belize, over the years. My wife and I purchased property on Ambergris caye two years ago. Last year we paid our property taxes while we were in San Pedro for vacation. This year we will not be down in the country (we live in Florida). My question to you is can I send my tax payment to San Pedro (we got our bill last week) and pay with a personal check from my Bank of America account? Thank you for your help.*

A. Property taxes in Belize are normally due on April 1. If not paid by the end of April there is a 1% per month late charge. You can pay property taxes at one of about eight Department of Lands and Surveys offices. Most of the tax records in Belize are now on computer. You can pay by check or wire transfer. Your Bank of America check should be okay and should be sent to San Pedro Town Council, P.O. Box 54, Barrier Reef Drive, San Pedro Town, Ambergris Caye, Belize, Central America. If you decide to make a wire transfer you could check with the Town Council on details of how to do it. The number is 501-226-2198 and email sptb@btl.net.

Q. *While traveling around the country, should we rent a car, take a bus, fl, or hire a taxi?*

A. Each has advantages and disadvantages. With a rental car, you go when and where you want, including remote areas that don't have air or bus service or to sites that would otherwise require an expensive guided tour. However, auto rental costs are high, and gas is near US$5 a gallon. Buses provide a true local experience and fares are dirt cheap, but buses mainly run on the major roads and stop frequently to pick up and drop off passengers. Buses take up to twice as long as a private car. Flying is the fastest way to get around the country; service is frequent on most routes, and the views from low altitudes are often dramatic. The downside? Fares—especially if you're traveling with a family—can add up, and not all destinations have service. In some cases, transfers by taxi can be an option, although taxis generally are quite expensive. For most long-distance trips, there are no set fares, so the rate is a matter of negotiation and can vary considerably, depending on your bargaining skills. Drivers may also ask a little more if there are three or four going together, rather than just one or two. Expect to pay around US$1.50 a mile for longer trips in Belize.

Magnificant ruins of Tikal are only 1 ½ hours from Cayo

APPENDIX A:
RECOMMENDED READING ABOUT BELIZE

Many of these books are available from Amazon.com, either as new books or through their used-book sellers system. Also, try ABE (www.abebooks.com) for out-of-print books. In the case of books published by Cubola, a Belize publishing company, visit www.cubola.com.

Archaeology

Awe, Jaime. *Maya Cities, Sacred Caves,* Cubola Productions, 2005, 104 pp. A guide to 10 noted Maya sites in Belize, by the director of Belize's Institute of Archaeology.

Coe, Michael D. *The Maya,* Thames and Hudson, 7th ed., 2005, 224 pp. Originally published in 1993, this is the best general introduction to the subject.

Coe, William R. *Tikal, A Handbook of the Ancient Maya Ruins,* University Museum at the University of Pennsylvania, 1967. Useful when touring Tikal.

Ferguson, William M. and Adams, R.E.W. *Mesoamerica's Ancient Cities: Aerial Views of Precolumbian Ruins in Mexico, Guatemala, Belize and Honduras,* University Press of Colorado, rev. ed., 2000, 272 pp.

Foster, Byron, Ed. *Warlords and Maize Men, A Guide to the Maya Sites of Belize,* Cubola Productions, Belize, 1992, 82 pp. The first popular guide focused entirely on Maya sites in Belize, by the late Dr. Foster (he was murdered at his farm in western Belize.) Maps, color photos.

Garber, James F., ed. *The Ancient Maya of the Belize Valley: Half a Century of Archeological Research*, University of Florida Press, 2003, 448 pp.

Guderjan, Thomas H. *Ancient Maya Traders of Ambergris Caye*, Cubola Productions, 1993, 40 pp.

-- *The Nature of an Ancient Maya City: Resources, Interaction, and Power at Blue Creek, Belize*, University of Alabama Press, 2007, 244 pp.

Hammond, Norman, Ed. *Cuello: An Early Maya Community in Belize*, Cambridge University Press, 1991 (hardcover), 2009 (paper). 284 pp.

Harrison, Peter D. *Pulltrouser Swamp: Ancient Maya Habitat, Agriculture and Settlement*, University of Utah Press, 2000, 294 pp.

Henderson, John S. *The World of the Ancient Maya*, Cornell University Press, 1981, 271 pp.

Kelly, Joyce. *An Archaeological Guide to Northern Central America: Belize, Guatemala, Honduras, and El Salvador*, University of Oklahoma Press, rev. ed. 1996, 352 pp. Includes coverage of many smaller sites. Photographs by Jerry Kelly.

McMillon, Bill. *The Archeology Handbook: A Field Manual and Resource Guide*, Wiley, 1991, 259 pp. Not specific to Belize, but provides the amateur archeologist or volunteer with information on excavation techniques, tools, methods, etc.

Montgomery, John. *Tikal: An Illustrated History of the Ancient Maya Capital*, Hippocrene Books, 2001, 275 pp.

Sharer, Robert and Traxler, Loa. *The Ancient Maya*, Stanford University Press, 6th ed. 2005, 931 pp. A classic in the field, this is the most comprehensive work on the Maya.

Thompson, J. Eric S. *The Maya of Belize: Historical Chapters Since Columbus*, Cubola Productions.

Boating

Calder, Nigel. *The Cruising Guide to the Northwest Caribbean*, McGraw-Hill, 2nd ed., 1991, 272 pp. Navigational and anchorage information on the Caribbean Coast of Mexico, Belize, Guatemala and Honduras. Unfortunately this has not been recently updated.

Copeland, Liza. *Comfortable Cruising Around North and Central America*, Romany Enterprises, 2001, 312 pp. Several chapters on cruising the Caribbean Coast of Central America, including Belize.

Rauscher, Freya. *Cruising Guide to Belize and Mexico's Caribbean Coast*, Windmill Hill Books, 3rd ed., 2007, 312 pp. with 117 charts and 185 photos. Comprehensive cruising guide, the best available to this region, from Isla Mujeres in Mexico to the Rio Dulce in Guatemala. Includes large charts of Belize's coast and Mexico's Caribbean Coast.

NOAA-28004 *Nautical Chart of Caribbean Sea, Northwest Part*, 1:1300,000 scale, undated. Includes Belize.

Waterproof Chart # 4, *Caribbean and Gulf of Mexico*.

Cookbooks

Burns, E. L. *What's Cooking in the Belizean Kitchen,* Angelus Press, 74 pp.

De Langan, Tracey Brown. *Mmmm ... a Taste of Belizean Cooking,* Cubola Productions, 2003, 142 pp. Chefs from leading Belizean restaurants contributed to this cookbook.

Nord, Alice, Martinez, Myrna and Shrine, Kaaren. *Cooking Belize,* self-published, c. 1995, 126 pp.

A Guide to Belizean Cooking, by Belize Cookbook Committee, *self-published*

Belize Hospital Auxiliary Cookbook, Angelus Press, 126 pp.

Belizeous Cuisine, Delicious Belizean Recipes, by Los Angeles Belizean Educational Network (LABEN), 1997, 102 pp.

To Catch a Cook, by South Ambergris Caye Neighborhood Watch, self published, 2009

Silly Bug & Bittle Recipes, Crooked Tree Village Creative Women's Group, self-published, 100 pp.

U Toucan Cook Belize Cookbook, self-published, 126 pp.

Fiction, Drama and Poetry

Auxillou, Ray. *Blue Hole,* self-published, date unknown, 479 pp. A collection of tales about mercenaries, drug runners and adventure. Other books in the same vein by Auxillou include *Belize Secret Service, Belize Connection* and *The Belize Vortex.*

Crone, Andrew. *Chameleon War,* Booksurge Publishing, 2008, 244 pp. You'll want to wash your hands after you read this garbage.

Coxe, George Harmon. *With Intent to Kill,* Knopf, 1964, 180 pp. Action/adventure.

Edgell, Zee. *Beka Lamb,* Heinemann, 1982, 192 pp. Classic novel about ordinary life in British Honduras.

— *In Times Like These,* Heinemann, 320 pp. English-educated Belizean returns home.

— *The Festival of San Joaquin,* Heinemann, 1997, 155 pp. Explores domestic violence in Belize.

Ellis, Zoila. *On Heroes, Lizards and Passion, Seven Belizean Short Stories,* Cubola Productions, 1994, 130 pp. "White Christmas an' Pink Jungle" is one of seven deliciously Belizean stories, from a distinguished Belizean/Garifuna writer.

Esquivel, Cathy. *Under the Shade,* Angelus Press, 192 pp. Tales of the drug trade.

Godfrey, Glenn D. *The Sinners' Bossanova,* Cubola Books, 1987, 269 pp. Action/adventure.

Hagerthy, Tim, and Parham, Mary Gomoz, Eds. *If Di Pin Neva Bin, Folktales and Legends of Belize,* Cubola Productions, 128 pp.

Hernandez, Felicia. *Those Ridiculous Years,* 64 pp. Short stories about Garifuna life.

Heusner, Karla. *Food for Thought, Chronicles of Belize,* Cubola Productions, 2004, 207 pp. Collection of weekly newspaper columns by a Belizean journalist who now lives in the U.S.

Koerner, Nancy R. *Belize Survivor: Darker Side of Paradise,* NK Marketing, 2007, 300 pp. A novel, based on a true story, of a young woman who comes to Belize, lives in the bush and gets more than she bargained for.

Lindo, Louis. *Tales of the Belizean Woods,* Cubola Productions, 82 pp. Short stories set in backabush Belize.

McKay, Claudia. *Twist of Lime, A Lynn Evans Mystery,* New Victoria Publishers, 1997, 188 pp. Mystery featuring lesbian newspaper reporter on Maya dig in Belize.

Miller, Carlos Ledson. *Belize, A Novel,* Xlibris Corp., 1999, 402 pp. Fast-paced saga of father and sons over four decades, beginning with Hurricane Hattie in 1961.

Miller, Harold R. *The Belize File,* Taylor-Dth Publishing, 2008, 372 pp. An ex-DEA agent turned private eye is hired to find a friend's daughter, missing on her honeymoon in Belize.

Mueller, William Behr. *Operation Belize,* CreateSpace, 2008, 358 pp. The U.S. Secretary of State is kidnapped in Belize, and American Special Forces attempt a rescue.

Patrick, William. *The Five Lost Days,* Pearhouse Press, 2008, 336 pp. A documentary film maker travels to the Maya Mountains of Belize to get footage of a Maya healer.

Phillips, Michael, Ed. *Of Words, an Anthology of Belizean Poetry,* Cubola Productions, 1997, 104 pp. A collection of poems by more than three dozen Belizean poets.

-- *Ping Wing Juk Me, Six Belizean Plays,* Cubola Productions, 2004, 120 pp. A collection of plays by George Gabb, Carol Fonseca Galvez, Evan X. Hyde, Glady Stuart, Shirley Warde and Colville Young.

-- *Snapshots of Belize, an Anthology of Belizean Short Fiction,* Cubola Productions, 2004, 122 pp. A collection of short stories by seven Belizean writers.

Rimmer, Stephen. *The Way to Go: Four Men & Three Women Sailing from Florida to Cozumel & Belize – A Story of Sex, Lust & Drug Trafficking, with a New Kind of Morality about Sinning of All Kinds!,* IUniverse, 2000, 428 pp. This novel is an example of the downside of the new print-on-demand technology.

Ruiz Puga, David Nicolas. *Old Benque,* Cubola Productions, 160 pp. Short stories in Spanish.

Stray, P.J. *The Danger on Lighthouse Reef,* Silver Burdett Press, 1997, 144 pp. Children's mystery story.

Theroux, Paul. *The Mosquito Coast,* Houghton-Mifflin, 1982. Obsessed American drags his family to Central America. Actually set in Honduras, not Belize, but the movie of the same name was filmed in Belize.

Vasquez, Ian. *In the Heat,* St. Martin's Minotaur, 2008, 245 pp. Caribbean Noir mystery set in Belize City and Cayo, by a talented new Belizean writer who now lives in Florida. *In the Heat* in 2009 won the Shamus Award for best first novel from the Private Eye Writers of America.

-- *Lonesome Point,* Minotaur Books, St. Martin's Press, 2009, 263 pp. Vasquez's second novel is set in Florida, with flashbacks to Belize.

Westlake, Donald. *High Adventure,* Mysterious Press, 1985. Dope, dummies and deliverance in Belize, by popular adventure writer.

Wilentz, Gay. *Memories, Dreams and Nightmares, Vol. 1, a Short Story Anthology by Belizean Women Writers,* Cubola Productions, 2004, 164 pp. Collection of stories by 13 Belizean female writers.

-- *Memories, Dreams and Nightmares, Vol. 2, a Short Story Anthology by Belizean Women Writers,* Cubola Productions, 2005, 124 pp. The second volume.

Young, Colville. *Pataki Full,* Cubola Productions, 120 pp. Collection of short stories by noted Belizean writer and scholar.

ZooDoc. *War Star Rising: Legend of Toucan Moon,* Star Publish, 2008, 216 pp. Young adult novel about a Maya princess at Xunantunich who speaks out against human sacrifice.

Guidebooks/Travel Guides

Berman, Joshua. *Moon Belize,* Moon Handbooks, Avalon Traveling Publishing, 2009, 347 pp. Excellent, up-to-date guide.

-- *Moon Spotlight: Belize Cayes Including Belize City,* Avalon Travel Publishing, 2009, 80 pp. Pullout of cayes and Belize City material from the *Moon Belize* guide.

Eltringham, Peter. *Belize, The Rough Guide,* 3rd. edition, Rough Guides, 2007, 400 pp. Thoroughly researched guide by knowledgeable writer who spent many years in Belize and Guatemala. Peter Eltringham passed away in 2008.

Glassman, Paul. *Belize Guide,* Open Road Publishing, 12th ed. 2006, 295 pp. Glassman was a pioneering guidebook author to destinations in Central America, including Costa Rica, Nicaragua and Belize.

Greenspan, Eliot. *Frommer's Belize,* 3rd edition, Wiley Publishing, 2008, 352 pp. Excellent and generally up-to-date guide.

Harvard Student Agencies, *Let's Go Guatemala & Belize: The Student Travel Guide,* Let's Go, 2009, 304 pp. Budget-oriented guide researched by intrepid Harvard students.

Hennessy, Huw, and Bell, Brian, Eds. *Insight Guides Belize,* Insight Guides, 2nd. ed., 2008, 341 pp. Unmatched photos and good general background on the country; weak on hotels and restaurants.

King, Emory. *Driver's Guide to Beautiful Belize,* Tropical Books, 2007, 40 pp. Mile-by-mile guide to most roads in Belize. Not updated since Emory King's death.

Lougheed, Vivien. *Adventure Guide to Belize,* Hunter Publishing, 6th edition, 2006, 555 pp. Tons of good information by the author of *Central America by Chickenbus.*

Middleton, Ned. *Diving Belize,* Aqua Quest Diving, 1998, 128 pp. Better than Lonely Planet's dive guide though an update is needed.

Morris, Charlie. *Open Road's the Best of Belize,* Open Road, 2nd. ed. 2009, 256 pp. New guidebook series claims to cut to the chase and give only what's best at the destinations.

Rock, Tim. *Lonely Planet Diving & Snorkeling Belize,* 4th. edition, Lonely Planet, 2007, 144 pp. Improved from earlier editions, but overlooks some dive and snorkel sites.

Sluder, Lan. *Fodor's Belize,* Fodor's/Random House, 2010, 352 pp. Up-to-date guide to Belize.

— *Belize Islands Guide,* Equator, 2010, also available as an eBook and on Kindle, 204 pp. Guide to Ambergris Caye, Caye Caulker and all the islands of Belize.

— *San Pedro Cool, Guide to Ambergris Caye, Belize,* Equator, 2002, updated as an eBook in 2009, 201 pp. Comprehensive guide to Ambergris Caye, with short section on Caye Caulker and other islands.

— *Belize Book of Lists 2000,* Equator, 1999, 112 pp. Lists the 5 to 10 best in each category — jungle lodges, seaside resort hotels, beaches, etc.

— *Belize First Guide to Mainland Belize,* Equator, 2000, 288 pp. Focuses on the mainland of Belize.

— *Best Belize Hotels and Restaurants,* Equator, 2008, 156 pp. This eBook reviews and rates the best hotels and restaurants in Belize.

Stratman, Steve. *Belize to Guatemala: a nine-day adventure guide,* The Artful Nomad Company, 2006, 60 pp. The author narrates a short trip from Caye Caulker via San Ignacio to Flores and Tikal, Guatemala.

Vorhees, Mara and Brown, Joshua Samuel. *Lonely Planet Belize,* Lonely Planet, 3rd. ed. 2008, 336 pp. A significant improvement over previous LP Belize editions.

History and Culture

Balboni, Barbara. *Taking Stock: Belize at 25 Years of Independence,* Cubola Productions, 2007, 343 pp. Noted Belizeans take a look at what Belize has achieved in its first 25 years of independence.

Barry, Tom with Vernon, Dylan. *Inside Belize,* Resource Center Press, 2nd. ed., 1995, 181 pp. Useful but now somewhat dated overview of history, politics, media, education, economy and the environment.

Burdon, Sir John Alder (ed.). *Archives of British Honduras* (3 vols.), Sifton Praed, 1931-35. This controversial history of British Honduras by Sir John Burdon, a governor of the colony, helped create and perpetuate myths about British colonialism and "benign" slavery in Belize that continued to influence historians for decades.

Burnworth, Joe. *No Safe Harbor: The Tragedy of the Dive Ship Wave Dancer,* Emmis Books, 2005, 256 pp. The story of the 21 people who died on the Wave Dancer live-aboard in Hurricane Iris in October 2001.

Cayetano, E. Roy. *The People's Garifuna Dictionary,* Angelus Press, 82 pp. Work in progress —a dictionary of the Garifuna language.

Cayetano, Sebastian. *Garifuna History, Language & Culture of Belize, Central America & the Caribbean,* Angelus Press, 170 pp.

Crosbie, Paul, editor-in-chief; Herrera, Yvette; Manzanares, Myrna; Woods, Silvana; Crosbie, Cynthia; and Decker, Ken, eds. *Kriol-Inglish Dikshineri English-Kriol Dictionary,* Belize Kriol Project, 2007, 465 pp. First comprehensive dictionary to the Belize Kriol language.

Dobson, Narda. *A History of Belize,* Longman Caribbean, 1973, 362 pp. History from Early Maya period to 1970.

Foster, Byron. *The Baymen's Legacy,* Cubola Productions, 2nd. ed., 1992, 83 pp. A history of Belize City.

— *Heart Drum,* Cubola Productions, 60 pp. A look at dagu and other aspects of Garifuna life.

Henderson, Peta. *Rising Up: Life Stories of Belizean Women,* Sister Vision Press, 1998, 302 pp.

Kane, William and Stanton, John. *A Jesuit in Belize: The Life and Adventures of Father Buck Stanton in Nineteenth Century Central America,* CreateSpace, 2008, 422 pp.

King, Emory. *Diary of St. George's Caye,* Tropical Books, 32 pp.

— *The Great Story of Belize,* Volume 1, Tropical Books, 1999, 53 pp. The first in what was to be a four-volume set, this volume covers the history of Belize from 1511 when the first Europeans arrive until 1798, when the Baymen won the battle of St. George's Caye.

— *The Great Story of Belize,* Volume 2, Tropical Books, 1999, 87 pp. Volume 2 tells the history of Belize from 1800 to 1850, the period which shaped Belize's history for generations to come.

— 1798 *The Road to Glory,* Tropical Books, 1991, 348 pp. Fictionalized and somewhat glorified account of the Battle of St. George Caye's.

Koop, Gerhard S. *Pioneer Years In Belize,* Angelus Press, 144 pp. History of the Mennonites in Mexico and Belize.

Leslie, Robert, Ed. *A History of Belize: Nation in the Making,* Cubola Productions, rev. ed., 1995, 125 pp. First published in 1983, this history of Belize is written for Belize schoolchildren.

McClaurin, Irma. *Women of Belize: Gender and Change in Central America,* Rutgers University Press, 1996, 232 pp. Three women describe their experiences in Belize.

Merrill, Tim. *Guyana and Belize Country Studies,* Federal Research Division, Library of Congress, 2nd. ed.,1993, 408 pp. One in the Area Handbook series sponsored by the U.S. Army; nevertheless, the historical, cultural and economic information is first rate.

Peedle, Ian. *Belize, A Guide to the People, Politics and Culture,* Interlink Books, 1999, 100 pp. Tries to cover everything in a small volume, and fails.

Setzekorn, William David. *Belize, Formerly British Honduras,* Ohio University Press, 1981, 300 pp. A profile of Belize's folklore, history, culture, economics and geography.

Shoman, Assad. *Thirteen Chapters of a History of Belize,* Angelus

Press, 1994, 4th. printing 2000, 297 pp. Somewhat left-wing interpretation of Belize history, by a prominent Belizean intellectual and politician.

Simmons, Donald C. Jr. *Confederate Settlements in British Honduras,* McFarland & Co., 2001, 176 pp. Discusses ex-Confederates who settled in Belize after the U.S. Civil War.

Sutherland, Anne. *The Making of Belize, Globalization in the Margins,* Bergin & Garvey, 1998, 202 pp. An American university professor with long family ties to Belize looks at "postmodern" Belize.

Thomson, P. A. B. *Belize, A Concise History,* MacMillan Caribbean, 2005, 192 pp.

Twigg, Arthur. *Understanding Belize: A Historical Guide,* Harbour, 2006, 240 pp. Arthur Twigg is the editor of a Canadian book magazine.

Waddell, D.A.G. *British Honduras, A Historical and Contemporary Survey,* Greenwood Press, 1961, reprinted 1981, 151 pp. An academic history.

Wilk, Richard R. *Household Ecology: Economic Change and Domestic Life Among the Kekchi Maya in Belize,* Northern Illinois University Press, 1997, 280 pp.

Young, Colville. *Creole Proverbs of Belize,* Cubola Productions, 44 pp.

Maya Atlas: The Struggle to Preserve Maya Land in Southern Belize, compiled by the Maya People of Southern Belize, Toledo Maya Cultural Council, 1997.

Living in Belize

Gallo, Roger. *Escape from America,* Manhattan Loft Publishing, 1997, 352 pp. Devoted to living/retiring abroad. Includes chapters on Belize. Roger Gallo later established the EscapeArtist.com website.

Golson, Barry and Golson, Thia. *Retirement Without Borders,* Scribner's, 2008, 432 pp. Looks at retirement options in a number of countries around the world. Lan Sluder contributed the chapter on Belize.

Gray, Bill and Gray, Claire (pseudonyms). *Belize Retirement Guide,* Preview Publishing, 4th ed., 1999, 140 pp. Guide to "living in a tropical paradise for $450 a month." Somehow, we kinda doubt it.

King, Emory. *"Hey, Dad, This Is Belize,"* Tropical Books, Belize, 4th printing, 114 pp. Collection of vignettes about Belize and Belizeans. Originally appeared in the Belize Times and other publications.

— *How to Visit, Invest or Retire in Belize,* Tropical Books, 1989, 32 pp. Early booklet on the subject, still being sold at about US$1 a page.

— *"I Spent It All In Belize,"* Tropical Books, 194 pp. More sketches of Belizean life. Emory King was a genius at picking book titles.

Peham, Helga. *Escaping the Rat Race – Freedom in Paradise,* World Audience, 2007, 344 pp. A series of interviews with expats and others in Belize, by a woman who lived in Corozal. Also available in a Kindle edition.

Sluder, Lan. *Living Abroad in Belize,* Avalon, 2005, 367 pp. Comprehensive guide to living, retiring, working, and investing in Belize.

— *Adapter Kit: Belize,* Avalon, 2001, 261 pp. The predecessor edition of *Living Abroad in Belize.*

-- *Easy Belize: How to Live, Retire, Work and Invest in Belize, the English-Speaking, Frost-Free Paradise on the Caribbean Coast,* Equator, 2010, 252 pp. This is the revised edition of the best-selling eBook on living or retiring in Belize. Also available as a paperback and in a Kindle edition.

-- *Island Living in Belize,* Equator, 2010, 201 pp. This revised edition of the eBook focuses on retiring, living and investing on Ambergris Caye, Caye Caulker and other islands in Belize. Also available as a paperback and in a Kindle edition.

Memoirs

Conroy, Richard Timothy. *Our Man in Belize,* St. Martin's, 1997, 324 pp. Fascinating, highly readable memoir of life in former British Honduras in the late 1950s and early 60s.

DeMarks, Dean Fortune. *The Tourist: Who's Too Dangerous for Belize,* BookSurge Publishing, 2009, 354 pp. Semi-literate account of why Belize is such a terrible place, by a would-be Placencia real estate developer who was deported from the country.

Fry, Joan. *How to Cook a Tapir: A Memoir of Belize,* University of Nebraska Press, 2009, 294 pp. Fascinating recollections of a young American woman's experiences in Toledo in the early 1960s.

King, Emory. *The Little World of Danny Vasquez,* Tropical Books, 1989, 134 pp. Emory King's presentation of his father-in-law's memoirs.

Salisbury, Christina and Salisbury, Kirby. *Treehouse Perspectives: Living High on Little,* Mill City Press, 2009, 324 pp. Memoir of a couple's 36 years living in a treehouse in Toledo.

Natural History

Ames, Oakes and Correll, Donovan Stewart. *Orchids of Guatemala and Belize,* Dover Publications, 1985, 779 pp. with 204 black-and-white illustrations. Republication of Chicago Natural History Museum 1953 field guide and 1965 supplement. Exhaustive, covering 527 species.

Arvigo, Rosita and Balick, Michael. *Rainforest Remedies, One Hundred Healing Herbs of Belize,* Lotus Press, 1993, 221 pp. Guide to traditional Mayan/Belizean herbal remedies.

Arvigo, Rosita with Epstein, Nadine and Yaquinto, Marilyn. *Sastun, My Apprenticeship with a Maya Healer,* HarperSanFrancisco, 1994,190 pp. Story of Arvigo's time with Don Elijio Panti.

Arvigo, Rosita with Epstein, Nadine. *Rainforest Home Remedies: The Maya Way to Heal Your Body and Replenish Your Soul,* HarperOne, 2001, 240 pp.

Barcott, Bruce. *The Last Flight of the Scarlet Macaw: One Woman's Fight to Save the World's Most Beautiful Bird,* Random House, 2008 hard cover, 2009 paper, 336 pp. Remarkable, gripping story of Sharon Matola's fight against the Chalillo dam.

Beletsky, Les. *The Ecotravellers' Wildlife Guide, Belize and Northern Guatemala,* Academic Press, 1999 hardcover, 2004 paper, 487 pp. Lavishly color-illustrated guide, oriented to the amateur, to the most commonly spotted mammals, birds, amphibians, reptiles, fish and corals.

Campbell, Jonathan A. *Amphibians and Reptiles of Northern Guatemala, the Yucatán, and Belize,* University of Oklahoma Press, 1998, 380 pp., with 176 color photographs. The best guide to herpetofauna of the region.

Emmons, Katherine. *Cockscomb Basin Wildlife Sanctuary: Its History, Flora and Fauna for Visitors, Teachers and Scientists,* Community Conservation Consultants, 1996. Definitive on the subject.

Greenfield, David W. and Thomerson, Jamie E. *Fishes of the Continental Waters of Belize,* University Press of Florida, 1997, 311 pp. Comprehensive guide, with black-and-white illustrations.

Edwards, Ernest Preston, illustrated by Butler, E.M. *A Field Guide to the Birds of Mexico and Adjacent Areas: Belize, Guatemala, and El Salvador,* University of Texas Press, 1998, 288 pp. This is used by many local guides in Belize.

Harris, Kate. *Trees of Belize,* self-published, 2009, 120 pp. Handy guide to common and notable trees of Belize, with color photos of most of them.

Horwich, Robert H. *A Belizean Rain Forest,* Orang-utan Press, 1990, 420 pp. A look at the Community Baboon Sanctuary and the northern forests of Belize.

Jones, H. Lee and Gardner, Dana. *Birds of Belize,* University of Texas Press, 2004, 445 pp. The new gold standard of Belize bird books.

LaBastille, A. *Birds of the Mayas,* West of the Winds Publications, 1993.

Lee, Julian. *A Field Guide to the Amphibians and Reptiles of the Maya World: The Lowlands of Mexico, Northern Guatemala and Belize,* Cornell University Press, 2000, 488 pp.

Mahler, Richard. *Adventures in Nature Belize,* Avalon, 1999, 362 pp. A guidebook that focuses on nature travel in Belize. This was a good idea that was canned by Avalon. Someone should do the concept again, as this guide is now badly out-of-date.

Matola, Sharon. *Birds of Belize, A Field Handbook,* Belize Zoo, 28 pp.

Meyer, John R. and Foster, Carol Farneti. *A Guide to the Frogs and Toads of Belize,* Krieger Publishing, 1996.

Miller, Carolyn M. and Miller, Bruce W. *Exploring the Tropical Forest at Chan Chich Lodge Belize,* Wildlife Conservation Society, 2nd. ed., 1994, 51 pp.

Peterson, Roger Tory and Chalif, Edward L. *A Field Guide to Mexican Birds: Mexico, Guatemala, Belize, El Salvador,* Peterson Field Guides/Houghton-Mifflin, 1999. The birder's pal, though it lacks Spanish names of birds.

Rabinowitz, Alan. *Jaguar,* Arbor House, 1986, 368 pp. Fascinating story of effort to establish the Cockscomb Preserve.

Reichling, Steven B. *Tarantulas of Belize,* Krieger Publishing Co., 2003, 148 pp. Everything you ever wanted to know about tarantulas in Belize.

Stafford, Peter J. and Meyer, John R. *A Guide to the Reptiles of Belize,* Academic Press, 1999, 356 pp.

Stevens, Kate. *Jungle Walk.* Birds and animals of Belize, with many illustrations

Woods, R.L., Reid, S.T. and Reid, A.M. *The Field Guide to Ambergris Caye.* Near exhaustive study of the island and surrounding sea.

Wright, Charles. *Land in British Honduras: A Report of the British Honduras Land Use Survey Team,* Her Majesty's Stationery Office, 1959, 327 pp. What began as a soils survey by Toledo resident Charles Wright became a detailed analysis of farming practices and land use in mid-twentieth century British Honduras.

Snakes of Belize, Belize Audubon Society, 55 pp.

Travel

Canby, Peter. *Heart of the Sky, Travels Among the Maya,* Harper-Collins, 1992, 368 pp. Modern classic on the modern Maya.

Chaplin, Gordon. *The Fever Coast Log,* Simon & Schuster, 1992, 229 pp. Couple sets sail aboard the Lord Jim to sail the Caribbean Coast. You know it's all going to end badly.

Faber, Carol and Perlow, Paula. *2 Jamericans Travel to San Pedro, Belize,* Trafford Publishing, 2006, 136 pp. Little book on the experiences of two women vacationing in San Pedro.

Davis, Richard Harding. *Three Gringos in Venezuela and Central America,* Harper & Brothers, 1896. Early travelogue begins in British Honduras.

Heistand, Emily. *The Very Rich Hours: Travel in Orkney, Belize, the Everglades and Greece,* Beacon Press, 1992, 236 pp.

Janson, Thor. Belize, *Land of the Free by the Carib Sea,* Bowen & Bowen, 2000, 96 pp. Published in Belize, this book has wonderful photos of the country and the people.

Huxley, Aldous. *Beyond the Mexique Bay,* Greenwood, 1975. First published in 1934, this book by the author of Brave New World holds the record for the most-quoted comment on British Honduras: "... if the world had any ends, British Honduras would surely be one of them."

Pride, Nigel. *A Butterfly Sings to Pacaya,* Constable. A 1970s trip through Mexico, Belize and Guatemala.

Roberts, Orlando W. *Voyages and Excursions on the East Coast and in the Interior of Central America,* University of Florida Press, reprint 1965 (originally published in 1827).

Straughan, Robert P. *Adventure in Belize,* A.S. Barnes & Co., 1975, 215 pp. Explorations in Belize, by a pet store and tropical fish store owner.

Stephens, John L. *Incidents of Travel in Central America, Chiapas and Yucatan,* Harper and Brothers, 1841. The great classic of early Central American travel books.

Sluder, Lan. *Rambles Around Belize,* 2005-2009.

Wright, Ronald. *Time Among the Maya: Travels in Belize, Guatemala and Mexico,* Grove Press, 2000, 464 pages. Travel diary in impressionistic style.

Maps and Atlases

Atlas of Belize, Cubola Productions, 20th ed., 1995, 32 pp. with 11 maps and 80 photographs. Prepared for use in schools.

Belize Traveller's Map, ITMB, 2005. The best general map of Belize. Scale 1:250,000.

British Ordnance Survey, Topographical Map of Belize, 1991. Two sheets, with maps of Belize City and towns on reverse. 1:250,000-scale.

British Ordnance Survey, Area Topographical Maps, various dates, 1970s-1990s. Country is divided into 44 sections, each 1:50,000-scale.

Insight Fleximap Belize, American Map, 2003. Sturdy and water-resistant but not fully up-to-date.

Laminated Belize Map, Borsch, 2008. German cartography company produced this handy, durable map. Scale 1:500,000. Would have been nice if the scale were a little larger.

APPENDIX B:
ATTORNEYS IN BELIZE

The following list of attorneys practicing in Belize was provided by the United States Embassy in Belize. Neither the Embassy nor the author assumes any responsibility for the professional ability of the individuals or firms listed here. Names are listed alphabetically, and the order in which they appear has no other significance. The information in the list on professional credentials, areas of expertise and language ability are provided directly by the lawyers. You may receive additional information about the individuals by contacting the Belize Bar Association at 501-227-2785.

ARGUELLES, EMIL of ARGUELLES & COMPANY LLC, 35 New Road, Belize. Born July 4, 1972, Belize. Graduated from Marquette University, B.A.; U.W.I., LL.B.; Norman Manley Law School, C.L.E. Trust & Estate Practitioner (TEP). Admitted to Belize Bar in 1998. Appointed Speaker of House of Representatives in 2008. Corresponds in English. Corporate, Tax, Intellectual Property, Real Estate and General Practice. Can provide translator/reporter/ stenographer/notary. Will take cases outside Belize City. Office Phone: 501-223-0088, 223-0858. Fax: 223-6403. Cell Phone: 610-2961. Email: info@belizelawyer.com Website: www.belizelawyer.com Personal Email: belizelawyer@hotmail.com

ARNOLD, ELLIS R. LL.B. (Hons) CLE 52 Albert Street, Belize City, Belize. Graduated from the Norman Manley Law School, C.L.E.; University of the West Indies LL.B. in 1977. Admitted to Belize Bar in 1983. Corresponds in English. General Practice and criminal matters. Notary Public. Will take cases outside of Belize City. Office phone 501-227-0810; 227-1106; Fax: 227-1119; Cell: 610-1276 E-mail: ellisarnold@hotmail.com

BARROW, DYLAN, of the LAW OFFICES OF RAYMOND H. BARROW, 121 Albert Street, Belize City, Belize. Born January 24, 1950, Belize. Graduated from U.W.I. C.L.E. Admitted to Belize Bar in 1985. Corresponds in English. General Practice and Criminal Matters. Can provide translator / reporter / stenographer / notary. Office Phone: 501-227-2912. Fax: 227-1270.

BRADLEY, JR., LEO, 90A New Road, Belize City, Belize. Born December 31, 1967, Belize. Graduated from St. Thomas University, B.A. U.W.I., LLB. Norman Manley Law School, C.L.E. Admitted to Belize Bar in 1998. Corresponds in English and Spanish. General Practice and Criminal Matters. Can provide translator / reporter / stenographer / notary. Office Phone: 501-223-3014

CHEBAT, MICHELLE of SHOMAN, CHEBAT, & ASSOC., 53 Barrack Road, Belize City, Belize. Born January 27, 1964, Belize City, Belize. Graduated from U.W.I., C.L.E. Admitted to Belize Bar in 1988. Corresponds in English and Spanish. General Practice with specialty in commercial / corporate / offshore. Can provide translator / reporter / stenographer / notary. Will take cases outside Belize City. Office Phone: 223-4160 / 223-4161 Fax: 223-4222. Email: attorney@btl.net www.shomanchebat.com

COURTENAY, S.C., DEREK of W. H. COURTENAY & CO., 1876 Hutson Street, Belize City, Belize. Corresponds in English and Spanish. Commercial and General Practice. Can provide notary. Office Phone: 501-223-5701; 224-4248. Fax: 223-9962. Email: derek@courtenaylaw.com

COURTENAY, S.C., DENISE of W. H. COURTENAY & CO., 1876 Hutson Street, Belize City, Belize. Corresponds in English and Spanish. Commercial and General Practice. Can provide notary. Office Phone: 501-223-5701; 224-4248. Fax: 223-9962. Email: denise@courtenaylaw.com

COURTENAY, JEREMY of W. H. COURTENAY & CO., 1876 Hutson Street, Belize City, Belize. Corresponds in English. Commercial and General Practice. Office Phone: 501-223-5701; 224-4248. Fax: 223-9962. Email: jeremy@courtenaylaw.com

RETREAGE, VANESSA of W. H. COURTENAY & CO., 1876 Hutson Street, Belize City, Belize. Corresponds in English. Commercial and General Practice. Office Phone: 223-5701; 224-4248. Fax: 223-9962. Email: vanessa@courtenaylaw.com

LINDO, DEAN R. of LINDO'S LAW FIRM, 7 Church Street, (P.O. Box 558, Belize City, Belize. Born September 4, 1932, Belize. Graduated from Wesley College. NYU, BSc and LL.M. University of Durham, England, LL.B. (Hons.). Gray's Inn. Admitted to the Belize Bar in 1964. Corresponds in English and Spanish. General Practice. Can Provide translator / reporter / stenographer / notary. Will take cases outside Belize City. Office Phone: (501) 227-7388 Fax: (501) 2275168 Home Phone: 224-4217 Email: linlaw@btl.net

LUMOR, FRED of MUSA & BALDERAMOS, 3750 University Blvd Edem Place, P.O. Box 2577, Belize City, Belize. Born November 17, 1952, Ghana. Graduated from Rivers State in Nigeria, LL.B. (Hons.) Ministry of Justice 4.5 years. Corresponds in English. General Practice. Can provide translator / reporter / stenographer / notary. Will take cases outside Belize City. Office Phone: 501-223-6024 Fax: 501-223-6001. Email: flumor_co@yahoo.com

MARIN, MAGALI G. , 99 Albert Street, P.O. Box 617, Belize City, Belize. Born November 18, 1971, Belize City. Graduated from University of Oklahoma, B.A. U.W.I., LL.B. Norman Manley Law School, C.L.E. Admitted to the Belize Bar in 1997. Corresponds in English and Spanish. General Practice. Can provide translator / reporter / stenographer / notary. Will take cases outside Belize City. Office Phone: 501-227-5280 Fax: 501-227-5278. Email: attorneys@barrowandwilliams.com Website: www.barrowandwilliams.com

MARSHALLECK, E. ANDREW of BARROW & COMPANY, 23 Regent Street, Belize City, Belize. Born July 23, 1969, Kingston, Jamaica. Graduated from Regis College, Bs. U.W.I., LL.B. Norman Manley Law School, C.L.E. Admitted to Belize Bar in 1996. Corresponds in English. General Practice. Can provide translator / reporter / stenographer / notary.

Will take cases outside Belize City. Office Phone: 223-5900/ 22-35903/ 22-35908 Fax: 223-5913 Email barrowco@btl.net

MOORE, ANTOINETTE of the LAW OFFICES OF ANTOINETTE MOORE, Cassian Nunez Street, Dangriga Town, Stann Creek District. Born June 3, 1955, Brooklyn, New York. Graduated from Lawrence University, B.A. Loyola University of Chicago, J.D. Norman Manley Law School, C.L.E. Admitted to Belize Bar in 1996. Corresponds in English and some Spanish. General Practice and Criminal Matters. Can provide translator / reporter / stenographer / notary. Will take cases outside Belize City. Office Phone: 522-2457 Fax: 522-2457 Email: moorelaw@btl.net

MUSA-POTT, SAMIRA Suite 308 Marina Towers, Newtown Barracks Belize City, Belize. Born April 29, 1971, Belize City, Belize. Graduated from Florida Int'l University, B.A. U.W.I., LL.B. Norman Manley Law School, C.L.E. Admitted to Belize Bar in 1996. Corresponds in English and some Spanish. General Practice. Can provide translator / reporter / stenographer / notary. Will take cases outside Belize City. Office Phone: (501) 223-2238 35924 Fax: (501) 223-2360 Email: smusapott@btl.net

SABIDO, OSCAR A. of OSCAR A. SABIDO & CO., #5 New Road, Belize City, Belize. Born January 7, 1949, San Ignacio Town. Graduated from U.W.I., LL.B. Norman Manley Law School, C.L.E. Admitted to Belize Bar in 1979. Corresponds in English and fluent Spanish. General Practice and Criminal Matters. Can provide translator / reporter / stenographer / notary. Will take cases outside Belize City. Office Phone: 223-5803 Fax: 223-5839. Home Phone: 227-2901 Email: oasabido@btl.net

SOOKNANDAN, LUTCHMAN of SOOKNANDAN'S LAW FIRM, 3 Barrack Road, Belize City, Belize. Born March 21, 1948, Guyana. Graduated from U.W.I., LL.B., C.L.E. Admitted to Belize Bar in 1986. Corresponds in English. General Practice and Criminal Matters. Office Phone: 223-2469. Home phone: 223-2625 Fax: 223-5164 Email: lsooknan@btl.net

TWIST, OSWALD H. of the BELIZE LEGAL AID CENTER, 16 Bishop Street, Belize City, Belize. Born June 9, 1959, Belize. Graduated from U.W.I., LL.B. Norman Manley Law School, C.L.E. Admitted to Belize Bar in 1996. Corresponds in English. General Practice and Criminal Matters. Can provide translator / reporter / stenographer / notary. Office Phone/Fax: 227-5781 BELMOPAN OFFICE: Phone: 822-1475 Fax: 822-1476 Home Phone: 802-3471

WILLIAMS, RODWELL of BARROW & WILLIAMS, 99 Albert Street, Belize City, Belize. Born September 29, 1956, Belize City, Belize. Graduated with B.A., LL.B., C.L.E. Admitted to Belize Bar in 1985. Corresponds in English. General Practice. Can provide translator / reporter / stenographer / notary. Will take cases outside Belize City. Office Phone: 227-5280. Fax: 227-5278 Email: attorneys@barrowandwilliams.com Website: www.barrowandwilliams.com

YOUNG, MICHAEL CLARENCE EDWARD of YOUNG'S LAW FIRM, 28 Regent Street, Belize City, Belize. Born January 7, 1955, Southhampton, England. Graduated from U.W.I., LL.B. Norman Manley Law

School, (Hons) C.L.E. Admitted to Belize Bar in 1977. Solicitor of the Supreme Court of Belize. Corresponds in English. General Practice. Office Phone: 227-7406 / 72408 / 72544 Fax: 227-5157 Home Phone: 223-2519 Email: services@younglaw.bz Website: www.younglaw.bz

Lois Young Barrow & Company 120 A New Road, PO Box 565, Belize City, Belize Tel: 501-223-5924 Email loisblaw@btl.net

APPENDIX C:
BEST WEB SITES ABOUT BELIZE
Here are some of our favorite web sites about Belize:

www.ambergriscaye.com Impressive site with massive amount of material about Ambergris Caye. Good links to other sites, including most hotels, dive shops, real estate firms and other businesses on the island. Active message board.

www.corozal.com Pretty good information about Corozal District, provided by students of Corozal Community College. A sister site, www.corozal.bz, has business listings and information.

www.hopkinsbelize.com Information on Hopkins village.

www.placencia.com Good tourist information on the Placencia peninsula.

www.destinationsbelize.com All kinds of news and information about Placencia.

www.puntagordabelize.com The official web site of the town of Punta Gorda.

www.belmopanbelize.com Information on Belize's capital city.

www.belizefirst.com On-line magazine about Belize (Lan Sluder, editor and publisher) with dozens of articles on travel, life and retirement in Belize.

www.belize.gov.bz Official site of the Government of Belize – not always up-to-date, unfortunately.

www.belizeinvest.org.bz Site of Beltraide, which is charged with attracting business investment to Belize.

www.belizenet.com Well-done site on Belize travel and other information, by folks who provide a lot of Web design services in Belize. Associated with an active message board, Belize Forums at www.belizeforum.com.

www.belizenorth.com Terrific resource for anyone considering moving to the Corozal Town area. Lots of nitty-gritty information on daily life by people who live in Belize, though the web site developer left Belize several years ago.

www.belizeretirement.org Basic information on the Qualified Retired Persons incentive program provided by the Belize Tourism Board.

www.channel5belize.com This Belize City TV station provides the most definitive and reliable source of news on Belize. The weekday evening news broadcast is provided in transcript form and also in video.

www.7newsbelize.com Another good Belize City TV station with transcripts of the evening news broadcasts.

www.belizenews.com This site has links to most newspapers, TV and radio stations, magazines and other media in Belize.

www.stonetreerecords.com Stonetree has been making Belize music since 1995.

www.travelbelize.org Official site of the Belize Tourism Board, with tons of information on hotels and sightseeing.

www.toucantrail.com Although this site focuses on budget and low-moderate priced accommodations (hotels with rates of US$60 and less), it also has wonderful information on travel in Belize regardless of budget. It's affiliated with the Belize Tourism Board and was done by the Belize by Naturalight group.

www.escapeartist.com Site with helpful information of all types on expat life.

www.fodors.com Some guidebooks authored or co-authored by Lan Sluder, including *Fodor's Belize, Fodor's The Carolinas and Georgia,* and the new *InFocus Great Smoky Mountains National Park* are published by this Random House division.

BEST BELIZE BLOGS

http://belizebus.wordpress.com Excellent site with up-to-date information on bus, water taxi, air and other transportation options in Belize.

http://winjama.blogspot.com Run by a man who moved to Corozal, this very helpful blog focuses on living in Belize.

http://tropicat.wordpress.com This blog is about living in the Belize bush.

http://bubbasbirdblog.blogspot.com Elbert Greer's blog on birding in Belize.

http://exploringbelizecontinues.blogspot.com Adventures of two expat women in San Pedro.

http://barnaclesbelize.blogspot.com Great Belize photos on this blog by Barnacle Bill Taylor in Maya Beach.

http://latitudesbelize.blogspot.com Put together by the owners of Changes in Latitudes B&B in San Pedro.

http://moonracerfarmbelize.blogspot.com A young couple with a small lodge in Cayo near the Mountain Pine Ridge blog on living and running a hotel in Belize.

http://www.caribbean-colors.blogspot.com Lee Vanderwalker, who divides her time between Caye Caulker and Chetumal, Mexico, blogs about her life and art.

http://www.investinbelize.com/blog1/ The San Pedro couple who run this blog are in the real estate business, but the site has a lot of good information on relocating to Belize.

Rose Lambert-Sluder and Lan Sluder
on Caye Caulker
Photo by BROOKS LAMBERT-SLUDER

ABOUT LAN SLUDER

Lan Sluder is an old Belize hand. The author of more than a half dozen books on Belize, Sluder has helped thousands of travelers plan the vacation of a lifetime in this fascinating little English-speaking country on the Caribbean Coast of Central America. He also has advised many people on the pros and cons of new life in Belize. Among Lan Sluder's Belize books are *Fodor's Belize, Living Abroad in Belize, Adapter Kit: Belize, Belize Island Guide, Easy Belize, San Pedro Cool* and *Belize First Guide to Mainland.* Sluder is also founder, editor and publisher of *Belize First Magazine* -- web edition at www.belizefirst.com.

A former business newspaper editor in New Orleans, where he won a number of New Orleans Press Club awards, Sluder has contributed articles on travel, retirement and business subjects to publications around the world, including *The New York Times, Chicago Tribune, Miami Herald, Where to Retire, Globe and Mail, St. Petersburg Times, Bangkok Post, The Tico Times, Newsday* and *Caribbean Travel & Life.* In addition, he also authored the travel guides *InFocus Great Smoky Mountains National Park* and *Frommer's Best Beach Vacations: Carolinas and Georgia* and co-authored several editions of *Fodors's The Carolinas & Georgia.*

Sluder was educated at Duke University and in the U.S. Army in Vietnam. When not in Belize or traveling elsewhere, he lives on a mountain farm near Asheville, North Carolina. Questions to Lan Sluder can be sent to him at lansluder@gmail.com.